Language in the Light of Evolution 1

The Origins of Meaning

SIMIA FEROX.   THE LION TAILED MONKEY.

'The Lion-Tailed Monkey' from George Shaw, 'Museum Leverianum, containing select specimens from the Museum of the late Sir Ashton Lever'. (Special Collections, Edinburgh University Library)

The Origins of Meaning

JAMES R. HURFORD

OXFORD
UNIVERSITY PRESS

OXFORD

UNIVERSITY PRESS

Great Clarendon Street, Oxford OX2 6DP

Oxford University Press is a department of the University of Oxford.
It furthers the University's objective of excellence in research, scholarship,
and education by publishing worldwide in

Oxford New York

Auckland Cape Town Dar es Salaam Hong Kong Karachi
Kuala Lumpur Madrid Melbourne Mexico City Nairobi
New Delhi Shanghai Taipei Toronto

With offices in

Argentina Austria Brazil Chile Czech Republic France Greece
Guatemala Hungary Italy Japan Poland Portugal Singapore
South Korea Switzerland Thailand Turkey Ukraine Vietnam

Oxford is a registered trade mark of Oxford University Press
in the UK and in certain other countries

Published in the United States
by Oxford University Press Inc., New York

British Library Cataloguing in Publication Data
Data available

Library of Congress Cataloging in Publication Data
Data available

Typeset by SPI Publisher Services, Pondicherry, India
Printed in Great Britain
on acid-free paper by
Biddles Ltd., King's Lynn, Norfolk

ISBN 978-0-19-920785-5

3 5 7 9 10 8 6 4

Contents

Acknowledgements

The Language Evolution and Computation Research Unit (LEC), within the Linguistics and English Language subject area at Edinburgh University, is a lively group constantly on the lookout for new developments in the field, which they approach critically and eclectically. The environment provided has been invaluable in putting this book together. More specifically, and further afield, I am grateful to many colleagues who have taken the trouble to read substantial parts of this book in draft, and to offer very helpful comments which I am sure have improved the final version. These readers and advisors, very roughly in order of their influence on the final form of this book, are: Alan Grafen, Juan-Carlos Gómez, Simon Levy, Kathleen Gibson, Chris Knight, Dave Hawkey, Robbins Burling, Jean-Louis Dessalles, Ian Underwood, Marina Rakova, Clare MacCumhaill, Maggie Tallerman, Fritz Newmeyer, Thom Scott-Phillips, Mike Dowman, Karola Kreitmair, Robert Seyfarth, Cyprian Laskowski, Graham Ritchie, and Bill Wang. Of course, though all have been influential, I take full responsibility for being influenced, and they are not to blame for the flaws.

All of the following have also helped in some way, either by providing inspiring thoughts, by generous donation of resources, such as offprints of hard-to-find papers, or by answering my dumb questions: Joseph Arko, Alan Barnard, Dick Byrne, Ronnie Cann, Andy Clark, Nicky Clayton, Greg Cogan, Terry Deacon, Robin Dunbar, Tecumseh Fitch, Kalanit Grill-Spector, Brian Hare, Emma Healey, Wolfram Hinzen, Sue Hurford, David Kemmerer, Simon Kirby, Andreas Kyriacou, Bob Ladd, David Leavens, Gary Lupyan, Dario Maestripieri, Karen McComb, April McMahon, Paul Meara, Alicia Melis, Geoff Miller, Nathan Oesch, Joe Poulshock, Stuart Semple, Andrew Smith, Kenny Smith,

Michael Stirrat, Mike Tomasello, Alex Weiss, Andy Whiten, and Jelle Zuidema.

I thank them all heartily, as well as thanking John Davey for his efficient management of an awkward author, Alison Kelly for a great copy-editing job, keeping me on my stylistic toes, Google for its amazing free service, my ailing computer for just hanging on long enough to let me finish, and my dear Sue again for always being there, even when I was here.

Preface

This book covers some of the same ground, now much more brightly illuminated by the light of modern research, as the passages on language in Darwin's *The Descent of Man*. The central message of the continuity between non-human animals and humans is the same. Darwin was aware of the great gulf between human language and animal communication, but touched on many of the relevant aspects of animal behaviour that give us clues about the origins of language. In the intervening century and a third, a vast amount of more thorough and less anecdotal evidence has accrued, pointing in the same direction as Darwin urged. Darwin would have delighted in the enormous body of empirical knowledge now built up by genetics, neuroscience, ethology, comparative psychology, and anthropology. I have raided these subjects to try to spell out a detailed and up-to-date account (as of 2006) of the evolutionary foundations of language. I have also raided the more speculative subjects, in particular philosophy (including logic) and computer modelling, where their ideas help to illuminate the origins of language. With a more principled carving of language into its natural parts by twentieth-century linguistics, we are able to spell out in more detail the probable animal precursors for various components of the language faculty (in its broad sense, of course). We have to admit that there is still a gap in our knowledge of the precise mechanism by which some accumulation of small changes brought about the apparent discontinuity between us and animals. But I hope this work, in its two volumes, will show how research has, especially in the last few decades, substantially narrowed that gap.

Books on 'the evolution of language' are expected to tell a story, preferably with dates. Though a rough sequence can be postulated for the order in which various elements of the modern human language capacity emerged, we do not have enough data to tell **when** they emerged, to closer than a few hundred millennia. There is nevertheless a broad chronological organization of this volume and its successor, Volume 2. The discussion of pre-linguistic animal concepts and social lives in this volume will take us to the brink of modern human language, when the species became for the first time 'language-ready'. The conceptual capacities discussed in Part I here were certainly in place for our first bipedal ancestors, the australopithecines, who lived about 4–5 million years ago. We can be certain of this because much of the basic conceptual apparatus can be found, in a simple form, in related apes, and even in some birds. The specific conceptual abilities that accrued to humans as a direct result of going public with their thoughts, via the medium of shared symbolic languages, are of course not present in animals; but much that can be reasonably labelled 'propositional' and 'conceptual' existed before modern public language.

The social changes discussed in Part II of this volume, by which our later ancestors became willing to open up their private concepts to others, would have happened during the several million years before the second great migration out of Africa, about 150,000 years ago. Language is a bridge between meanings and vocal sounds or manual signs. Pre-humans established evolutionary bridgeheads to language-readiness at both ends: the phonetic and the semantic/pragmatic. The phonetic bridgehead to language-readiness has received more attention (e.g. by Lieberman 1984) than the equally crucial semantic/pragmatic one. This volume gives a picture of the semantic and pragmatic aspects of pre-human language-readiness. The final processes tipping us over the brink of language, the emergence of a shared lexicon and then of complex linguistic forms, morphosyntactic and phonological, will be the subject of Volume 2.

Besides following this broad chronological framework, this book is at least as much about showing how we can begin to see language in a new light. Unique though it is, language emerges from known aspects of animal behaviour and more abstract organizational principles ('self-organization'). The title I have given to the work as a whole echoes Dobzhansky (1973)'s title 'Nothing in Biology Makes Sense Except in the Light of Evolution'. Thinking of language in the light of evolution helps to make much more sense of it. Mysteries of discontinuity from non-human animals begin to dissolve—though they still haven't entirely disappeared.

'In the beginning was the Word,' wrote St John at the beginning of his gospel. Goethe's scholar-hero Faust, sitting down to translate this gospel, couldn't accept this mysterious aphorism, and neither can I, if it expresses transparently anything to do with the evolution of language. Faust at first replaced 'the Word' with 'Sense' or 'Meaning', thus agreeing with the view taken here that **meaning** precedes human words, as I argue in Part I, on (proto-)semantics. But Faust wasn't satisfied with that, either, and ended up translating the sentence as 'In the beginning was the Act', thus agreeing with the view taken here that **action** is a precursor to human language, as I argue in Part II, on (proto-)pragmatics. Unlike Faust, I accept that **both** meaning and action, on parallel tracks, laid the basis for human words.

In researching this book, I have been impressed by the emerging consensus in the field of language evolution. Disagreements do exist, but much evidence, gathered laboriously in many far-flung corners, points in very similar directions. I have relied very heavily on this mass of empirical research, and have quoted it liberally. I hope you won't object to my extensive use of quotations. Important contributors to the field deserve their own voice, rather than being paraphrased. I have gathered together a lot of original material. What virtue may be seen in the book lies in my assembling the labours of others into what I hope is a coherent argument of my own about how language use and structure got to be the way they are.

A few linguists (e.g. Derek Bickerton, Phil Lieberman, Jean Aitchison, Mike Beaken, Andrew Carstairs-McCarthy) have written books on the evolution of language. Now that these pioneering frontierspeople and trailblazers have given us charts of their chosen valleys, we can begin to compile an atlas of the whole landscape. The difference between their works and mine is that I have tried systematically (in this volume and the next) to cover, at least in outline, all the compartments into which linguists habitually divide language structure and behaviour: semantics, pragmatics (both in this volume), and phonetics, phonology, and morphosyntax (in Volume 2). With some reservations, linguistics has carved nature at her joints. Each part of this book thus spends a little time on explaining the basics of each compartment (e.g. what the central themes of semantics, or of pragmatics, are) and then examines in detail how that aspect of language behaviour or structure could have got to be that way. It might be thought that this importation of boundaries established within linguistics is already biased against possible ideas from other subjects such as anthropology or psychology. I have a double-barrelled reply to this. Firstly, I believe, with some reservations, that linguistics has got the carve-up of linguistic phenomena pretty much right, and that evolutionary accounts of **all** these components of language are crucial to a picture of how language evolved. Language is all of pragmatics, semantics, morphosyntax, phonology, phonetics, and more besides. The study of language evolution has suffered in the past from insufficient acknowledgement of this rich multi-component nature of language. This is evident in studies which, while sometimes ambitiously labelled 'the evolution of language' or 'the origins of language', in fact just focus on one domain, such as phonetics (larynx-lowering), pragmatics (grooming, or Theory of Mind), phonology (syllable structure), or syntax (recursion). The second barrel of my defence of using the broad subdivisions accepted by linguistics is that I have, where necessary, modified them **in the light of evolution**. An example is my definition of semantics for evolutionary purposes, which I do not define as essentially relating to the meanings of words and sentences. If this seems provocative, read on, especially Part I.

For a book written by a linguist, there is rather little linguistics in it, as a glance at the bibliography will show. Modern linguistics naturally deals with fully developed modern languages, and has given scant thought to the question of how they got to be the way they are, or how the language faculty got to be the way it is. This volume, in dealing with the foundations of meaning, both communicated and non-communicated, inevitably deals with rather distant, but essential, precursors of modern human language. Linguistics tends very strongly to focus on linguistic **form**, be it phonetic, phonological, or syntactic. Phonetics, phonology, and syntax are more distinctive of human language than are semantics and pragmatics, which have clear foundations, as we will see, in animal concepts and animal social life. (This is not to say, of course, that there are not also distinctively human aspects of conceptual structure and social interaction.) The second volume, dealing with the phonetic, phonological, and morphosyntactic form of languages, will engage more fully with literature written by linguists.

Who is this book for? Well, it is clearly interdisciplinary. Many philosophers write only for other philosophers, linguists write for linguists, and anthropologists for anthropologists. This is a linguist writing for any philosopher, psychologist, anthropologist, cognitive scientist, ethologist, linguist, or other intellectually curious person with an interest in the foundations of humans' most distinctive ability: language. Consequently, I spend a bit more space explaining some basic ideas than would be spent in a monodisciplinary monograph. I hope that more linguists will be encouraged to expand their horizons beyond formal synchronic theorizing about structure. I hope that more philosophers will be encouraged to grapple with the continuities between non-human and human mental life. And I hope that others will begin to appreciate the various complexities hidden behind the cover-all term *meaning*.

Drawing ideas and facts from so many disciplines into a single story has its problems. Terms with very precise definitions in one subject, and around which debate has often centred, so that they have especially loaded connotations, can be innocently used by an outsider in an everyday sense without any intention of taking sides in hoary old intra-disciplinary debates. Thus *drift* and *linkage* have quite special meanings for biologists, as does *association* for psychologists, *reference* for linguistic semanticists, and *identity* and *representation* for philosophers. In the most pernicious cases, the **same** term is used in different senses by different disciplines. Thus linguists and philosophers often mean different things by *subject* and *predicate*. I have benefited from the advice of specialist readers in avoiding some of these pitfalls. But, just in case there are still some such problems, try to be an interdisciplinary reader, as I have tried to be an interdisciplinary writer. That is, if from the viewpoint of your own subject area, you find some statement puzzling or provocative, try taking any offending term in its everyday, non-technical sense. In the same vein, keep in mind that this work is not intended to solve problems that only crop up within the traditions of a single discipline. So I have no interest here in discussing theory-dependent issues in linguistics. Likewise, I am not aiming to solve any purely metaphysical problems, though the work as a whole reflects my stance that satisfactory answers to many apparently metaphysical questions should be sought naturalistically in empirical facts about brains and social life. Except where precision requires otherwise, I have written in everyday language, to make the book accessible to students and other intellectuals, and I have also tried rigorously to back up my arguments and statements with references to well-researched primary sources.

The explosion of knowledge, and access to knowledge, due to the internet has revolutionized scholarship, especially in the natural sciences. What one used to have to trudge through library bookstacks for, often to find that someone else had borrowed the crucial tome, can often now appear in seconds on one's desktop. Without this facility, many of the claims I have made in this book would have been more speculative and less well backed up by empirical studies, or not ventured into at all.

Finally, I urge all readers to seek out the gaps and inconsistencies in the argument that I present here, and to try to remedy them constructively, in the light of available empirical findings. Of course there will be new visions and revisions, and I look forward to them.

This book is the first of two closely linked but self-contained volumes. The second, on the origins of linguistic form and structure, will be published in 2008.

PART ONE

Meaning Before Communication

We are sometimes alone. In our everyday lives we often deal privately with practical tasks that we don't bother to tell anyone else about. There would be no point; we can manage. Some of our thinking through these tasks is informed by our enculturation and language. Perhaps we use simple mental arithmetic. Often we are guided by ethical notions of what is right, because even private tasks have consequences for other people. But some of what goes on in our heads when doing everyday tasks is naturally solipsistic, even primitive, using mechanisms that preceded the emergence of our societies. We share this kind of mental activity with (non-human) animals. Fitch (2005, p. 206) writes of 'rich cognitive abilities in non-human primates' showing them as 'having quite complex minds, particularly in the social realm, but lacking a communicative mechanism capable of expressing most of this mental activity'.

The ancestors of humans had no shared languages. The more distant ancestors lived in social groups much more simply structured than ours. They had to deal individually with practical everyday tasks. And they evolved to be very good at solving the most pressing problems of individual survival. This first part of the book, the first five chapters, tries to sketch out the elements of a kind of animal thought about the world before communication with others began to trim thinking in newer ways. Thus the goal of these chapters is very similar to that indicated by José Luis Bermúdez's title *Thinking without Words* (2003). At a level of technical detail I come to somewhat different conclusions from Bermúdez.

So these first five chapters will be non-social. Be in no doubt that part of human meaning is intensely social. We will get to the social aspect of meaning later, in Part II, after exploring the kinds of mental structures that animals can build up for purely non-social ends. The implied sharp separation between individual and social is largely for practical purposes of exposition. Here in Part I, we will see the seeds of human concepts and propositions. We will also see the still large gap that exists between us and other species.

CHAPTER ONE

Let's Agree on Terms

1.1 DEFINING SEMANTICS WITH EVOLUTION IN MIND

A language is a system for translating meanings into signals, and vice versa. Thus language is anchored in non-language at two ends, the end of 'meanings' and the end of signals. I will deal with the signals end of language in a later volume, to include phonetics. It is convenient, and now a practice generally followed by linguists, to divide the other end of language, namely 'meaning', into two parts, semantics and pragmatics. I will follow this division and deal with semantics in this part, and pragmatics in the next (Part II). But I will modify the traditional definitions of semantics and pragmatics; this is necessary because we are dealing in part with the pre-linguistic origins of these aspects of human capability.

Within philosophy, a dominant tradition defines semantics as a relation between language and the world (e.g. Russell 1905; Wittgenstein 1922; Carnap 1942; Montague 1970). 'Semantics ... is where the rubber meets the road, where language gets all the way to the world and words refer to the things and events therein' (Dennett 2003a, p. 673). This is opposed to pragmatics, which tends to be defined more variously, but always involves a relation between language, its **users**, and its **contexts of use**.

[A]n investigation which refers explicitly to the speaker of the language—no matter whether other factors are drawn in or not—falls into the region of *pragmatics*. If the investigation ignores the speaker but concentrates on the expressions of the language and their designata, then the investigation belongs to the province of *semantics*.   (Carnap 1958, p. 79)

This distinction roughly corresponds to that made by Halliday (1985) between ideational meaning ($\approx$ semantics) and interpersonal meaning ($\approx$ pragmatics).

All languages are organized around two main kinds of meaning, the 'ideational' or reflective and the 'interpersonal' or active. These components . . . are the manifestations in the linguistic system of the two very general purposes which underlie all uses of language: (i) to understand the environment (ideational), and (ii) to act on the others in it (interpersonal).

(Halliday 1985, p. xii)

The key component of both the mainstream philosophical take on semantics and Halliday's ideational meaning is the involvement of things, events, and situations in the world that can be **referred** to. This link with an external world is **extensional**. While much goes on inside an animal's brain when it attends to some object or event in the world outside, the relation of this mental activity to the outside world is essential to an evolutionary account of it. Animals survive in the world, among objects, and assailed by events, and the neuronal activity within their skulls is an evolutionary adaptation to this environment. In these chapters on semantics, I will start by reviewing what we know about animals' or humans' representations, of states of affairs, rather than the tactics and politics of animals' behaviour towards each other, which is the domain of pragmatics, to be dealt with in Part II.

Now here we meet the necessary modification of earlier definitions of semantics, which have been concerned with meaning in fully fledged modern languages. Language, a system relating meanings to vocal sounds or hand movements, emerged from a situation in which there was no language. Obviously, before language, some vocal sounds and hand movements existed, and these were the first to be recruited in the service of this new emerging human capacity, language.[1] It is not so often recognized that some of the other end of a language system, meanings, also existed before the advent of language. The term 'meaning' itself lends itself to this kind of denial, because we habitually attach it to words and sentences. We tend to think of meaning as like the smile on a face. Lewis Carroll was teasing us in suggesting that one could see the smile of the Cheshire Cat after the cat had disappeared. Likewise, it is perhaps hard to see how the meaning of a word could be present before the word exists. But in fact, substantial parts of both ends of language, the vocal sounds or hand movements **and** the meanings they later came to convey, existed

---

[1] Modern human vocal agility is far in excess of what apes can manage, and it seems likely that the full range of sounds accessible to modern humans evolved rather late, probably co-evolving with the full range of meanings we can now express.

before language came along to build a bridge between them. A central purpose of this book is to present a case for this pre-existence of some 'meanings'.

The evolutionary foundations of semantics lie in the internal mental representations that animals have of the things, events, and situations in their environment. The traditional philosophical conception of meaning as a direct connection between language and world bypasses the mind. This is a strong tradition in semantics, especially formal semantics, which is embarrassed to speculate about what might go on inside people's heads, and prefers to abstract the study of meaning away from 'psychologizing'. I subscribe to a different view of semantics, namely that the relationship of meaning between language and the world is indirect, and is mediated by the mind, which is host to such things as concepts, ideas, and thoughts. In this way, Halliday's term 'ideational meaning', explicitly acknowledging the role of the mind in mediating between signals and their meanings, is more in keeping with my approach. This approach, placing mental representations between expressions in language and the world they describe, is also in line with the approach taken under the banner of 'Cognitive Linguistics' (see e.g. Allwood and Gärdenfors 1999; Talmy 2000). A natural evolutionary approach pushes one towards a more specific position, namely that mental representations of things and events in the world came before any corresponding expressions in language; the mental representations were phylogenetically prior to words and sentences. This is in the same spirit as, and goes one step further than, Fodor (1998, p. 7), who, in rather fancy abstract lingo, insists: 'Both ontologically and in order of explanation, the intentionality of the propositional attitudes is prior to the intentionality of natural languages; and both ontologically and in order of explanation, the intentionality of mental representations is prior to the intentionality of propositional attitudes.'[2] Rudimentary concepts, ideas, and thoughts (or something very like them), about things, events, and situations in the world, can reasonably be said to exist in animals' minds, even though they may not ever be publicly expressed in language, or indeed in any kind of communication whatsoever. Thus my thesis here is diametrically opposed to an aphorism of Wittgenstein's: 'The limits of my language mean the limits of my world'

---

[2] *Intentionality* here can be glossed as the property of being **about** something in the world. I will use *Intentionality* with a capital *I* for aboutness. The word *intentionality*, derived from the verb *intend*, meaning an animal's capacity to intend to do things, will be spelt with a small *i*.

(Wittgenstein 1922, 5.6). This would imply that a languageless creature has no world.[3]

Aboutness is known to philosophers and cognitive scientists as 'Intentionality', spelt with a capital 'I' to distinguish it from 'intentionality', which is the capacity to have intentions and to act on them. Aboutness or Intentionality is primarily a relation between mental states and 'objects' or propositions. I put 'objects' in scare quotes, because philosophers, in particular, have discussed a wide range of things which could conceivably be on the receiving end of the 'about' relation from mental states. The mental states concerned are such as **believing, knowing, imagining**, and **desiring**. A person can desire a particular apple; in this case the desire is 'about' the apple. A person can know that it is raining outside his window; here the knowledge is about the situation outside the window. With more difficulty, one can imagine a unicorn; here the act of imagination is about something that does not exist, but is nevertheless said to be 'about something'.

I will assume that the pre-linguistic ancestors of humans had a whole range of different mental states, including beliefs and desires, which were 'about', and could even 'be true of', states of affairs in the world. Truth is classically seen as a relation between linguistic expressions and the world. The sentence *It's raining* is true if, in the world at the time of utterance, it is raining; otherwise, it is false. But we can also speak of someone having in their mind a 'true picture' of the world, or a 'true belief' about some situation. I advocate the view that truth, as applied to language, originates in truth as applied to non-language, in particular to private mental representations of things, events, and states of affairs.

We can reasonably attribute beliefs and desires to non-human animals closely related to us. 'Many animals other than humans, especially mammals and birds, possess well developed knowledge-of-the-world (declarative memory) systems, and are capable of acquiring vast amounts of flexibly expressible information' (Tulving and Markowitsch 1998, p. 202). Animals remember, and thus can be in mental states relating to past circumstances. There are many studies, in laboratories and in the wild, of memory for places and things in animals who cache food for later

[3] See Abbott (1995) and Hauser (1995) for a lively and compact exchange on the issue of whether thought requires public language, with Abbott taking the view I espouse here, that genuine thought is possible without public language. See also Bermúdez (2003) for a concerted philosophical argument that thinking without words is indeed possible, an overall argument that partially overlaps with, and partially diverges from, my own, developed in this book.

retrieval, or who parasitize the nests of other birds. These include studies of scrub jays (Griffiths et al. 1999), cowbirds (Clayton et al. 1997), and tits (Healy and Suhonen 1996). Experiments with garden warblers (Biebach et al. 1989) demonstrate reliable ability for judging time of day and memory for associations between particular feeding places and times of day. The neural basis for memory even in species quite distantly related to humans, such as birds, is very similar, with substantial involvement of the hippocampus in all cases (Reboreda et al. 1996; Clayton et al. 1997). Their technicalities apart, all such studies confirm the common 'folk' assumption that non-human animals, especially mammals and birds, while falling short of humans in many of their mental abilities, nevertheless learn, remember, and plan. The garden warblers who remember where to find food at particular times of day also plan. Even honeybees can be said to remember and to plan (von Frisch 1974). The scout bees remember where they found nectar and signal it to their hive-fellows, who plan their forays accordingly.

These beliefs and memories stored, at least for a while, in an animal's head are rooted in instances of perception that happened at particular prior times in the animal's life. 'Perception is in all likelihood the primary form of intentionality,[4] the one on which all others depend ... ' (Searle 1979, p. 135). Perception causes mental states. When an animal perceives some object or state of affairs, it is in a particular mental state relating to that bit of the world. Apart from any innate concepts, an animal's concepts are learned through experience, the gateway to which is perception. It is through repeatedly perceiving salient objects and states of affairs of certain types, that the animal comes to have regular patterns of learned behaviour in relation to them. The reservation about salience is necessary because an animal presumably need have no concept of the air it breathes, or of the constant smell of its own body. It seems reasonable to suppose that (apart from any innate concepts) an animal only has concepts of those types of things that it has at some time perceived (and only some of those). In the case of innate concepts, as in people with an instinctive fear of snakes or spiders, these are either just evolutionary accidents or (more likely) are the products of natural selection favouring ancestors who did perceive (harmful) snakes or spiders, took evasive action, and survived to pass on their genes. Thus, although humans can be in mental states relating to fictitious objects such as unicorns, it seems most unlikely that any non-human animal could be in such a state, having had no actual

---

[4] Searle means 'Intentionality' here.

experience of unicorns or other fictions. The brand of Intentionality applicable to non-humans is more limited than that applicable to humans.

Humans have a great variety of words describing Intentional mental states, but it is not always clear that different words actually describe different mental states. What, for instance is the difference between the state described by *hope* and that decribed by *want*? Can you ever want something to happen and not hope it will happen, or hope something will happen and not want it to happen? *Want* can take a non-sentential object, as in *Jenny wants an ice cream*, but this is equivalent to *want to have*. Although the meanings of the two verbs overlap significantly, *want* typically indicates a more short-term desire than *hope*. The overheated and thirsty Jenny on the beach doesn't just **hope** to have an ice cream— she **wants** one, now. But the significant similarity between *hope* and *want* shows that, if we grant that non-human animals can want things to happen, then, as far as wanting overlaps with hoping, they can also hope for things to happen. Similarly, it might be possible to drive a thin wedge between the meanings of *expect* and *anticipate*, and though we grant that non-human animals can expect things to happen, they might not, for some cases of anticipation, be able to anticipate that things will happen. Can a non-human animal **regret** something? It seems reasonable to say that under some circumstances an animal can be **unhappy** about some current state of affairs, for instance a cat being shut out in the rain.

The human words for Intentional mental states do indeed show a richness that we cannot easily attribute to non-human animals, but the difference seems to be a matter of degree of elaboration and differentiation of the mental states. Humans can no doubt introspectively distinguish between a great variety of mental states which bear on situations in the world. For non-humans, there is only evidence of a relatively crudely carved-up space of possible Intentional mental states, and these can perhaps be classified along a very small number of dimensions.

In this Part I of the book, I will review what we know about such private mental representations in pre-linguistic creatures, concluding that they show, in embryonic form, characteristics that are sometimes thought to be unique to humans. Some of the semantic properties that we see in modern human languages can be traced back to these pre-linguistic foundations. However, with the advent of the two central components of language, the extensive use of learned arbitrary meaning–form connections and their combining by syntactic systems, additional semantic capacities came to exist. Humans, uniquely, now had access to new additional ways of representing the outside world in their minds. These additional semantic capacities, made possible by language, will be discussed in Volume 2.

I.2 HEALTH WARNING ABOUT 'CONCEPTS'

Be warned: I will not be too shy about attributing concepts to some animals. Much of the resistance to attributing concepts to animals comes from philosophers and other scholars in the humanities.[5] Until quite recently, the detailed workings of the brain have been *terra incognita*, and introspection by humans about their own mental activity was the main source of theorizing about concepts. Thinkers for whom their own mental activity is the foundation of all knowledge have some distance to travel before they can be convinced that other people have minds, let alone that animals have them, and let alone that the contents of animal minds include entities like our own concepts. The Cartesian tradition emanating from *cogito ergo sum* still has a strong grip. The main objection to solipsism[6] is that it flies in the face of common sense. **Obviously** other people have minds. Neuroscientists and animal researchers have their own more advanced common sense, and most start from a common assumption of continuity between animal and human minds. It can be added that many workers in another modern field, Artificial Intelligence, also have no qualms about attributing mind-like properties even to machines,[7] as the name of their discipline implies. Besides radical scepticism, another aspect of Cartesianism, dualism, is sometimes implicit in debates over animal concepts. 'A certain Cartesian residue might be detected here: if we have an associative "mechanism" we can avoid attributing (unsubstantiated) rational thought' (Allen 2006, p. 181). In a philosopher's essay on the mental lives of non-human animals, Dupré (1996, p. 323) writes of the 'powerful and pernicious influence [of] Cartesian assumptions'.

Attributing concepts to animals does not imply that animal concepts are identical in their range to human concepts. We can identify things that we call 'legs' in spiders, centipedes, quadrupeds, and humans, because of an overall similarity in shape and function. But this does not amount to a claim that spiders' or centipedes' legs have all the same properties as

---

[5] Not all philosophers and humanists, of course, resist granting animals some conceptual or quasi-conceptual knowledge.

[6] Solipsism can be defined as the belief that the only thing whose existence one can be certain of is oneself.

[7] Though, as Simon Levy has pointed out to me, 'At this point in the checkered history of AI, all but its most extreme practitioners would probably concede that their programs have very little in common with real human or animal minds.'

human legs. Analogously, we can identify behaviour in animals similar enough to the human behaviour that prompts us to say that humans possess concepts, so it is natural to say that these animals possess concepts too. Wordless creatures may, in this view, have concepts. Possession of words is not a necessary criterion for identifying possession of concepts. I am sure that I have separate concepts for about five different kinds of weeds that grow in my garden, which I can deliberately seek out, and whose characteristics I can take advantage of when dealing with them; but I don't know what they are called, and I don't need to. But words, if used successfully between people for communication, are a **sufficient** criterion for possession of corresponding concepts. Clamping possession of concepts firmly to the possession of language, as some philosophers do,[8] removes one possible hypothesis for the origin of language. If concepts only appear with language, the origin of language itself is that much more of a mystery.

Donald Davidson (Davidson 1975, 1982) was a prominent exponent of the view that, without language, animals cannot have beliefs. Setting the scene by describing a dog chasing a cat, which disappears up a tree, and asking whether the dog believes the cat is in the tree, he writes:

[C]an the dog believe of an object that it is a tree? This would seem impossible unless we suppose the dog has many general beliefs about trees: that they are growing things, that they have leaves or needles, that they burn. There is no fixed list of things that someone with the concept of a tree must believe, but without many general beliefs, there would be no reason to identify a belief as about a tree.   (Davidson 1982, p. 3)

Well, just how many general beliefs does it take? At what stage in a child's growing up, as it acquires more and more general beliefs about trees, do we decide that now, but not before, it can entertain a specific belief about a particular tree? And Davidson's argument is surely prone to infinite regress. He argues that you cannot have a belief about an object that it is a tree without having previously acquired general beliefs about trees. But how could the allegedly prior beliefs 'about trees' have been acquired unless the creature knew, while acquiring them, that it was dealing with a tree or trees? Dupré (1996, p. 332) has an answer to Davidson's argument. He concedes to Davidson, as I do, that we would not wish to attribute to

---

[8] I'll quote an apt footnote from Fodor (1998, p. 28) here: 'Just why feelings run so strongly on these matters is unclear to me. Whereas the ethology of all other species is widely agreed to be thoroughly empirical and largely morally neutral, apriorizing and moralizing about the ethology of our species appears to be the order of the day. Very odd.'

a dog the full complement of beliefs that a human has who believes that there is a cat up a particular tree. But, Dupré argues, it is reasonable to say that the dog has some belief which has significant content in common with the human belief. Davidson's position is conservative. A more recent wave of philosophers, including Dupré, is more inclined to attribute a **degree** of conceptual knowledge to animals and pre-linguistic infants. Alva Noë is one; he argues against thinking of 'concepts as brought into play only in the context of what we might call *explicit deliberative judgment*' and continues, 'But conceptual skills can also enter thought as background conditions on the possession of further skills of one sort or another' (Noë 2004, p. 187). As is to be expected in a work of this sort, looking for precursors of human meaning in our pre-human ancestors' capacities, this issue of whether animals have concepts (or propositions, or predicates) will crop up again and again. It will be picked up in several of the following chapters.[9]

From the empirical psychological side of the topic, Shettleworth and Sutton (2006, p. 235) express a compatible view, discussing experiments in which animals behave in ways similar to human behaviour typically described in terms of distinctive mental states.

The term *functional similarity* (Hampton 2001) captures the idea that the best we can do in such investigations is to define rigorously the behaviour accompanied by a given mental process and see if the animals show it. If the process is one usually assessed by a verbal report, we will never be able to have the same kind of evidence for it in other species as in humans. . . . People may never agree on the degree to which similar nonverbal behaviour implies similar mental events in very different species (c.f. Griffin 2001), but when the phenomena under study are well enough defined, agreement on functional similarity may be possible.

'[I]n general one should expect that an organism's internal representation system is far more elaborate than its external communications indicate' (Harms 2004, p. 43). There is now empirical evidence that some animal species have mental capacities far in excess of what we previously thought, and of a kind significantly approaching the special properties that we want to retain for 'concepts'. We can reasonably seek the origin of human-like concepts in such animal behaviour. I will label the simplest and earliest

---

[9] One of the hardest questions my daughter Eve ever asked me was, of our cat Bubble, 'Does Bubble know she's a cat?' I am happy with the idea that a dog may have a belief **like**, but not identical to, ours, that some object is a tree, but I'm not at all sure in what sense a dog can know that it is a dog. Self-knowledge is a more complex issue than knowledge of other things.

precursors 'proto-concepts'; these can be found in many animals. Recent experimental evidence shows that some species go beyond proto-concepts, to mental representations of a more sophisticated sort. I will follow this trail of increasing sophistication to a point where it is more clearly an arbitrary terminological issue whether to award the more complex representations the label 'concept'. As we will see, the advent of language does change the nature and range of concepts, but I will use the term *concept* broadly enough to attribute concepts to some animals. In brief, it will be useful to talk in terms of an evolutionary succession: proto-concepts → pre-linguistic concepts → linguistic concepts.

Note that in speaking of 'animal concepts' or 'human concepts', or even of 'my concept of so-and-so' as opposed to 'your concept of so-and-so', I locate concepts in minds. There are no concepts outside minds. So I interpret the term 'concept' differently from Davidson, for whom 'Concepts themselves are abstractions and so timeless' (Davidson 2001a, p. 123). For Davidson, the concept of the element iron, for example, has existed for all time, but its **instantiation** only occurred some time after the formation of the universe; likewise the concept of a human being is timeless, but was instantiated only a few hundred millennia ago. I can't see the use in this kind of Platonism. Davidson's definition includes 'abstraction', but in his view this can have no connection with the mental activity of abstracting, in the sense in which a symphony is an abstraction over performances of it. Abstracting is an activity carried out by a mind. But Davidsonian 'concepts', which he says are abstractions, existed before any minds existed, and so cannot be the outcome of any mental activity of abstraction. Thus, using the term 'abstraction' in the definition of allegedly timeless concepts cannot be an allusion to any mental activity that we are familiar with under the heading of 'abstracting', and so does not get us any closer to the meaning of the term 'concept', as Davidson sees it. Maybe this is all a terminological quibble, for in another essay in the same collection Davidson (2001b) writes of 'conceptual schemes' as if they exist in minds, which makes our positions seem closer. I will use the term 'concept' to indicate a certain subpart of a state of mind.

Treating concepts as subparts of states of mind is in line with Fodor (1998), and my position is very similar to his. He sets out five 'non-negotiable' requirements for concepts, and I part company with him only on his fifth condition, which is 'Concepts are *public*; they're the sorts of things that lots of people can, and do, *share*' (Fodor 1998, p. 28). I'm talking about animal concepts, before any communication of concepts takes place. Fodor's work is only about human concepts, so here a distinction between pre-linguistic concepts and post-linguistic concepts is in order. Fodor, of course, makes no such distinction, but maybe he would grant the status of pre-linguistic concepts to anything that satisfied the first four of his conditions but not the fifth.[10] For an allegedly non-negotiable condition, there is a bit of a hedge in Fodor's formulation; is the 'can' of 'the sorts of things that lots of people can, and do, *share*' redundant? If it is redundant, the strict condition is that concepts **are** shared by lots of people. But if the 'can' is not redundant, this lets in the possibility of some concept that **could** be shared, but as a matter of contingent fact **isn't** shared by any two people, let alone 'lots'. In this case Fodor's fifth condition is not so non-negotiable after all. The modifications of pre-linguistic concepts that the addition of public labels brings to them will be discussed in detail in the sequel to this book. In many cases, as we will see much later, there really is a difference, perhaps slight but important nonetheless, between pre-communicational concepts and public concepts.

Researchers have approached the cognition underlying language from both ends. In the linguistic, logical and Artificial Intelligence literature, starting naturally at the language end, there has been a strong tendency to assume a one-to-one correspondence between words and the underlying concepts. Recognizing that the words and the underlying concepts are not the same thing, notations have flourished which simply transform (typically English) words by some device such as capitalizing them, as in Jackendoff (1990, 2002) and Schank (1982). For human researchers working in a natural language (often English) this is a very convenient notation, even for referring to the non-linguistic concepts of babies or animals. I will follow this practice, embedding the capitalized terms in a box notation, to be explained in Chapter 5. There, we will meet diagrams such as $\boxed{\text{LION CROUCH}}$, intended as a useful research notation for a pre-linguistic animal's representation of a scene with a lion crouching. We just need to bear in mind that, in the context of evolution, words came later, and had a modifying effect on the pre-linguistic mental representations.

A problem that lurks behind quarrels over the term 'representation' is that in ordinary language usage, representations are static and relatively permanent, like pictures in an art gallery (which are iconic) or letters in a printed book (which are symbolic). The formulae to be developed

---

[10] Fodor's other conditions are that concepts are (1) mental particulars, (2) categories, (3) compositional, and (4) often learned. What I call concepts conform to these conditions, as far as I can see. Fodor's criteria won't be systematically discussed in this work, except in passing where appropriate.

in Chapter 5 are intended as snapshots of partial transient states of a dynamic neural system at some point in time. The formulae above bear the same general kind of relation to the neural activity in the animal's brain as the chemical formula H_2SO_4 bears to the state of some liquid in a flask at a particular time. The letters are **our** scientific symbols standing for atoms of various elements, in numbers indicated by the subscripts. If the acid is diluted, or something is dissolved in it, the substance changes, and the formula H_2SO_4 no longer describes what is in the flask. A better example of chemical formulae describing transient states of a dynamic system is in diagrams representing catalytic cycles.[11] In these diagrams, chemical formulae represent transient stages of the catalyst and reagents involved in the cycle. In some cases, the diagrams mention that some stages shown are not experimentally confirmed but hypothesized. This is a similarity with our formulae, which represent hypotheses about brain activity. An important difference is that, in the case of chemical formulae, statements embodied in the notation are very exact: the inclusion of H_2 in the formula for sulphuric acid definitely denotes the presence of two hydrogen atoms in the acid molecule. Chemical formulae are nonetheless higher-level abstractions, as they don't explicitly mention electrons, for example.

In the notation to be developed, the capitalized terms are more like theoretical, and so far non-explanatory, place-holders: ROCK stands for whatever goes on in an animal's brain when it recognizes, or thinks about, things roughly coextensive with what we would call a rock. This implies that a generalization will be found about rock-invoked brain activity in some species of animal. Admittedly, there is likely to be variation between individuals in a species, so the notation has to be understood as standing for some statistical distribution over types of brain activity. Nevertheless, it is reasonable to expect that such generalizations can be found. The concept RED, for example, is likely to involve significant activation of the known colour recognition areas, and minimal activation of the motor area sending signals to the left thumb.

In choosing which terms to use, and capitalize (like ROCK), as a way of describing the environmental objects and events that an animal's intentional states are about, we make practical and revisable decisions about likely approximate correspondences between how we and the animal categorize things. To take an example from Fodor (1990), a frog that reflexively flicks out its tongue to catch flies is in a particular brain state.

---

[11] For some good examples, do a Google search on the phrase 'catalytic cycle'.

It is natural and practical to say that this state is **about** flies, which I would write, as an interim measure, FLIES. Fodor rightly claims, 'there is nothing to stop you from telling the story quite a different way. On the alternative account, what the neural mechanism is designed to respond to is little ambient black things (or, mutatis mutandis, characteristic patterns of ocular irradiation as of little ambient black things).' Well, yes, of course, but why should we, until we know any better? We pick the term FLY from a large set of possibilities all equally consistent with experimental facts, because it will be helpful to convey to other scientists what we are talking about. As experiments proceed, it is certain, in the froggy case, that we will change our minds about the most useful term, and narrow it down well beyond LITTLE-AMBIENT-BLACK-THINGS, because we find that frogs respond the same way to artificial stimuli that we wave in front of them. And of course, we have to specify as exactly as possible just how LITTLE and just how BLACK.[12] I apply here, as a matter of practicality, what Dennett (1991) calls 'a certain "interest-relative" tactic of interpretation— roughly, the decision to ignore nitpickers. Hence such considerations will not serve to rule out heroically Pickwickian interpretations, e.g., the sort of phenomenalistic interpretation that insists that the frog lives its whole life caring only about "little ambient black things"' (p. 93).

So far, these capitalized terms for concepts are not explanatory. They resemble the *virtus dormitiva* that Molière ironically puts in the mouth of his aspiring doctor in *Le Malade imaginaire* to 'explain' how opium puts one to sleep.[13] But they are nevertheless useful in theorizing, just as the phrase *the source of the Nile* was usefully distinguished from *the source of the Congo* before either of these places had been located precisely. The interior of Africa was once *terra incognita*, just as the workings of the brain still mostly are. At the edges of Africa, big rivers visibly emerged, and arbitrary names such as *Nile* and *Congo* became accepted for these rivers. Common knowledge about rivers entailed that they had sources, but no one knew exactly where in the unexplored interior these sources were. The phrases *the source of the Nile* and *the source of the Congo* were, and remain, meaningful, and useful for describing the goals of expeditions. Analogously, we observe complex behaviour in ourselves and animals, and we know that particular patterns of behaviour are caused by patterns of activity in their brains, but, of course, we don't know

[12] Research has already raced on, and the appropriate PREY stimulus for frogs and toads has been described as 'bar-shaped objects elongated in the direction of movement with W- or H- orientation'. (See Ewert 1987; Beauquin and Gaillard 1998.)

[13] See Mumford (1996) for a philosophical defence of *virtutes dormitivae*.

exactly what this cerebral activity is. Nevertheless, it is useful to have terms denoting such activity, whatever it is, in advance of its being perhaps pinned down in the future by neuroscience.

No analogy is perfect, and of course there are significant differences between an expedition to locate the source of the Nile and a search for the patterns of brain activity underlying behaviour. In our case, it is hoped one day to be able to specify weighted **potentials** for neural activity. The brains of different individuals vary in their instantiation of concepts, but not unconstrainedly, so that statistical distributions over patterns of (potential) brain activity could be specified. The evidence comes from complex, but in some sense regular behaviour, in well-described environmental (natural or experimental) contexts, all suitably classified, augmented where possible by forays into the interior with the kit of neuroscience. Clearly there are systematic connections between the internal activity and the externally observed behaviour and environmental conditions. In this sense, I am almost at ease with Wittgenstein (1953, ¶580)'s well-known dictum 'an "inner process" stands in need of outward criteria'; but I would like to replace *criteria*, with its connotation of defining by necessary and sufficient conditions, with *evidence*. An acceptable formulation by a commentator on Wittgenstein is that he 'argues that the epistemic criteria for the applicability of mentalistic terms cannot be private, introspectively accessible inner states but must instead be intersubjectively observable behavior' (Marras 1995, p. 68). I agree.

1.3 A SCALE FROM NO-BRAINERS TO COGNITIVE CONCEPTS

It is necessary, but not sufficient, for attribution of a concept of something to an animal, that the animal show (or have shown) regular and systematic behaviour in connection with that thing. At least one further step is necessary, which I will describe later. But before we go on, let's emphasize the importance of this first step of regular and systematic behaviour in connection with some class of entities from the environment. I will say that the existence of such regular behaviour is evidence of '**proto-concepts**'. The next step, to be described, is built upon the foundation of such proto-concepts. Without proto-concepts, no full concepts can evolve. As an example, a cat has (at least) some proto-concept of its habitual prey because it adopts the same behaviour towards it when it encounters it. This is not to say, of course, that a cat has the exact human concepts MOUSE or BIRD that a human has. Indeed they may be all the same to a cat, unless of course we can observe behaviour towards mice differing in a regular way from behaviour towards birds. So, when a cat is watching a bird, and acting as it usually does (crouching low, perhaps muttering), it seems reasonable to say that the cat's behaviour is guided by, and thus the cat possesses, some mental category or proto-concept of PREY. Of course animal concepts such as PREY are entirely private, except for a tiny number such as the vervets' concepts of specific predators, which do get externalized in public signals. My choice of the terms 'concept' and 'category' allows the possibility (indeed the probability) that these mental entities are fuzzy.

I can go a certain distance along with philosophers who argue for a narrow interpretation of 'concept':

[having a concept] is not just a matter of being natively disposed, or having learned, to react in some specific way to items that fall under a concept; it is to *judge* or *believe* that certain items fall under the concept. If we do not make this a condition on having a concept, we will have to treat simple tendencies to eat berries, or to seek warmth and avoid cold, as having the concepts of a berry, or of warm, or of cold. I assume we don't want to view earthworms and sunflowers as having concepts. This would be a terminological mistake, for it would be to lose track of the fundamental distinction between a mindless disposition to respond differentially to members of a class of stimuli, and a disposition to respond to those items *as* members of that class.

(Davidson 2004, pp. 137–138)

As long as terms such as *judge* and *believe* and the preposition *as* in the last sentence here are not necessarily tied to language, I can agree. Like Davidson, I don't want to attribute the concept of a fly-like object to a Venus flytrap, because a flytrap has no brain. From an evolutionary point of view, it is useful to distinguish, as Davidson apparently does not, between sunflowers and earthworms,[14] between plants and animals with brains. Any animal with a brain has the rudiments of a system which can evolve to play host to concepts, whereas a plant does not. Proto-concepts and concepts are instantiated (in a way shortly to be discussed) in brains. Plants (and sea sponges and jellyfish) don't have brains.

Now, what are some examples of behaviours indicating the possession of proto-concepts, but not of concepts? Reflex actions, like kneejerks and eyeblinks, are systematic responses to external stimuli, but cannot reasonably be said to indicate concepts of those stimuli. We want more

---

[14] I wonder if Davidson was aware of Darwin's discussion of intelligence in earthworms (Darwin 1881).

from concepts than that. But reflex actions **lie on the evolutionary path** to more complex behaviours that do indicate possession of concepts.

The behaviour of some animals seems to consist mainly, and perhaps only, in reflex actions. A fly behaves in a regular and systematic way in response to certain classes of input. Chan et al. (1998) have shown that this systematic behaviour is managed by a direct linkage between the fly's eyes, through its halteres (club-shaped oscillators acting as gyroscopes), to its wings. Further, three of the most important activities that a fly engages in, turning, landing, and collision-avoidance, can be satisfactorily described as reflex responses to certain classes of visual input from the optic flow (Tammero and Dickinson 2002). Thus, where a fly goes in the world is largely determined by reflexes. Compare this with our own movements: walking about, sitting, and standing. Though the details of putting one foot in front of the other may have reflex components, the overall direction of travel, and where in the world we end up, is not governed by reflexes, unlike most of the fly's path through life.

In the limit, whether animals have concepts is a doubly slippery question, because the normal intuitive understanding of the 'concept of a concept' assumes answers to two profoundly deep, and perhaps insoluble, philosophical questions: (1) the question of what counts as a valid generalization, i.e. the problem of induction, and (2) the question of whether we, or any organisms, have 'free' access to, and control over, our mental states. Now, as this is a book about language evolution, I'm not going to claim to give answers to those thorny philosophical problems. Instead, I will appeal to the idea of scales of complexity, one for induction and one for 'freewill', on which researchers can practically agree whether some behaviour is more or less complex than some other. Then I will pin the possession of 'genuine' concepts above some arbitrary point on each of these scales; these points, though arbitrary, nevertheless command the agreement of a number of animal researchers and some philosophers, if not those determined to preserve concepts for language-using humans. This strategy for deciding whether concepts can be attributed to animals is similar to Herrnstein's (Herrnstein 1991): he defined a scale with five points, and labelled the fourth point on the scale 'concepts'.[15] He concluded that many animals showed evidence of having concepts, but that only humans reach his fifth point, the level of abstract relations. More recent work, as we will see, indicates that some non-humans can represent

---

[15] See Allen and Hauser (1991) for some further discussion of attributing concepts to animals, including discussion of Herrnstein's experiments.

abstract relations. I will review some results in animal research that show that some animals (a) make inductive generalizations of a quite complex ('abstract') sort, and (b) can be responsive to their own internal states, both these capacities reflecting the beginnings of a level of cognition that is often demanded for possession of concepts. The motivation for all this, of course, is that such animal concepts provide a foundation for the meanings of words, when these eventually evolve.

CHAPTER TWO

Animals Approach Human Cognition

(This chapter title is not meant to suggest a *scala naturae* on which humans occupy the pinnacle, with other species sitting on various lower rungs, and, over the course of evolution, 'approaching' humans' exalted status. Rather, in our own line of descent, our animal ancestors approached modern human cognition to various degrees, and our best clues to what these evolutionary stages might have been can be found in currently available animals more of less closely related to us.)

Depending on their evolutionary closeness to us, animals live in the same physical world as us, in more than the most vacuous physical sense.[1] They have evolved ways of categorizing many of the same phenomena as us. Their organs of perception are similar to ours, but differ in some ways. Thus we can expect the pre-linguistic concepts of those vertebrates whose habitats overlap with ours to resemble ours, but of course we don't expect identity. Any claim of resemblance between an animal concept and a human concept is based on their apparent extensions in the world. For example, we can test whether an animal can distinguish between the numbers 1, 2, and 3 by giving it real-world stimuli consisting of these numbers of objects. Similarly, to test an animal's possession of a concept of sameness, we give it real-world exemplars that are the same for us.

---

[1] An idea once popular in biology, due to Uexküll (1909), was that of the 'Umwelt' of an organism: the totality of aspects of the world meaningful in some way to it. This is a valid idea, but it can be taken too far, especially in the case of closely related species. An extreme version would hold that even if some animal species live in the same physical world, their Umwelts, what they sense and attend to, may be so different that they might as well live in different physical environments. For humans and sea-slugs there may be an interesting element of truth in this, but even sea-slugs are subject to gravity, friction, and the temperature range of liquid water, like us. It seems more interesting, in the present project, to concentrate on the **similarities** between human Umwelts and those of birds and mammals, with special emphasis on apes.

Wittgenstein (1953, p. 223) famously wrote, 'If a lion could talk, we could not understand him.' This is far too extreme. If the lion (or any other animal) had been sufficiently motivated to communicate with us, and if somehow a set of conventions had been adopted by both sides, there could be some meaningful communication. A lion is an unlikely candidate, but something of the sort has been achieved with Kanzi, the bonobo who lives in a 'Pan/Homo culture' (Segerdahl et al. 2005), the product of interaction between him and his keepers. It is clear that Kanzi can communicate to humans and that they can understand him. In Wittgenstein's terms, a particular form of life, or language game, has evolved between Kanzi and the humans he deals with. On the same page, the ever-enigmatic Wittgenstein puts his finger on how this is possible: 'There is a game of "guessing thoughts".' This is what we all do, our guesses being well-informed by confident knowledge of a common code, of a shared set of background assumptions, and the relevant context of situation. We are very good at it.

As for animals, the most we can show is similarity between an animal's concept and some human concept. In keeping with a general principle of scientific discovery, any claim to identity of concepts between two organisms can always be falsified by the next datum to come along. This in fact applies even among humans speaking the same language, as there is no absolute certainty that any two people share (or perhaps better, agree on) identical concepts. Communication between people is approximate, and usually close enough for government work. Depending on one's trade, people take greater or lesser care to communicate exactly. In some cases, of course, the falsifying instances are already with us, and we can be certain that some animal concept is not identical in its extension to its closest human counterpart. For example, many primate species have concepts of relative social rank, in terms of dominance and subordination, but the social world of humans is far more textured, and our own roughly corresponding concepts of dominance and subordination are much subtler than a chimpanzee's. (See Dennett 1996's section on 'The Misguided Goal of Propositional Precision' for concurring arguments.)

Note the appeal to extension. The brain mechanisms underlying different organisms' possession of similar concepts may be quite different. At least while we know so little about brain mechanisms, we have to rely on extensional criteria to decide whether two organisms are dealing with a similar concept. And this will probably still apply even when at some future time we have a good map of how the brain is activated when various concepts are brought to mind, or attended to.

After this cautionary preamble, this chapter will survey several domains in which we can see an approach by animals to the content of human concepts. In the animal concepts to be mentioned, we can see foreshadowings of some human semantic universals. Many things that animals find it useful and possible to discriminate are also universally discriminated by humans.

2.1 INDUCTION, GENERALIZATION, AND ABSTRACTION

Even reflex actions involve some kind of generalization over stimuli. No two stimuli are ever exactly the same. The various slightly different stimuli prompting reflex actions are at the bottom of a scale of complexity in classifying things or events. Such stimuli can be readily classified as the same because they involve a small number of easily measured physical parameters, such as the strength of the airpuff giving rise to an eyeblink, or the force of the hammer blow giving rise to a kneejerk.

On a generous interpretation, many animals in the wild may be thought to generalize over inputs to their senses that are far more heterogeneous than the stimuli producing reflex actions. Swallows, for instance, mob both aerial predators, such as hawks, and ground predators, such as cats. A hawk flying quite high and apparently nonchalantly near nesting swallows will attract this mobbing behaviour; the swallows repeatedly dive close to it, interrupting and disturbing its smooth flight, until the hawk goes far enough away. A cat sitting immobile in open ground gets the same treatment, the swallows diving low enough to make the cat duck its head and eventually slink off. The behaviour seems selective for predators. Pigeons and ducks don't get mobbed by swallows, nor do dogs, not even cat-sized dogs. The behaviour is regular enough to make one suspect that the swallows have a high-level concept of PREDATOR, generalized from past experience of hawks going for fledgling swallows before they can fly very well, and cats snooping around under their nests. An airborne hawk and a sessile cat don't present very similar visual appearances. The problem is, of course, that the swallows may not have actually made a generalization, and may have evolved separate cat-mobbing and hawk-mobbing behaviours in parallel. This seems likely, as it has been shown in classic ethological work by Konrad Lorenz that even naive chicks (domestic fowl) respond instinctively to a very specific aspect of the shape of an aerial stimulus, namely 'short neck', a very short protrusion in the silhouette at the front relative to the direction of movement of the stimulus (Lorenz 1939, cited by Tinbergen 1948).

Likewise, it may be tempting to attribute a higher-level category FOOD to many omnivorous animals, since they display the same stuff-it-in-the-mouth behaviour towards a wide range of different things. But without experiment there is no way of telling whether they have made a genuine generalization rather than just having independent but parallel behaviour to lots of different things. Nevertheless the fact that they associate the same eating behaviour with a range of different objects surely makes them closer to attainment of a generalization over all foods. Savage-Rumbaugh et al. (1978a, 1980) found that the chimpanzees Sherman and Austin, after learning to label a training set of different food items with a lexigram for food, could generalize this label appropriately to new food items. In some cases it has been possible to demonstrate somewhat structured animal knowledge of food categories and their relation to other categories, such as colour and shape. Santos et al. (2001, p. 149) showed that 'After learning about a novel food object, rhesus monkeys selectively approach objects of the same colour, but not objects of the same shape.' These authors also mention previous work (Hauser 1998a; Hauser and Marler 1993) indicating a two-level organization of rhesus monkeys' knowledge of the food domain: the monkeys distinguish a category of food from other categories, and within the FOOD category, they distinguish between high-quality food and low-quality food, as indicated by different calls. This shows a rudimentary semantic hierarchy.

In the wild, it is impossible to tell whether generalizations get formed inside an animal's head. Carefully controlled experiments in the lab, however, can provide stronger evidence. There is now an enormous amount of experimental data showing that in laboratory conditions animals **can** learn to make generalizations across classes of inputs. Some of the earliest classic results were obtained by Herrnstein et al. (1976), who showed that pigeons could learn to distinguish pictures containing people from pictures not containing people. Training was carried out with many pictures, making rote memorization of the stimuli unlikely, a conclusion confirmed by the pigeons' significantly accurate performance on novel stimuli. Some later experiments (Watanabe et al. 1995) achieved surprising and amusing results, showing that pigeons could learn to discriminate correctly between novel presentations of paintings by Monet and Picasso. Commenting on this work, Wynne (2001, p. 90) summarizes: 'In the first study of the categorization of schools of art by a non-human subject, paintings by Cezanne and Renoir were spontaneously categorized as belonging to the Monet school, while paintings by Braque and Matisse were categorized as belonging to the Picasso school.' These experiments are only a small subset of those that have been reported. It is now clear that a wide range of mammals and birds can generalize over classes of stimuli in ways similar, if not identical, to the generalization that the human trainers have in mind. When tested, it turns out that, not surprisingly, the animals in question are always much better at generalizing over genuine classes of stimuli than over randomly assembled classes of stimuli, at which they perform no better than chance. Of the experimental work mentioned here so far, I am tempted to attribute learned concepts to the pigeons who have been trained to discriminate between schools of painting. But, if the bar is to be set even higher, see just below on animal learning of abstract relations, and in the next section on some animals' ability to 'stand outside' their own generalizations.

The stimuli given to animals in such experiments are, being tightly controlled, not rich in all the extra information that would come an animal's way in roaming the wild. Most stimuli, for example, are two-dimensional pictures, are bland in smell, and make no noise. Occasionally, the animals make a generalization that is not exactly what the human investigators had in mind, but usually this can be traced to some accidental property in the range of stimuli that escaped the researchers' meticulous planning (D'Amato and van Sant 1988). Of course, when we look for evidence of concepts in animals, we shouldn't expect them to have exactly the same concepts that we do, just as we naturally don't expect animals' legs or brains to match exactly with human legs or brains. Animals' sensory experiences, which form the basis of concepts, differ from ours, to a greater or lesser degree. For example, apes share with us trichromatic vision, with red-, green-, and blue-sensitive receptors, whereas New World monkeys such as marmosets have only receptors for two colour foci; and primates generally have a reduced sense of smell compared to other mammals such as dogs or rodents (Rouquier et al. 2000).

A simple extension of classification tasks involves 'reversal learning'. Here an animal is first trained to associate one stimulus with a reward and another stimulus with lack of a reward. When the animal has attained a certain degree of success, the relations between stimulus and reward are reversed. The animal has to unlearn the old associations, and learn the opposite associations. The idea is that if an animal can quickly reverse its associations, it does so on the basis of some concept of oppositeness. If, on the other hand, an animal takes just as long, or longer, to learn the reversed associations as it took to learn the initial pairing, no application of some concept of OPPOSITE, used as a mental shortcut, can be attributed. Furthermore, the experiments can be varied according to how successful you let the animal get in the first round of training. With animals that make no use of the OPPOSITE conceptual shortcut, the better they have learned the first set of associations, the longer they will take to unlearn it and learn the reverse matchings. On the other hand, with animals that seem to make use of this conceptual trick, the better they have learned the first set, the more quickly they will be able to reverse it. Rumbaugh and Pate (1984a, 1984b) compared different species of primates with this technique, showing great apes performing better than monkeys, and monkeys better than prosimians. Oppositeness is an abstract relation, and our closest relatives seem able to apply this relational concept.

The reversal learning experiments show more than an ability to apply the relation of oppositeness. An animal that quickly learns the second, reversed, association is, fairly clearly, not learning a whole new set in the same painstaking way as it learned the first set. It seems to be keeping its old mental representation (concept) of the general class of stimuli acquired in the first training regime and relating the new set to that acquired concept. Diagrammatically, and of course simplifying somewhat:

Training regime	Prosimians	Great apes
First session:		
Stimulus-1 > reward	Association of	Formation of Concept of
Stimulus-2 > nothing	Stimulus-1 with reward.	Stimulus-1, and association with reward.
Second session:		
Stimulus-1 > nothing	Association of	Application of negation,
Stimulus-2 > reward	Stimulus-2 with reward. (Difficult unlearning and relearning.)	or oppositeness to Concept of Stimulus-1. NOT(STIMULUS-1) associated with reward. (Relearning facilitated by use of acquired concept.)

In the (unconventional but insightful) terminology of Deacon (1997), the prosimians are learning an **indexical** connection in both training regimes, whereas the great apes, in the second training regime, are learning a **symbolic** connection to a previously acquired inner representation. In relation to a different, but closely related, set of experiments, Deacon (1997, p. 89) comments:

the shift from associative predictions to symbolic predictions is initially a change in mnemonic strategy, a recoding. It is a way of offloading redundant details from working memory, by recognizing a higher order regularity in the mess of associations, a trick that can accomplish the same task without having to hold all the details in mind.

(We will return to closely related ideas in Volume 2, in connection with vocabulary learning.)

Besides the oppositeness relation, some animals have also shown themselves capable of learning other relational concepts, too. Premack and Premack (1983) reported an early study in which chimpanzees learned to match one of a pair of different objects to a sample object previously shown to them (the 'Match-to-Sample', MTS, paradigm), thus exhibiting a capacity to control the sameness relation. Thompson et al. (1997) went a step further, and showed that chimpanzees could master a **relation between relations**. In this case, rather than single objects, the samples and potential matches were **pairs** of objects, either identical or different. For example, a chimpanzee was shown a pair AA as a sample, and then given two further pairs, say BB and CD, as potential matches, being required to choose BB, because that pair exhibited the same internal relation (sameness) as the sample AA. It is relevant to point out that these chimpanzee subjects were said by the authors to be 'language-naive', i.e. they had not been given language training; but they had been **previously trained with symbols for the concepts** SAME **and** DIFFERENT. This is important, because the animals had been artificially given 'mental tools' labelling the same pairs and the different pairs. It seems likely that they called up these mental tools in the more abstract decision-making task. In Clark (2003, p. 70)'s terms, the chimpanzees were provided by humans with a 'cognitive shortcut': a shortcut or mental tool that doesn't come to them in their wild state. By contrast, humans, in initiating their babies into a linguistic environment, provide them with thousands of such cognitive shortcuts. (This is explored in more detail in the sequel to this book.)

This behaviour in chimpanzees contrasts with that of macaques. Macaques, investigated by some of the same authors (Washburn et al. 1997; Kuczaj and Hendry 2003), could learn to make the required responses to individual pairs, but could not generalize the same/different concepts across new pairs; essentially, the macaques had not learned what is common to the SAME relation. Capuchin monkeys, on the other hand, have been shown to be able to master generalized SAME/DIFFERENT tasks to a limited extent. (D'Amato and Colombo 1985; Tavares and Tomaz

2002): 'in [capuchin] monkeys, the matching (or identity) concept has a very limited reach; [these results] consequently do not support the view held by some theorists that an abstract matching concept based on physical similarity is a general endowment of animals' (D'Amato and Colombo 1989, p. 225). Thompson and Oden (1998) found that macaques could not succeed at the relations-between-relations task successfully performed by chimpanzees, as mentioned above. The gap between monkey and ape abilities is stated somewhat more extremely by Thompson and Oden (2000, p. 363): 'There is no evidence that monkeys can perceive, let alone judge, relations-between-relations. This analogical conceptual capacity is found only in chimpanzees and humans.' There is a tension in the literature between researchers who claim qualitative differences between species and those who assert that the differences are only quantitative. Thus, counter to Thompson and Oden (2000), Katz et al. (2002, p. 367) write, on the basis of training sessions of different lengths with rhesus monkeys:

The proposal made here is that most species (e.g., most vertebrates) ultimately have a set-size function for abstract-concept learning. Some species (e.g., pigeons) may have a set-size function that is lower than that for rhesus monkeys and would require larger set sizes to achieve full abstract-concept learning. Other species (e.g., chimpanzees) may have a set-size function that is elevated relative to that for rhesus monkeys. If the set-size function is sufficiently elevated, then that species under those conditions might be able to learn an abstract concept with very few items. Humans can demonstrate equivalence relationships after being trained with small stimulus sets (e.g., Sidman et al. 1982).

The abstract concepts that these authors experimented with are SAME versus DIFFERENT.

It has been shown that a California sea lion, trained to make same–different judgements, can remember the concept of sameness/difference, and make correct responses to novel stimuli after a complete gap of ten years after the initial training. 'In the 10-year memory test, the sea lion immediately and reliably applied the previously established identity concept to familiar and novel sets of matching problems' (Kastak and Schustermann 2002, p. 225). Bermúdez (2003, pp. 112–114) argues that *identity* is the wrong term to describe what these sea lions had mastered, pointing out that there is no evidence that they had learned the logical notion of identity, a relation between a thing and itself. What the sea lion had learned was an equivalence relation, i.e. sameness in some respect.

This illustrates a typical interdisciplinary problem; by an innocent choice of term, you risk appearing to workers in another discipline to be making a stronger claim than you are actually making. I'm sure that Kastak and Schustermann (2002) would be happy to give up *identity* and settle for *equivalence relation*.

The famous trained African grey parrot, Alex, can top the performance of some primates such as macaques (Pepperberg 2000). The advantage of experimenting with Alex is that he can speak his responses. (This is in fact highly relevant, because it has been argued, e.g. by Premack (1983) and others, that language training actually changes an animal's cognition from some pristine natural state. This point is also relevant to the example of allegedly non-language-trained chimpanzees from the paragraph above. The effect of learning public labels on thought will be discussed in Volume 2.) Straightforwardly, Alex can name the colours, shapes, and materials of objects presented to him. Not every object you might think of, but a range of middle-sized (to a parrot) objects that can fit on a tray, with fairly salient colours, shapes, and materials. Then, given three such objects on a tray, in answer to the question 'What's same?', Alex can correctly (usually) reply 'Colour' if they all have the same colour, but are of different shapes and materials. Likewise, he can correctly reply 'Shape' or 'Matter' if those are the properties common to all the displayed objects. Furthermore, if the objects are different in all their properties, he can correctly reply 'None' to the question 'What's same?' He also replies 'None' to the question 'What's different?' if all the objects are identical. Alex is not simply memorizing particular training instances; he is able to generalize to novel items. '[Alex] correctly answered 12 of 15 queries of "What color?" and "What shape?" for first-time ever presentations of objects that varied in newly acquired colors and shapes (e.g. at the first ever presentation of a blue pentagonal piece of rawhide' (Pepperberg 2000, p. 60).

Note that these abilities of Alex's go beyond classical first-order predicate logic (FOPL), if we assume that the words Alex uses express predicates in the same way as they do for humans.[2] Alex, given a green object, can clearly report that it is green. This only indicates first-order logical competence, applying a predicate to an individual object, as in $\text{GREEN}(x)$, where 'x' stands for the object he is attending to. But the question put

---

[2] It is hard to see how Alex's words such as *green* and *square* could not express predicates in pretty much the human sense, but a logician has argued to me that what is a predicate for a human may not be for a parrot, even though both agree on applying the same symbol to the same external object in the world, in response to similar questions.

to Alex is 'What colour?' This means that he is capable of making the second-order judgement COLOUR(GREEN), corresponding to 'Green is a colour', because he does not respond to the 'What colour?' question with a word for a shape or a material. Further, he is capable of a judgement that can only be represented in quite abstract terms logically:

$$P_1(x) \ \& \ P_2(y) \ \& \ P_1 = P_2 \ \& \ \text{COLOUR}(P_1) \ \& \ \text{COLOUR}(P_2)$$

Roughly paraphrasing: 'Object X has a certain property, object Y has an identical property, and this property is a colour.'

Further experiments on birds (back to pigeons again) have also shown strong evidence for an ability to learn the concepts of sameness and difference (Cook et al. 1995; Wasserman et al. 1995; Cook and Wixted 1997; Young and Wasserman 1997). To my mind, these experiments are convincing of the animals' ability to attain such abstract concepts as SAME and DIFFERENT. Commenting on these and similar results, Shettleworth (1998, p. 227) has expressed the cautious experimental psychologist's view that 'consideration of this line of research suggests that the line between abstract concepts and direct perception of relationships may not be easy to draw. Implicit knowledge of some abstract relationship may be embedded in a highly specific perceptual module without the animal being able to access it to control explicit, arbitrary, discriminative responses.' This brings us to the topic of the next subsection, where I will discuss the further requirement on concepts that they be accessible for the control of explicit discriminatory responses.

2.2 FREEWILL, OR AT LEAST SOME METACOGNITION

I confess: 'Freewill' is a come-on heading. My question is not whether any organisms have absolute freewill, being able to act independently of external causation. It's really a question of the depth and complexity of control exercised by an animal over its actions and internal representations. An animal governed entirely by a set of simple reflexes has, we agree, no concepts. Having a concept involves some ability to 'stand outside' one's immediate behaviour, possibly to choose one's next move, or evaluate alternative possibilities. This is at the heart of Davidson's insistence, quoted earlier, on the necessity of **judgement** or **belief**. Concepts should be 'stimulus free'; working with them (i.e. thinking) should be somewhat voluntary, not completely involuntary or reflexive or automatic. Of course, the very term 'voluntary' is problematic; I shall use it as a scalar term, where a more voluntary act is one less immediately subject to external stimuli, and correspondingly more determined by hidden inner mental processes. This allows, of course, that these hidden processes are subject eventually and indirectly to external stimuli.

'When an organism knows what it knows, its actions are different from an organism that is locked out of its library of knowledge' (Hauser 2003, p. 80). A recent report of research on dolphins (Smith et al. 1995) and macaques (Smith et al. 1997) concludes that '[T]here is a strong isomorphism between the uncertainty-monitoring capacities of humans and animals. Indeed, the results show that animals have functional features of or parallels to human metacognition and human conscious cognition' (Smith and Washburn 2005, p. 19). 'Uncertainty-monitoring' refers to the capacity to recognize how sure or unsure one is in making a judgement. In other words, it has been shown that these higher animals are not only able to register a 'Yes' or 'No' answer to a challenge put to them by a researcher, but also to register an 'I don't know' response. They know whether or not they know something. This reveals a degree of self-awareness, or **metacognition**, previously unsuspected in non-humans.

These same authors (plus a third) wrote a slightly earlier paper on metacognition in *Behavioral and Brain Sciences*, where it attracted a number of peer commentaries. In their summary of the commentaries Smith et al. (2003b, p. 358) conclude:

There was a strong consensus in the commentaries that animals' performances in metacognition paradigms indicate high-level decisional processes that cannot be explained associatively. Our response summarizes this consensus and the support for the idea that these performances demonstrate animal metacognition.

This summary is somewhat partisan, as Shettleworth and Sutton (2006, pp. 238–239) note: 'We emphasize more than they do the methodological issues . . . , and we are accordingly less inclined to interpret the results as evidence for human-like awareness or meta-cognition.' But even these cautious commentators conclude: 'Thus only primates and perhaps a dolphin have been proven rational in a strong sense that requires having access to the reasons for their behaviour' (Shettleworth and Sutton 2006, p. 245).

The phrase 'animal metacognition' is too loose. Only some animals have it. It has not (yet) been convincingly shown in birds. Sole et al. (2003) carried out an experiment with pigeons similar in structure to those claiming to establish metacognition in monkeys. They write:

Like monkeys and people in related experiments, the birds chose the uncertain response most often when the stimulus presented was difficult to classify correctly, but in other respects their behavior was not functionally similar to human behavior based on conscious uncertainty or to the behavior of monkeys in comparable experiments. Our data were well described by a signal detection model that assumed that the birds were maximizing perceived reward in a consistent way across all the experimental conditions.

(Sole et al. 2003, p. 738)

In other words, rather than being aware of their own uncertainty, the pigeons were probably simply learning associations with three classes of stimulus, the middle one of which the human experimenters had labelled 'uncertain'.

The idea that some animals may respond to their own uncertainty has only recently become acceptable as a topic of debate in psychology. Smith et al. (2003a, p. 320) have a wry comment on the history of the idea:

It is possible that animals' ancillary behaviors would betray their uncertainty or conflict on threshold trials. These hesitations and waverings do sometimes occur, and they made behaviorists uncomfortable because they suggested that animals might be in mental turmoil over difficult trials. Tolman even suggested that these 'lookings or runnings back and forth' (Tolman 1938, p. 27) could be taken as a behaviorist's definition of animal consciousness (Tolman 1927). As a behaviorist, Tolman sometimes misbehaved. Moreover, twelve years later, Tolman retracted this claim (Tolman 1938, p. 27), thereby completing his own theoretical 'looking or running back and forth'.

A version of this running back and forth has been observed in pigs, strongly correlated with an immediately recent wrong response. Keddy-Hector et al. (2005) trained piglets on a same–different task. To make their choices the piglets had to enter either the left or the right arm of a T-maze. Here is what the experimenters report (in a so far unpublished paper):

Half of the animals used in the study attempted to immediately back out of a T maze arm once it was entered. There was no movement or sign by the experimenter to indicate whether or not the pig's choice was a correct response. A strong, positive correlation was found between the likelihood of backing out and the percentage of correct responses by the same individual within a given trial ($r = .819$, $p < .01$, Spearman). Backouts were not performed, however, during individual runs where the piglet made a correct response. Instead backing out occurred almost exclusively during those runs where the piglet made an incorrect choice (21/22 runs). Overall, the average percentage of correct responses by piglets who attempted to back out of a T maze arm was greater than those piglets who never exhibited any backout behavior ($p < .05$, $n = 13$, $m = 17$, Mann-Whitney test).

(Keddy-Hector et al. 2005).

In other words, it could be argued that these piglets seemed to realize immediately that they had just made a mistake, and attempted to correct it by backing out of the wrongly chosen arm of the maze. An alternative explanation[3] is that the piglets did not make their initial decision until after they had already randomly entered one or other arm of the maze, and then did what was necessary to enter the correct arm. If they had randomly entered the incorrect arm, this necessitated backing out. In this case, the piglets are 'thinking', for example, 'I need to go to the left-hand arm', and then going there, from wherever they happen to be, which might be the right-hand arm. In this case, the piglets are not 'thinking' anything like 'Oh, damn, I made a mistake—I'm in the wrong arm.'[4] I have given this unpublished example so much space because it is clearly suggestive, though in need of independent replication, and illustrative of the difficulties of interpretation. Myself, I don't know which interpretation to prefer.

A capacity for metacognition involves the ability to take different **attitudes** to the content of propositions. In linguistic semantics, propositional attitudes are expressed by such verbs as *believe*, *know*, *wonder-whether*, *want*, and *expect*. The same proposition can be contemplated with any of these attitudes. You can believe that John came, or know that he came, or wonder whether he came, or want him to come, or expect him to come. In each case, the same proposition[5] is present to the mind, and the organism can use a different part of its mind to take an attitude to this proposition. Bermúdez (2003, pp. 38–39), quite reasonably, makes the ability to take different propositional attitudes to the same propositional content a criterion for full human-like propositional thinking. It seems to me that familiar examples of animals' behaviour are consistent with them being able to take different attitudes to the same proposition. Animals that give alarm calls indicating the presence of predators, such as chickens and vervets, seem to some degree to be able to choose whether to give

---

[3] Pointed out to me by Dave Hawkey.

[4] The inclusion of first-person expression, such as *I*, in such a gloss is hard to avoid. It should not be assumed that metacognition of one's own internal states necessarily involves representation of a separate entity that is 'doing the cognizing'. See three paragraphs below (p. 34) on *self*.

[5] Ignoring tense.

the alarm call or not, depending on whether there is an audience ready to hear, especially if the audience is close kin (Karakashian et al. 1988; Cheney and Seyfarth 1990). This can be read as the animal knowing the proposition that there is a predator present, and in some cases deeming this fact worth giving an alarm call for, and in other cases deeming it not worth the labour of an alarm call. The animal, in other words, is making some implicit judgement about the urgency of the proposition that there is a predator present.

In all of this discussion of metacognition, the bogeymen of awareness and consciousness frequently creep in. Animal experimenters keen to emphasize the fact that their animal subjects are not responding directly to some external stimulus, but to some internal state generated by the problematic nature of the stimuli, sometimes use the terms 'know' and 'aware'. When they do, they get immediately pounced on by philosophers. Here's an example, from a commentary on Smith et al. (2003a)'s seminal article: 'Granted, the animal needs to have some way of telling when it is in a state of the required sort [uncertainty]...But this doesn't mean that the animal has to conceptualize the state *as* a state of uncertainty' (Carruthers 2003, p. 243). Carruthers' use of the preposition *as*, like Davidson's, quoted earlier, seems to require some explicit label, presumably linguistic. Notice, incidentally, that in avoiding saying that animals need to have some way of **knowing**, Carruthers has little choice but to use the more colloquial and less philosophically controversial *telling*, a word which, etymologically at least, is even more language-bound than *knowing*. Oddly, for Carruthers then, an animal can 'tell' when something is the case, but not 'know' that it is the case. Attribution of awareness, even of belief, desire, and intention, are often linked to possession of language. I take the position that while the use of coherent language is the strongest indicator of awareness, there can be awareness without language. One can be 'dimly aware' of many things. The animal experiments on metacognition have established that some animals can become aware (perhaps only dimly, but enough to affect their behaviour) of their own inner states. It is clear that the levels of metacognition discovered, with some effort and ingenuity, in animals, are far below what normal adult humans are capable of. Yet the seeds of human metacognitive capacity are present in some animals. If one were to go further into this topic, it might be held that animals display metacognitive **regulation** but not metacognitive **knowledge**, a distinction made by Flavell (1979). That is, possibly some animals can plan, monitor, and correct their own ongoing mental activity, without having a permanent store of 'known' facts about their own cognition in general, such as knowing that they can always find the way home. I am sceptical whether this latter kind of knowledge can be disentangled from possession of language.

In speaking of animals 'regulating their own behaviour', we need, of course, to avoid falling into the dualistic trap of supposing that there are somehow two entities, the regula**tor** and the regula**ted**. I suppose that the self-regulation of behaviour in animals works in a way analogous to a thermostatic control on a heating device. One part of the machine responds to heat and switches another part of the machine on or off; but it is all just one (complex) machine, with differentiated parts. A regulatory mechanism such as a thermostat does not regulate **itself**. When a thermostat goes haywire, the thermostat doesn't notice. Absolute reflexivity is not possible where cause and effect are involved.

There is another trap implicit in the *self-* of terms like *self-awareness*, *self-control*, and *self-regulation*. By linguistic convention, for English at least, *self* refers to the very same entity as some antecedent in a sentence. For example, *Mary scratched herself* is usually logically translated as SCRATCH(MARY, MARY), thus identifying the exact same entity as both the agent and the patient of the scratching. Even in such a simple case, different parts of Mary initiate the scratching and suffer it; Mary's mind initiates manual actions that result in her (own) body getting scratched— not *Mary's body initiates manual actions that result in her (own) mind getting scratched! If there is in any animal a metacognitive mechanism, X, that knows what other mechanisms, Y, Z, ..., in the same animal know, X does not know how much X itself knows.[6]

Bickerton (1995, pp. 135–138) also lays the blame on the structure of language for the illusion of a self that is somehow **part of**, yet simultaneously **wholly in control of**, 'itself'. Bickerton singles out the universal subject–predicate distinction. He doesn't mention Descartes, but Descartes obviously thought that *cogito* could be analysed into a cogitating subject and the separate action of cogitating (despite the absence of an overt subject pronoun in the Latin). Bickerton, by contrast (and I agree with him), claims that language deceives us here. 'Instead of holistic descriptions, "bird-flying", "cow-chewing", and so on, we are obliged to separate an actor or topic from an action, an event, or a state: "The bird flew", "The cows chew", and so on' (p. 137). Bickerton's eloquent

---

[6] I chose to put it this way, with *how much X knows*, to avoid one of the two interpretations of *what X knows*, which would have made the claim contradictory. Consider the ambiguity of *Bill knows what John knows*. On one reading *I know what I know* is a tautology, and its negation is a contradiction; it is the other reading that I claim cannot be the case.

summary of his section 'The inevitable invention of the self' is 'What I intuitively feel myself to be [is] a web made up of stunningly different types of property (mental phenomena, physical phenomena, attributions by others, abstract relationships, and so on) that are somehow held together to yield the illusion of a single self-conscious self' (p. 138).

Metacognition should be distinguished from metarepresentation. Being aware of some inner state of one's own is still solipsistic. It is a step towards, but still short of, being aware of the mental states of others, covered by the term *metarepresentation*. This distinguishes a simpler kind of metacognition from that argued by by Gopnik (1993) to be involved in children's understanding of their own intentional states. Gopnik argues that children's representations of their own beliefs and desires are mediated by the same internal representations as their understanding of the intentional states of others. So, according to Gopnik, children's knowledge of their own mental states is not a step short of knowing others' mental states. I would argue that the logic of the two kinds of knowledge can be different, one not necessarily involving representation of a knowing entity and the other necessarily doing so. For example, the piglet who backed out of the wrong arm of the T-maze might have had the thought expressed in the ungainly quasi-logical sentence *That this is the correct arm is wrong*—in a more logical notation WRONG(CORRECT(THIS)). Here the first (or inner) clause represents the basic first-order thought, and the outer predicate WRONG represents a second-order judgement about that basic thought; there is no representation of the knowing piglet itself. But an animal attributing a thought to another animal necessarily has some representation of the other animal, as in the thought expressed by *Mary thinks the food is in the left-hand bucket*. In this part of the book, on (pre-linguistic) semantics, we are just considering how an animal solitarily conceives its relationship to objects and events in its surroundings. The issue of animals' social dealings with conspecifics, which involves mind-reading, or metarepresentation, will be taken up in Part II, on pragmatics.

This is a story about what some animals are capable of that can provide an evolutionary foundation for human concepts. I'll call the relevant animal mental states 'pre-linguistic concepts'. A couple of further remarks are in order. Firstly, many of the results reported here describe what animals can do in unnatural situations contrived by humans. These experiments show what animals **can** do, if pushed. We don't know how far animals in the wild exploit their own latent abilities. By contrast with humans, animals' concepts are poorly developed and patchily distributed across species. Somehow or other, in the evolution of humans, abilities latent in animals **were** pushed by some contingency or other, and our ancestors started to move along the road to language. But there is a lot more of this story yet to sketch out, in subsequent chapters. Secondly, many researchers comment that there is a lot of individual variation in their animal subjects. There are smarter pigeons and dumber pigeons, savvy piglets and slower piglets, clever macaques and not-so-clever macaques. We can be sure that there was similar individual variation in our ancestors. Some had better abilities to work with abstract relational concepts than others, and some sometimes had more vivid awareness of their own inner mental states than others. Individual variation is the fuel of natural selection. In the area of ability to entertain concepts approaching human concepts, the top-performing animals were presumably our ancestors. Many other abilities had to fall into place, but an ability to entertain concepts of things and events in the world was one necessary evolutionary building block for human language as we know it.

2.3 OBJECT PERMANENCE AND DISPLACED REFERENCE

For us, and for all higher animals, objects exist. To the best of our knowledge, and we are pretty certain, the world is structured in such a way that physical matter very frequently forms into aggregations with clearly defined boundaries separating them from their surroundings. Hard and not-so-hard surfaces exist, defining the boundaries. How objects get formed varies. It can be as simple as a chip of rock flaking off a cliff. In the most complex case, biological objects such as human beings are assembled by unfathomed processes and delivered into the world, exquisitely formed. Physics, chemistry, and biology conspire and contrive to make it happen.

There are objects within objects: objects have parts, which are also objects. Here the prototypical boundedness of objects bends a little, and the relativity of the concept of an object begins to show. A finger is clearly an object, and so is a fingernail, but I am not happy to call an arbitrarily defined stretch of skin, unseparated from its body, a proper part, or indeed an object. If we create boundaries round it, by slicing it out from its body, it becomes clearly an object, a piece of skin. Human ideas of what are objects change with cultures. The planet Earth is an object; this was discovered by the Greeks, forgotten in the Dark Ages, and rediscovered in the Renaissance. Language is not a good guide; the sky is not an object, or at best is a marginal case. Nor, in a few cases, is perception even an absolutely reliable guide; our visual systems can be tricked into perceiving things as objects which closer inspection, or rational inference from other evidence, tells us are not what we really want to call objects.[7]

Perhaps for some very primitive organisms there are no objects, their environment being to them all just stuff to be sucked in or swum through. In a psychologically well-informed philosophical discussion, Clark (2004) distinguishes 'three different schemes of reference relevant to understanding systems of perceptual representation: a location-based system dubbed "feature-placing", a system of "visual indices" referring to things called "proto-objects", and the full sortal-based individuation allowed by a natural language' (p. 451.[8]). An evolutionary progression of ways of representing the world can be seen through these three schemes, taken as successive evolutionary stages. A 'feature-placing' system is a very primitive form of mental representation, which just registers the presence of qualities incoming from the world, without assigning them to particular objects. For some sensations, this is adequate, and the best one can do, for example noticing that it is hot where one is—not that any particular object is hot, just that 'it', where one is, is hot. A feature-placing system has no representation of individual objects. Strawson (1959) entertained the idea of a language consisting solely of feature-placing propositions, and concluded that it was inadequate for the purposes to which actual languages are put. The main reason for the inadequacy of simple feature-placing is that it has no way to accommodate the clusters of features, bound together, that we recognize as particular objects, and which are certainly psychologically real for us. In terms of the psychological theory of attention, to be discussed in Chapter 4.3, it might be said that a feature-placing system has only global attention, with no capacity for local attention to individual objects.

Particular objects exist for even so lowly a creature as an earthworm, as Charles Darwin noticed. In his book *The Formation of Vegetable Mould, through the Action of Worms* (Darwin 1881), he makes it very clear that worms are able to size up objects, check out their shapes, and drag them into their burrows in the most efficient way. The objects they drag are leaves and petioles of various kinds, pine needles, and little round mini-pebbles. Darwin discusses the role of intelligence in this task, and experimented by giving worms leaves from imported plants that would

---

[7] Have a look at the website http://www.scientificpsychic.com/graphics/ for some great fun examples of optical illusions, some of which involve 'seeing' objects, such as grey spots, which aren't really there. (This website was still active on 23/08/2006.)

[8] See also Clark (2000), where these ideas are developed.

not have figured in earthworm phylogeny.[9] It seems likely that earthworms can only manage to represent one object at a time, unlike many mammals and birds, who are capable of representing **scenes** or **events** with several objects (see Ch. 4).

More complex animals with eyes clearly have their attention drawn to objects and respond to their boundaries, by picking them up or moving around them. And animals of roughly human size, say between mouse-sized and elephant-sized, respond to objects in basic ways very similar to humans. If they didn't, most psychological experiments with animals wouldn't work. But there are differences in degree among mammals and birds with regard to how much information about the nature of objects is reflected in the animal's behaviour. Munakata et al. (2001) found that rhesus monkeys correlate independent movement with objecthood in the same way as children; they also found some differences between the monkeys and humans, indicating that children are more affected than monkeys by seeing hands manipulate objects, and that the monkeys are more responsive than children to changes in colour and texture in detecting object boundaries.

In the enormous body of work on object permanence in humans and animals, two principal experimental conditions stand out. These are 'visible displacement' and 'invisible displacement'. In the visible displacement condition, an object is visibly (to the animal subject) moved behind some obstruction, such as a screen, and the animal is tested to see whether it searches for the object behind the obstruction. The invisible displacement condition is more complex. Here the object is, in sight of the subject, placed inside a box, then the box is moved behind the obstacle and the object is surreptitiously removed from it (but the object stays behind the obstacle); the subject is then shown the empty box, and the experimenter observes whether the animal looks behind the obstacle.[10] There are many local variations on these broad classes of experimental conditions.

The results, by the standards of results in animal behaviour, are relatively clear-cut, although disputes remain about the abilities of particular species in subtly varied subtypes of the experiments. Naturally enough, every animal that can succeed at the invisible displacement task can also succeed at the visible displacement task. Some birds cannot even do the

---

[9] This little work is a great example of Darwin's incredible curiosity, thoroughness, systematic thinking, and humanity. It is a joy to read.

[10] Note that these experiments implicitly rely on lack of biological motion (see next subsection) in the hidden object. Hauser (1998b)'s cotton-top tamarins, mentioned below, were not surprised when live mice appeared in a novel location.

visible displacement task; these include domestic chicks (Etienne 1973). Parrots, among the smartest of birds, can even succeed at the invisible displacement task (Pepperberg et al. 1997), as can domestic dogs (Gagnon and Doré 1992; Watson et al. 2001). As for the visible displacement task, 'The tracking of an object moved visibly to a hiding location seems to be a capacity shared by most vertebrates tested, including avians, nonprimate mammals, and primates' (Neiworth et al. 2003, p. 28). Neiworth et al. (2003) provide an excellent thorough summary of results up to 2003. Their findings are that apes are unequivocally capable of succeeding at the invisible displacement task.[11] Depending on experimental procedures, different results are obtained for monkeys. Neiworth et al. (2003) found that cotton-top tamarins could manage all but the most complicated versions of the invisible displacement task, an ability which previous studies with these animals had not revealed. Squirrel monkeys, as so far tested (de Blois et al. 1998), have not been able to succeed at the invisible displacement task. Within primates, the closer the genetic relationship to humans, the more likely it is, roughly, that an animal can solve the invisible displacement task. But the patchy mosaic pattern often found across animal behaviour can be seen in the relatively advanced abilities of parrots, better than some monkeys. Human children typically manage the invisible displacement task by about age 3.0 at the latest (Baillargeon 1995; Hood et al. 2003).

Although dogs, like children over age 3.0, can succeed at an invisible displacement task, it has been shown by experiment and clever reasoning that children accomplish the task by a kind of logical deduction, whereas dogs use a 'less logical' association mechanism. Watson et al. (2001) showed a desirable object to their child and dog subjects, then put it in a container, then passed the container behind three screens, while surreptitiously tipping the object out of the container behind one of the screens; finally the subject was shown the empty container and expected to search for the object behind the screens. The children, after not finding the object behind the first two screens, tended to speed up their search when looking behind the last screen. This can be accounted for by assuming that the children were reasoning by logical negation of disjunction—either A or B or C, and not A and not B, so it must be C. The assumption is that having failed to find the object behind the first two screens, the children were certain that it must be behind the third, and,

---

[11] Tomasello and Call (1997, pp. 42–46), in an earlier survey, are more sceptical about the abilities of apes at the invisible displacement task.

given this certainty, moved quickly to retrieve it. The dogs, on the other hand, though they did continue searching after looking unsuccessfully behind two screens, tended to search more slowly behind the third screen. The authors attribute this behaviour to a different 'non-logical' associative process. The dog vaguely associates the object with a location somewhere behind the screens, but tires of searching as this association weakens, and searches less quickly after successive failures. But this does not invalidate the more basic conclusion about object permanence in dogs: they can keep an object in mind even when it has disappeared from sight.

Chimpanzees, our closest relatives, have no trouble at all with these tests. Panzee, experimented on by Menzel (2005), routinely remembered the type and location of hidden objects, sometimes overnight. By contrast, in dogs, memory for the location of a hidden object declines as a function of the interval between hiding and seeking, even for intervals as short as one minute, though they still perform better than chance with intervals of up to four minutes (Fiset et al. 2003). Menzel's experimental target with the chimpanzee was episodic memory (memory for specific events—see next chapter) rather than object permanence. The issues are intertwined, as it is hard to imagine episodic memory without the capacity for object permanence. It is surprising that this connection is not often made in the literature.

Knowing that an object is permanent takes a cognitive step beyond simple perception of the object. It involves knowing something about an object even when it is inaccessible to perception. During perception, the brain tracks perceived objects by attending to them, concurrently absorbing some information about them. When objects disappear behind a screen, they can no longer be attended to, and only the absorbed information remains, as a representation of the no-longer-present object. Even if an attended-to object does not disappear, but the eyegaze is quickly distracted away to another object, this distraction does not impede processing of the information taken in about the first object focused on and used to recognize what it is (Irwin and Brockmole 2004). See Santos et al. (2002) for experiments showing that rhesus macaques apply stored information about an object to maintain its identity, just as humans from about 1 year of age do. The ability to solve the displacement tasks, especially the invisible displacement task, shows that apes, humans (over age 3.0), and surprisingly parrots can maintain a representation of an object in a mental space controlled by knowledge, rather than perception. The capacity to know something about an object, even when 'it isn't there', is a first step along the road to the impressive characteristic of human languages: their capacity for displaced reference. 'Displacement' was noted by Hockett as one of his list of 'design features of language' (Hockett 1960; Hockett and Altmann 1968). We can talk about things very distant from our senses, such as the far side of the Moon and last year's potato crop. An animal that cannot represent an object out of its view cannot begin to work with displaced reference. Humans' ability to create labyrinthine mental models of spaces, and the movement of objects within them, without direct appeal to perception, exceeds the capacity of any non-human. As the difference between the psychologist's visible and invisible displacement tasks is a matter of the amount of mental computation involved, the impressive abilities of humans in this regard may be seen as a quantitative, rather than a qualitative advance over non-human animals. Displaced reference in language starts its evolutionary trajectory with an intuition of object permanence.

The topics of displaced reference and object permanence interact with the issue of whether pre-linguistic mental representations need a special category such as the individual constants of Predicate Logic. Logical individual constants correspond roughly to proper names in language, but also convey the absolute uniqueness in the universe of the individual object denoted. This will be taken up in Chapter 5.2.

In language, nouns prototypically denote solid physical objects, available to perception. But languages also stretch the noun category far beyond physical objects. It is possible that the escape from perception-dependence, seen in the intuition of object permanence, also brings with it the seeds of an ability to create abstract mental spaces, populated by abstract objects, such as virtues, numbers, nationalities, religions, and grammatical rules.

2.4 BIOLOGICAL MOTION AND ANIMACY

Stimuli prompting reflex responses are typically relatively simple. There are some behaviours which are automatically triggered by considerably more complex inputs. 'Biological motion' is a label attached to a kind of motion typical of an animal; it is distinct from trees waving in the wind, rocks tumbling down a cliff, waves in the sea, or eddies in a stream. Recognizing biological motion is not just a matter of certain sensors being excited. There has to be a quite complex calculation of the temporal and spatial relations among the moving parts. In many animals, including humans, a disposition to recognize biological motion is hardwired: there is no question of learning a concept of biological motion; we recognize it instinctively without training:

Here we report that newly hatched chicks, reared and hatched in darkness, at their first exposure to point-light animation sequences, exhibit a spontaneous preference to approach biological motion patterns. Intriguingly, this predisposition is not specific for the motion of a hen, but extends to the pattern of motion of other vertebrates, even to that of a potential predator such as a cat. The predisposition seems to reflect the existence of a mechanism in the brain aimed at orienting the young animal towards objects that move semi-rigidly (as vertebrate animals do), thus facilitating learning, i.e., through imprinting, about their more specific features of motion.   (Vallortigara et al. 2005)

Perception of biological motion in chicks appears to be a case such as described by Shettleworth (1998, p. 227), quoted earlier, of 'implicit knowledge of some abstract relationship . . . embedded in a highly specific perceptual module without the animal being able to access it to control explicit, arbitrary, discriminative responses'. The story is more complicated, however, because chicks respond better to simultaneous visual and acoustic imprinting stimuli than to the same stimuli presented in sequence (Honey and Bolhuis 1997). Can we interpret Shettleworth's 'highly specific perceptual module' as involving both vision and hearing?

The biological motion studies take off from a paper by Johansson (1973), who showed that human babies attend preferentially to mobile patterns generated by lights attached to the joints of moving animals. Biological motion is a basic component of higher-level perceptual judgements. Jokisch and Troje (2003) showed that in human subjects the particular stride frequency of an example of biological motion (in a simulated dog) was used as a clue to size and distance from the observer.

Two parallel literatures deal with essentially the same topic, under the headings of 'biological motion' or 'animacy'. Reporting results under the term *animacy*, Hauser (1998b) watched the reactions of cotton-top tamarins to the appearance of four different kinds of object in a novel location after the object had moved (or been moved) out of sight. Of the four different kinds of object, only one type, the animate ones, such as live frogs and mice, evoked no apparent surprise (as measured by looking time[12]) when they appeared in a novel location. Self-propelled but inanimate objects, such as clockwork mice, did evoke an apparent surprise

---

[12] Looking time is the period during which an experimental subject continues looking at some stimulus before looking away, presumably because the stimulus no longer commands attention.

reaction. Hauser summarizes, rather cautiously, 'Some feature other than self-propelled motion accounts for the tamarins' looking time responses and at least one candidate feature is whether the object is animate or inanimate' (Hauser 1998b, p. 31).

A disposition to treat animate objects differently does not necessarily correlate with expectations that an observed object will behave rationally. Gergely et al. (1995) showed that 12-month-old children interpreted the movement of computer-animated shapes without human features as a case of goal-directed rational action. Indeed it is common for people to attribute human goals to robots that are obviously machines. Human babies at 9 months react differently to moving images depicting causal events from the way they react to similar images depicting non-causal events, suggesting a very early grasp by human infants of the quite abstract relation of CAUSE (Schlottmann and Surian 1999). To my knowledge, no non-human animal has shown such a capacity.

Biological motion and animacy differ in degree of abstraction. Biological motion involves an immediate perceptual (possibly multimodal) response to an experience, whereas animacy reflects a more permanent, and less perception-dependent, judgement. A sleeping dog is animate, but (except for dreaming twitches) does not exhibit biological motion. Animacy is a generalization from biological motion. Anything which **could** exhibit biological motion, though it may be inert at the time of referring to it, is credited with animacy. Animacy is **potential** biological motion.

The step from biological motion to animacy involves more than just perception; it involves forming a hypothesis about objects exhibiting biological motion. Barrett (2004) lists a number of criteria giving clues to agency (equivalent to animacy here). As he argues, there are strong evolutionary pressures on any animal to detect animacy in the objects around it, and clearly almost all species have solved the problem quite well. 'There are benefits associated with success and costs associated with failure (e.g. realizing or failing to realize that what appears to be a log is really a crocodile), and these, summed statistically over time, have shaped the evolution of agency detection systems that are present in all or most animal species' (Barrett and Behne 2005, p. 95). Barrett (2005) also emphasizes the adaptivity of detecting agency in an environment where one is constantly likely to be on the lookout for either predators or prey. Biological motion is salient for many animals.

A particularly problematic case is that of dead animals, which show conflicting clues to animacy and inanimacy. Barrett and Behne (2005) have investigated this cross-culturally in human children, finding that

German children and Shuar children living in the Ecuadorean Amazon discriminated in significantly similar ways between sleep and death, when presented with these two conditions in stories. It is not clear from Barrett's study how much this coincidence between German and Shuar children is a matter of similar cultural traditions in the two societies. The children were **told** whether the protagonist in a story was asleep or dead, and then asked questions about it. What was not investigated was any actual perceptual mechanisms that might be involved in deciding between sleep and death in the case of encountering a real body. Gärdenfors (2003, pp. 131–132) reports chimpanzee mothers carrying their dead babies around for several days, appearing 'perplexed rather than mourning', and also a case of a baboon mother carrying its dead infant around. It seems likely that the features that prompt a mother to look after her baby, such as small size and a very particular smell, override the importance of (non-existent) signs of biological motion in a dead baby.[13] And of course humans can be deceived about death, both ways: living people are sometimes given up for dead, and buried, and conversely dead bodies are sometimes kept in the hope that they will 'wake up'.[14]

What remains an open question is how many non-humans make the cognitive inferential step from biological motion to animacy (a.k.a. agency), rather than relying on purely perceptual reflex-like mechanisms to take the beneficial action, such as flight from a predator or pouncing on prey. Inferring animacy in objects is the first step towards a full-blown 'Theory of Mind' necessary for communications of one's inner representations to other members of one's community, a topic to which we will return in Part II, on pragmatics.

Biological motion and its more abstract derivative, animacy, impinge strongly on linguistic structure, in at least three ways. Firstly, many human languages discriminate grammatically between words denoting animate objects. The ANIMACY feature is deep-seated in semantic universals. Many noun-classification systems use the category of animate things. In pathology, access to words denoting animates may be selectively impaired or selectively spared (Hillis and Caramazza 1991). Mandler (1992, 1994) has proposed that pre-linguistic infants have access to perceptual features

---

[13] See also sections 3 and 4 of Allen and Hauser (1991) for discussion of animal behaviour in response to death, and the question of whether animals can have a concept DEAD.

[14] Particularly touching is the episode in the Third Millennium BC *Epic of Gilgamesh*, in which the hero king Gilgamesh refuses to believe in the death of his friend Enkidu until a worm appears from Enkidu's nostril.

giving rise to their subsequent command of the category of animacy. These perceptual features are of the same kind as described in experiments on animals' susceptibility to biological motion. The foundations for the ANIMACY feature were laid down in our pre-human ancestors. Secondly, there is also, of course, a very strong tendency for words denoting biological motion to be verbs. This is a one-way inclusion relationship: many verbs (such as *sleep, lie, rest, own, belong, know*, and *think*) do not denote biological motion. There is not a simple correlation between grammatical verbs and the semantic category of actions, but any biological motion is extremely likely to be expressed by a verb. A third connection between biological motion and linguistic structure is seen in the theta-role (or participant role) labelled 'Agent'. Many theories postulate a level of linguistic structure in which the objects or persons involved in some event are labelled with terms indicating their manner of participation in the event. These terms include 'Agent', 'Patient', 'Instrument', and many others, but the 'Agent' role is the most commonly mentioned and the least controversial. Identification of the Agent in an event is strongly correlated with biological motion. The Agent in an event described by *The cat caught the mouse* or *The mouse was caught by the cat* is the cat. And in such an event, the participant displaying most biological motion is the cat. Though the mouse may move, it may just cower, whereas the cat has to move to be the Agent in an act of catching.

2.5 STRUCTURED CONCEPTUAL CONTENT AND TRANSITIVE INFERENCE

We saw earlier that Alex the parrot showed second-order knowledge in his ability to tell, for instance, that green is a colour, and that square is a shape. Another possible, and more powerful, instance of animals' ability to work with second-order judgements involves **transitive inference**. If Eve is older than Jack and Jack is older than Rosie, it follows that Eve is older than Rosie. This relies on an assurance that the relation 'older than' is transitive. We humans know that a chain of inference like this can be continued as long as necessary, involving tens or even thousands of 'links' in the chain.[15] It is this potential to generate an unlimited number of inferences that makes the transitivity of a relation more powerful than, for instance, the classification of red, green, and blue as belonging to the

---

[15] Hurley (2006, p. 139) has labelled this unbounded capacity to follow a chain of reasoning 'inferential promiscuity'.

class of colours. Humans can learn the transitivity of a relation without necessarily being aware in any explicit sense of what they are learning, as an experiment by Greene et al. (2001) has shown. They gave students pairs of unfamiliar Japanese characters, and required them to pick one character. The 'correct' character was always the 'greater' one in an artificial hierarchy set up by the experimenters. Thus choice of character C was correct if it was presented with the character D, but incorrect if it was presented with the character B. Subjects only ever saw pairs, and some were not told that a hierarchy was involved. Of these uninformed subjects, some worked out that a hierarchy was involved, as they told the experimenters after the experiment, but others did not show any explicit awareness of a hierarchy. Even these 'unaware' subjects learned to pick the correct symbols. In some sense, they had internalized the hierarchical rule without it reaching a level of conscious awareness.

Can animals do it? If they can do it beyond any reasonable doubt that they are not just memorizing lots of separate associations, then this ability would show that they can not only learn a **relation** (e.g. STRONGER-THAN) but also make an inductive second-order generalization about this relation, namely that it is transitive. Further, an animal with this capacity would be able to follow through the deductive consequences implied by the transitivity of the relation, and have access to items of information not individually memorized. In another context, this would be called 'generativity'. Not surprisingly, there is an extensive literature on whether non-human animals can do transitive inference.

The issue is well surveyed by Allen (2006): 'It is widely accepted that many species of non-human animals appear to engage in transitive inference, producing appropriate responses to novel pairings of non-adjacent members of an ordered series without previous experience of these pairings. Some researchers have taken this capability as providing direct evidence that these animals reason. Others resist such declarations, favouring instead explanations in terms of associative conditioning' (Allen 2006, p. 175). Allen points to the conflicting traditions and styles of laboratory experimental psychologists and field ethologists. Lab studies usually involve training on ecologically unnatural stimuli, and typically cannot work with chains of more than about five possible inferential links.

As far as lab studies are concerned, there is some strongly suggestive evidence that some animals, especially those that live in large social groups, are capable of transitive inference. The pioneering work was by McGonigle and Chalmers (1977), working with squirrel monkeys. Trained on five separate adjacent pairs from a sequence devised by the experimenters, the monkeys were able to make the 'correct' responses when presented with a non-adjacent pair. Bond et al. (2003) found that both pinyon jays and scrub jays were capable of some degree of transitive inference. Birds from both species were trained to know the order in pairs of colour stimuli, an arbitrary order determined by the experimenters, for example red precedes green, green precedes blue, blue precedes magenta, and so on, for seven different colours, hence six 'adjacent' pairs. Then the birds were given non-adjacent pairs, to see if they could respond consistent with transitive inference, for example knowing that red precedes magenta. Both species managed the task, but pinyon jays, who live in large colonies of up to 500, were better at it than scrub jays, who live in pairs. The two species are closely related.

Lab results are dogged by problems of alternative interpretation. In relation to a study on pigeons, von Fersen et al. (1991) argue that a hypothesis of 'value transfer', an inherently 'less cognitive' (my phrase, not theirs) hypothesis, can account for the data. This value transfer hypothesis is explained in an intuitively clear way by Wynne (2001, pp. 155–156). Interestingly, Wynne advocates this value transfer hypothesis not as an alternative to transitive inference, but rather as the mechanism by which certain animals, in certain situations, achieve transitive inference. Wynne also notes the correlation between social species and an ability to do transitive inference.[16] In fact, there are a number of different mechanisms theoretically capable of achieving transitive inference, each making somewhat different predictions about the error patterns. Treichler et al. (2003) trained macaques on three separate lists of five items, then gave them examples of lists linked at the edges, and the monkeys immediately inferred an ordered fifteen-item list, thus transferring within-list transitive inference to new items as soon as relevant data appeared. Hogue et al. (1996) showed that hens could make the appropriate inference about a stranger hen's probable dominance relation to themselves, on witnessing the stranger interact with another hen already known to them. Thus a hen would steer clear of a stranger whom she had witnessed defeating a hen dominant to her; and she would risk attacking a hen whom she had seen being defeated by a hen dominant to her. This can be taken as evidence of transitive inference. Dusek and Eichenbaum (1997) trained rats on

[16] In case the phrase 'social species' brings to mind a worry about insects, you may be relieved to know that Benard and Giurfa (2004, p. 328) found, not surprisingly, that 'bees do not establish transitive inferences but, rather, guide their choices by the joint action of a recency effect and the associative strength of the stimuli'.

a set of four overlapping odor discrimination problems that could be encoded either separately or as a single representation of orderly relations among the odor stimuli. Normal rats learned the problems and demonstrated the relational memory organization through appropriate transitive inferences about items not presented together during training. By contrast, after disconnection of the hippocampus from either its cortical or subcortical pathway, rats succeeded in acquiring the separate discrimination problems but did not demonstrate transitive inference.   (Dusek and Eichenbaum 1997, p. 7109)

The transitive inference literature naturally overlaps with reports of work on animals' ability to infer serial order in lists, since pairwise information on order plus transitive inference **is** a list. Brannon and Terrace (2000) found that rhesus monkeys could infer the 'correct' order of objects of five different magnitudes in the range 5–9, having been trained on the ordering of a different but comparable set of objects with magnitudes in the range of 1–4. The monkeys were applying a kind of transitive inference, beside translating size information into serial order information.

Field ethologists base their claims for transitive inference on observation and experiment in connection with social dominance hierarchies. Baboons, for example, live in troops as large as eighty, and the animals display an accurate and immediately accessible knowledge, for any random pair of individuals, of who dominates whom. See, for example, Seyfarth and Cheney (2003). The number of possible pairs in a population of eighty is 3,160. It is most implausible that a baboon would store 3,160 separate facts about dominance relations in its troop. For knowledge of social hierarchies, at least, it seems inescapable that some animals are capable of transitive inference.

In conclusion, animals, especially social species, have access to internal representations that are internally generated by inference. The correlation between this mental activity and the animals' social circumstances is interesting, and will be taken up in the next part of the book, on pragmatics. Note for the present that this is a form of semantic knowledge about the outside world; conspecifics are no less objects in the outside world for being conspecifics. And animals capable of transitive inference are also capable of recruiting this ability to perform satisfactorily on ecologically unnatural materials, like coloured cups hiding nuts. So, although there is a tendency to domain-specificity in the transitive inference capability, it can 'escape' the domain of social relations and be applied to other tasks, even by animals.

Social primates' inner representations of the social relations in their troop are more complex than a simple one-dimensional ranking. Embedded in the rank hierarchy is information about family relationships, and this relates systematically to the ranking information. Baboon females in a troop, for example, are ranked from topmost to humblest. The offspring of a superior female outrank the offspring of an inferior female. This adds a second dimension to the hierarchical knowledge that must be attributed to the socially competent baboon (and they are all pretty socially adept, by baboon standards). Individuals are classified by others simultaneously according to both individual rank and kinship (Bergman et al. 2003). The reasoning that it seems plausible to attribute to a socially competent baboon can be expressed in traditional logical terms like this, with the premises above the line, and the conclusion below it:

| Given: | OFFSPRING(A, B) |
| | OFFSPRING(C, D) |
	OUTRANK(B, D)
Therefore:	OUTRANK(A, C)

Here, the OUTRANK premiss may itself be the conclusion from a chain of transitive inference. Furthermore, baboons are also able to distinguish troop members from non-troop members and conspecifics from non-conspecifics. This suggests that they have a taxonomic hierarchy of concepts: CONSPECIFIC < TROOP MEMBER < INDIVIDUAL.

2.6 SEMANTIC MEMORY, A STORE OF NON-LINGUISTIC KNOWLEDGE

A central idea of this part of the book is that there can be a kind of semantics independent of language, an idea which is no doubt strange to linguists, in particular. Linguists are used to thinking of semantics as dealing with the meanings of **words** and **sentences**. This section fleshes out the idea of semantic memory as the set of representations in an organism's brain corresponding to regularities experienced in external objects and situations. Here I will explore the ways in which such permanent **cognitive** representations may be stored in brains, and how they relate to fleeting **perceptual** experiences.

The representation of hierarchy that we saw in the last section goes beyond the permanence of objects and inference of agency from biological motion. Further still, animals can bring to mind wished-for situations that do not exactly fit their immediate perceptual experience. Kanzi, for example, signed fairly explicitly that he wanted the group room unlocked so that he could see his mother, Matata (Segerdahl et al. 2005, p. 59). Animals can creatively synthesize representations of wished-for situations from the stored conceptual components in their 'semantic memory'. Interestingly, trained apes such as Kanzi are quite good at utterances with present-time imperative force, but more reticent than humans at giving information about events that happened yesterday or earlier, and mostly they don't offer information about the future beyond the next few minutes. There are attested exceptions which, by their very remarkableness, show at least the large quantitative gap between humans and apes. Sue Savage-Rumbaugh[17] tells of promising Kanzi a treat tomorrow and then being reminded of the promise the next day. Kanzi is no ordinary animal, but 'prospective object permanence' (Gómez, 2004)—i.e., the ability to look for objects you have not yet seen, whose existence you are assuming—may be demonstrated in many foraging activities by animals. An alternative explanation for foraging behaviour is that animals simply cruise their environment without any representation of desired food in mind, and are stimulated to act accordingly when they happen to encounter it. Such a weaker account does not require any prospective representation, but does involve some kind of prior categorization of objects perceived, in order to account for the systematic selective response, for example, eat or don't eat. Most surveys of foraging behaviour (e.g. in Shettleworth 1998) attribute some memorial representation of good foraging locations to some animals.

Maybe the typically unforthcoming nature of ape communication with humans beyond immediate needs is just a pragmatic matter of motivation: generally they can't see the point of communicating about anything other than the here-and-now. But any pragmatic limitation is likely to have had knock-on effects on apes' characteristic cognition; they just don't **readily** store information about episodes that happened in the past yesterday or earlier. They certainly lack the voracious acquisition of memories of past events that is found in humans (see the next chapter). The lack-of-motivation explanation without at least a modest lack-of-cognitive-capacity account is implausible, as any animal with the capacity would surely find some occasion to use it. The social motivation to communicate and the cognitive wherewithal for communication co-evolve.

[17] Personal communication.

Many have attributed to animals 'small-scale models of external reality' (Craik 1943) or 'inner worlds' (Gärdenfors 2004). I am very sympathetic to such claims, especially for mammals. For those still stuck in scepticism, there needs to be some fleshing out of how a languageless animal **can have** small-scale models of external reality, or an inner world of concepts, and of the mechanisms by which these internal structures interact with the outside world. So, with the reservation that animal concepts are still in several ways short of human concepts, I will briefly give it a try. The first hurdle to overcome is to grant that what is private is nevertheless real and can be intruded upon by science. The second step is to realize that when we penetrate the barrier between public and private, we enter a new territory where familiar public instruments don't help us to navigate. Outside the brain there are colours, smells, noises, touchable surfaces, hot and cold.[18] All these external stimuli get **transformed** in the brain to patterns of firing of neurons. By carefully watching the firing of an animal's sensory neurons while controlling its outside environment, clear correlations can be found between patterns of neural activity and classes of external stimuli. This is on the perception side, what is input to the brain. On the output side, in the public world, animals blink, swallow, reach, grasp, turn their heads, move their arms and legs. Inside the brain there are no arms and legs to move, but classes of an animal's bodily movements can be correlated with patterns of motor neurons firing. We can't explore human brains in such detail, for ethical reasons, but correlations between brain damage and sensory or motor impairments confirm a wide range of similarities between the workings of animal, especially primate, brains and ours.

Given a fair idea of how neurons work, it becomes possible to construct computer models, to test out the internal consistency of hypotheses about brain workings, and to find what predictions these hypotheses make, for checking against empirical data. In parallel with the advances of neuroscience, there have been significant advances in computer modelling of brain activity.[19] In short, new technologies have opened up a Pandora's box. Now that we are able to look inside the brain, we realize how dauntingly much there is to discover. We are also strongly reinforced in our belief in the fundamental similarities between animal and human mental workings.

---

[18] I choose to put it it this realist way, rather than resort to more cumbersome phenomenological wordings, such as 'there are causes of the experiences of colours, noises, touchable surfaces, hot and cold'.

[19] Tyler et al. (2000) and Wu and Levy (2001) are good examples of a combination of experimental psychology and computer modelling.

At a basic level, pioneering work by Hubel and Wiesel (1959) showed that different individual neurons in cats were responsive to diagonal lines at different angles. Information from such cells is fed forward to cells which combine input from both eyes (Hubel and Wiesel 1968); this is an early instance of the integration of simple information into a more complex assemblage of information. Again at a basic level, photorecep-tor neurons with different pigments in the retina are sensitive to differ-ent wavelengths and different intensities of incoming light. But a given photoreceptor cannot distinguish a bright light with a little green in it (say) from a dimmer light with more green in it, so its firing response is ambiguous as to the 'real' colour input. Real-colour vision is achieved by higher levels of the visual system integrating whole patterns of signals from many different photoreceptors, sensitive to different wavelengths. The overall message is that the sensations that we can become consciously aware of, such as the colour or shape of an object, are the result of much transformation, via many integrating and differentiating way-stations. Nevertheless, after all this transformation, persistent correlations are seen between overall patterns of activation in various brain centres and classes of external stimuli. It seems reasonable to say that these firing patterns **represent** the classes of input stimuli, in the animal concerned.

Brains are excellent integrators of multisensory information. Inde-pendent stimuli coming from the eyes, the ears, and the skin can be integrated into unified responses. Stein et al. (1998, p. 440) mention an example in which 'the visual stimuli and the auditory stimulus are not very effective when presented individually within their respective receptive fields. However, when presented at the same time, their combined response is enhanced far beyond the sum of the two unimodal responses'. This is an example of a single neuron (in the superior colliculus) integrating coherent information from two different senses. The superior colliculus is an integrating way-station. It is easy to see how such integration could facilitate unified internal representations of complex happenings outside the body. Stein et al. (1998) also note the extremely ancient evolutionary foundations of such multisensory convergence and integration, which, they say, 'are evolutionary ancient schemes that antedate mammals and even the evolution of the nervous system' (p. 440).

Detection of biological motion is very complex, involving tracking different shapes moving in rough, but not perfect, unison. In humans, it has been shown that different parts of the brain are actively involved in the processing of different types of biological motion. Bonda et al. (1996, p. 3737) showed that the interpretation of different types of biological motion engages brain systems in a differential manner. . . . The perception of scripts of goal-directed hand action selectively activated areas in the posterior part of the left hemisphere within the intraparietal sulcus and the caudal superior temporal sulcus. By contrast, the perception of signs embedded in expressive body movements involves interaction between temporal neocortex and limbic areas critical for emotional effector patterns of behavior.

It should not surprise us that different gestures that we can recognize and talk about are registered by different brain mechanisms. As far as can be seen, other primates also react systematically to similar ranges of gestures, and it is natural to suppose that the complex biological motion gestures recognized by primates likewise activate characteristic brain areas, and activity in these areas can be said to represent these categories of action, which are meaningful to the animals.

Different types of biological motion play a part in recognition of specific categories of animal. Say I see a small brownish shape on my lawn and am not sure, from a distance, what it is. It jumps, so I realize it is a frog. Alternatively, it scurries along the ground, and I conjecture that it could be a mouse. Or a breeze picks it up, and I realize it is a leaf. Jumping and scurrying are types of biological motion, for us.[20] An ability to distinguish at a distance between a frog and a mouse, by its characteristic motion, shows that specific types of motion are components of our concepts of these creatures. At other times, other characteristic features come into play: we can tell a dead frog from a dead mouse. Our concept of a mouse, say, is a complex of many different features, its size, its shape, its colour, its way of moving, maybe the texture of its fur, each of which we can be separately aware of, and in some cases name with a word. But naming with a word is only incidental. I can distinguish the flight of a pigeon from that of a crow, but I can't easily put the difference into words. Here is a hint from a dedicated birdwatcher: 'You can turn to another trick of the birder's trade: the art of identifying birds by "jizz". Jizz is basically the "feel" of a bird; some indefinable characteristic based not on plumage detail, but on shape, movement and habits' (Moss 2005). 'Jizz' is the *je ne sais quoi* that we use in the familiar experience of not being able to describe a certain kind of thing, but nevertheless clearly knowing one when we see one.

---

[20] Presumably cats, who sometimes chase wind-blown leaves, have a different conception, one that is less adaptive, because they don't eat leaves. But maybe cats are just playing.

The point to emphasize here is that animals can make such categorial distinctions, too, and do so by using component features of the categories. An animal that can distinguish a mouse from a leaf has categories of MOUSE and LEAF[21] and also has some category of biological motion which we can label MOUSY-MOTION, and it uses the category MOUSY-MOTION in its attribution of the category MOUSE to some perceived object. It is all done, in non-humans, without the help of language. And in fact for humans, much of this work is also done without the help of language. Many of the features involved in recognizing different classes of objects have no convenient linguistic labels, although we can concoct clumsy multi-word expressions which roughly capture the features we use.

Jackendoff (2002, p. 350) makes this point, too, using as an example actions described by the English verbs *walk*, *jog*, *limp*, *strut*, and *shuffle*. It would be artificial in the extreme to try to invent distinct 'semantic primitive' verbal labels for what distinguishes these actions from each other. As Jackendoff says, 'we can distinguish [the meanings of] these words by their appearance (and how they feel in the body)'. This is achieved in us by a somewhat modality-independent system which

can be thought of as the 'upper end' of the visual system [and] it also receives and integrates inputs about shape and spatial layout from the haptic system (sense of touch), auditory localization, and the somatosensory system (felt position of one's own body). This integration is what enables you to know by looking at an object where to reach for it, and what it should feel like when you handle it.   (Jackendoff 2002, p. 346)

All such machinery can safely be taken to exist, in some form or other, in animals closely related to us. Animals just have not taken the human step of applying linguistic labels to some combinations of features regularly delivered by their senses.

The appeal to a language-independent system for storing usable regularities in the environment is not mere hand-waving. Details of such a system have been spelled out in neurological terms by Damasio (1989) in his 'Convergence Zone' (CZ) approach to storage and retrieval of concept-like entities in the brain. Kemmerer (2006) provides a very clear example, which is worth quoting at length:

It [CZ] assumes that the various instances of a conceptual category are represented as fluctuating patterns of activation across modality-specific feature maps in primary and early sensory and motor cortices. . . .

---

[21] Not necessarily exactly the same as the similar human categories, of course.

Thus, to return to the example of watching a dog run across a field, the following stages of processing can be distinguished: first, activation patterns across visual feature maps are detected by modality-specific CZs that store purely visual knowledge about dogs; these modality-specific CZs then feed forward to a cross-modal CZ for the more general concept of a dog; next, the cross-modal CZ triggers the engagement of related modality-specific CZs in other knowledge domains; finally, the various modality-specific CZs may, depending on the task, generate explicit representations across the appropriate feature maps—e.g., auditory images of what dogs typically sound like, motor images of how one typically interacts with them (like reaching out and petting them), somatosensory images of how their fur feels, and so on. The evocation, whether conscious or unconscious, of some part of the large number of such neuronal patterns, over a brief lapse of time, constitutes activation of the conceptual knowledge pertaining to the category of entities at hand, namely dogs.   (Kemmerer 2006, pp. 356–357)

Bickerton (1995) also mentions Damasio's convergence zones, in particular cross-modal ones. He discusses the idea of a mental 'holistic cat', unifying all the auditory, visual, olfactory, and tactile properties of cats into a single concept. Bickerton suggests, however, that it is only with the advent of linguistic labels that such cross-modal 'holistic' concepts get built: 'there are at least a few reasons for thinking that the only holistic cat is the linguistic cat—or in other words that it takes some kind of arbitrary symbol to tie together all the representations of all the attributes that make up our idea of "cat"' (p. 24). Bickerton is correct that the advent of public linguistic labels influences private representations; but unified cross-modal concepts do exist before language, in animals and in babies.

What Kemmerer is describing in the quotation above is what happens when we perceive a dog running across a field **as** a dog running across a field. This is the case where a perceptual experience is fitted to stored mental categories. But how do such mental categories get formed and stored in the first place? Barsalou (1999), in harmony with much other modern research, has put forward a theory of **perceptual symbols** by which the structure of stored conceptual representations derives from perceptual experience:

During perceptual experience, association areas in the brain capture bottom-up patterns of activation in sensory-motor areas. Later, in a top-down manner, association areas partially reactivate sensory-motor areas to implement perceptual symbols. The storage and reactivation of perceptual symbols operates at the level of perceptual components—not at the level of holistic perceptual experiences. Through the use of selective attention, schematic representations of perceptual components are extracted from experience and stored in memory (e.g., individual memories of *green, purr, hot*). As memories of the same component become organized around a common frame, they implement a simulator that produces limitless simulations of the component (e.g., simulations of *purr*). Not only do such simulators develop for aspects of sensory experience, they also develop for aspects of proprioception (e.g., *lift, run*) and for introspection (e.g., *compare, memory, happy, hungry*).

(Barsalou 1999, p. 577)

The idea behind Barsalou's 'simulators' and 'simulations' here is that the brain, having learned from perceptual and/or proprioceptive experiences, is able to recreate or rehearse versions of those experiences in the absence of the original perceptual or proprioceptive stimulus. In emphasizing the perceptual basis of conceptual systems, Barsalou does not dissolve the distinction between perception and cognition. Perceptual symbols are the permanent cognitive traces (in the form of activation potentials) of fleeting perceptual experiences.

Barsalou emphasizes the continuity between non-human and human conceptual representational systems, implicitly granting (and I agree) that non-human animals have conceptual systems. It is known that many animals have attention and both working and long-term memory, and it seems likely that they can apply these to the formation of Barsalovian perceptual symbols to 'produce useful inferences about what is likely to occur at a given place and time, and about what actions will be effective' (Barsalou 1999, pp. 606–607).

Barsalou's account posits a stored connection, based on perception and subsequent abstraction, between the non-linguistic concepts PURR and CAT, and between GREEN and LEAF. This application, usually below any level of awareness, of the features that contribute to recognition of different categories of object is **semantic**, and stored in what many psychologists call 'semantic memory'. Tyler et al. (2000, p. 198) converge on the same idea as Barsalou: 'concepts are represented as patterns of activation distributed over multiple units corresponding to different semantic properties or "micro-features".' Gallese (2003a) also argues, on the basis of a non-human primate brain's interaction with the world, that conceptual knowledge can be attributed to non-linguistic animal species, and he labels this as 'semantic content'. This common use of the term *semantic* by non-linguists is not necessarily about the meanings of words, although it can be.[22] '[T]he normal process of retrieving words that denote

---

[22] See also Hodges and Patterson (1999) for a survey of 'semantic memory disorders', which are deficits in factual memory, rather than specifically linguistic deficits.

concrete entities depends in part on multiple regions of the left cerebral hemisphere, **located outside the classic language areas**' (Damasio et al. 1996, p. 499, emphasis added). For humans, then, retrieving the meaning of a word involves going outside the classic language areas. The areas involved are those shared with non-human primates, for coding conceptual information about their environment. Meanings existed in our pre-linguistic ancestors before the application of linguistic labels to them by humans.

Much more is known about how brains implement perception than about how they implement cognition. If perception underlies cognition, then what we know about perception can be used to understand cognition. Neural accounts of color, form, location, and movement in perception should provide insights into the neural mechanisms that represent this information conceptually. Much research has established that mental imagery produces neural activity in sensory-motor systems, suggesting that common neural mechanisms underlie imagery and perception. (Barsalou 1999, p. 607)

Production is much harder to investigate experimentally than perception. The processes that lead human minds to conjure up memories are not so easy to control as the stimuli presented in perception experiments. A common technique is to ask subjects to imagine some experience and compare the resulting brain activity with what happens during the real experience. This has been done in both visual and auditory modalities.

In the visual modality, Kosslyn et al. (1995) PET-scanned the brains of subjects while they closed their eyes and imagined objects. They report: 'the primary visual cortex is activated when subjects close their eyes and visualize objects. . . . These findings . . . indicate that visual mental imagery involves "depictive" representations, not solely language-like descriptions' (p. 496). The activity in the primary visual cortex was topographically related to the image that a real object **would have projected** onto the retina.

In the auditory modality, also using a PET-scanning method, Zatorre et al. (1996) got subjects to judge the change in pitch between two words in a song they were listening to. They also asked the subjects to judge the change in pitch between these same two words when they were not listening to the song, though presumably rehearsing the tune in their mind.

In the imagery condition, subjects performed precisely the same judgment as in the perceptual condition, but with no auditory input. Thus, to perform the imagery task correctly an internal auditory representation must be accessed. Paired-image subtraction of the resulting pattern of CBF [cerebral blood flow], together with matched MRI for anatomical localization, revealed that both perceptual and imagery tasks produced similar patterns of CBF changes, as compared to the control condition, in keeping with the hypothesis. More specifically, both perceiving and imagining songs are associated with bilateral neuronal activity in the secondary auditory cortices.

(Zatorre et al. 1996, p. 29)

Of course, perceiving and imagining are different.

Because perception, imagery, and cognition are not identical behaviorally, their neuroanatomical bases should not be identical. Theorists have noted neuroanatomical differences between perception and imagery (e.g. Farah 1988; Kosslyn 1994), and differences also certainly exist between perception and cognition. The argument is not that perception and cognition are identical. It is only that they share representational mechanisms to a considerable extent.

(Barsalou 1999, p. 607)

The obvious lack of a complete overlap between perception and cognition is neatly set out by Hummel (1999, p. 85): 'We may remember where we parked our car last Tuesday, but it is unlikely that the neurons representing our car have been firing in synchrony with those representing our parking space continuously since then.' Goldenberg (1998) also specifically discusses the overlaps and differences between visual recognition and visual imagery.

One clear difference between actually perceiving a visual scene and summoning it to mind without perception is that the motor mechanisms for visual tracking of the objects involved in the imagined scene may interfere with the ongoing activity of tracking real visual input simultaneously. This is why it was important for Kosslyn et al. (1995) to get their subjects to close their eyes while imagining objects. Elsewhere, I have offered the following analogy:

Consider a robot programmed to roam the world, taking and storing digital photographs of kinds of things that its programmers have determined. Such a machine would have mechanisms for directing its lens, zooming, focussing, and adjusting exposure for light conditions. Having directed, focussed, and adjusted exposure, then 'Click!'—the photo is taken, and downloaded (say as a JPEG or GIF) to its memory. If the machine is also programmed to search its data-bank of photos and to provide descriptive summaries of what they contain, there is no reason to suppose that the lens-directing, zooming, focussing and exposure-adjusting mechanisms will be involved in this latter task. No analogy is perfect . . .

(Hurford 2003b, p. 304)

The key point to take away is that the semantic content represented in the brain when it entertains non-present situations and events is strongly rooted in perception, and involves sensory and motor brain activity common to real-world engagement with actual situations and events. That is, 'detached representations' (so long as language is not yet involved) are not symbolic in the sense of the hoary old debate between 'Logical versus Analogical or Symbolic versus Connectionist or Neat versus Scruffy' (Minsky 1991).[23] In Chapter 5, I will be using symbols quite freely, as schematic representations of animal brain activity, but bear in mind that it is we investigators who interpret the symbols; they are our handy shorthand notation for hypothesized brain activity.

The term 'semantic memory' is usually applied to a subtype of so-called 'declarative memory', which contrasts with 'procedural memory'. Procedural memory is associated with 'knowing how', as opposed to 'knowing that' (Ryle 1949). Stanley and Williamson (2001) have argued on philosophical grounds that there is no fundamental distinction between 'knowing how' and 'knowing that'. Interpreting their argument psychologically, this would entail no fundamental distinction between procedural memory and semantic memory. In linguistics, a parallel to the semantic/procedural distinction is the distinction between **competence** and **performance**. Adult native speakers are said to have 'tacit knowledge' of the lexicons and rules of their language; this is their competence, usually envisaged by linguists as a kind of declarative knowledge of the facts of the language system. Contrasting with this competence is speakers' performance: their actual behaviour on specific occasions, including all the mental computations that lead them to make particular utterances. A speaker's performance is based on, but not identical to, his competence. The speaker mentally follows the permanent declaratively known rules, assembling the words in their right order, with any required affixes and phrase boundaries, finally setting the motor articulatory phonetic processes in action, in real time, as suits the occasion. A knowledge of how to perform these last operations is procedural, not declarative. Performance includes the receptive, as well as the productive side of language use, so the picture is of a listener parsing the sequence of input sounds by somehow consulting his tacit knowledge of the language, his competence. This is how linguists typically see the relation between the grammar of a language and the behaviour of its speakers; see Jackendoff (2002, pp. 29–34) for a nice summary. The competence/performance distinction has been a cornerstone of mainstream linguistic research for at least half a century.

[23] Barsalou (1999) chooses to make the same distinction using the terms 'perceptual symbols' versus 'amodal symbols'. So long as we always remember who uses what terminology, no confusion should arise.

Here is not the place to discuss this distinction in detail, but I will point out that there is a growing tendency in psychology to talk in terms of complex interactions between declarative and procedural knowledge, to the point where originally declarative knowledge becomes 'hardwired' or automatized procedural knowledge. A case in point is the 'motor learning' by an animal of the topology of its home range. Knowledge of how the barriers, obstacles and tracks are related to each other gets built into rapid routine behaviour patterns that no longer involve consulting the original declarative knowledge of the territory; Stamps (1995) is one study of such phenomena.

In the next section, I will press the case for the involvement of motor (procedural) information, as well as perceptually based semantic information, in the representation of concepts. Perceptuo-motor (i.e. procedural-semantic) memory is, however, still to be distinguished from another type of memory, usually also classed as 'declarative', namely episodic memory, to be discussed in the next chapter.

2.7 SENSORY-MOTOR DECLARATIVE-IMPERATIVE CO-INVOLVEMENT IN CONCEPTS

In several places above, I have mentioned that conceptual representations in animals may involve both sensory and motor information. There are (at least) two different ways in which this can be envisaged, one more primitive than the other, but both ways are probably still in evidence in animal and human behaviour. The more primitive kind of motor-sensory co-involvement is discussed by Millikan (1996, 2004) and Harms (2004); Millikan adopts the whimsical term 'pushmi-pullyu'[24] for her kind of representation involving both sensory and motor information. The second, more advanced, kind of motor-sensory co-involvement is suggested by the discovery of mirror neurons (Gallese et al. 1996; Rizzolatti et al. 1996). I will briefly discuss both types below.

The basic idea of pushmi-pullyu representations (PPRs) is expressed thus: 'Mental representations, then, can be used either to reflect states of affairs or to produce them' (Millikan 2004, p. 17). 'These representations tell in one undifferentiated breath both what the case is and what to do about it' (Millikan 2004, p. 20) PPRs have two kinds of content, which Millikan calls 'indicative' and 'imperative'.

---

[24] The pushmi-pullyu is a rare kind of African antelope, with a head at each end of its body, from Hugh Lofting's children's books about the adventures of Doctor Dolittle.

Consider any behavior triggered by an environmental releaser—for example, the feeding behavior of the songbird triggered by the sight of the red inside of the open beak of its young. This behavior is mediated by a mental PPR whose indicative content is that *a hungry baby of mine is right here and at this time needy and ready to receive food*, and whose imperative content is the directive *at this time drop food into this baby's mouth*—or something of that sort. But none of that complicated content is articulated, of course. . . . Indeed, the bird may have, as we might say, 'no idea' what it is doing, as *we* would conceive what it is doing.   (Millikan 2004, p. 20)

PPRs, then, are as basic and simple as reflexes, but it interesting that Millikan, a philosopher, grants them the status of 'representations'.

Harms (2004) expresses very similar views. As an example, he proposes that the best, if still imperfect, translation of the vervet alarm call for a leopard is the conjunction of both *There is a leopard nearby* (the declarative or indicative aspect) and *Run up a tree* (the procedural or imperative aspect). He calls this kind of mental conjunction 'primitive content'. This suggests a degree of integration, if not a complete conflation, of different types of memory hitherto labelled as 'semantic' and 'procedural'.

The discovery of mirror neurons, which fire both when an animal is observing an action, and when it is carrying out that same action itself, also suggests that an animal's conceptual representation of an action is coded in both sensory and motor terms. But this kind of sensory-motor co-involvement is significantly different. A macaque's concept of grasping is represented in terms of what grasping (by another) looks like, and of the motor activity that initiates grasping (by oneself). The same argument can be applied to a number of other common activities engaged in by animals, such as running, standing, sitting, licking the lips, defecating, and so forth. This has very significant implications for the evolution of language. It suggests that an animal such as a macaque conceptualizes its own actions and those of other animals in closely related ways. Seeing a conspecific grasping a nut, for example, can cause the brain of the observing animal to be in some kind of partly similar state to that of the observed animal. This is the beginnings of the kind of empathy required in communication at the level of human language. One of the discoverers of mirror neurons, Vittorio Gallese, has articulated this connection between mirror neurons and empathy (Gallese 2003b, 2003c, 2004). Compare Millikan's scenario of the bird feeding its young with a human mother spoon-feeding her baby. A human mother often involuntarily opens her mouth on seeing the baby open its mouth and may swallow when the baby swallows. The bird's kneejerk reaction (do birds have knees?) is functionally adaptive, but it is not empathetic with the baby's situation, as the human mother's mimicking reaction is.

In evolution, old mechanisms are typically not completely replaced by newer mechanisms. Often old and new mechanisms continue to co-exist. It seems likely that actions are sorted into those for which a mirror imitative response is appropriate (such as humans tending to laugh when others laugh) and those for which a more primitive pushmi-pullyu-like correlation obtains (such as ducking when someone throws a punch at you).

A non-mirror co-involvement of sensory and motor information occurs in the mental representations of objects. This was already implied above, in the quotation from Kemmerer, where it was suggested that part of the (human) concept of a dog involves the characteristic actions towards dogs, such as stroking them. The idea can be extended to inanimate objects, especially tools. Martin et al. (1996) found that 'naming tools selectively activated a left premotor area also activated by imagined hand movements'. Similarly, Mecklinger et al. (2002) report: 'When contrasted directly, manipulable relative to non-manipulable objects activated the left ventral premotor cortex and the anterior intraparietal sulcus, a circuitry that is assumed to mediate the transformation of movement-relevant object properties into hand actions. These results indicate that visual working memory for manipulable objects is based on motor programmes associated with their use' (p. 1115). Of course, nothing in the brain is simple, and Grossman et al. (2002) point to complications in the overall picture, as well as a host of other relevant literature.[25]

The mirror neuron phenomena and the combined sensory-motor representations of tools highlight an important feature of behaviour which is especially prominent in humans, namely **inhibition**. The brain of a monkey who observes grasping begins to go through the same firings as are involved in actual grasping, but the animal doesn't 'follow through' and actually carry out a real grasping action itself. The mirror neurons are in **pre**-motor cortex, with the suffix *pre*- serendipitously expressing both brain location anterior to primary motor cortex and temporally previous

---

[25] Some of these last ideas are reminiscent of Gibson's affordances. Gibson (1979) writes that apples afford eating and mailboxes afford letter posting. These affordances of objects depend crucially on perception–action coupling. In philosophy, a school of thought known as 'Enactive Perception' also emphasizes the involvement of action in perception; see Noë (2004) for arguments in favour, and Prinz (2006) and Edelman (2006) for some not wholly positive commentary. A more detailed, explicitly sensory-motor theory of the brain's representation of concepts has now been proposed by Gallese and Lakoff (2005), and my view is entirely consistent with theirs.

involvement in initiating voluntary action. When a human contemplates a tool, such as a screwdriver, the declarative knowledge partly expressed by *That is a screwdriver; it is a tool* is invoked,[26] and the pre-motor areas involved in its actual use are also activated; but the final carrying out of an appropriate action, for example, right-hand-twisting, is (usually) inhibited. In Millikan's pushmi-pullyu terms, both indicative and imperative types of content are involved.

Now, I prefer *declarative* to Millikan's *indicative*, for reasons of consistency with the terminology of 'declarative memory', and to highlight the **linguistic** relevance of this conflation of two types of content. In linguistics, *declarative*, *imperative*, and *interrogative* denote the commonest sentence-types found in the world's languages, and they are defined in terms of their typical communicative function between people (making statements, issuing commands, and asking questions). But note the naturalness of using, as Millikan and Harms do, *declarative* and *imperative* when there is absolutely no question of any communication between people. Their discussion is only about internal representations in a single brain. The declarative (semantic) content of a concept, such as the vervet's concept EAGLE, includes the features that trigger (passive) recognition of eagles, such as its shape, position in the sky, and manner of movement; the imperative (procedural) content of that concept tells the vervet what to do when it knows there is an eagle around (dive under the bushes!). The imperative content of a primitive conceptual representation doesn't communicate a command to anyone else, but it does communicate a command to the animal itself. Thus a distinction normally held to be pragmatic, about communication between people, has a precursor in solipsistic conceptualization. What happens later in language evolution, when public signals get conventionally associated with concepts, is that it becomes possible for one animal to stimulate the imperative content of a concept in the mind of another animal. In fact, for a small number of alarm calls, natural selection has already accomplished this trick for the vervets. If there had been no imperative content to the vervet proto-concept EAGLE before the alarm calls evolved—that is, if vervets had not had a combined SHAPE-IN-SKY/DIVE-UNDER-BUSHES serial pattern of brain firing—the alarm calls could not have evolved.[27]

A similar story can be told in relation to the empathic involvement of pre-motor cortex in proto-concepts of actions such as grasping, running,

---

[26] Of course, I am not suggesting that these actual **words** come to mind, just their non-verbal meanings.

[27] And of course, many more vervets would have been caught by eagles.

laughing, and yawning. If a public signal becomes associated with the concept GRASP, it is more natural to imagine a basic imperative use for such a signal than a declarative use, although both are conceivable. The signal could be used for the purpose of evoking the declarative content of the concept, to express something like *There's grasping going on* or *Someone is grasping something*. In this case the communicative event has what Searle (1975) calls a 'words-to-world' direction of fit: the speaker utters words chosen to fit the observed state of the world. But equally, and probably more commonly in the first uses of public signals, the signal associated with the GRASP concept could stimulate in the receiver its motor/imperative content, leading the receiver to carry out the action, i.e. to grasp something. In this case the communicative event has what Searle calls a 'world-to-words' direction of fit: the speaker wants the world to change so that there is grasping going on. (The crucial pragmatic question of why a receiver of such a signal would be disposed to cooperate with the signaller by bringing about the desired world-to-words match will be discussed in Chapters 8 and 9.)

In sum, the distinction in public communication between declarative and imperative acts, and the sentence-types conventionally associated with them in the languages of the world, has, I claim, ancient roots in the co-involvement (in varying proportions) of sensory and motor components in primitive proto-concepts.

CHAPTER THREE

A New Kind of Memory Evolves

We have seen how the capacities of some animals have begun to expand out of the narrowly constraining territory of automatic behaviours, into areas of new mental representations acquired by learning and generalization, sometimes to rather abstract concepts. And we also saw animals beginning to get metacognitive glimpses into their own mental states and to be able to act in response to them. Before language, some higher animals had become able to represent aspects of their world in terms of such concepts as we can anthropocentrically[1] label SAME, DIFFERENT, and OPPOSITE. Learning gives rise to new enduring mental states. The animal that has learned a new behaviour has laid down in its brain some new lasting linkages between classes of experience. And an animal that has learned, say, to distinguish different categories of prey by combinations of their perceptual features, such as specific types of biological motion, colour, size, and texture, has laid down enduring linkages between the prey-categories and the features. Such linkages constitute semantic memory. The animal may or may not have metacognitive access to these connections. And the animal may retain no specific memory of the individual experiences (training episodes in the lab, formative experiences in the wild) that caused its brain to be rewired. The value of generalizing is in data-compression. You don't need to burden your memory with all those formative experiences if you can distil what is important in them into an economical set of principles automatically guiding your future behaviour.[2] Also, having a store of concepts detached from the specific

---

[1] As human investigators, what else can we do but take an anthropocentric point of view? We only claim that the animal pre-linguistic concepts are **similar**, not identical, to human concepts.

[2] For instance, it seems certain that the gosling who is imprinted with the nearest large moving object in the first few days of its life does not remember the specific event of seeing

episodes that formed them gives them a 'timeless' quality that turns out to be an indispensable foundation for thinking (or later talking) about things happening other than now.

Classic amnesics, people with memory loss, typically cannot remember who they are, what their name is, where they live, or where they were at previous times in their lives. And yet they typically maintain full competence in their native language and skills such as playing a musical instrument. They can tell a scurrying mouse from a wind-blown leaf by the characteristic motion, but they can't remember the mouse getting into the cellar last winter. They often can't remember who their parents were, but they know what the words *mother* and *father* mean and how they are related to *parent*. The brain treats two different kinds of enduring representations quite differently. Amnesics have not lost semantic memory, the kind resulting from a distillation of past experiences and laid down as generalized principles guiding behaviour. But they have lost all memory of individual experiences, tagged with some representation of where and when they happened. The kind of memory lost by amnesics is called 'episodic' memory. Semantic memory is the kind in which generalized principles are stored, formed by previous experience but with no representation of the individual formative experiences themselves. Episodic memory is what stores traces of individual experiences, like the face of the person opposite you on the train last night, or the empty taxi that went past you in the rain.[3]

Tulving (2005) gives a thorough, recent survey of the theoretical issues and some empirical data on episodic memory. An amnesic patient, K.C., is a striking case, allowing us to see rather clearly the difference between episodic and other kinds of memory. K.C. can name his parents and his birthplace, along with various other learnt facts about his life and the world in general. But he cannot remember anything that happens to him more than a few minutes before. It is not a memory for facts that is impaired. K.C. has a specific inability to store his own experiences as recallable facts.

It is usually held that episodic memory came late in evolution. Tulving (1999, p. 278), one of the pioneers in this area, writes, 'Episodic memory

that object at that time; it just lays down an automatic behaviour of following such a thing (Lorenz 1937).

[3] Horner (1990) casts doubt on the validity of the distinction between semantic and episodic memory, but this remains, to my knowledge, a minority view. There is a (mercifully shallow) terminological quagmire surrounding the different classifications of memory. My own choice of terminology doesn't make any loaded or controversial assumptions.

is a recently evolved, late developing, past-oriented memory system, probably unique to humans.'

There must be some question as to why it might be adaptive to travel mentally into the past when phylogenetically older forms of memory already allow for learning from a single event. Part of the answer may lie in the nature of the information extracted. Sherry and Schacter (1987) argue that the older form of memory (procedural) is essentially concerned with extracting invariances from stimulus events, as in pattern recognition, whereas the newer form is concerned with preserving the individuality of events. Since these characteristics are mutually incompatible, the later form of memory evolved as a separate system.   (Suddendorf and Corballis 1997, p. 153)

Suddendorf and Corballis (1997, pp. 153–154) advocate a kind of cyclical co-evolution of procedural and declarative memory: 'since other species seem to be capable of at least a primitive form of semantic memory, we agree with Tulving (1983, 1984, 1985) that episodic memory emerged later, but then allowed the semantic memory system to develop more fully.' We will see that this kind of co-evolution is very pertinent to the evolution of meaning.

Klein et al. (2002) also discuss the evolution of various types of memory, along with references to several surveys of the area. They support the typical independence of episodic and semantic memory, but point to atypical tasks for which 'absolute statements about the independence between the episodic and semantic stores may not be possible: One finds independence in some domains but not in others' (p. 322). They stress the necessary interdependence of both summary generalizing information, as held in semantic memory, and specific information, as held in episodic memory.

Full episodic memory involves being able to retrieve, for several remembered and related events, the order in which they occurred. Humans can do this to a limited extent. You can somewhat accurately retrace all the main things you did last last Saturday, in order. This is helped by the existence in human affairs of a routine structure to the day, held in semantic memory. But often we cannot remember whether we did one thing before, or after, another thing. Time is a more abstract dimension than space, and much of our command of temporal ordering of distant events is aided by a metaphorical extension of the spatial dimension. (See Boroditsky 2000.) It would be very surprising to find any capacity for this kind of full episodic memory in animals, and a lively literature exists debating the extent to which animals have episodic memory; I will review key studies from this literature in this chapter. One fascinating question is how humans managed to transfer a grasp of space to a grasp of time, and how this process related to the emergence of language.

There is a clear connection between episodic memory and ability to bring memories back to conscious awareness. Even amnesic patients, who cannot explicitly recall events that have happened to them, show signs of having registered some unconscious take-home message from the experience. In the late nineteenth century, the Russian neurologist Korsakoff noted that a patient who could not explicitly recall being in a situation where he was given an electric shock nevertheless showed an aversion to the room in which it had happened and to the neurologist who had administered the shock. (See Victor and Yakovlev 1955; Schacter 1987.) Such examples do not invalidate the notion of episodic memory. Korsakoff's patient presumably formed a connection in his semantic memory between the room, the doctor, and an unpleasant experience, but kept no episodic memory of the specific experience that gave rise to this connection being formed.

There is also a connection between episodic memory and some sense of the self. My episodic memories are memories of what I experienced—I was there. It is an open question how much the involvement of the ego is retained in, or central to, the content of episodic memories. Great care must be taken to clarify the notion of 'self' or ego involved in episodic memory. Compare the meanings of the two sentences *X happened* and *I saw X happen*. A person who saw X happen probably knows thereafter that X happened, and a normal adult also knows that he or she saw that X happened. But the two items of knowledge are definitely separable. The question arises what exact entity is referred to by the *I* in the second sentence. If a person entertains the (true) thought expressed by *I saw X happen*, it may seem obvious that the *I* in question refers to the thinker herself. But one difference is also obvious: the times of the seeing and the subsequent thinking are different. Some past events can be ascertained by their consequences in the present. Thus if X = HENRY DIED, we can check the truth of proposition X by seeing whether Henry is dead. But the truth of *I saw X*, whatever *X* is, can only be ascertained by what has been called 'mental time travel' on the part of the person referred to by *I*. Somehow, the knowing subject has to relive the experience— not completely, because that is physically impossible, but the experience has to be rehearsed in the mind in enough detail for it to be clearly distinguished from other experiences. Normal adult humans are familiar with this reliving of experiences, but it is intensely subjective, so how can we know whether other beings do it, especially if they can't talk? It is also clear that the entities encountered in this subjective reliving of experience are not directly observable entities in the world in the same way as the original entities causing the experience. Further, during the actual experience, at the time it happened, no 'I' was part of the event objectively experienced. Simply being able to relive an experience does not entail an objective view of the reliving self on a par with more objectively available entities, such as the Henry who died in our hypothetical event X. For such reasons, I remain cautious about a necessary connection between episodic memory and reflective self-awareness or 'autonoesis'.

Linked to the ideas of self and consciousness, there may be a close connection between language and episodic memory. Most people's 'first memories' of the earliest experiences in their lives are of events happening after about two years of age, after the first onset of connected language. There is now a body of evidence indicating that episodic memory matures in children around the age of four years. Gopnik and Graf (1988), for example, showed some children objects being put into a drawer and, for comparison, just told other children the contents of the drawer. Then they asked the children, aged 3, 4, and 5 years, (1) what was in the drawer, and (2) how they knew. All the children managed reasonably well on the first question, so across all the ages tested, memory for facts about the world was good. On the second question, children at age 5 managed to report well how they knew what was in the drawer, while children at age 3 performed barely better than chance. The younger children could not recall what specific experience had given them their good knowledge of what was in the drawer.

Episodic memory seems to come onstream after the beginnings of language in normal children. But it also seems that having language is not a prerequisite for the laying down of episodic memories. The memories are not laid down **in language**. Merlin Donald makes this point by referring to Helen Keller:

Language was completely absent from her life. There was no story-telling, no questioning, no wordplay, no stream of word thoughts. However, this did not prevent her as an adult from remembering a fair amount from this period. Her later recall of events that occurred during her early life was sometimes quite vivid, and she recounted many memories that must have been formed without any mediation by language.   (Donald 2001, p. 240)

With the appearance of episodic memory, the ancestors of humans acquired another route by which representations of non-present events and situations could be brought to mind. For modern humans these representations are stored either as a result of a prior perceptual experience or by dint of believing someone else's report of such an event or situation. We might (anticipating somewhat) call these different sources of knowledge *de facto* and *de dicto*. At this stage, we are only considering representations of the world in the minds of non-linguistic creatures. So I will focus here on *de facto* knowledge and how it might be represented in the brain. *De facto* knowledge is knowledge transferred from momentary perception of a particular event or situation, by mechanisms of episodic memory, to a permanent store. This process has been expressed by Peter Gärdenfors as the move from **cued** representations to **detached** representations (Gärdenfors 1996, 2004).

A cued representation stands for something that is present in the current external situation of the representing organism. When, for example, a particular object is categorized as food, the animal will then act differently than if the same object had been categorized as a potential mate. . . . In contrast, detached representations may stand for objects or events that are neither present in the current situation nor triggered by some recent situation. A memory of something that can be evoked independently of the context where the memory was created would be an example of a detached representation.

(Gärdenfors 2004, p. 238)

Bickerton (1995)'s parallel and closely corresponding terms are **online** thinking (= cued) and **offline** thinking (= detached). Just as Tulving maintains that probably only humans have episodic memory, Bickerton (1995, p. 59) claims that only humans are capable of offline thinking. I will argue that small beginnings of such detached/offline representation can be found in some animals. The later advent of human language no doubt gave a massive boost to such capacities, but it cannot be claimed that language fundamentally enabled detached/offline representation. The mechanisms by which cued representations get stored, in some stripped-down and abstracted form, in long-term memory, both semantic and episodic, are not well understood. Animal research is unlikely to help us much here, because animals' long-term representations don't approach humans' in terms of depth of abstraction, and animals, unlike humans, have little or no episodic memory. For humans, we know that the hippocampus is involved (see e.g. Shastri 2001, 2002; Burgess 2002; Eichenbaum 2002). We simply have to acknowledge, at this stage in science, that this process does happen in humans, and that just how it happens remains largely unknown. For some preliminary results, see Nyberg et al. (2000).

In what follows I will mention some recent evidence showing that something like episodic memory, though undoubtedly recently evolved, is not unique to humans, and then explain what this has to do with the evolution of linguistic semantics.

3.1 EPISODIC MEMORY IN ANIMALS: KNOWLEDGE OF PAST AND FUTURE

We have all seen squirrels burying nuts, and have probably wondered whether they actually remember where they have buried them. It seems unlikely that evolution would have selected a behaviour so costly in energy without some payoff. Empirical work on another food-storing species, American scrub jays (Clayton and Dickinson 1998), has shown, not only that the birds can remember where they stored food, but also what kind of food was stored in which location. This is because jays store two kinds of food, one more perishable than the other, and after a certain lapse of time, they do not bother recovering the more perishable food from caches, but only go back to the stores of less perishable food. This study was conducted under controlled experimental conditions, and so escapes the anecdotal character of many observations in the wild.

On the basis of a single caching episode, scrub jays can remember when and where they cached a variety of foods that differ in the rate at which they degrade, in a way that is inexplicable by relative familiarity. They can update their memory of the contents of a cache depending on whether or not they have emptied the cache site, and can also remember where another bird has hidden caches, suggesting that they encode rich representations of the caching event. They make temporal generalizations about when perishable items should degrade and also remember the relative time since caching when the same food is cached in distinct sites at different times. These results show that jays form integrated memories for the location, content and time of caching. This memory capability fulfils Tulving's behavioural criteria for episodic memory and is thus termed 'episodic-like'.[4] We suggest that several features of episodic memory may not be unique to humans.
(Clayton et al. 2001, p. 1483, see also Griffiths et al. 1999.)

Millikan (2004) sounds a correct cautionary note on such facts about food-caching by birds: 'many species of birds can remember hundreds and even thousands of caching places in which they have left food for future

[4] The term 'episodic-like' usually expresses a reservation that the animal need not be 'aware', in a fully human sense, of the recalled event, or, even more demandingly, aware that it is recalling it.

use. It does not follow that they are capable of collecting and remembering any other kinds of facts. Nor does it follow that they can use knowledge of these kinds of facts for any purpose other than finding food when they are hungry' (p. 26). True enough, birds' episodic (or episodic-like) memory is very domain-limited, compared to ours, but it is a step in the human direction.[5] It only requires generalization to other domains. If a mechanism is already used for one purpose, it is a lesser evolutionary step to apply it for some new purpose than it was to invent it in the first place.

Schwartz and Evans (2001) followed Clayton's criteria and surveyed eight studies of great apes, concluding: 'We summarize the evidence that is compatible with the existence of episodic-like memory, although none of the data completely satisfy the Clayton et al. criteria. Moreover, feelings of pastness and feelings of confidence, which mark episodic memory in humans, have not been empirically addressed in non-human primates' (p. 71). I take a positive message from this quotation, that great apes have episodic-like memory, but to counter their last reservation about what has not been empirically addressed, see above (Chapter 2.2) on uncertainty monitoring in some animals, and see below on animals distinguishing between past and future.

Menzel (2005) describes the impressive performance of a chimpanzee, Panzee, who was shown various food items being hidden outside her enclosure, and later, sometimes several days later, accurately directed a person (who did not know where the food was) to the hiding place. There seems little doubt that Panzee spontaneously recalled the individual events of food hiding, as and when she felt the need for the hidden items. She was not prompted to recall them by being shown sets of alternatives, from which she was supposed to choose. Thus an important criterion, **recall** rather than **recognition**, was met. A sceptic might still reasonably object that we do not know which of the two following propositions Panzee stored, on seeing, for instance, a kiwi fruit being hidden under leaves to the left of the pine tree. Did she just store a **static fact**, THE KIWI IS UNDER LEAVES TO THE LEFT OF THE PINE TREE, in which case she is not using episodic memory; or did she store the **experience of seeing** SOMEONE HIDING THE KIWI UNDER LEAVES TO THE LEFT OF THE PINE TREE in such a way that she could relive the experience as much as a few days later? The same problem affects other experiments on animal memory, such as those described in MacDonald (1994) and Gibeault and

---

[5] No teleological claim is intended here, of course.

MacDonald (2000), in which gorillas were tested on whether they could remember where food had been hidden. These gorillas could remember where food had been hidden up to twenty-four hours later.

The question of whether animals are remembering a state of the world inferred from some observation, or storing an episodic memory of the actual experience of observation, is not at all easy to answer empirically. If an event is stored for the purpose of later episodic recall, presumably only the aspects of the event selectively attended to at the time are stored. So for instance, Panzee may only have stored the bare bones of this event, while not attending to inessential factors, such as the expression on the face of the human hider, or his shirt buttons, or whether he used his right or left hand. The argument against episodic memory would be that at the time of the initial observation, Panzee also interpreted the event in a way that was relevant to her, storing the inference that the kiwi was likely to remain where she had seen it placed, and not storing a memory of the event itself. In fact a very large number of inferences can be drawn from any observed event, and one may ask whether it is economical to do a lot of instant inferencing and throw away the premiss (a representation of the event). The alternative would be not to do any on-the-spot inferencing and to store the raw observed information about the event (filtered by selective attention), leaving any inferencing for later, whenever it may be needed. This argument may seem to push towards an attribution of episodic memory to Panzee, but we should also remember that the number of inferences from a food-hiding event that are highly relevant to the life of a chimpanzee may be very constrained. In Hurley (2006, p. 139)'s terms, Panzee and the rest of her species may not be 'inferentially promiscuous'. Perhaps the likely location of food is the only highly relevant inference from a chimpanzee's point of view. Chimpanzees, like scrub jays, are highly motivated by food.

This suggests that the difficult issue could be resolved by an experiment of the following kind. (1) Show an animal some event, contriving to make the event salient in its attention. (2) Later, teach the animal some highly specific and artificial inference involving objects used in such events, associated with a reward; the idea would be that the inference is unlikely to have been made by the animal when observing the event earlier, because it had no relevance then to the animal's normal life. (3) Test the animal for recall of the event. For example, with an animal with no experience of keys and their function, (1) prominently show it a key being stored somewhere. (2) Later, train the animal to expect food when this key is used to unlock a food cupboard; during training the animal should not see the key being taken from its store—it should just be in the trainer's hand. Finally (3) one day the trainer seems to have lost the key, shows the animal his open hand, and looks puzzled standing by the food cupboard. If the animal communicates the whereabouts of the key, the argument would be that it remembered the actual event of the key being stored there at a time in its life when it had no reason to make any highly relevant inference about food—it just remembered the event. This, or its formal equivalent, could be done with a chimpanzee like Panzee, accustomed to interaction with humans. To avoid accusations of anecdotalism, repeat the experiment enough times to satisfy some sceptics, although you'll never satisfy them all. An experimental procedure somewhat like this has actually been used, by Zentall et al. (2001), testing whether pigeons had any memory of whether they **had just** pecked or not pecked. Their experimental setup was quite abstract, involving only arbitrary associations on which the pigeons had to be trained, and furthermore, only tested very short-term memory. But the pigeons did show that they could, with significantly better than chance frequency, answer the 'question' 'Did you just peck or not?'

Schwartz (2005) reports experiments (Schwartz et al. 2004) with a captive gorilla, King, who was made to experience unique events, such as eating a novel food, or seeing a human doing a novel trick, and then later (but not much later, no more than 15 minutes) was asked to pick one from three photographs. One photograph depicted some aspect of the prior event, and the other two photos were distractors. King performed at better than chance on this. But the intervening period was quite short, so this is certainly not a test of long-term episodic memory. This experiment had one advantage over Menzel's experiments with Panzee however. The events observed by King had no lasting consequence for the state of the world about which he was interrogated after the delay. The food had been eaten, the man skipping had stopped skipping. So King could not have been storing an inference about the state of the world consequent on the observed event.

In a further experiment with King the gorilla, Schwartz et al. (2005) tested whether he could recall the order in which he had, fairly recently, been given three food items. The three givings of food were spaced approximately five minutes apart. A necessary feature of the experimental design shows up a clear difference between this gorilla and humans:

King was required to first respond with a card corresponding to the last food he was given by the experimenter, then respond with the food he had been given second in the sequence, and finally with the food he had been given first in the sequence. We did it in reverse order because when we initially required King to do it in forward order, he always responded with the last food item and grew quite frustrated that he was not getting reinforced for this response.

(Schwartz et al. 2005, p. 235)

Humans can, without frustration, name the actual order in which events occurred, and are not constrained by this Last-In-First-Out restriction. But correctly recalling the arbitrary order of novel events, even though insisting on doing it backwards, does seem to show episodic memory, rather than inferences about the state of the world stored at the time of the event(s). And King managed this task with significantly greater than chance success. Again, however, the time period over which he had to operate was relatively short, under half an hour. Hoffman (2004) also experimented with King, to see if he could remember the location of a witnessed novel event. He could, but with a performance only barely statistically significant, and he seemed to get bored with the experiment, as his first results were much better than later results.

In all this discussion of episodic memory, we should keep in mind that, although humans can do it, and apparently far better than animals, we are still pretty bad at it. Eyewitness testimony to crimes is notoriously unreliable (Wells and Olson 2003).

An interesting point, put to me by Karola Kreitmair, is whether honeybees who signal the location of food (nectar) at a distance from the hive can be said to have the same kind of episodic memory as is attributed to scrub jays who remember where they hid food. The bee has an individual experience of finding food. It reports the crucial properties of this experience (distance, direction) to its hivemates. On its flight back to the hive is the bee not remembering where it discovered the food? Episodic memories can be long-lasting or short-lived, and perhaps the only difference is the length of time for which bees store their memories of food-finding. They presumably forget them as soon as they have discharged their signalling duties. This retention of a memory is in most cases considerably longer than the five-to-eight-second limit on working memory discovered in the honeybee by Zhang et al. (2005). Evolution has converged on versions of episodic (or episodic-like) memory in anatomically very different brains.

Evidence of a completely different sort for something like episodic memory in non-humans comes from neurophysiological studies of rats dreaming. (No, don't switch off—this is fascinating stuff.) Louie and Wilson (2001) trained rats to run a maze, and implanted tetrodes in the rats' brains to record the activity during the running of the maze.

About a dozen brain cells per animal were recorded in this way, and the researchers stored the complexes of temporal firing patterns reflecting the rats' experience in running the maze. Then, they also recorded activity from the same brain areas during the rats' REM sleep. The significant conclusion, thoroughly screened against the possibility of mere chance coincidence, is that during REM sleep, the rats' brains went through many of the same long sequences of complex firing patterns as while awake and running the maze. 'We show that temporally sequenced ensemble firing rate patterns reflecting tens of seconds to minutes of behavioral experience are reproduced during REM episodes at an equivalent timescale. . . . These results demonstrate that long temporal sequences of patterned multineuronal activity suggestive of episodic memory traces are reactivated during REM sleep' (Louie and Wilson 2001, p. 145). Obviously, the question of awareness doesn't arise, as this is about sleep. But the research does show that episodes from the rat's past experience are re-run in its mind/brain when the rat is no longer actually experiencing the original episode.

Memory is usually associated with the past, but, as we shall see, there is some evidence for memory-like mechanisms representing future events. Recently the pioneer of this field, Endel Tulving, rather adventurously but possibly correctly, identifies episodic memory closely with both past and future (i.e. planned) events. Thus his proposed experimental test for (all kinds of) episodic memory in animals involves seeing whether an animal can plan to bring a tool to a situation in which, by previous experience, it has been at a disadvantage for lack of the tool (Tulving 2005). Let's briefly consider animals' mental representations of possible future events.

Byrne (1995, pp. 154–158) argues on the basis of anecdotal observations in the wild that chimpanzees behave as if they anticipate the future, for example by killing a leopard cub (to prevent it being a danger when grown up?).[6] On their own, anecdotes like this (and there are many of them) are not as convincing as we would like, because the observed events may just be coincidences, and there is no control of the circumstances. Long-distance migration might seem to be a candidate for planning by animals, but there is no evidence at all that the animals (e.g. swallows, whales, turtles, geese) know where they are going and figure out how to get there.

Nevertheless, it is clear from observation of domestic pets that they can find alternative routes home if the most direct path is blocked, and it seems

---

[6] Gärdenfors (2004, pp. 253–254) is also very doubtful of Byrne's interpretation of this episode.

likely that this is accomplished by means of a mental map of the place and a representation of the goal. Some kind of representation of where the animal wants to be in the immediate future seems to be involved. Mulcahy and Call (2006) report on experiments in which bonobos and orangutans collected and hoarded appropriate tools for tasks as far ahead as fourteen hours before the task was carried out. They comment that 'These findings suggest that the precursor skills for planning for the future evolved in great apes before 14 million years ago, when all extant great ape species shared a common ancestor' (p. 1038).

Cook et al. (1983) experimented with rats in a 12-arm radial maze. The rat is placed in a space from which 12 different arms lead to different trays, only one of which is baited with food.[7] The rat's job is to find the food. It does this by exploring the arms of the maze in turn until it finds food. The experimenters watched the rat exploring and then interrupted its search (always before it had found the food) and kept it out of the maze for a little while. Now the rat has to restart its search, but if it is smart, it doesn't revisit arms that it had already explored before it was interrupted. Cook et al. (1983) found, not surprisingly, that rats restarted their search in the right place better if they only had 2 arms to remember rather than if they had 4 arms to remember; and performance on remembering 4 visited arms was better than on remembering 6 visited arms. This shows that rats can remember, to some extent, their own previous searching episodes. The decline in performance with number of arms to remember is not surprising.

What was even more interesting is that the rats were actually better at restarting their search in the right place when they were interrupted after exploring 10 arms than when they were were interrupted after exploring 8 arms, and better if interrupted after exploring 8 than if interrupted after exploring 6. The most plausible interpretation of these results is that the rats not only have a **retrospective** memory for the arms they have visited, but also what is called a **prospective** memory[8] for the arms they have yet to visit. For both kinds of memory, there is a quantitative deterioration in performance correlated with the load placed on it (2 arms visited or yet to visit, 4 arms visited or yet to visit). The rats knew pretty well where to restart searching both when they had searched just 2 arms

---

[7] If you want to see what these mazes look like, go to http://wwwo8.homepage.villanova.edu/michael.brown/galleryram.htm. (This website was still active on 23/08/2006.) For a general discussion of the conclusions that can be drawn from experiments with animals in radial mazes, see Shettleworth (1998, pp. 242–246).

[8] The term *prospective memory* was introduced by Meacham and Singer (1977).

and when they had only 2 arms left to search, and didn't manage so well when they had either already searched 4 arms or still had 4 arms left to search. And their worst performance was when they had already searched 6 arms, and thus still had another 6 to search. This shows that the rats' behaviour is guided by memory, and furthermore that they are sensitive to whether this is memory of past episodes or memory of future plans.[9] The rats' behaviour shows that they distinguish past from future.

This claim that rats can distinguish past from future, though technically true, disguises a large quantitative gap between humans and non-humans. 'Current evidence, although indirect or based on anecdote rather than on systematic study, suggests that non-human animals, including the great apes, are confined to a "present" that is limited by their current drive states. In contrast, mental time travel by humans is relatively unconstrained' (Suddendorf and Corballis 1997, p. 133). As we have seen, the evidence is in fact not merely anecdotal, but Suddendorf and Corballis do have a good point. The rats in Cook et al.'s experiments were motivated by a very present drive to find food. Gärdenfors (2004, pp. 239–240) summarizes: '[A]ll examples of planning among animals available in the ethological literature concern planning for current needs. Animals plan because they are hungry or thirsty, tired or frightened. Their motivation comes from the present state of the body.' Gärdenfors is not quite right in this last statement, as Mulcahy and Call (2006) showed that some, but not all, bonobos in their experiment collected a specific tool for use on a specific food-retrieving task as much as fourteen hours later.

The literature on 'mental time-travel' (MTT), to which Suddendorf and Corballis' article belongs, stresses the ability of humans to plan **long** into the future, and to remember events long in the past. It seems likely that language plays a role in this enhanced ability of humans. See Suddendorf and Busby (2003a, 2003b) and Clayton et al. (2003) for a lively, but largely terminological, debate on the relationship between episodic memory and MTT. The idea that the difference is at least partly a matter of degree, that MTT is based on episodic memory expanded in scope, is not mentioned. Suddendorf's agenda is to find, in MTT, a unique distinguishing feature of humans, so he has to insist on the qualitative difference between it and episodic memory.

---

[9] Note that rats' ability to smell where they have been in the past does not account for their different performance on 2, 4, and 6 arms searched or yet to be searched.

The theoretical possibility of a qualitative difference between episodic memory and MTT is raised by considering the different roles of the hippocampus during sleep and the waking state.

In the awake brain, information about the external world reaches the hippocampus via the entorhinal cortex, whereas during sleep the direction of information flow is reversed: population bursts initiated in the hippocampus invade the neocortex. We suggest that neocortico-hippocampal transfer of information and the modification process in neocortical circuitries by the hippocampal output take place in a temporally discontinuous manner associated with theta/gamma oscillations [the wake–sleep cycle, JRH].

(Buzsaki 1998, p. 17)

Humans, as we all know, can store memories of episodes that happened before the last period of sleep. There is a correlation between sleep-deprivation and the different types of memory discussed here. 'In humans, there is now evidence that different types of tasks are differentially sensitive to rapid eye movement sleep deprivation (REMD). Memory for declarative or explicit types of tasks appear not to be affected by REM sleep loss, while memory for cognitive procedural or implicit types of material are impaired by REMD' (Smith 1995, p. 137).

One may hypothesize, then, that an instance of human uniqueness is the inability of non-humans explicitly to recall episodes before the last period of sleep, related to a qualitative difference between MTT, which perhaps only humans can do, and short-term episodic memory, which some animals have. Tulving (2005, p. 20) also speculates along these lines: 'A special evolutionary leap may have been necessary to produce brains that were capable of bridging the remembering across the diurnal divide.' Here the asymmetry between past and future may seem to be a problem. Why should the (in)ability to remember things yesterday and before transfer to the (in)ability to plan things tomorrow and after? The answer could be simple. The prospective plans formulated by non-humans could be forgotten during sleep, just like retrospective memories, so that any plans formulated today can never get carried out tomorrow. Sleep, according to this hypothesis, puts a natural boundary around both past and future time travel in (some) non-human animals. I wonder if this is true. The evidence of Menzel (2005)'s chimpanzee Panzee, who could remember where food had been hidden on an earlier day, would indicate that chimpanzees have crossed this boundary to the human side, at least in the domain of events involving food.

On the issue of the evolutionary timing of semantic and episodic memory, it is unfortunately necessary to try to resolve a discrepancy between my account here and that of Merlin Donald (1991), in a well-received book. By my account, and that of many others, semantic memory preceded episodic memory. A hot question in the literature is whether episodic memory is uniquely human. Tulving thinks it is, while others claim to have found 'episodic-like' memory in animals. I believe that some tiny seeds of episodic memory, restricted by time (perhaps to same-day or even same-hour experiences) and by domain (e.g. only for food), can be found in some animals. Furthermore, I argued in the previous chapter for co-involvement of semantic (perceptual, declarative) and procedural (motor, imperative) information in an animal's permanent brain-store. So my story is that semantic/procedural memory evolved before episodic memory.

By contrast, Merlin Donald's account of human evolution is that our ancestors passed through four stages in sequence: first, a stage of 'episodic culture', characteristic of apes; next 'mimetic culture'; then 'mythic culture'; and finally with fully modern humans 'theoretic culture'. There is much to recommend in Donald's account, especially his emphasis on the interaction of individual minds and social cultures, and also especially the later stages of his evolutionary trajectory. My difficulty is with his use of *episodic* and *semantic*, and the implied reverse evolutionary ordering to what I, and many others, envisage. To a large extent, the disagreement is terminological, but it needs sorting out.

Donald's use of *episodic* and *semantic* is clearly at odds with the literature reviewed earlier, which debates, as a live issue, whether any non-human animals have episodic memory, while granting that they have semantic memory. Here are some characteristic passages of Donald's:

Most animals, including humans, possess procedural memories, and therefore the term is not particularly useful in characterizing the dominant feature of mammalian culture. Episodic memory is probably unique to birds and mammals ... Humans possess both procedural and episodic memory systems, but these have been superseded in us by semantic memory, which is by far the dominant form of memory in human culture ... In contrast, episodic memory is dominant in most mammals, including apes. Animals do not seem to possess the systems of representation that would allow them to have elaborate semantic networks. Their experience, in this light, is entirely episodic. The pinnacle of episodic culture, the culture of the great apes, marked the starting point of the human journey.   (Donald 1991, p. 152)

'From a human viewpoint, the limitations of episodic culture are in the realm of representation. Animals excel at situational analysis and recall but cannot re-present a situation to reflect on it, either individually or collectively. This is a serious memory limitation; there is no equivalent of semantic structure in animal memory, despite the presence of a great deal of situational knowledge. Semantic memory depends on the existence of abstract, distinctively human representational systems. The cognitive evolution of human culture is, on one level, largely the story of the development of various semantic representational systems.   (Donald 1991, p. 160)

Contrast these quotations with Tulving, the modern pioneer of this field, who believes that episodic memory may be uniquely human: 'Many animals, other than humans, especially mammals and birds, possess well developed knowledge-of-the-world (semantic memory) systems' (Tulving 1999, p. 278).

So Donald and Tulving (and I) agree that animals have 'a great deal of situational knowledge' (Donald) or 'well developed knowledge-of-the-world' (Tulving). Tulving, like many other researchers, is happy to call this semantic memory, while Donald is not. Hence this difference is indeed terminological, and regrettably confusing. From his books (Donald 1991, 2001), it appears that Donald reserves the terms *semantic* and *declarative* exclusively for **symbolic** knowledge and behaviour. For example: 'It is certainly true that in general, animals lack detailed declarative knowledge about the world. Whatever knowledge they do have remains implicit because they cannot express, or declare, their knowledge in any form of symbolic representation' (Donald 2001, pp. 119–120). My position from the outset of this book has been that the modern human 'semantic' link between public symbols and entities in the world is indirect, and was preceded in evolution by a more direct link between private mental representations and the world. I and others call such developed systems of real-world knowledge 'semantic'. Some of this knowledge can also reasonably be called 'declarative', too, because it involves knowledge of **facts** rather than just fixed action patterns triggered by releasing mechanisms. For example, when an experimenter plays a recording of a dominant baboon making a submissive noise while a subordinate baboon makes a threatening noise, other baboons register surprise, by looking longer at the source of the noise (Cheney and Seyfarth 1999; Bergman et al. 2003). This demonstrates knowledge of a social fact, who-dominates-whom.

Turning now to the use of *episodic*, there are also grounds for seeing agreement on the basic facts, with divergent uses of terminology. Donald writes: 'In fact, the word that seems best to epitomize the cognitive culture of apes . . . is the term *episodic*. Their lives are lived entirely in the present, as a series of concrete episodes' (Donald 1991, p. 149). So Donald agrees with Suddendorf and Corballis that 'current evidence . . . suggests that non-human animals, including the great apes, are confined to a "present" that is limited by their current drive states' (Suddendorf and Corballis 1997, p. 133). But their point was to deny non-humans episodic memory, or mental time-travel, whereas Donald makes a point of emphasizing the 'episodic' nature of ape lives. Donald does admit to using the term *episodic* 'in a rather idiosyncratic sense' (Donald 1991, p. 149). In his usage, it is crucially linked with the representation of experienced events, concurrent with the time they happen, rather than with recalling them after they have happened. Using *episodic* in this sense, with no implications for mental time-travel, I am in substantial agreement with Donald on apes' ongoing representations of current scenes and events; see Chapters 4 and 5.

Donald's exposition does not distinguish between the hypotheses which have exercised researchers such as Clayton (working on scrub jays), Schwartz (studying a gorilla), and Menzel (experimenting with a chimpanzee). Do these animals recall specific events, locating them somehow in the past? Or do they just store static information about the world learned from their experience of events? Donald does not discuss the distinction. Tomasello, a commentator on this work, complains that 'Donald's lack of familiarity with current theory and research on ape (especially chimpanzee) social cognition and social learning has led him seriously astray' (Tomasello 1993, p. 771). Other commentators on Donald's theory have taken issue with his claims about episodic memory. 'Donald seems intent on preserving the idea of episodic memories largely for primates: "Episodic memory is apparently more evolved in apes than in many other species . . . " (p. 151) As far as we know, this notion is unfounded. . . . There is no comparative evidence for Donald's view of the progressive evolution of episodic memory systems' (Cynx and Clark 1993, p. 757). Vauclair and Fagot (1993), without using the term *semantic*, emphasize the generality and abstractness of non-linguistic animals' mental representations.

Before ending this section, here is one more thought on human uniqueness and episodic memory. The hippocampus is known to be involved in human episodic memory. Fortin et al. (2002) show that hippocampal lesions in rats impair their ability to recall a sequence of stimuli. Control of sequences is, of course, also crucial for human syntax. Perhaps there is **some** connection between humans' unique episodic memory capacity and their unique syntactic abilities.

Summarizing this section, there is evidence, from experiments with chimpanzees and gorillas, from studies of scrub jay food-caching and rat maze-searching, and from neurophysiological studies of rat dreaming, for a kind of episodic memory in non-humans, certainly not attaining the level of mental time-travel or domain-generality that humans are capable of, but providing a seed from which the human capacity could evolve.

3.2 EPISODIC MEMORY AND KANTIAN ANALYTIC/SYNTHETIC

In the eighteenth century, Immanuel Kant (1783) tapped into a fundamental intuition about language when he propounded his distinction between **analytic** judgements and **synthetic** judgements.[10] The distinction has since Kant's time been applied to sentences, i.e. to publicly available objects, rather than to private judgements. But, interestingly, Kant thought that judgements still had language-like structure, in that he defined the analytic/synthetic distinction in terms of Subject and Predicate. The distinction is this: analytic sentences are sentences that are necessarily true by virtue of the meanings of the words in them. For example, *Cats are animals*, *Gold is a metal*, and *Water is a liquid* would all have been held to be analytic sentences. By contrast, synthetic sentences are true or false according to the state of the world they describe. For example, *Our cat has fleas*, *We bought gold rings in Dakota*, and *The water at Portobello beach was cold yesterday* are synthetic sentences. They are not true or false (whichever they are) simply because of the relationships between the words in them.

Gallons of philosophical blood have been spilt over the analytic/synthetic distinction. The most authoritative and philosophically correct position is Quine (1951)'s, who argued that the distinction cannot, in the philosophical limit, be maintained. Philosophically, Quine is entirely right (except for a few atypical kinds of sentence) but he is fighting a losing battle when it comes to native speakers' intuitions about the meanings of words in their language. Ask anyone (untutored in philosophy or semantics) 'Does the concept of a cat somehow contain (or invoke) the concept of an animal?' or 'Can you think of gold without thereby thinking of some metal?' I'd be surprised if anyone answered No to the first or Yes to the second question. The intuition that there are necessary

---

[10] Other philosophers had made a similar distinction. Aristotle (*c.* 350 BC) distinguished between essential and accidental properties; Leibniz (1714) (Rescher, 1991) distinguished between truths of reason and truths of fact; Hume (1739) distinguished between relations of ideas and matters of fact.

components of the meanings of words is very strong. We use these connections between concepts in our everyday reasoning. If I see a notice saying 'No animals allowed beyond this point', I know that I can't take my dog there. If I see a sign saying 'Please put all metal objects in the tray', I know I should put my gold ring in. Of course, there are practical context-dependent limits on how far people follow such inferences. Most travellers don't actually take off their wedding rings when going through airport security gates. But the strict sense in which a gold ring is held by native English speakers necessarily to be a metal object is indisputable (except in impractical Quinean philosophical terms). Note here the qualification 'held by native speakers'. We are not speaking of a necessary relationship in any way independent of language.

There is a beautiful saying by Otto Neurath about the meanings of words: 'We are like sailors who have to rebuild their ship on the open sea, without ever being able to lay it up in a dock and remake it with the best materials.'[11] The ship is our language, that we use every day to negotiate with. If I say to you 'I need some liquid' and you pass me a brick, you have not respected the meanings of the words I used. So we need the meanings of most words to hold constant in their relations with the meanings of other words, just in order to communicate with each other. But we do also renegotiate the meanings of words, often in strained circumstances. To take one example, the word *marriage* is now undergoing a change in meaning. It was previously necessarily linked in the minds of native English speakers to the union of a man and a woman. That is changing. But we can't change the meanings of all words simultaneously. Gently does it. In changing the meanings of a few words, we need to hold onto the shared assumptions about the necessary meanings of other words. So, though *marriage* is changing in meaning, we have to hold fast to our understanding of the meanings of words such as *man*, *woman*, and *union*. We, like Neurath's sailors, have to keep the ship of our language afloat, even while reshaping it.

The distinction between the (held-to-be) necessary meanings of words and merely incidental facts about the world that we express in synthetic sentences, using those same words, is absolutely fundamental to the human capacity for meaningful language. Occasionally, it is useful to strive for clarification by saying 'It depends what you mean by X'. But if the meanings of **all** words were up for grabs, all of the time,

---

[11] The original German was 'Wie Schiffer sind wir, die ihr Schiff auf offener See umbauen müssen, ohne es jemals auf einem Dock zerlegen und aus besten Bestandteilen neu errichten zu können.'

including the meanings of *depend*, *you*, and *mean*, we absolutely could not communicate. Humpty Dumpty was, of course, wrong when he said to Alice 'When I use a word, it means just whatever I want it to mean.' I suggest that the semantic relationships that we agree to keep unchanged, for the moment, are the connections captured by the idea of an analytic sentence.

Now, what has this to do with the psychological distinction between semantic and episodic memory? Note that particular facts that we store in episodic memory, such as that the taxi that drove past me in the rain last night was going north, or that the man opposite me in the train had a moustache, are expressed by synthetic sentences. They are remembered facts about the world, but the world might have been otherwise, in which case the sentences concerned would be false. Facts held in episodic memory are expressed in synthetic sentences. One of the most obvious uses of language is to give each other new information, to tell people about events that we know happened, but that they don't know about. Such informative messages are expressed in synthetic sentences, and are reports of episodes held in episodic memory. If we didn't have episodic memories, we wouldn't have much to tell each other. By contrast, uttering analytic sentences, such as *Lions are animals*, is pretty useless in factual communication, though it can serve a purpose in educating the young about the commonly held meanings of words.

Men are male, *Wolves are animate*, and *Taxis are vehicles* are analytic sentences. We don't store the knowledge that taxis are vehicles, or that men are male, in the same way as we store episodic memories. That is 'semantic' knowledge, stating, for the time being at least, facts that we hold to be necessary. It is, of course, significant that the term *semantic* was chosen to describe this kind of memory, although it is not only manifested in language. Semantic memory is widely attributed to animals: 'Many animals, other than humans, especially mammals and birds, possess well developed knowledge-of-the-world (semantic memory) systems' (Tulving 1999, p. 278). Of course, animals cannot make the specifically linguistic connections between concepts that humans can make. But the learned connections between different classes of experience that animals have internalized as automatic guides to their behaviour are, for the animal, necessary.

I have suggested a parallelism between the psychological notions of semantic and episodic memory and the philosophical notions of analytic and synthetic sentences. The parallelism is imperfect, because memory, of both kinds, is an individual private psychological matter, whereas the sentences of a language are public socially conventional entities. A pre-linguistic individual, in learning to navigate the world, may form many permanent 'semantic' associations that are idiosyncratic to it, and not necessarily shared by others. Everybody builds a mental map of his home, and navigates pretty automatically around it, so that the particular relations between rooms, hallways, stairs, and front and back doors become part of the individual's semantic memory store. The relations between rooms are permanent and static. There is no question here of this being memory of 'things that happened to me' (although of course memories of things that happened to me can be related to objects in this memory store). A sentence such as *The dining room is at the foot of the stairs* is not analytic, but if all the people in a society build similar semantic memories relating to certain aspects of their environment, we can expect the sentences describing those memories to be analytic in the language of the community, if the language has developed words sufficient to talk about them. An example would be *The roots of a tree grow in the ground*. The following generalizations seem to hold. No individual episodic memory (e.g. that Fido bit me) is described by an analytic sentence. Semantic memories shared by all members of a community (e.g. that snow feels cold) are described by sentences likely to be judged analytic.

A belief in the necessary truth of analytic sentences is a kind of essentialism. It would maintain, for instance, that being an animal is an essential feature of being a cat. Most people (apart from philosophers, and even philosophers in their everyday linguistic practice) intuitively subscribe to essentialist assumptions, for better or for worse. Barrett (2001, p. 1) argues that, in our evolutionary history, it was for the better:

[P]sychological essentialism results from a history of natural selection acting on human representation and inference systems. It has been argued that the features that distinguish essentialist representational systems are especially well suited for representing natural kinds. If the evolved function of essentialism is to exploit the rich inductive potential of such kinds, then it must be subserved by cognitive mechanisms that carry out at least three distinct functions: identifying these kinds in the environment, constructing essentialized representations of them, and constraining inductive inferences about kinds.

In keeping with the arguments in this section, constructing essentialized representations of natural kinds would include, for example, forming a representation of the category MOUSE with a mental feature corresponding to certain kind of scurrying biological motion as an essential property. Another, more fundamental, example of an essentialized representation would be that of PERSON with its connection to ANIMATE. This last example is taken from Chomsky (1975, pp. 45–52), with whom I concur that our essentialist intuitions derive from 'systems of language and common-sense understanding'. My point here is that some (not all) of a human system of common-sense understanding precedes a system of language, both ontogenetically and phylogenetically.

Amnesics don't forget the meanings of words. They can't remember whether a particular man had a moustache, but they know that men are male. The faint beginnings of an ability to store two kinds of information, semantic and episodic, can be seen in some animals, such as scrub jays, rats, and chimpanzees. This ability is one lying at the heart of human language. Somehow in our evolution this separation of two memory types was emphasized and selected for.

CHAPTER FOUR

Animals Form Proto-propositions

Animals cannot think all the same kinds of thoughts as humans. Some thoughts only come with language. Examples are the thoughts expressed by *Christmas is on a Thursday this year* and *The square root of minus one is an imaginary number*. However, animals do think and animal 'proto-thought' laid part of the evolutionary foundation for human language. In this chapter and the next, we will look at approaches to describing and circumscribing animal thoughts in order to illuminate how they paved a way for the later human developments. In other words, the transition from non-human to human was not such a drastic jump as some have imagined. The term *proto-thought* is used by Dummett (1993); in his view animals are capable of proto-thought but cannot entertain **propositions**, which are more closely associated with language. I will argue to the contrary that animals are capable of proposition-like cognition; much hinges on how one defines *proposition*, and this is surprisingly not well pinned down in philosophy.

Within philosophy and linguistic semantics, there is a curiously paradoxical attitude to the relationship between propositions and sentences of natural languages. On the one hand, it is insisted that they are not the same thing. For example, the same proposition can be expressed by very many different sentences. Any sentences which are true in exactly the same set of circumstances as each other express the same proposition. Thus active/passive pairs, such as *A bus ran over John* and *John was run over by a bus* express the same proposition.[1] This same proposition would also be expressed by *I was run over by a bus*, if spoken by John, and by *You were run over by a bus* if addressed to John. And if we were to translate any of

---

[1] If the John referred to is indeed the same person when these sentences are uttered; the same condition applies to the other examples below.

these sentences faithfully into other languages, those translations would all express this same proposition that I have mentioned. So a proposition is something abstract, a **possible fact**. A proposition is not necessarily an **actual** fact, as *There is ice in the Sun* also expresses a proposition, which happens to be false. These are standard examples intended to show the independence of propositions from natural language sentences.

On the other hand, it is also often assumed that propositional thoughts are significantly tied to natural language sentences. For example: 'All the *propositional* thoughts that we consciously introspect... take the form of sentences in a public language' (Bermúdez 2003, pp. 159–160, italics in original). This comes down to a belief that propositions have the same (or similar) predicate-argument structure as natural language sentences. Apart from simple feature-placing propositions with zero-place predicates, as typically expressed in sentences about the weather, like *It's raining* or *It's hot*, the idea is that propositions are **about particular objects**. And a common assumption is that, like sentences, a proposition must have at least two parts, some of which serve to identify the objects that the proposition is about, and one of which, the predicate, expresses a property or a relation. Typical examples in familiar notation are TALL(JOHN) and TALLER-THAN(JOHN, MARY). What is neglected in this assumption is that, within standard predicate logic, there are even simpler propositions in which, while they do have a separation between a predicate and its argument(s), no specific term actually identifies the argument in any universal context-free way. These propositions are existential, as in $\exists x$ LION(x), translatable as *There's a lion*.

In the rarefied vision of traditional logic, a proposition stating that at least one lion exists is taken as relating to a whole **universe of discourse**, an assumed world in which the users of the logic operate. Such a universe of discourse is held constant for all uses of the logical language, so that the statement that a lion exists, for example, makes a sweeping claim about the whole world assumed. The aspiring omniscient global scope of early twentieth-century logic is seen in the opening aphorisms of Wittgenstein's *Tractatus Logico-Philosophicus*: 'The world is everything that is the case' (Wittgenstein 1922, 1) and 'The facts in logical space are the world' (Wittgenstein 1922, 1.13). In particular, there is no adjustment of the semantics of the logical language to suit different occasions of use. For bounded mortal human interaction, this is impractical. If I say 'There's a lion!' on some particular occasion, I am not taken to be making a statement that, as of now, lions are not extinct. More likely, I am saying something relevant to the immediate situation, such as that, as we tour the safari park, I have spotted a lion. Pragmatically, such an utterance would be accompanied by some gesture to indicate what I am talking about. Traditional logic makes no distinction between *There's a lion* and *That's a lion*, as, being designed to be universal and context-free, it has no way of building in a deictic expression with the function of the English pronoun *that*, which takes its reference from the immediate situation in which it is used. I will argue that non-human animals are capable of representing propositions, which do respect a separation between logical predicate and argument, but where there is no specific kind of mental term serving to identify, in any universal or context-free sense, the object(s) that the proposition is about. Identifying objects as recurring from one occasion to the next can be done reliably enough without recourse to specifically nominal terms. When it comes to any public expression of internally represented propositions (a stage that animals have not reached), successful **reference** to particular recurring objects is achieved pragmatically, by principles deriving from assumptions about communication being relevant to the current situation.

This last discussion illustrates a concern to relate the logical idea of a proposition to plausible settings of communication and to psychologically realistic constraints on what kinds of facts and events animals, including humans, can entertain in their minds. This chapter will pursue this concern, starting with a numerical limit on the size of simple propositions.

4.1 THE MAGICAL NUMBER 4—HOW BIG IS A SIMPLE THOUGHT?

In this section, psychological facts about simple judgements of numerosity are brought to bear on a limitation that it seems necessary to impose on any psychologically implementable conception of a proposition. In Chomsky's classical view of linguistic **competence**, factors such as memory limitations are not relevant, but belong to a theory of **performance**. According to this classical generative thinking, a million-word sentence could be perfectly grammatical, even if impossible to utter. Similarly, though to my knowledge, nobody has discussed memory limitations on the size of simple propositions, it would be consistent with the generative stance that a predicate could in principle take a million arguments, with the limitation to a maximum of about four arguments being regarded as a matter of performance.[2] In practice, the simple propositions discussed by

---

[2] To put this in the kind of terms used by generative linguists, UG imposes no constraint on the number of arguments a predicate may take.

linguists and logicians alike are almost entirely limited to cases where the predicates take four or fewer arguments. I will show a psychological basis for this limitation.

How many items can you take in at a quick glance, and say how many there are?[3] If I quickly uncover, and then re-cover, four coins on a plate in front of you, can you tell me how many you saw? Now, what if there were ten coins on the plate? The answer would be much less certain, if you even tried to give an answer. And when your computer beeps at you, can you say how many beeps there were? If there were four beeps, you could get it right. If there were ten beeps, you probably couldn't, unless you are a musician and used a chunking strategy to break the sequence of beeps up into musical bars. Recognizing at a glance how many objects are in a group, without verbal counting, was labelled 'subitizing' by Kaufman et al. (1949) and there is now a massive psychological literature on it. It is established that people vary somewhat, but the limit to subitizing is around four or five items. People can train themselves to perform and get better up to about eight or nine items. But the natural untrained limit of subitization is around four or five.

Subitizing must be strictly distinguished from counting. Counting involves reciting a verbal sequence, and simultaneously associating each word with one of the objects in the group, until all the objects have been visited just once. The last word you utter expresses the number of objects in the group. When we hear anecdotes of crows being able to 'count' to some number, this is a misuse of the term 'count'. Crows don't count, they subitize. In fact no animals, apart from humans, count, as only humans have words to use in the recited counting sequence. All animal whole-number ability is based on subitizing. And humans have about the same subitizing range as animals. When it comes to subitizing, we are with the monkeys and dogs. 'In summary, the system used by human adults to apprehend small, exact numerosities is present and functional both in human infants and in two species of non-human primate. These findings suggest that this system is both ontogenetically and phylogenetically primitive' (Hauser and Spelke 2004, p. 861). These same authors, along with Dehaene (1997) and Dehaene et al. (1998) present copious evidence for the strikingly similar basic (i.e. non-linguistic) numerical abilities of humans and a range of animals. Humans, of course, can specify exact numbers higher than the subitizing range of about four, but only using language. The primitive limit of about four, being found in animals, applied

---

[3] The ideas in this section are set out rather more fully in Section 4 of Hurford (2003a).

to humans before the emergence of language. Without using language, we still can't go any further.

It has been part of the folklore of psychology for many years that the limit on short-term memory is 'the magical number seven, plus or minus two', stemming from a highly influential article by George Miller (Miller 1956). More recently, Nelson Cowan has revisited the issue, and by thorough control of auxiliary devices such as chunking, concludes that the real limit of human short-term memory is in fact much less. 'The preponderance of evidence from procedures fitting these [chunking-controlled] conditions strongly suggests a mean memory capacity in adults of 3 to 5 chunks, whereas individual scores appear to range more widely from about 2 up to about 6 chunks. The evidence for this pure capacity limit is considerably more extensive than that for the somewhat higher limit of 7 + 2 stimuli' (Cowan 2001). Cowan relates these findings to subitization, concluding: 'it seems that a focal attention strategy involving eye movements is important for visual enumeration of over 4 items, but not at or below 4 items, the average number that subjects may be able to hold in the limited-capacity store at one time'.

We have moved from the narrow topic of subitization to the wider topic of general limits on short-term memory (Cowan's work). We can now take this line of thought further, applying it to the task of keeping track of a number of moving objects in a visual scene. Here the major research is by Zenon Pylyshyn (see Pylyshyn 1989, 2000; Pylyshyn and Storm 1988). Pylyshyn's typical experiments involve presenting subjects with an array of objects (on a screen), and identifying a subset of them as 'targets' to be tracked while all the objects move around (not necessarily with 'common fate'). The general finding is that people can successfully keep track of a maximum of four objects. Successful keeping track is measured by subjects' reporting sudden small changes in the objects they are attending to. It turns out that the number of other, untracked, or background, objects is irrelevant, having no effect on subjects' abilities to track the target objects. Pylyshyn hypothesizes that the mind has available a very small number of indexes (I find it easy to think of them as variables over individuals), which can be temporarily assigned to individual objects for the purpose of tracking them. These indexes are like mental labels (think of them as w, x, y, and z in an algebra exercise) attached to the objects for the duration of the tracking task in hand. Given another task, the mind throws away any former assignments of the indexes and reassigns them to whatever objects are used in the next task. 'Visual indexing thus provides a means of setting attentional priorities when multiple stimuli compete for attention, as indexed objects can be accessed and attended before other objects in the visual field' (Sears and Pylyshyn 2000, p. 2). 'There is a limit of 4 or 5 such indexes available. The indexes are object-based in that they do not point to the locations of objects but to the objects themselves, and, as a result, indexes keep referencing objects as the latter move around. The purpose of indexes is to bind objects to internal references or names' (Sears and Pylyshyn 2000, p. 13). The same idea has been developed by a number of other psychologists. One prominent way of expressing it is that the mind has available a small number of initially blank 'object files', and temporarily stores information about tracked objects in these files. Such a file is updated as new information about an object comes in (e.g. if it approaches, or changes shape), and is emptied for allocation to a new object when an object ceases to occupy attention. (See Kahneman and Treisman 1984, 1992.)

Pylyshyn's results are backed up by other research:

When presented for 250 ms [milliseconds] with a scene containing 10 distinct objects, human observers can remember up to 4 objects with full confidence, and between 2 and 3 more when forced to guess. Importantly, the objects that the subjects consistently failed to report elicited a significant negative priming effect when presented in a subsequent task, suggesting that their identity was represented in high-level cortical areas of the visual system, before the corresponding neural activity was suppressed during attentional selection.

(VanRullen and Koch 2003, p. 75)

This shows that the limit at the magical number 4 is a limit on what is attended to with some kind of awareness—the 'non-target' objects are in some sense also unconsciously present to the mind.

Neuroscientific research has now located a very small area in the posterior parietal cortex responsible for encoding and maintenance of this small number of items in short-term visual memory: see Todd and Marois 2004; Vogel and Machizawa 2004. The former writers relate their findings to everyday visual experience: 'At any instant, our visual system allows us to perceive a rich and detailed visual world. Yet our internal, explicit representation of this visual world is extremely sparse: we can only hold in mind a minute fraction of the visual scene' (Todd and Marois 2004, p. 751). (We shall see the involvement of the posterior parietal cortex again in the next section.)

And here, finally, is the connection to the light that evolution can shed on semantics. Humans and monkeys have a common limit on subitizing. Hauser et al. (2000) let semi-wild rhesus monkeys watch while they baited different opaque containers with different numbers of apple slices and waited to see which container the monkeys would approach. 'The monkeys chose the container with the greater number of apple slices when the comparisons were one versus two, two versus three, three versus four and three versus five slices. They failed at four versus five, four versus six, four versus eight and three versus eight slices' (Hauser et al. 2000, p. 829). Humans and monkeys also share a very similar visual system. It is reasonable to suppose that the human limit to roughly four trackable items in a visual scene is also shared by monkeys, or if humans are different, the difference is only of small degree. The limitation on how many objects can be actively attended to when taking in a visual scene is, then, very ancient, long pre-dating language. And this limitation has had a firmly constraining influence on language structure.

Typical sentences describe states of affairs—events and situations. *A priori* there is no upper bound on how many individual objects may be involved in a 'state of affairs'. How big is a state of affairs? How big is a situation, or an event? Logic certainly cannot provide an answer. Imagine that Martians had evolved in a completely different way from us and that they could take in as many as thirty separate objects at a glance and keep reliable visual track of that many objects in a visual scene. To be sure, the Martians' brains would have to be wired up differently from ours, but it is a logical possibility. Whatever we understand by the word *event* it is not analytically constrained to involve only four objects at maximum. Here's a description of a complex event: *Mary was flirting with Billy on the sofa, which Sara was scrubbing with liquid from a bucket held by Sam, who was watching the European Cup final on the TV.* A lot is going on here, involving nine things: Mary, Billy, the sofa, Sara, the liquid, the bucket, Sam, the soccer match, and the TV set. All the participants are in some way involved with each other in the same scene. It's what is happening, or what we have deemed to mention is happening, in the room (where no doubt many other things are also happening). Notice that in describing this complex situation we were forced to use subordinate clauses. It couldn't be done in a simple main clause.

An old schoolbook definition of a sentence[4] is that it expresses 'a single thought'. Sensible people have always worried that this definition is circular, because what is a single thought, if not something that can be described in a sentence? The results I have summarized above give us an

---

[4] This should really be a definition of a **clause** rather than a sentence, but schoolbooks are not strong on the difference between clauses and sentences.

escape from this circularity. There **is** a language-independent definition of a 'single thought'. It is derived from the limits of our ancient visual attention system, which only allows us to keep track of a maximum of four separate objects in a given scene.

The limitation to four objects of attention is respected in the practice, but not the theory, of logicians. Traditional logic has an ambivalent attitude to psychology and natural language. In the dominant tradition, propositions are non-mental timeless abstract entities, which may nevertheless be grasped or entertained by a mind. Propositions may be, for example, the objects of belief. And when it comes to analysing the internal components of propositions into predicates, arguments, and quantifiers, logic in theory stipulates no limit on the number of arguments that a predicate may take. 'Two-termed relations are called *dyadic*, three-termed *triadic*, etc. Some relations have a minimum of more than two, but no maximum, number of terms; they are called *polyadic*' (Langer 1967, p. 61). In theory, there can be fourteen-place predicates,[5] or even million-place predicates. But it is striking that the practical examples given by logicians never exceed four argument places, and even the four-place examples are linguistically strained. An example of Carnap's is 'Let "T(0, 8, 4, 3)" mean: "the temperature at the position 0 is as much higher than at the position 8 as the temperature at the position 4 is higher than at the position 3" ' (Carnap 1937, p. 13). Mostly, the examples used by logicians translate into very everyday sentences such as *Sue is married to Bill*, *Sue killed Bill*, and *Everyone applauded Sue*. The pedagogical practices, if not the theories, of logicians respect the psychological limit of the magical number 4. They seem to have been guided in their practice by an intuition that psychologically tractable propositions are strictly limited in size. This size limit, as we have seen, corresponds closely with an evolutionarily ancient limit on the number of objects in a scene that can be tracked at once. The bare 'Who did what to whom' information contained in a simple proposition is limited to four participants. (The idea here is close to that of a 'minimal subscene', introduced by Itti and Arbib 2006.)

The evolutionary processes leading from limitations on visual attention to syntactic limitations on the clause structure of public language will not be discussed in detail here. At this point, we are concerned with what mental representations of the outside world were available to pre-linguistic creatures, before they ever started to communicate their internal

---

5 Indeed, it is common practice, if not good programming style, in logic-based computer programming languages, such as Prolog, to have predicates with large numbers of arguments. I admit to once having used a fourteen-place predicate in a Prolog program.

mental states publicly to one another. It seems reasonable to say that a
pre-linguistic ancestor of humans, at the moment of attending to some
visual scene, could mentally represent what it saw as a complex entity (call
it a 'proto-proposition') with up to four separate parts, corresponding to
the perceived participants in the situation, plus perhaps another overall
term covering the relation holding among them. Four participants was
probably a bit of a stretch, and probably the norm was less complex events
with one or two participants.

An animal's brain during the perception of an event with several participants, for example, an alpha male dragging a branch in front of a female,
is in a certain complex state. Interestingly, besides the upper limit on the
number of participants attended to, something is also known about the
temporal 'size' of perceived events, in humans, and it seems likely that the
facts are not very different for closely related primates. The lower limit is
about 30 milliseconds. 'Sensory data picked up within 30ms are treated as
cotemporal, that is, a relationship of separate stimuli with respect to the
before-after dimension cannot be established (Pöppel, 1997). Temporal
order threshold being identical in different sensory modalities (Hirsh and
Sherrick, 1961), thus, also indicates a lower limit for event identification'
(Pöppel and Wittmann 1999, p. 841). The upper limit is about 3 seconds.
'A low-frequency mechanism . . . binds successive events up to approximately 3 seconds into perceptual and action units. . . . Metaphorically, the
brain asks every 3 seconds "what is new?"'' (Pöppel and Wittmann 1999,
p. 842).

If an animal perceiving an event were capable of episodic memory, of
bringing this event to mind at a later time (a big 'if'), its brain would be
in some similar state when recalling that event. And, given a motivation
to tell someone else about this event (another big 'given'), this cognitive
recalled representation would have formed the basis of the message. Obviously, there are still some gaps in this story to be filled in, but we have
now seen a plausible candidate for the precursors of simple propositional
messages. This theme will be followed up in the next section.

4.2 PREDICATE-ARGUMENT STRUCTURE IN ANIMAL BRAINS

I claim, so far, to have established that categories corresponding to
classes of objects and events in the world are represented in the brains
of animals close to humans, such as the great apes, but also to a lesser
extent in other animals. It seems reasonable to call these 'pre-linguistic
concepts', reflecting such reservations as that they may not be very far

abstracted from experience, and the animal may be able to exercise little or no metacognitive regulation over them. A vervet monkey, for instance, has the pre-linguistic concepts we might translate approximately as LEOPARD/RUN-UP-TREE, EAGLE/DIVE-UNDER-BUSH, and PYTHON/WATCH-GROUND. I see in these pre-linguistic concepts the forerunners of **predicates** such as logicians use to analyse the meanings humans express in language.[6]

The English speaker's concept associated with the word *leopard* has a lot in common with what the vervet has in its head that makes it respond systematically to sight of a leopard or sound of a warning bark. Certainly, the English speaker can entertain the concept when no leopard is present. But we have seen that rats probably dream of mazes, so might not a vervet dream of a leopard? We don't know. The **extension** in the world of the English word *leopard* is the class of leopards. There is a class of things in the world, corresponding almost exactly, as it happens, with what we call leopards, that causes a certain pattern of neural firing in the vervet's brain. Adopting the logician's terminology, the extension in the world of this particular cluster of neural potentials in the vervet monkey is the class of leopards. For the vervet there is more, as its concept also triggers (or includes?) the typical motor response of running up a tree. Human concepts associated with words are usually, but not always, freer of any closely associated bunch of motor responses; we and our concepts are less stimulus-bound, but it is a matter of degree.

This is an argument, then, that pre-linguistic predicates can be identified in animal minds. They are not, of course, associated with words, and they may be missing some of the sophisticated baggage associated with human predicates, which is why I cautiously call them 'pre-linguistic'. They have the key quality of corresponding to classes of input stimuli. They may have fuzzy extensions, in that marginal cases of the stimuli may only trigger the associated neural firings in a probabilistic way. But in reality this is also the case with almost all human predicates.

Animal pre-linguistic predicates come at various levels of generality. Thus (using an obvious ad hoc notation) we can expect the vervet monkey to have, not only LEOPARD$_{vervet}$, but also LEOPARDY-MOTION$_{vervet}$ and LEOPARDY-SMELL$_{vervet}$. None of these pre-linguistic predicates is necessarily simply translatable into the words of any human language, but LEOPARD$_{vervet}$ is pretty close to an English speaker's LEOPARD. The

---

[6] This section sets out ideas with which I have a closer historical affiliation than I have with many of the other ideas set out in this book. I paraphrase here much of my argument from Hurford (2003a, 2003b).

pre-linguistic predicates don't correspond to grammatical categories such as Noun, Adjective, and Verb, either. This is in keeping with the logician's traditional notion of predicates, which cuts across all grammatical categories. To a logician, common nouns, verbs, adjectives, and prepositions all express predicates. In short, keep in mind that we are dealing with **pre-linguistic** entities here. The vervet monkey has no grammatical system to relate to its mental predicates. But, I maintain, logicians (and especially Frege) were psychologically on the right track in identifying the notion of a logical predicate, as it is understood today. This is not to say that we start with a logical analysis and look to find it in animal behaviour. Rather we notice in this case, but not necessarily elsewhere, a happy convergence of theory between logic and the psychology of animal behaviour.

All this talk of animal pre-linguistic predicates raises the obvious question: What about their arguments? A fundamental principle of logical analysis is a dichotomy between two essentially different types of term: predicates and arguments. These two are combined in an asymmetric relationship to form propositions. A simple proposition consists of a predicate with one or more arguments.[7] Examples, in a transparent notation, are TALL(JOHN) and BETWEEN(PARIS, LONDON, MARSEILLE), translatable as *John is tall* and *Paris is between London and Marseille*. Here, the predicates are TALL and BETWEEN, and the argument terms are JOHN, PARIS, LONDON, and MARSEILLE.

Logicians distinguish between two types of argument in first-order logic: individual constants and individual variables. Both individual constants and individual variables denote individual things, in different ways. In the logician's scheme of things, individual constants denote particular objects, such as particular people, particular cities, particular stars, particular chairs, and so on, as seen in the examples above with the terms JOHN, PARIS, LONDON, and MARSEILLE. Each separate object that can be talked about in the universe of discourse (the world that the logician is concerned with) can have its own logical proper name. In explaining their notations in textbooks, logicians typically start with individual constants such as these illustrated, as they are somehow pedagogically simpler, and closer to language.

The other type of argument is an individual variable. This is used to pick out individual objects, but **not any specific** object. A variable, as its name implies, has variable reference. Logicians use the alphabetic symbols

---

[7] Or zero arguments, to accommodate woefully under-discussed predicates like those corresponding to states of the weather, like HOT and RAIN, underlying English sentences such as *It's hot* or *It's raining*.

w, *x*, *y*, and *z* for individual variables. Simplifying somewhat, a formula such as TALL(*x*) would be translated into English as *Something is tall*. Now, this is not so odd as it might seem. Let's face it, we don't have individual names for most of the things we deal with in life. Say you are watching a tranquil scene, and suddenly something moves; you don't know what it is, and all you can be sure of is that something moved. This perception would readily be expressed by the logician's MOVE(*x*), translatable[8] as *Something moved*. Now put yourself in the vervet's place, sighting a leopard. You don't know **which** leopard it is, and you don't care, so conjuring up its proper name, if it ever had one, is not possible or at best a waste of time. The crucial information in this situation is that there's a leopard about, neatly expressible in the logician's formula LEOPARD(*x*).

All this may sound like dangerous anthropomorphism, thrusting man-made logical categories onto poor dumb beasts. But in fact a case can be made that exactly this split between predicates and their arguments (individual variables, not individual constants) has psychological reality for a large class of mammals (and probably many other animals, but we don't know about them). What do we need to identify something like propositional predicate-argument structure in the brains of animals? Recall the crucial principle that all stimuli from the outside world suffer a sea-change in the brain into something rich and strange. Less poetically, stimuli are **transformed** into interacting chains of firings of neurons. In a previous section on semantic memory, a few examples were given. Is it possible to identify separate processes in the brain, one for picking out any arbitrary object (as an individual variable does) and another for delivering some contentful judgement about the object (as a predicate term does), and integrating these two processes? Yes.

Here's how, in brief.[9] In the visual systems, and to a lesser extent in the auditory systems, of primates and other mammals, including cats, two separate neural pathways can be identified. One pathway, known as the 'where stream', simply identifies the location of an object in the space around the animal; it gives no further information about the object—just that it, whatever it is, is there. The information about what the object is is delivered by a separate pathway, the 'what stream'; this gives the animal much richer information, for example, that it is a leopard, or an eagle, or a leaf, or a person,[10] or even, for a human, a person with all the properties necessary to identify it as a unique individual, such as your mother.

---

[8] Ignoring the past tense feature, to avoid unnecessary complication.

[9] For much more detail, see Hurford (2003a, 2003b).

[10] To reiterate a familiar point, not, of course, necessarily exactly what a human would categorize as a leopard, or an eagle, or a leaf, etc., but probably things pretty close, since

The 'where stream' is known as the dorsal pathway. It takes signals from the retina, via several intermediate stations, to posterior parietal cortex, where motor responses are triggered directing saccades (fast eye movements) or head-turning towards the relevant object. (Recall from the previous section the role of posterior parietal cortex in keeping track of up to four objects in a visual scene.) The object concerned need not have been in foveal (central) vision. It can be glimpsed out of the corner of one's eye. The activation by the dorsal stream of eye saccades or head-turning has the effect of getting the object 'in full view', with the most sensitive part of the retina taking input from it. Now the 'what stream', known as the ventral pathway, kicks in. Information from the retina is also routed, by the ventral stream, to the infero-temporal cortex and beyond, where it is acted upon by the kinds of classificatory mechanisms we saw in the earlier section on semantic memory (pp. 49–60).

There is wealth of evidence, of various sorts, for this separation of function in human and some animal brains. I will just mention some of the most fascinating here. There can be a dissociation between the function of locating an object in the space around you and the function of deciding what it is. Some patients, suffering from what is known paradoxically as 'blindsight', cannot tell an experimenter whether a postbox slot in front of them is horizontal, vertical, or diagonal, or even whether the thing in front of them is a postbox; but they can hold an envelope at exactly the right angle to post it in the slot whose angle they cannot, with one visual subsystem, see. For such patients, the dorsal stream is intact, but the ventral stream has suffered an injury. (See Sanders et al. 1974; Weiskrantz 1986; Goodale et al. 1994; Milner and Goodale 1995; Weiskrantz 1997; Marcel 1998. See also Ramachandran and Blakeslee 1998 for a popular account.) Conversely, Goodale et al.'s patient RV could discriminate one object from another, but was unable to use visual information to grasp odd-shaped objects accurately (Goodale et al. 1994); RV's dorsal stream was impaired. For a survey of other evidence for separate dorsal and ventral streams in vision and audition, see Hurford (2003a, Section 2); Milner (1998) gives a brief but comprehensive overview of the evidence from vision, up to 1998.

The psychological distinction between predicates and their arguments can be expressed less technically, in terms of **attention**. Clearly, many animals attend to objects in their environment. This involves **first** an

our visual systems and basic aspects of our lives are similar to those of the higher animals we are comparing.

orienting reflex, making whatever movements bring the object into sharpest focus, and **then** paying close ('focal') attention to it, gathering in whatever information it offers. Psychologists distinguish between pre-attentive processes and processes involved in focal attention. (See Julesz and Schumer 1981; Bergen and Julesz 1983; Treisman 1985; Trick and Pylyshyn 1993, 1994). Pre-attentive processes are those involved in the orienting reflex, such as an object being glimpsed in the periphery of the visual field, followed by a saccade[11] or head orientation to look at the object head-on. Once the object is being looked at full-on, with light from it entering the fovea, the part of the retina most densely packed with receptors, the object is said to be in focal attention. Dudai (2002, p. 23) eloquently emphasizes the evolutionary significance of pre-attentive processes: 'the most precious niches of our inner world owe their existence to the emergence in evolution of the primitive, elementary orienting reflex.'

For my purposes, Pylyshyn (2000) sums up the facts well:

the most primitive contact that the visual system makes with the world (the contact that precedes the encoding of any sensory properties) is a contact with what have been termed visual objects or proto-objects... As a result of the deployment of focal attention, it becomes possible to encode the various properties of the visual objects, including their location, color, shape and so on.   (Pylyshyn 2000, p. 206)[12]

This is basically still the conclusion held by neuroscientists, although inevitably some complications have arisen and reservations need to be expressed. In particular, there is evidence that the dorsal stream does register some properties of objects, albeit at a level inaccessible to awareness. This is not so surprising. The dorsal stream houses the attention-grabbing mechanism, and there must be something about objects, as opposed to the background, that grabs attention. I mention some of these complications below.

Grill-Spector and Kanwisher (2005) got subjects to detect whether a quickly presented gray-scale photograph contained a picture of an object or was merely 'texture', and simultaneously to 'categorize' or 'identify' such objects, if they detected them. For gross 'category' judgements,

[11] A saccade is a movement of the eyes.

[12] There are some similarities between the 'proto-objects' mentioned by Pylyshyn here, and the metaphysical construct 'thin particular' or 'bare particular' suggested by the philosopher Armstrong (1989). It is important to distinguish, however, between metaphysical speculation about what exists in the world (ontology), and psychological hypotheses about the mental states involved in focal attention and pre-attention.

such as birds versus vehicles, it was found, as the article's subtitle has it, 'as soon as you know it is there, you know what it is', contrary to the point of the quotation from Pylyshyn above. For more fine-grained 'identification', such as between pigeons and other birds, 'detection occurs prior to identification' (Grill-Spector and Kanwisher 2005, p. 157). The absolute distinction between 'categorization' and 'identification' is a false dichotomy; this is a continuum. The reaction time and accuracy results for detection and categorization were strikingly similar, leading the authors to conclude that 'detection and categorization are linked'. This may have been a ceiling effect. A problem, as I see it, is that the subjects were directed from the start to attend to a relatively small display immediately in front of them, so that 'object detection' here is not a matter of focal attention being drawn to an object somewhere in the field of vision.

Fang and He (2005) exposed subjects to 'invisible' stimuli, in a clever experiment, capitalizing on rivalry between the two eyes. When one eye receives a clear bright picture of an object, and the other eye just receives optic fuzz, the clear bright picture dominates, and the subject sees it. Lateral dominance makes a difference, and given conflicting stimuli, the picture seen by the subject's dominant eye (usually the right) is the one that the subject reports. The authors presented pictures of objects to subjects in two conditions: a 'visible' condition and an 'invisible' condition. In the invisible condition, the dominant eye was shown high-contrast dynamic optic noise, i.e. lots of brightly coloured or dark pixels shifting about, while the non-dominant eye was shown a very faint image of a stationary object. In this condition, the faint picture was 'invisible' or inaccessible to conscious awareness. But fMRI imaging nevertheless showed a broad distinction between pictures of faces and pictures of tools. Invisible images of tools, but not of faces, evoked activity in the dorsal stream.

The brain of any vertebrate is enormously more complex than any simple dichotomy between two kinds of logical terms can capture. Scholars and researchers have for centuries been investigating cognition from different starting points and using different tools. The philosophical tradition, including logic, has gained deserved prestige in analysing thought without fancy mechanical or electronic instruments. For human thought, analysis in terms of a fundamental dichotomy between predicate and argument terms (largely due to Frege) enabled great strides to be made in describing the semantic relations between human sentences, and their relations to an outside world. Neuroscience didn't impinge on the logical tradition, because it had not reached a sufficiently detailed level.

Interestingly, given the connection between logic and neuroscience that I have proposed, some detailed problems of description and analysis are shared, or intertranslatable, between the two disciplines. For instance, in discussing the separate functions of the 'where' (dorsal) and 'what' (ventral) streams, it is generally stated that the ventral stream delivers properties of the object attended to, while the dorsal stream delivers its location. But isn't location itself a property? Correspondingly, in logic, the existence of an object is expressed by an 'existential quantifier', ∃, rather than by a predicate, but a classic question asked in the theory of logic is 'Isn't existence a predicate?' This question has occupied philosophers from ancient times to the present, including Aristotle, Avicenna, Aquinas, Hume, Kant, and Quine; see Miller (2002) for a comprehensive survey. It is fair to say that the majority of philosophers have concluded that the existence of an object is not one its properties, in the sense that its shape, colour, or size is. This is consonant with excluding the egocentric location of an object in the perceptual space of a perceiver from the properties delivered for it by the ventral stream. (In many languages, there is an etymological connection between existence and spatial location, as with English *There is*....)

It is now possible to see connections across the divide between disciplines. Aha, so the logicians, in the case of predicate-argument structure at least, were onto something that has **approximate** neuropsychological correlates, always keeping in mind that what we can find in the brain is only structured neural activity. The interdisciplinary task is to see how such structured neural activity can plausibly be interpreted as encoding some theoretical construct that had been thought of outside of neuroscience.

4.3 LOCAL AND GLOBAL ATTENTION TO OBJECTS AND SCENES

The arguments in these sections are driven by the goal of articulating a possible bridge between formal logic and neuroscience. More specifically, I am trying here to consolidate the two logico-neural links already claimed. These are: (1) the link between dorsal stream, pre-attentional processes, which assign mental indices to a small number of tracked objects, and the individual variables of logic, w, x, y, z, which I assume here to be in very limited supply—only up to four available at any one time; and (2) the link between ventral stream recognition areas, where categorization of tracked objects takes place, and logical one-place predicates. The restriction to one-place predicates is necessary for this analogy, because categorization only affects one object at a time; typically the small number of objects tracked in a scene belong to mutually exclusive categories (e.g. PERSON, ARTEFACT, PLANT), and so there would be conflict in trying to pass information to the recognition areas from several different objects at once. Once objects have been noted and categorized, for as long as the animal is 'globally attending' to the whole scene, it is possible to keep the assignments of categories to visual indices current in the mind, until they are ditched when attention switches to another scene. But these assignments are to single indices, corresponding to single objects in the environment. Thus the requirement, so far, to deal only in terms of one-place predicates.

But clearly there is a difficulty here, because the minds of animals and humans can grasp **relations between** objects, such as MOTHER-OF, DOMI-NATE, EAT, GROOM. And in speaking of animals taking in whole scenes, we presume it is possible for animals to categorize events of different kinds differently. Thus a baboon can distinguish a chasing event from a grooming event, and both of these from an eating event. In considering events such as these, clearly we are dealing with entities at different levels: the level of the whole event and the level of the participating objects. Events are dynamic, involving change, but static scenes can also involve several participant objects. Thus a chimpanzee can distinguish between a ball being on a table and a ball being under a table. How can we reconcile complex multi-participant events and scenes with the idea of attention delivering one-place judgements about the object(s) of attention?

The answer lies in a distinction between two types of attention recognized in the psychological literature: **local** attention and **global** attention. The general idea of the distinction between global and local attention is given by Treisman (2004, p. 541): 'An initial rapid pass through the visual hierarchy provides the global framework and gist of the scene and primes competing identities through the features that are detected. Attention is then focused back to early areas to allow a serial check of the initial rough bindings and to form the representations of objects and events that are consciously experienced.' The theory was pioneered by Navon (1977), whose title, 'Forest before the trees', expresses the phenomenon vividly. He summarizes: 'global structuring of a visual scene precedes analysis of local features' (p. 353) and 'global processing is a necessary stage of perception prior to more fine-grained analysis' (p. 371). A slightly different theory, still consistent with my overall purpose, is suggested by Humphreys (1998). He provides evidence for different, and parallel, visual processes of between-object coding and within-object coding. The coordination of the two levels of processing, one attending to elements of what is attended to by the other, is common to both theories, and is what will be exploited for proto-semantic purposes here. For expository simplicity, I will stick with the 'global/local' terminology.

Global attention takes in a scene very quickly and can note features in it, but does not necessarily bind these features consistently to the right objects. Treisman and Schmidt (1982) showed that in scenes presented very briefly, observers could often detect the presence of features, for example, red, yellow, a square, a triangle, but would incorrectly report their conjunction: a briefly presented scene with a red circle and a yellow triangle might be reported as containing a yellow circle.

The perceptual distinction between global and local attention shows a kind of 'doublethink' that is alien to logic. Animals capable of this two-level functioning are actually using two separate systems, one parallel and one serial, in tandem, and integrating their outputs into a single whole representation. Global attention directed at a whole scene delivers one or more monadic (one-place) judgements about the scene; in tandem, local attention to the participants delivers monadic judgements about them. It is in this sense that it is possible to claim that concepts traditionally held to be relational are monadic: they apply to a **single scene**, which in its turn, when analysed at a different level of attention, may contain several participants. These claims will be fleshed out in more detail in Chapter 5.4; a few quick examples can be given now. The idea is, for example, that an animal seeing one animal grooming another perceives this whole scene, via its global attention system, as a 'grooming scene', a scene in which grooming is happening. Thus, the predicate GROOM is a one-place predicate that applies to a scene (or event). Within this scene the observing animal registers, via its concurrent local attention system, two participants, each individually taking a particular role. As another example, an animal seeing a lizard on a rock globally perceives an 'on-ness situation', with two participant objects tracked by the local attention system. Thus ON, or some other appropriate translation, is a one-place predicate applying to the whole situation or scene, and the asymmetric participation of the rock and the lizard can be expressed by individual (one-place) properties of each. These ideas will be developed in the next chapter; for the moment it is interesting to explore the psychological evidence for the global/local distinction in more detail.

The mechanism which (sketchily and perhaps inaccurately) takes in a whole scene at a rapid glance is attributed with the power of parallel search for single features. Thus the red objects in a display can be quickly identified without much interfering effect of the number of distracting non-red objects also in the display, so subjects cannot be inspecting each object in the display in sequence. The target objects 'pop out' from a parallel search of the whole display. But search for **conjunctions** of features (e.g. finding all the red squares) is affected proportionally by the number of distractors, so it seems that subjects must need to focus attention on each object in turn (serial search) to check whether they satisfy the conjunction of features (Treisman and Gelade 1980). Nakayama and Silverman (1986) extended these results of Anne Treisman and her colleagues to conjunctions of colour and motion. They write: 'the visual system is incapable of conducting a parallel search over two stimulus dimensions simultaneously' (p. 264). (This widely accepted account has been shown to have complicating, but not falsifying, factors by Carrasco and Yeshurum 1998.)

The phenomenon of left spatial neglect[13] can be seen as a disorder of global attention. In this condition, patients consistently fail to notice, or direct focal attention to, objects on their left. The condition affects not only vision but also tactile, proprioceptive, and auditory modalities (Vallar 1998). Experiments with such patients show that they are capable of attending to individual objects in (the right side of) a scene; they can pick out targeted objects and mark them, but on the right side only. The psychological literature often relates this condition to attention, but not explicitly to global attention. It is clear, however, that the deficit is not a problem with mechanisms of local attention: 'Whereas true visual field cuts (or other sensory losses) cannot be alleviated by directing attention to the affected region, performance for otherwise neglected stimuli can often be improved by cuing covert[14] attention there (Posner et al. 1984)' (Driver et al. 1999, p. 595). Attention is, of course, an extremely complex topic, and there are many poorly understood subtleties in the various deficits that have been observed. But at the gross level in which we are interested here, left neglect phenomena indicate a separation between two mechanisms, one for taking in a whole scene (in normal patients) and another for attending to specific objects within that scene. Most interestingly, the condition also affects memory and imagery, indicating some carry-over from perception to more permanent cognitive representational capacity.

---

[13] See Driver et al. (1999) for an excellent survey of the spatial neglect condition.

[14] Covert attention is attention to an object or location without concomitant shift of eyegaze or head position. Think of a teacher watching a miscreant pupil at the side of a classroom out of the corner of her eye.

A dissociation between the superficial, gross taking in of a scene and the registering of all the scene's major details as reflected in conjunctions of features associated with each object is seen in **simultanagnosia**. Some patients with this disorder are permanently in the state that normal subjects are in when they are presented with a scene very briefly. They are aware of the presence of features, but cannot tell what features go with each other, or with which object. Informal brief descriptions of simultanagnosia can be puzzling, and must be treated with caution. It is commonly described as an inability to see more than one object at a time, with concomitant failure to take in a whole scene. A more careful definition is 'a failure to perceive multiple concurrent stimuli, sometimes even for superimposed objects (e.g., seeing the examiner's face but not his or her glasses, or vice versa), with awareness shifting only slowly between distinct objects or object parts' (Driver et al. 1999, pp. 597–598). In some sense, simultanagnosics do take in a whole scene, but only at a superficial level, failing to integrate all the component objects coherently. Simultanagnosia is typically associated with ocular apraxia, or 'psychic paralysis of gaze', an inability to direct voluntary eye movements, such as are involved in tracking objects in a scene, already mentioned several times in previous sections. That this is not always the problem is shown by Rizzo and Hurtig (1987), who tracked eye movements in three simultanagnosic patients and found them to be normal. Laeng et al. (1999, p. 109) made the alternative suggestion that their simultanagnosic patient AMA's 'problem could be a consequence of the loss of multiple spatial indices (whose purpose is in fact to direct attention)'. Dehaene and Cohen (1994, p. 958) likewise identify the problem as 'a fundamental inability to use spatial tags to keep track of previously explored locations'.

Farah (1990) gives an extended and careful discussion of two different types of simultanagnosia, dorsal and ventral, which are not often distinguished in the literature. While the symptoms are very similar, they are not identical, and the conditions are associated with injury to quite different parts of the brain, as the terms suggest. Both types of simultanagnosic have trouble integrating multi-participant scenes into wholes, but their difficulties lie in different parts of the various subsystems to be integrated, according to Farah. By her account, dorsal simultanagnosics cannot **see** more than one object at a time, whereas ventral simultanagnosics cannot **recognize** more than one object at a time.

When [Luria's] patient [a dorsal simultanagnosic] was shown a rectangle made up of six dots, the patient was unable to count the dots. Recall that dorsal simultanagnosics cannot count objects because this requires seeing more than one object at a time. In contrast, this patient could see the rectangle made up of the six dots, as well as recognize other geometric forms drawn with broken lines. Apparently the patient could view the stimulus as dots, and hence see a single dot at a time, or he could view it as a rectangle, and hence see the entire rectangle. In the latter case, the patient was still unable to count the dots, presumably because once he started to count the dots, he would again be seeing them as dots and see only one at a time. In other words, the organization of the dots into a rectangle did not increase the patient's attentional capacity to more than one object; rather it allowed the patient to view the set of dots as a single object. An implication of this is that the attentional system of dorsal simultanagnosics is sensitive to voluntary 'top-down' determinants of what constitutes an object.

(Farah, 1990, pp. 22–23)

(This relates to the dorsal simultanagnosic patient discussed in Luria 1959.) By contrast, 'Although ventral simultanagnosics cannot recognize multiple objects, they differ from dorsal simultanagnosics in that they can *see* multiple objects. This is evident in their ability to count scattered dots (Kinsbourne and Warrington 1962), as well as in their ability to manipulate objects and walk around without bumping into obstacles' (Farah 1990, p. 25).

In terms of our earlier discussion of individual variable arguments of predicates, or temporary indices assigned by the visual system to objects, from a limited available set of four (w, x, y, z), some simultanagnosics seem only to have one index available to them. To repeat, Laeng et al. (1999, p. 109) suggest that their patient AMA's 'problem could be a consequence of the loss of multiple spatial indices (whose purpose is in fact to direct attention)'. AMA had most brain damage within the ventral system, a complicating fact, as her symptoms resemble those of dorsal simultanagnosics. Laeng et al. (1999) hypothesize that the damage may have resulted in some kind of disconnection between the dorsal and ventral systems.

Simultanagnosia is reflected pervasively in the sufferers' everyday lives. Farah cites Luria again: 'looking out a window, Luria et al. (1963)'s patient was able to see one car at a time, saying, "I know there are many but I see only one" (p. 222)' (Farah 1990, p. 18). Farah (1990, pp. 18–19) cites several other cases (from Godwin-Austen 1965 and Tyler 1968) of patients being shown pictures of familiar scenes and failing to 'make sense of them as a whole'. Boutsen and Humphreys (1999) report on a simultanagnosic patient, GK, who was 'typically unable to interpret complex thematic pictures (e.g. the Boston "cookie theft" picture was described just in terms of the people present; cf. Goodglass and Kaplan 1983)' (Boutsen and Humphreys 1999, p. 659). GK, then, lacked the ability to form a complete representation of a scene, including all the who-did-what-to-whom information regularly conveyed by normal speakers in sentences; but he could identify the participant persons (without being able to describe **how** they participated). A general conclusion reached by the authors is that 'it appears that GK has difficulty in selecting between local and more global descriptions when they conflict' (p. 669). Normal adult humans have no such problem in shifting back and forth between local and global attention, so that the total representation of a scene is synthesized from both its gross overall configuration and the conjunctions of features associated with each of its constituent objects.

Striking evidence of the dissociation between global and local visual processing is seen in the difference between Williams Syndrome and Down Syndrome subjects. 'Mentally retarded subjects with Williams Syndrome are considerably more impaired in global relative to local analysis, whereas subjects with Down Syndrome display the opposite pattern' (Bihrle et al. 1989).

[Experimental] items were composed of local components that together constituted a global form (i.e. a big D constituted of little Y's). . . . When asked to draw the designs, both groups failed, but in distinctively different ways. In these paradigms, Williams syndrome subjects typically produced only the local forms sprinkled across the page and were impaired at producing the global forms. Subjects with Down syndrome showed the opposite pattern; they tended to produce the global forms without the local forms (Fig. 4, bottom). This was true whether subjects reproduced forms from memory (after a five-second delay) or whether they were asked to copy the form placed in front of them. In perceptual matching tasks as well, Williams syndrome subjects showed a local bias. These results suggest an unusual processing pattern in Williams syndrome, a bias towards attention to detail at the expense of the whole (Wang et al. 1995; Bellugi et al. 1994; Bihrle et al. 1989).

(Bellugi et al. 1997, p. 338)

The relevant part of Bellugi et al. (1997)'s 'Fig. 4' is reproduced as Figure 4.1 below. The global/local difference between the two syndromes is very striking.

In normal adult humans, the relationship between local and global attention is controlled and subject to direction by higher-level goals. Depending on what we are looking for, or interested in, normals can direct attention to a whole broad scene, or to some specific object in that scene.

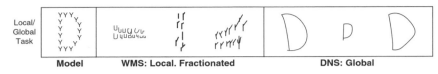

Figure 4.1 Williams Syndrome and Down Syndrome subjects' copied drawings reflect local and global emphasis respectively.

Some brain-damaged patients can readily recognize short words, but have trouble counting the letters in them; this shows an inability to individuate the parts of a whole stimulus. Other patients have a converse problem. These cases are reported in Humphreys (1998).

Having focused on one object, normal observers can 'zoom in deeper', treating the object as the scene and focusing on its parts. This potentially recursive zooming in is limited in practice by the small size of the subparts. (Microscopes were invented to overcome this limitation.) Topdown expectations about the things we are supposed to be attending to play a part in priming the appropriate level of attention. Deciding whether we like a new wallpaper design, we typically keep to a global level of attention to the whole pattern; but given a page of print, we immediately plunge to a level of attention to the words on the page, and sometimes to the individual letters. Most higher animals have global and local attention systems and can shift between them, so this setup is ancient.

Humans can shift attention between parts and wholes, as shown in experiments with complex hierarchical stimuli, such as larger, global letters constructed from smaller, local letters. In these experiments, a target stimulus appears at either the local or the global level, with a distractor at the other level. A shift of attention between levels is said to be demonstrated through a form of priming, whereby targets at one level are presented with a higher probability than at the other level. This base-rate type of priming can facilitate speed of responding to targets, as seen in shorter reaction times to targets at the primed level.   (Fremouw et al. 1998, p. 278)

Cerella (1980, 1986) concluded from experiments on pigeons inspecting objects that they do not attend to the global relationships between parts or features of the objects. To the contrary, Kirkpatrick (2001) argues strongly against the lack of any global visual mechanisms in pigeons, on the basis of ordinary observation and further experiments.

It is difficult to imagine how an organism that flies about in the world could successfully navigate without using any information about the spatial organization of the surrounding environment. The pigeon actually possesses two perceptual systems: (1) a long-range guidance system; and (2) a shorter-range (food) detection system. It is possible that a particulate mechanism may operate on the grain-seeking system, which is invoked when closer range, smaller objects are being detected and identified. Perhaps, the long-range guidance system does make use of global organizational properties of the surrounding environment.   (Kirkpatrick 2001, Section 1)

Fremouw et al. (1998) found that pigeons, as well as humans, can shift their attention between local and global levels. In a later experiment, they found that pigeons can shift their level of attention very fast: 'pigeons can shift attention between local and global levels of perceptual analysis in seconds. . . . [P]igeons, like humans, can display highly dynamic stimulus-driven shifts of local/global attention' (Fremouw et al. 2002, p. 233).

Given that both pigeons and humans can do it, there is presumably no problem in assuming that apes closely related to humans also have this ability, and that our primate ancestors also had both local and global visual attention systems and were able to shift fluently between them. There are, however, differences of detail among primates in the division of labour between global and local attention. In a series of publications (Deruelle and Fagot 1997; Fagot and Deruelle 1997; Deruelle and Fagot 1998; Fagot and Tomonaga 1998), Joel Fagot and his colleagues have discovered that baboons tend to attend immediately at a local level, by contrast with humans, for whom the first visual pass is at a global level. '[D]ata from baboons, chimpanzees and humans suggest a phylogenetic trend in the way compound stimuli are processed' (Fagot and Tomonaga 1998, p. 3), with humans favouring a global pass, at least as a first approximation. These studies also found lateralization effects, with global attention showing a right hemisphere advantage (stimuli from left visual field); this is consistent with the phenomena of left spatial neglect, seen as a disorder of global processing.

An intriguing fact about the distinction between global and local visual processing is a tendency to emphasize the former in happier moods and the latter in sadder moods (Gasper and Clore 2002).

Normal adult humans can deploy the two visual attention systems, global and local, fluently in tandem, rapidly noting the major participants in a complex scene, together with their salient features, and conflating all the information gleaned into an apparently seamless whole. The whole mentally represented scene is still, however, highly underrepresentative of the actual scene in the world. Studies in 'change blindness' show that normal people fail to notice very obvious (after they are pointed out) changes between two consecutively presented scenes. One sensational example is reported by Simons and Chabris (1999): in this study about half of the observers failed to notice a woman in a gorilla suit walk for five seconds among a group of six basketball players. The observers had been instructed to watch the dynamic scene and count the passes made by either the black or the white team. Evidently, close attention to the players prevented them from seeing the gorilla! See Simons and Levin (1997) for a review of change blindness. The high fallibility of attention to a scene is also notoriously evident in the unreliability of eyewitness testimony to crimes (see Wells and Olson 2003 for a survey).

Finally, here is the main idea that I want to develop from this review of global and local attention. Property judgements, corresponding to one-place predicates, can be made of a whole scene, as well as of the individual objects in it. Quick global attention delivers such properties; on subsequent focal attention to individual objects, as in normal people, some of these properties may be reassigned to the constituent objects of the scene, but some may be kept as applying to the scene as a whole. Here is some evidence.

Recall an earlier quote from Nelson Cowan, about subitizing numerosities up to about 'the magical number 4', repeated here: 'it seems that a focal attention strategy involving eye movements is important for visual enumeration of over 4 items, but not at or below 4 items, the average number that subjects may be able to hold in the limited-capacity store at one time' (Cowan 2001). The implication is that the number of participants in a visual scene with four or fewer salient objects can be taken in at a glance by the global attention process. Given a scene with three objects, quick global attention can discern its 'threeness'. That is, a (numerical) predicate is associated with the scene as a whole, by the global attention mechanism. This is consistent with global attention involving parallel processing of a scene in normal people. This is backed up by a study of five simultanagnosics by Dehaene and Cohen (1994). They write:

Numerosity naming time and errors were measured in 5 simultanagnosic patients who suffered from severe difficulties in serial counting. Although these patients made close to 100% errors in quantifying sets comprising more than 3 items, they were excellent at quantifying sets of 1, 2, and sometimes 3 items. Their performances in visual search tasks suggested that they suffered from a deficit of serial visual exploration, due to a fundamental inability to use spatial tags to keep track of previously explored locations. The present data suggest that the patients' preserved subitizing abilities were based not on serial processing but rather on a parallel algorithm dedicated to small numerosities.   (Dehaene and Cohen 1994, p. 958)

In these patients, global parallel-processing attention can deliver the 'one-ness', 'twoness', or 'threeness' of a whole scene, but they cannot serially attend to individual objects in the scene. By contrast, Laeng et al. (1999)'s simultanagnosic patient AMA seemed to need to do a serial search to enumerate objects in the normal subitizing range 2-4, according to the statistical test applied. As mentioned earlier, this patient may be atypical, having damage in a ventral region not usually associated with parallel search.

Sometimes a scene may only consist of a single object. Here again evidence from simultanagnosia is relevant. 'Simultanagnosics generally have difficulty identifying objects in a scene, although they may successfully identify objects when they are presented alone' (McMullen et al. 2000, p. 407). This can be interpreted as applying a judgement to a whole scene (which simultanagnosics can do) which just happens to contain a single object. In the one-participant case the distinction between scene and object is neutralized. Visually, a one-participant scene **is** an object.

We have concentrated on the global/local attention in vision, but parallel effects can be found in audition as well. In a noisy room, for instance, one can concentrate on one particular voice, or just take in the whole noisy scene—the 'cocktail-party effect' (Cherry 1953). Listening to an orchestra, one can pay global attention to the whole orchestral sound, or concentrate attention on the sound of one instrument. Janata et al. (2002, p. 121), reporting fMRI studies of listening to complex musical 'scenes', state: 'direct comparisons of the listening conditions showed significant differences between attending to single timbres (instruments) and attending across multiple instruments'. The features used for segregating out one particular sound stream include rhythm, pitch, and location of the source (Bregman 1990).

The next chapter will capitalize on the global/local distinction to advocate a notation for the representation of scenes in which all predicates are one-place, some applying globally to the whole scene, and others applying locally to specific objects with a scene. This builds on the theme developed in this chapter of the evolutionary basis of proposition-like representations in the perception of scenes.

4.4 ANIMAL TRUTH, REFERENCE, AND SENSE

In Chapter 1, I argued against an essential connection between concepts and beliefs, and language, so that we can reasonably speak of animals having certain kinds of concepts and beliefs, even though they have no language. If we dislodge the idea of a logical proposition from any necessary connection with language, then it is possible to find activity correlating with propositional structure, of the required predicate-argument form, in non-linguistic animals' brains. In previous sections, we have considered (1) how an animal can store generalized semantic information about the categories of objects that it interacts with, and their component features; (2) how an animal can represent in its mind an event or situation involving up to four participating objects, of which it is keeping visual track, and (3) an argument that the tracking (or pre-attentional) dorsal mechanism combines with categorizing ventral mechanisms to give an analogue, in structured neural activity, of predicate-argument structure. These capacities, taken together, are enough to produce immediate perception-bound representations with the same structure, and same relation to the world, as propositions discussed by philosophers. Adopting a familiar logical notation, we can, for example, represent part of what a baboon perceives when it contemplates a scene containing a crouching lion and a rock as

$$\text{LION}_{baboon}(x) \ \& \ \text{CROUCH}_{baboon}(x) \ \& \ \text{ROCK}_{baboon}(y)$$

The subscripts indicate that these are baboon predicates/concepts, not (of course) human ones; mostly I will omit such relativizing subscripts, but only for expository convenience. But we can expect the baboon's concepts to have quite similar extensions to ours, as it lives in the same world and has a similar body. The individual variables x and y stand, in our notation, for the mental indices of these objects in the baboon's brain as it tracks them (probably realized as activity in its posterior parietal cortex). The observant reader will have noticed that these variables are unbound by any quantifier; I assume an implicit existential quantifier, $\exists$, so that roughly translating what this baboon sees into English, we would get *There's a crouching lion and there's a rock*. The formula above represents a compound proposition formed by the conjunction of three simple propositions (the order of the three conjuncts is immaterial). These ideas will be developed in a later section. As an animal such as a primate has no trouble tracking several objects at a time, and registering their properties, there is no problem in attributing a (limited) capacity for logical conjunction to such an animal.

Philosophers and logicians require of sentences expressing propositions that they be capable of being true or false. Thus *Water is wet* and *I am writing this book* express propositions and are true[15]; *Water is dry*

---

[15] Well, the latter was true when I wrote it, but isn't when you are reading it.

and *You are writing this book* express propositions and are false. In the evolutionary approach taken here, truth is fundamentally not a relation between sentences and the world but between non-linguistic mental representations and the world. We can speak informally of someone having in their mind a 'true picture' of the world or of some situation. Similarly, when a cat is watching a bird, and acting as it usually does (crouching low, perhaps muttering), it seems reasonable to say that the cat has a true belief that the thing it is watching belongs in some mental category which we will label $PREY_{cat}$.

Again to emphasize the point that animal concepts need not correspond to human concepts, we could fool a cat all of the time into acting towards some non-prey stimulus the same way it acts towards things in its $PREY_{cat}$ category, without it ever changing its behaviour; in this case we have to say, on the evidence, that the dummy object falls under the cat's $PREY_{cat}$ concept. From our point of view, but not from the cat's, the cat's concept is disjunctive. Contrariwise, where an animal has greater discriminatory powers than a human, and corresponding more highly differentiated behaviour, our human concepts would seem crudely disjunctive from the animal's point of view (if only it could study them). There is a lively discussion of such matters in Chapter 14 of Dennett (1995).

Truth is based on some standard. In the case of human sentences, the standard rests on conventional public agreement about the denotations of predicates. If I say 'My pen is on my desk', the truth of this depends in part on the somehow agreed range of the words *pen* and *desk*. If there is nothing on my desk that falls in the range we agree to call pens, the utterance is false. You and I share the same understanding, reinforced by frequent communicative interaction in the same large society, of what counts as a pen, and a desk, and so on. In the case of animals, of course, there is no such public standard. We are talking about the possible truth (correspondence to reality), not of public expressions, but of an animal's inner mental representations of the world. But glib mention of 'reality' will not do, for the world may present itself to an animal in different packages from the way a human perceives it. We know, for example, that dogs are red-green colourblind. I submit that we can, nevertheless, get glimpses of an animal's possibly alternative segmentation of the world by observing its **usual behaviour**, in and out of the laboratory, and allowing, at least in the case of higher animals, that it has goals and acts purposefully much of the time. This usual behaviour is the standard on which a private conception of truth is based. Investigating this kind of truth is much harder work and much more tentative than judging the truth of a simple declarative sentence expressing some concrete fact about nearby middle-sized objects. But it is possible.

In these terms, it is possible for an animal to have a false belief. We can present a cat with a fake stimulus, so that it acts as if it is seeing a bird, but then 'realizes' that the stimulus is not a bird, and changes its behaviour accordingly (stops crouching, looks bored). For the time before the change of behaviour, it seems reasonable to say that the cat has a false belief, believing wrongly that the thing it was watching belonged to the feline mental category $PREY_{cat}$.

Of course, the animal need never actually realize that it has a false belief. There are two senses to this. One involves metacognition: there is no reason to credit a non-human animal with any kind of conscious awareness corresponding to the human idea expressed by *Oh, I was wrong*. By the criteria used here, one could, in principle, discover that a non-human animal had some concept of having made a mistake. This could happen if, under a range of different conditions where the animal had entertained a false belief and then corrected it, it behaved in a regular and systematic way. For instance, if we always observed the same peculiar gait or pose after a cat had (a) walked into a glass window believing there to be no obstacle, (b) stopped acting frightened on recognizing the human figure approaching, (c) stopped lapping a white liquid on realizing it is something other than milk, then we could claim that the cat actually had some higher-level concept of the falsehood of its own (previous) beliefs. This level of metacognition is either nonexistent or very rare in non-human animals (but recall the backing-off behaviour of Keddy-Hector et al. 2005's piglets mentioned earlier).

The other point in saying that an animal need never actually realize that it has a false belief is that the 'realization', indicated by a change in behaviour, is not criterial for a theorist's claim that the animal did indeed have the false belief. The animal enticed to a sudden death by a lure or bait does not realize its mistake; nevertheless it did entertain a false belief. So when a cat, on looking at a wind-blown leaf, entertains the representation $MOUSE_{cat}(x)$, it is grasping a proposition, which it believes at the time (seeing is believing), and which we can 'objectively' from our Godlike vantage point assign a particular truth value (in this case, false). It must be emphasized here that when a human investigator judges an animal to have a false belief, the judgement should be made in terms of **a well-rounded consideration of the animal's usual behaviour**, and not in terms of any human category. When pressed for time, we all make mistakes, and animals are no different. If a cat persisted in always treating wind-blown leaves exactly like mice, we should conclude that it has a mental category different from any of ours, and not that it entertained a false belief. But when a thing twitches momentarily, and you only catch sight of it out of the corner of one eye, anyone, even a cat, can be mistaken, and for a while have a false belief about the thing. By contrast, a stickle-back that consistently tries to attack anything red, including the postvan outside the window, cannot be credited with any concept of rival male stickleback. It never seems to realize the difference between different red stimuli.

Cases like those just discussed are admittedly very problematic, as they involve trying to map the boundaries of an animal's concepts. But other kinds of facts not so closely bound up with categorization are more clearly amenable to truth assignments. In the experiments on object permanence reviewed in Chapter 2, animals watched objects going behind screens, and then searched for them behind the screens. The basis for the psychologists' experiments was an assumption that an animal's mental representation could or could not correspond to reality. It seems perfectly reasonable to say that a puppy in such an experiment believes that the ball is behind the screen. If (we know that) the ball has been surreptitiously removed, the puppy has a false belief about the location of the ball. If the ball is still behind the screen, the puppy has a true belief.

Now take the philosopher's other relation between language and the world, namely **reference**. It would seem natural and consistent to claim that the neural index in the cat's posterior parietal cortex (presumably, if it's like a primate) which the individual variable x in this mentally entertained representation stands for **refers** to the wind-blown leaf, out there in the world. The kind of reference involved is **deictic**, or indexical, reference, as with the English demonstrative pronouns *this* and *that*. The mental index x refers to one particular object for just the duration of an episode of attention.

It also seems reasonable to claim that a relation of **denotation** holds between mental categories and the classes of object and event that they denote in the outside world. This is not a deictic relation, as it does not vary from one situation to another. A class of objects or events is denoted by a pattern of potential neural activity, which is consistently activated when events or objects from that class are encountered (or imagined).

If animal non-linguistic mental representations can be true, and if parts of them can refer and denote, one might ask whether there can be a distinction, in non-linguistic minds, between sense and reference, in the spirit of Frege (1892). Frege's classic example involved an object (the planet Venus) seen at different times of day, and described with reference to the time of observation variously as either *the Morning Star* or *the Evening Star*. These two expressions have different senses, but the same referent. The example is patently linguistic, involving a difference between two noun phrases. But could there be a corresponding phenomenon in the minds of animals prior to language? Possibly there could, and I will sketch this possibility below.

An animal could conceivably encounter the same entities in completely different types of situation, and develop different concepts triggered by the different contexts. For example, our animal might experience a certain type of predator charging silently in daylight often enough to build up a mostly visual concept of this predator type. The same predators might also operate by night, using a different technique, creeping up on their prey from behind with a loud roar, and our animal (if it escapes) might build up a mostly auditory concept from this experience. Its motor responses to these two experiences might be different, too, adapted to the different day/night circumstances. In the terminology of Gallese and Lakoff (2005), the animal develops different functional clusters, functioning as neurally realized units, corresponding to these different experiences, without making any connection between the two concepts, even though (**we** know *ex hypothesi* that) the concepts denote the same class of entities. In such a hypothetical case, it would seem reasonable to say that the animal has two different mental concepts denoting the same external reality. These could be seen as a non-linguistic analogue of Fregean senses. (For Frege, senses were not mental entities, in line with his general avoidance of psychologizing. Fodor (1998, pp. 15–22) replaces Frege's term *sense* with *Mode of Presentation* (MOP), and argues that, for Frege's overall conception to work, MOPs must be mental entities. I agree, so, if you like, replace *sense* above with *MOP*; in fact, I suppose that more superficial readers of Frege than Fodor have naturally taken Fregean senses to correspond to something mental, even though Frege himself might have winced at such an interpretation.)

But it seems likely that animals have also evolved a strong defence mechanism tending to prevent such cases from arising. As mentioned earlier, concept-formation involves generalization over stimuli occurring in different situations, for instance in different lighting conditions, with different ambient smells and temperatures, at different distances, from different angles, and possibly moving in different ways. The vervet that sees a leopard on different occasions **never** has exactly the same sensory experiences, but these different experiences nevertheless trigger the same concept. It is highly adaptive for an animal to be able to recognize the same entity or class of entities under different conditions. Another obvious example is colour: 'It is remarkable that we see an object as having a constant color even when viewed under a wide variety of illumination conditions' (Churchland 1986, p. 454). Judgement of an animal's size has also been shown to vary systematically as a function of the frequency of the animal's stride (Jokisch and Troje 2003). Fast-striding animals are seen as relatively small, and slow-striding animals are judged to be relatively big. Judgement of size, then, is not just a matter of the angle subtended by an object at the retina. Jokisch and Troje (2003) did not investigate this, but it may be presumed that a stimulus of a fast-striding animal subtending a wide angle at the retina would be judged anomalously big, or anomalously fast-striding. The judgements, put into words, would be *big for such a fast-striding animal* or *fast-striding for such a big animal*. It is well known that humans can make context-dependent judgements of size, such as 'short for a basketball player' or 'tall for a jockey'. Sarris (1998) has shown that chickens can be trained to make such context-dependent size judgements, and to develop internal 'frame-of-reference' systems. Sarris first trained chickens to select large or small cubes, then habituated them to differing expectations about the size of cubes dependent on their colour. Chickens were able to make perceptual judgements such as 'big for a red cube' or 'small for a green cube' of cubes of the same size but different colour. (See also Sarris 1990, 1994, 2000a, 2000b. A monograph (Sarris 2006) pulls much of this work together and sets it in a wider context.)

Finally, don't get me wrong: I am **not** proposing that anything like **linguistic** representations are formed in an animal's mind when it perceives a scene. The logical formulae above purporting to represent what goes on in the baboon's or the cat's brain are, of course, rough and ready. But they do represent a claim that the animal (1) in tracking the objects of its attention, assigns mental indices to them, and (2) binds stored categories to each of them (to a greater or lesser degree of detail, presumably, depending on its arousal or motivation). The conventions for interpreting a symbolic formula such as $\text{MOUSE}_{cat}(x)$ are conventions applied by us human researchers, not by the cat in whose brain the perceptual experience is registered. **We** both define and interpret x in our notation as referring to some object in the world outside the cat's brain that it is attending to via a tracking mental index or tag. And the non-linguistic predicate symbol MOUSE_{cat} is our crude way of indicating the complex of neural firings that happen when a cat mentally categorizes an object of attention in this way. This approach is adopted by, among others, Gallese and Lakoff (2005), who describe a concept (GRASPING) in terms of a neural schema, with various components such as 'initial condition' and 'final state'. Of this description, they write: 'we have written down symbols (e.g. *final state*) as our notation for functional clusters. This does not mean that we take functional clusters themselves to be symbolic. The symbols are only **our names** for functional clusters, which function as neurally realised units' (Gallese and Lakoff 2005, p. 469). In the terms used by Barsalou (1999), representations formed inside an animal are 'perceptual symbols', and not 'amodal symbols'. 'Amodal symbol' is Barsalou's way of characterizing an abstract mental entity devoid of any perceptual content, like the configurations of representations in a computer whose only input from the outside world is from a keyboard. I agree with Barsalou that concepts have perceptual content, but, along with Gallese and Lakoff, who also argue against amodal symbols, add that they may have motor content, too.

To emphasize the sensory-motor character of pre-linguistic concepts in animals and babies, as I have here, is not to deny the existence of some concepts, even in animals, which are not so directly captured in these sensory-motor terms. In Chapter 2.1, in connection with reversal learning tasks, I claimed that apes applied some concept of OPPOSITE. This is indeed abstract and amodal, or at least much less easily related to primary sensory-motor activations than concepts of objects and actions. Other relational concepts that some animals are capable of, such as SAME and DIFFERENT, seem likely to be similarly abstracted away from primary sensory-motor activations. The attaching of public linguistic labels to concepts adds some kind of abstract dimension to them, less directly rooted in perception and action; this is a matter touched on briefly earlier and to be further explored in the sequel to this book.[16]

This chapter has begun to make the case that neural correlates exist, in both humans and closely related non-humans, of something that linguists, philosophers, and logicians would recognize as having the properties of **propositions**. Propositional thought is sometimes held to be the special preserve of humans, for example by Dummett (1993). Propositions have size, shape, and function. To make the logical idea of a proposition fit well with primate psychology, we needed to cut logical propositions down to size. This was done by showing how the practice, if not the theory, of logic

---

[16] Volume 2 of *Language in the Light of Evolution*, titled *Origins of Linguistic Form.*

and linguistic semantics operates within the psychologically significant boundary set by the magical number 4, the limit of much mammalian (including human) and avian subitizing. As to the shape of propositions, it was argued that the two essential components of a simple logical proposition, a predicate and one or more arguments, have neural correlates, respectively, in the categorical judgements delivered by the ventral stream, and in the indices available to the brain for tracking a small number of attended-to objects, a process happening in the dorsal stream. In this argument, it was essential to relate the neural indices to logical individual **variables**, e.g. the logician's x, y, and z, rather than individual constants, e.g. JOHN, PARIS, VENUS. Here, a different kind of cutting down to size is involved, from **universal**, or context-free, to context-dependent. The scope of traditional visions of logic is universal, aiming to provide a notation usable (by scientists) about objects known by, and familiar to, **all users in any context of use**. Real animals, even humans, don't know the whole world; they constantly encounter fresh objects, and can categorize them. In this vital function, individual variables, which can be attached to whatever new objects come along, are the essential tool. So the version of logic practically usable by living organisms is not omniscient, i.e. does not have a known individual constant term for every individual object in the world in which it lives. This idea will be followed up in the next chapter.

Further concerning the shape of propositions, the approximate correlation of their predicate-argument shape with neural ventral and dorsal pathways required another cutting down to size, namely an elimination of all but one-place predicates. This is perhaps a bold step, and will be argued for in more detail in the next chapter. But I attempted to lay the groundwork for this step in this chapter by highlighting a psychological distinction between global and local attention. The idea is that global attention delivers one-place judgements about whole scenes, while local attention delivers one-place judgements about the individual objects within each scene, and the two processes, global and local, operate in parallel. Thus, there is no conflict (I will argue) between the one-place-ness of all predicates and the limit imposed by the magical number 4 on the number of entities involved in a simple proposition. A maximum of about four objects can be attended to in one scene; global attentional processes categorize the scene, and local attentional processes simultaneously categorize the participant objects. See the next chapter for further development of this argument, from the point of view of a linguistic semanticist. Finally, as to the logical 'function' of propositions, the closest that logic gets to any consideration of their function is their relation to an external world, a relationship captured in the notions of **reference** and **truth**. The last section of this chapter argued that it is still possible to maintain a clear sense in which mental propositions, cut down to psychologically motivated size and shape, have relations to the world which can reasonably be called truth and reference.

CHAPTER FIVE

Towards Human Semantics

This chapter will pursue the ideas of the previous chapter, from the perspective of a linguistic semanticist struggling to accommodate his familiar, and often quite rich, propositional notations to the rather severe psychological constraints outlined there. The arguments here will inevitably appeal to (or provoke) logicians and linguistic semanticists more than psychologists, much less anthropologists. The arguments here are rather an in-house business, concerned with the notation and terminology used by linguists for describing the meanings of sentences. If linguistic semantics is to relate to facts outside language itself, such as psychological and neuroscientific facts, it needs to put its own house in order. So if you are not a linguistic semanticist, peer in through the windows of this chapter, to watch a linguist trying to do some house-tidying, making the place fit to receive visitors in the shape of ideas and facts from psychology and neuroscience. If you **are** a linguistic semanticist, I expect plenty of argument about my proposed way of tidying the house. But don't forget the goal of establishing a framework for describing the continuous evolution of representations of meanings from pre-human to human.

5.1 A PARSIMONIOUS *BEGRIFFSSCHRIFT* FOR PROTO-PROPOSITIONS

Now for something completely different in flavour, starting from the other end of our topic.[1]

Investigation of meaning is a multidisciplinary business. It started, millennia ago, with logical study based on language; way back then,

---

[1] Using the term *Begriffsschrift* is meant to convey, not arrogance in borrowing Frege's term, but a similar intention to his, of devising a form of 'concept writing' for the representation of scenes. Frege would probably turn in his grave at the thought that anyone would apply his methods to **animal** concepts.

public language itself was the only available guide to the workings of the mind. And as public language is the most salient and pervasive outer manifestation of the workings of the mind, any theory of meaning must necessarily fit naturally and as economically as possible with the facts of language. It is also clear now that such a theory must fit naturally and as economically as possible with the machinery of the brain. So we have two anchor points: brain and language.

'The logician's distrust of the psychological aspects of reasoning has led to a de facto division of labor. The relationship between mind and representation is considered the subject matter of psychology, that between representation and world the subject matter of logic' (Barwise 1999, p. 483). Notice that both logic and psychology are here supposed to be concerned with the same thing, called 'representation'. But if the labour remains divided, who is to work on a common view of representations, the interface between logic and psychology, so that both sides can eventually talk to each other about their shared concern, the mind? It needs to be done; and it is not too early to start. I will volunteer a contribution. Consider these proposals on their merits.

The very publicness of language easily leads us to the dangerous idea that, since we use it so effortlessly, we must know all there is to know about it. Over the centuries, and even before anyone started seriously to consider how language is represented in the brain, it was recognized that the outer forms of language could be misleading. A separate discipline of logic grew, still largely responsive to language, but insisting on a gap between any logical notation and the superficial shapes of sentences. The most important modern advance was Frege (1879)'s shift to a generalized view of predication, whereby concepts corresponding to all major parts of speech—nouns, verbs, adjectives, and prepositions—are **predicates**. The move to a representation less slavishly tied to the superficial form of sentences makes it possible to envisage a rapprochement to the brain (although that was not Frege's motivation). In the previous chapter we have already made one proposal for interpreting the most basic core of Fregean logical notation, predicate-argument structure, in neural terms. This chapter will suggest a far-reaching extension of that idea of getting logical representations of meaning to be plausible in terms of what we know about the brain.

In what follows, I will make two assumptions. The first is that the logico-linguistic enterprise is essentially psychological; but linguists and logicians can make a contribution while keeping to their traditional verbal pen-and-paper tools and methods. Linguists and logicians, without getting drawn into neuroscience, stake out the territory of what the mind can do, what inferences and connections it can make, and sometimes express in language, about what kinds of objects and events. So long as an eye is kept on the ultimate goal of relating logical representations to psychology, linguists and logicians can carry on analysing language without being too distracted by questions of neural representation.

This leads to my second assumption, which is that the ontology of many currently proposed logical notations is too rich to support plausible neural instantiation. Formal semanticists propose representations which include many different types of term, such as quantifiers, individual constants, ordered multi-place predicates, participant-role labels (e.g. Agent, Patient), operators, referential indices, and so forth. It is unlikely that different brain mechanisms will be found corresponding to all the different interpretive conventions that these different notational devices require. If the linguists and logicians are to use notations that will eventually be interpretable psychologically, they ought not to multiply notational innovations beyond necessity.

One-place predicates[2] taking individual variables as arguments, have, I claim, a neural basis. Can we reduce all formal representations of propositions to this bare minimum? I will sketch an affirmative answer. If it turns out that such minimal representations are inadequate for all the subtle distinctions made by modern human languages, I have a fall-back position. This is that the bare minimal representations I will propose **are** adequate to capture the private mental representations of animals at an evolutionary stage just prior to the emergence of public language. How could we possibly know about those? By reasoning from what we know about human and animal perceptual and memory systems.

It is convenient to devise a somewhat new notation to bridge the gap between what is known about visual (and auditory) attention and conventional logical formulae. The notation I will propose follows Discourse Representation Theory (DRT, Kamp and Reyle 1993) in the use of boxes as a way of delimiting the part of the world represented. In DRT, the concern is with building up a 'universe' consisting of only the things mentioned in the discourse under analysis, typically beginning with a simple sentence of the *Jones owns Ulysses* sort. Correspondingly, the notation I will use here depicts just the set of entities that can be comprehended in

---

[2] Please read most instances of *predicate* in this chapter, especially when attributed to animals, as abbreviating *pre-linguistic predicate* or *proto-predicate*. Once public labels get attached to these, and they become integrated into human languages, they take on further properties, as will be seen in the sequel to this book.

one visual scene. My own notation, however, will be more constrained, in not using any variables at all. The use of variables in DRT enables that theory (and equivalently predicate logic) to capture certain facts about quite complex linguistic phenomena that go beyond anything that seems to be necessary for the comprehension of a scene. Further, the non-use of variables, augmented by the idea of the context-dependence of predicates mentioned at the end of the last chapter (Sarris 2006), will also make it possible to maintain the limitation to one-place predicates. Right, here goes, introducing the box notation for scenes.

Recall the scene mentioned earlier (and now suppressing the relativizing $_{baboon}$ subscript for simplicity):

$$\text{LION}(x) \,\&\, \text{CROUCH}(x) \,\&\, \text{ROCK}(y)$$

For starters, we'll redraw this as:

The outer box represents the whole scene to which global attention is paid. The inner boxes represent the individual objects in this scene, to which local attention is paid. In this notation, a box plays the same role as a variable in conventional notations. Inclusion of several predicate terms in the same box means that they all apply to the same individual. Separate boxes stand for different individuals. The two-level device of an outer box containing inner boxes corresponds to the two-level distinction between global and local attention.[3] As mentioned earlier, the 'threeness' of some group of objects can be detected by the parallel-search, subitizing mechanism of global attention. Correspondingly a scene containing three cows would be represented as:

Here the predicate THREE is in the outer box, hence representing a judge-ment about a property of the whole scene. The two-level outer/inner distinction, corresponding to objects **in** a scene, is the only iconic aspect of this notation. This element of iconicity in the notation is helpful to us because it roughly mimics scenes as we, and higher animals, see them. The box diagrams are not, of course, a literal picture of the represented neural activity in the brain of an observer seeing a scene.

---

[3] Or, following a slightly different theory (Humphreys 1998), the two-level distinction between between-object visual coding and within-object visual coding.

There are no pictures inside brains. The outer box represents global attention to a whole scene; the inner boxes represent local attention to the individual objects in a scene. This is not a thoroughgoing picture theory of propositional representations in the manner of Wittgenstein (1922). The relative positions of the inner boxes have no significance, and these boxes can be moved around with no effect on the claimed relation to the observed scene. The only element of **ordering** in these representations is the asymmetric relationship between outer and inner boxes.

Here is another illustrative example. Say an observer sees a pair of people walking in unison together near a rock; the pair, seen as a unit, moves. This could be represented as follows:

This attributes three levels of global–local 'zooming-in' to a pre-linguistic creature, which may be more than some animals are capable of. I assume that primates can manage scenes of this complexity.

A monkey can look at three birds and take in the whole scene, the global 'threeness' of it and the fact that the participants are all birds. Three or four is the limit of what a monkey can take in at a glance, but a monkey can represent something about a scene containing more than four birds, say a whole flock, without devoting any local attention to any individual bird, more or less as we can. This could possibly be represented as:

$$\boxed{\text{MANY BIRD}}$$

This supposes that there is no sustained zooming in to attend to individuals, but that global attention nevertheless delivers the information that the scene contains birds. The predicate MANY expresses something roughly corresponding to the human category Plural.

As mentioned earlier, the division between global and local attention applies to audition as well as to vision. A baboon mother can pick the cry of her own infant out of the background chattering hubbub, and we might represent her experience as:

A human auditory example, picking out the individual voices in a group, would be:

QUARTET	BASS	TENOR	ALTO	SOPRANO

The predicate labels in these diagrams are, as throughout this work, our own shorthand labels for whatever neural activity is involved in recognizing an object or scene as belonging to a particular mental category. It is not implied that a pre-linguistic primate would have exactly the same neural response on seeing a rock or a person as we do. And in fact there is individual variation among humans. But humans, by and large, can agree to common labels on what they are jointly attending to. Thus, the use of a term such as ROCK means 'whatever neural activity happens in a pre-linguistic creature that has a category of rocks more or less coextensive with ours, when it recognizes, or thinks about, a rock'.

5.2 GETTING RID OF INDIVIDUAL CONSTANTS

In the box notation just introduced, a box is the equivalent of an individual variable, e.g. x, y, or z, in standard logic, and the terms in the boxes correspond to (conjunctions of) predicates taking those variables as arguments. This leaves out of consideration individual constant terms, purporting uniquely to identify particular individuals, terms like JOHN, PARIS, and VENUS. In this section I propose to eliminate such terms, arguing from (1) first principles, (2) the lack of clinching psychological evidence, and (3) differences of opinions among philosophers.

5.2.1 The Principled Unknowability of Uniqueness

The **logical** idea of an individual constant is that it names a unique individual in the world with absolute reliability. Many of the founders of logic were aiming at an ideal notation in which the propositions of science could be expressed. The science concerned would make statements about objects such as the Sun, the Moon, and particular stars. (It is interesting how often astronomical examples are used.) In the scientific notation, predicates would be applied to the names for such individuals, as in STAR(SIRIUS), translatable as *Sirius is a star*. It was assumed that users of the logical language would have absolutely (and I mean 'absolutely') no problem in identifying, out there in the world, the unique object denoted by the individual constant. This is a psychologically untenable ideal.

Barsalou (1999, p. 584) sums up the psychological problem very clearly, in terms of his theory of Perceptual Symbol Systems: 'Perceptual symbols need not represent specific individuals ... we should be surprised if the cognitive system *ever* contains a complete representation of an individual. ... [W]e should again be surprised if the cognitive system ever remembers an individual with perfect accuracy.'

The killer problem is the possibility of identical twins. I mean identical twins in a broad sense, applicable to any sensible pair of objects. We recognize objects by their properties. And our sense organs are limited in the fineness of detail that they can detect. Given two paperclips from the same batch from the same factory, you can tell, if you have them both in your hand, that they are different individual objects. But shuffle them around a bit, or toss them in the air and catch them, and you can't tell now which one was previously on the left. You can't tell which is which. The logical idea of an individual constant embodies the 'whichness' of individuals, the separateness that they carry around distinguishing them from other individuals. We don't doubt that individuals, out there in the world, are distinct from each other,[4] so that the question 'Which paperclip was previously on the left?' is a perfectly meaningful question. But, in the limit, we can never answer such questions with any absolute certainty. Consider now something much more important to you, actually, some**one**, say your parent or your partner. You have good ways of telling this person from all others that you meet. You have never had any problem. Parents of identical twins can tell them apart. But ask them how they do it, and they will give you a list of properties, for example, Lesley is slightly heavier than Kim. Now conceivably there could be identical twins distinguished by no properties at all that a parent, or anyone else, could be sensitive to, given the sense organs we have. And yet they would still, we know, be separate individuals, because we sometimes see them together. So psychologically, individual constants, as logicians use them, that is as terms uniquely identifying individuals, are impossible, because there is no guaranteed reliable procedure for getting to the 'right' referent.

This killer problem of twins for reliably re-identifying the same individual is made worse by the fact that individuals inevitably change their properties over time. An extreme case is the tadpole who becomes a frog. Closer to home, nobody is physically the same person as they were thirty years ago, even though, paradoxically, we want and find it useful to say that they **are** the same person. There is a mountain of philosophical

---

[4] Note the relationship between this claim and object permanence, discussed earlier in Chapter 2.

literature on this, of course, which testifies to the enduring mismatch between our human intuitions and the evidence presented to us by the world. Ruth Millikan (1987, p. 293) eloquently sums up the arbitrary nature of human decisions in this domain:

> The principle of strict identity over time is not strong enough by itself to divide up the world into a determinate set of enduring objects. Or, more accurately, it divides the ongoing world into chunks that are far too numerous, overlapping, and crisscrossing to try to keep track of. So a great deal of room is left for decision on our part as to how to divide the world into sensible-sized and sensibly unified temporally extended wholes to be recognized and honored by coordination with common and/or proper names.

Animals have no common and/or proper names, so there is no evidence that they do mentally mark a difference between unique enduring individual objects and roughly enduring bundles of properties, perhaps sometimes very fine-grained. As far as characterizing animal thought is concerned, an alternative is available: to treat proper names as predicates. Traditional logic translates *Mary is tall* as TALL(MARY), using MARY as an individual constant, or rigid designator, in the terms of Kripke (1980). Here is where an evolutionary account of meaning has to start from different examples. We are concerned with the mental representations of pre-linguistic creatures. Mary is only known as 'Mary' because someone, probably her parents, named her thus, attaching a public label to her. Before language, nobody named anything. Remember that in this part of the work we are considering the mental representations of things in the world held by creatures, probably quite smart, with no public ways (yet) of signalling to each other about them. Let us, you and I humans, on a visit to the zoo, agree to label a specific chimpanzee in the troop 'Mary', and agree not to call anything or anyone else by that name.[5] Now what can be said to be present in the mind of another chimpanzee in the troop (call him 'Fred') when seeing Mary scratching? Fred doesn't know our name for Mary, and if we put Mary's identical-to-the-senses twin into the arena, Fred couldn't tell them apart. All that Fred knows is that a chimpanzee with a rich combination of features very familiar to him is scratching. Let's label this combination (with the usual reservations about imperfect translatability into human categories) MARY*fred*. What passes through Fred's mind

---

[5] This is not, of course, actually possible, for what if the chimp we agree to call Mary goes indoors and one exactly like her, as far as we can see, comes out? Is that Mary? We don't know.

on seeing Mary scratching is, in equivalent conventional and box notations[6]:

$$\text{MARY}_{fred}(x) \;\&\; \text{SCRATCH}_{fred}(x)$$ | MARY SCRATCH |

A claim is made here about animal cognition, namely that animals do
not have the cognitive equivalent of the human concept of a unique individual. This suggests the further claim that the human concept of a unique
individual came with the advent of public language. The most convincing
evidence that humans have concepts of unique re-identifiable individuals
is linguistic, in our strong intuitions about (non-)coreference in sentences
with reflexive and non-reflexive pronouns, as in *Mary$_i$ shot herself$_i$* versus
Mary$_i$ shot her$_{j \neq i}$. What use would a languageless animal have for the
concept of a unique individual that could not equally well be served, in
all practical circumstances, by a sufficiently distinctive bundle of features?
An animal needs to be able 'recognize' its own offspring. The scare quotes
here are necessary, because the word *recognize* is ambiguous as between
recognizing something as a unique individual (which we humans gullibly
think we can do) and recognizing something as belonging to a category
(an ability we share with many animals). But animals are not uniformly
good at recognizing their own offspring. The victims of parasitic birds
such as the cuckoo cannot tell that the egg in the nest is not one that they
laid.[7]

The **non-uniqueness** of an object in terms of its sensible properties can
be experienced. Given two identical twin objects presented together, one
knows that they are separate individuals, because there are two of them
right there present to the senses. But the **uniqueness** of an object can
never be experienced. Humans may mentally **postulate** the uniqueness of
certain objects,[8] because they never experience them together with a twin
indistinguishable to the senses. Postulating such uniqueness of an object
amounts to adopting a working hypothesis that one will never encounter
this object and an indistinguishable twin together. One could in theory
test whether an animal or a baby had taken this mental step in relation
to some object (say its mother) by seeing whether it somehow registered

---

[6] As noted earlier, there is no distinction between an object and a one-object scene. Also,
for simplicity, I have omitted the $_{fred}$ subscripts from the box version here.

[7] And, even more strikingly, appear not to be able to 'tell' that the giant hatchling they
struggle to feed could not be of their own kind.

[8] I have an idea that this is essentially what Kant (1781, p. 574) had in mind when asserting that 'the concept of an individual object . . . is completely determined by the mere idea,
and must therefore be called an ideal of pure reason'. This quotation and the page reference
are taken from *Immanuel Kant's Critique of Pure Reason. In Commemoration of the Cente-
nary of its First Publication*, trans. F. Max Müller, 2nd rev. edn. New York: Macmillan, 1922.

surprise when presented with two of them together indistinguishable to the senses. Surprise in the baby would be measured operationally by the usual criteria of longer looking time or increased sucking in response to some violation of expectations. [9]

No doubt, some bundles of features are far more important for an animal than other bundles of features. Especially in the case of social animals, who know the hierarchical ranking relations between all their group members, there must be, for each individual, a highly detailed mental descriptive representation. For the sake of an example, let's postulate that a dominant animal in a troop is effectively distinguished by the following set of predicates: {SLANTY-EYED, SCAR-ON-LEFT-CHEEK, TORN-RIGHT-EAR, SWEATY-SMELLING, MALE, BIG, STRUTS}. We do not need to suppose that all predicates in this set are necessary for 'recognition' of the animal. Probably, satisfying a good majority of them on any given occasion will be enough. This has to be the case if an animal is capable of registering occasional changes in the criteria by which it 'recognizes' other animals. And probably some predicates/properties are more dispensable than others. So the predicate STRUTS is not necessary if this dominant animal is observed obviously sleeping. But the same STRUTS feature will be useful for distinguishing the dominant in a group walking about, when perhaps the torn right ear is not so easy to see. This is the basis of a probabilistic, fallible 'recognition' procedure.

Following up the same example, this particular set of predicates may be so useful to the recognizing animal that it acquires a fast habitual response to any object simultaneously satisfying enough of them, as determined by the circumstances. That is, the animal acquires a higher-level predicate that experience tells it is pretty reliable in guiding its social behaviour, directing it, for example, not to pick a fight with this particular dominant member of its troop. Presumably, a social animal will have such effectively distinctive bundles of features for all the members of its troop. These bundles of features serve the same purpose as proper names, but we have not had to postulate a separate special kind of mental term to account for languageless animals' behaviour. [10]

---

[9] A long time ago, I heard of experiments in which babies were shown contrived movies depicting two or three images of their mother simultaneously, and were apparently unperturbed; but I have not been able to dig up a reference for this, so the story remains apocryphal.

[10] The arguments here about eliminating the equivalent of proper names from 'proto-thought' have been set out in a number of other publications, in various ways, with different emphasis, and in some cases at greater length. See Hurford (1999, 2001, 2003a, Section 1.3, 2003b, Section 6).

Even if it can be shown that an animal has taken the cognitive step of attributing uniqueness to some object, it would not be necessary to use the logician's device of an individual constant to represent this. If, for example, some companion of our slanty-eyed smelly friend mentioned above has 'decided' that he is one of a kind, that there is no one else exactly like him in all sensible respects, the companion's bundle of features for this individual could be augmented by a feature reflecting this decision, so that the animal in question is now known as {UNIQUE, SLANTY-EYED, SCAR-ON-LEFT-CHEEK, TORN-RIGHT-EAR, SWEATY-SMELLING, MALE, BIG, STRUTS}. Whether any animal in fact treats any other animal, or any object, in this way, remains an open empirical question, and of course the hypothetical predicate UNIQUE cannot be based on any properties derived from perception alone. Steven Pinker (1997, pp. 114–118) gives a clear exposition of the importance in human thought of a distinction between individuals, identified by their unique 'whichness', and mere bundles of properties. Later (p. 471), he attributes this distinction to animals: 'Males [animals] may not care *what kind of* female they mate with, but they are hypersensitive to *which* female they mate with. It is another example of the logical distinction between individuals and categories.' No reference is given for this assertion, and it should be pointed out that it would be very difficult to design an experiment to see whether animals really have a human-like concept of an individual, as opposed to a hyperfine discrimination of features. Unless there is evidence that animals make this distinction, it seems reasonable to assume that they don't, and my proposal for pre-linguistic mental representations will reflect this parsimony.

This view of the mental representation of particulars has its critics. (Bickerton 2007, p. 516) writes: 'But since (in life as opposed to logic) what words represent are concepts, not real-world entities, the fact that animals can be deceived about individual identities is wholly irrelevant; if a non-human has the concept of an individual, that concept can be named, and no real-world misapplication of the name affects it or its utility.' This is a bundle of confusion. Let's start with points of agreement. Yes, words represent concepts, as English *cat* represents the concept CAT. (The indirect relation between words and real-world entities, kinds and classes, etc., such as the cat kind, is indispensable, because we use words to talk about things in the world, but I guess that is not at issue here.) Yes, words don't represent real-world entities, if by this is meant that a word cannot pick out a particular real-world entity, such as Felix, the exact specific ginger tomcat that lived from June 1992 to July 2006 in Portobello, Edinburgh. For all I know, Felix might be alive still and the body I buried in the garden was his twin. So when we use a proper name like *Felix*, most of the time we are safe in communicating about the same entity, but it can't be guaranteed. If this is what is meant by 'what words represent are not real-world entities', then we agree; so far so good. The argument goes on with a conditional: '**if** a non-human has a concept of an individual . . .'. Note the hypothetical 'if'. That condition is, of course, exactly what is at issue, namely whether a non-human can have a concept of an individual (as opposed to a concept of a bundle of properties), so we can't take the condition for granted just because it has been introduced, lawyer-like, into the discourse. What follows the conditional is 'that concept can be named'. Hey, wait a minute, the condition was about **non-humans** having a 'concept of an individual'; non-humans don't have names for anything, let alone (hypothetical) concepts of particular individuals. So when 'animals can be deceived about individual entities' (a fact on which we agree), it is not a matter of the 'misapplication of a name', because animals don't use names.

When an animal is deceived about an individual entity, it is a matter of its concept of a very specific bundle of features matching the wrong entity in the world. I will repeat an example I have used before (Hurford 2001). The following quotation demonstrates the prima facie attraction of the impression that animals distinguish such individuals, but simultaneously gives the game away.

The speed with which recognition of individual parents can be acquired is illustrated by the 'His Master's Voice' experiments performed by Stevenson et al. (1970) on young terns: these responded immediately to tape-recordings of their own parents (by cheeping a greeting, and walking towards the loud-speaker) but ignored other tern calls, even those recorded from other adult members of their own colony.   (Walker 1983, p. 215)

Obviously, the tern chicks in the experiment were **not** recognizing their individual parents—they were being fooled into treating a loudspeaker as a parent tern. For the tern chick, anything which behaved sufficiently like its parent was 'recognized' as its parent, even if it wasn't. The tern chicks were responding to very finely grained properties of the auditory signal, and apparently neglecting even the most obvious of visual properties discernible in the situation. In tern life, there usually aren't human experimenters playing tricks with loudspeakers, and so terns have evolved to discriminate between auditory cues just to the extent that they can identify their own parents with a high degree of reliability. Even terns presumably sometimes get it wrong. '[A]nimals respond in mechanical robot-like fashion to key stimuli. They can usually be "tricked" into responding to crude dummies that resemble the true, natural stimulus situation only partially, or in superficial respects' (Krebs and Dawkins 1984, p. 384).

Bickerton's argument continues: 'A wealth of evidence from ethological studies of primates shows that apes have a very clear idea of the other individuals in their group and even the precise kinship relations of each person (if this were not the case, it would not be possible for A to avenge an action of B's by attacking C, who is B's nephew).' Yes, absolutely, I don't doubt those data. Note that field experiments which help to establish these facts (such as those reported in Cheney and Seyfarth 1999; Bergman et al. 2003; Seyfarth and Cheney 2003) **rely** on the animals being deceived about the individual entities they (think they) hear in played-back audio recordings. A mother monkey or baboon, hearing a recording of her infant, looks towards the loudspeaker, not towards her absent infant. Such animal behaviour, and all the rest of their complex social behaviour, can be accounted for perfectly easily by attributing to the animals highly specific bundles of mental predicates, rather than something ontologically distinct from predicates, such as individual constants.

A lot of the problem here stems from the original logical idea of an individual constant, a term in the logical language with a different status from predicates. The argument is about the specific idea of a unique individual, as embodied in the logician's idea of the denotation of an individual constant. A major motivation for developing logical representations in the late nineteenth and early twentieth centuries was to provide an ideal language for science, because ordinary language was deemed too vague. Scientists need to be as sure as possible that the particular individual entities to which they refer, for example, Venus, Alpha Centauri, are the same from one occasion of reference to the next. Of course, this can never be absolutely guaranteed, but the developers of logic pressed on regardless of this inconvenient psychological fact. Other scholars who have never been particularly bothered about logic may not grasp the enormity of the claim implicit in postulating individual constants, and much of their commentary reflects this. Of course, they say, animals can be deceived. But a (hypothetical) organism with the equivalent of an individual constant in its mental repertoire **would never be deceived**—that is what is meant by 'individual constant'. This shows the wrongness of adopting a scheme of mental representation incorporating individual constants.

My objective here is not to adopt a pre-existing logical formalism willy-nilly and to squeeze animal behaviour into it. On the contrary, I am **rejecting** a particular element of traditional logic, individual constants, as inappropriate to animal behaviour. Interestingly, all sides are agreed on the basic facts about animal behaviour. To those not professionally bothered by details of logical formalism, this argument may seem like a storm in a teacup, much ado about nothing. But my project is to outline a continuity between the mental representations of animals and those of humans underlying their natural language sentences. Thus it is necessary to try to spell out, in a similar style to the logical project for human thought, what elements animal thought could have consisted of.

The discussion so far has been of private non-linguistic mental entities that can be attributed to animals. Bickerton concludes his critical passage with 'We may therefore reasonably conclude that proto-language had proper as well as common nouns.' Now we are in a different realm, that of public expression of hitherto private representations. The question of whether proto-language had proper names is independent from the main focus of the discussion here, namely the private conceptual representations of animals. I will return to the topic of proto-language and syntactic categories in the sequel to this book.

5.2.2 No Clinching Psychological Evidence

The undoubted psycholinguistic fact that proper names are more subject to forgetting in old age than other words does not argue for a separate semantic category, distinct from predicate. Predicates form a large class of concepts, with many subtypes. There are specific anomias relating to various subcategories of predicate, such as fruit, body-parts, living things, artefacts, and others.[11] Indeed there are several reports of proper-name-specific anomia (Semenza and Zettin 1989; Semenza 1997; Fukatsu et al. 1999; Pelamatti et al. 2003).[12] I claim that proper names correspond to a special subclass of predicates, rather than to a distinct class, separate from predicates. If proper names correspond to a class distinct from predicates, we would expect to be able to find cases of anomia that impaired retrieval of all words corresponding to predicates, but selectively spared retrieval of proper names. Bredart et al. (1997) discuss three papers claiming to have found a double dissociation between processing of common nouns

---

[11] Among other sources, see a special issue of *Neurocase*, 4 (1998) for several case studies and a general discussion of their significance by Alfonso Caramazza (Caramazza 1998).

[12] Semenza et al. (1998) also give a good list of references to 'proper name anomia'.

and proper names and conclude that 'a double dissociation between the processing of proper names and common names has not been demonstrated for production. The evidence for a double dissociation between comprehension of proper names and common names is much stronger, but even this claim is limited' (p. 209). No clear case has been reported of an anomia affecting all words, of any syntactic category (nouns, verbs, adjectives, etc.), **except** proper names. If logical terms corresponding to proper names are as distinct from predicates as classical logic treats them as being, it should be possible to find such a case.

Chief among the special properties of proper names is that the linguistic semantic system provides extremely few inferences that can be drawn from the fact that a person bears a particular proper name. From the surname *Baker* one can infer nothing reliably about the person who bears it, except perhaps that he or she comes from an English-speaking culture. But from the common noun *baker* applied to a person, one can immediately infer a lot of information about that person. This fact is picked up by Proverbio et al. (2001), who compared brain activity by subjects retrieving common and proper names.

ERPs spatio-temporal mapping showed on one side a strong activation of left anterior temporal and left central-frontal areas for proper names, and on the other side a greater involvement of occipital areas for common names retrieval. The specific pattern of bio-electrical activity recorded during proper names retrieval might index the activation of neural circuits for recalling names of high contextual complexity, poor of sensory-motor associations and dependent on precise spatio-temporal coordinates.

(Proverbio et al. 2001, p. 815)

Note the implicit idea of a quantitative difference of degree here in 'contextual complexity [and poverty] of sensory-motor associations'. I would predict that proper names with great iconic status, like *Jesus*, *Hitler*, and *Einstein* would be retrieved with more activity in areas usually involved in common-noun retrieval. Such names are more frequently recruited grammatically as common nouns, as in *He's no Einstein* or *He's a real Hitler*.

Semenza et al. (1998, p. 51) correctly write: 'This distinction [common noun versus proper name] resembles closely that universally made between semantic and episodic memory mechanisms but with an important difference: the mechanisms in question are more peripheral and operate at the lexical level.' Animals, with little or no episodic memory, and no lexicon, are unlikely to have a specific class of predicates distinguished as it can be in humans.

A different psychological point has been thoughtfully made by Juan Carlos Gómez (personal communication). He writes:

There is a robust finding in primate literature that all great apes (excluding most gorillas) are capable of recognising themselves in mirrors by showing behaviours such as exploring otherwise invisible parts of their bodies or, more experimentally, by passing the red mark test (red painting placed on their forehead while anesthetised that they can only discover with the mirror once they wake up), whereas all monkey species as well as non-primates always treat mirror reflections as conspecifics. Could this be taken to entail a notion of individuals, as exemplified by one's own individuality?

I don't think this relates exactly to the question of knowing **other** individuals as unique. Undoubtedly the results that Gómez describes show some kind of qualitative differences between apes[13] and monkeys. I, in company with many others, am unsure how to interpret these mirror results. They could be taken to show that apes are ready to accept causally linked doubles of themselves, which at least somewhat undermines any argument for personal uniqueness. An awareness of one's own uniqueness may be the evolutionary starting point for attribution of uniqueness to others, but the uniqueness of others is still a matter of a kind of mental postulation, because, to reiterate the argument from first principles, the genuine uniqueness of some other is in the limit unknowable.

5.2.3 Philosophers Split both Ways

Within the philosophy of language, there has been a lively debate between those who interpret grammatically proper names as individual constants and those like me, who treat them, as predicates. Burge (1973, n. 3), a member of the 'predicates' camp, gives a list of classic sources in this debate: he includes Russell and Quine as proponents of the 'predicates' view. A more recent proponent of the predicate view is Elugardo (2002). The recent arch-proponent of the opposing view is, of course, Kripke (1980), with the view sometimes being originally attributed to J. S. Mill (1843). Since Burge's article, others who have leapt into the debate include Pendlebury (1990); Geurts (1997); Segal (2001); Abbott (2002); Reimer (2002); Soames (2002); Stidd (2004). It is also now common practice

---

[13] I believe that the difficulty with gorillas is that looking another gorilla in the eye is taken as a sign of hostility, and so they avoid looking themselves in the eye in a mirror. On the face of it, this might be taken as showing that the gorilla thinks that the image in the mirror is a different, possibly hostile, gorilla. But it may be more of an inbuilt inhibition, hard to overcome.

in Discourse Representation Theory (DRT, stemming from Kamp and Reyle 1993) to treat proper names as predicates, so that, for example, the representation of *Jones owns Ulysses* is the structure below (from Kamp and Reyle 1993, p. 64):

$$
\begin{array}{|l|}
\hline
\quad x \quad y \\
\text{Jones}(x) \\
\text{Ulysses}(y) \\
x \text{ owns } y \\
\hline
\end{array}
$$

Kamp and Reyle (1993, p. 132) emphasize the triviality of treating individual constants as predicates by noting the equivalence between MARY(x) and $x = $ MARY, an identity notation conventionally used in predicate logic.

It is significant that DRT, being a psychologically concerned theory about what speakers do when interpreting sentences, also treats proper names as predicates. In this theory, when hearers hear a proper name in the flow of discourse, they assign it an index (e.g. w, x, y, z) for temporary reference. This is very reminiscent of the way in which observers of a visual scene keep track of a small number of objects and assign them mental indices (for which I have earlier adopted the notation w, x, y, z). A theory closely related to DRT is Heim (1983)'s 'File Change Semantics'. In this theory, newly mentioned referents in discourse are assigned to a 'file', in which information predicated of them is kept, and updated as necessary. In Heim (1983)'s words:

A listener's task of understanding what is being said in the course of a conversation bears relevant similarities to a file clerk's task. Speaking metaphorically, let me say that to understand an utterance is to keep a file which, at every time in the course of the utterance, contains the information that has so far been conveyed by the utterance.   (Heim 1983, p. 167)

This is a strikingly similar idea to that proposed by psychologists working on visual attention. Kahneman and Treisman (1984 and 1992) hypothesize that the mind sets up temporary 'object files' in which information about objects in a scene is stored. The object files can be updated, as the viewer tracks changes in an object's features or location. The use of the same 'file' metaphor is not mere coincidence: there is a real convergence of ideas here, from the normally very distant fields of linguistic discourse processing and visual scene processing.[14] Kahneman and Treisman's idea of visual object files overlaps significantly, and consistently, with Pylyshyn

---

[14] A few merely terminological adjustments are necessary. For Heim, the objects corresponding to Kahneman and Treisman's 'files' are 'file cards'.

(1989)'s theory of FINSTs, which are indices assigned by the visual system for tracking objects in a scene.[15] So several independent theories of discourse processing (DRT and File Change Semantics) converge significantly with several independent theories of visual processing. This is exciting, and strongly suggests that one bit of language-processing machinery has been co-opted (and probably adapted somewhat) from pre-existing visual scene-processing machinery.

Returning now to proper names as expressing predicates, my argument here, unlike those of philosophers of language and formal semanticists, is not about how grammatically proper names in human languages should be interpreted. In particular, my replacement of individual constants by predicates does not appeal to the idea, commonly used in the philosophical debate, that such a predicate is an abbreviation for '(is a) person named X'. Animals don't give each other public names. My argument is for a way of conceiving the possible pre-linguistic mental representations that animals construct of their world. The argument is motivated by considerations of parsimony (don't multiply types of mental term beyond necessity) and feasibility (don't attribute impossible powers to any organism). The argument here does relate to the debates within the philosophy of language and linguistics, however, because it is natural to assume that human language evolved by building upon pre-existing representational schemes in animals.

5.3 GETTING RID OF ORDERED ARGUMENTS AND ROLE MARKERS

This section builds cumulatively on the previous section. (For this section it will be convenient to stick with a conventional linear notation, and return to box representations in the following section.) In the previous section, individual constants were replaced by predicate terms, and the examples given were all one-place predicates. We now turn to predicates which take more than one argument. So far, we can render traditional logical formulae as in the first batch below (p. 141) in the revised notation below it.

Logic insists that the arguments of a relation are **ordered**. This is necessary to distinguish between, for example STAB(BRUTUS, CAESAR) and STAB(CAESAR, BRUTUS), and between OWN(SCARLETT, TARA) and OWN(TARA, SCARLETT). Sequential ordering on the printed page is logic's way of making it clear how the referents of the arguments are related by the predicate. The logician's idea of the ordering of arguments

---

[15] FINST is Pylyshyn (1989)'s abbreviation for FINger of INSTantiation, highlighting the indexical (deictic) nature of these visual tracking devices.

Traditional Notation

STAB(BRUTUS, CAESAR)

OWN(SCARLETT, TARA)

ORBIT(EARTH, SUN)

TALLER-THAN(GOLIATH, DAVID)

BETWEEN(ATLANTIC, EUROPE, AMERICA)

English Translation

Brutus stabbed Caesar

Scarlett owns Tara

The Earth orbits the Sun

Goliath is taller than David

The Atlantic is between
Europe and America

Revised Traditional Notation without Individual Constants

BRUTUS(x) & CAESAR(y) & STAB(x, y)

SCARLETT(x) & TARA(y) & OWN(x, y)

EARTH(x) & SUN(y) & ORBIT(x, y)

GOLIATH(x) & DAVID(y) & TALLER-THAN(x, y)

ATLANTIC(x) & EUROPE(y) & AMERICA(z) & BETWEEN(x, y, z)

also has a more abstract aspect than mere graphical convenience. It is traditional to say that the denotation of a one-place predicate is the set of all entities satisfied by that predicate. Thus the denotation of the predicate CAT is the set of all cats. Correspondingly, but more challengingly to the imagination, the denotation of a two-place predicate is said to be a set of 'ordered pairs'. Thus the denotation of BIGGER-THAN is supposed to be the set of all ordered pairs in which the first member is bigger than the second; likewise the denotation of LOVE is the set of all ordered pairs such that the first member loves the second. We are meant to imagine that the world in some way **contains** these ordered pairs, and ordered triples for three-place predicates, and so forth. This kind of move stems from a non-psychologizing abstract logico-mathematical tradition. Quine (1960), coming from this tradition himself, was nevertheless somewhat uneasy about the idea of an ordered pair. He writes: 'We do better to face the fact that "ordered pair" is a defective noun, not at home in all the questions and answers in which we are accustomed to imbed terms at their full-fledged best' (p. 258). In the end, I think[16] Quine decided that the term 'ordered pair' was worth keeping, but in his discussion of it he offered another possibility:

We have, to begin with, an expression or form of expression that is somehow troublesome. It behaves partly like a term but not enough so, or it is vague in ways that bother us, or it puts kinks in a theory or encourages one or other confusion. But it also serves certain purposes that are not to be abandoned. Then we find a way of accomplishing those same purposes through other

---

[16] Quine's discussion is convoluted and allusive, so I only **think** that this was his conclusion.

channels, using other and less troublesome forms of expression. The old
perplexities are resolved.   (Quine 1960, p. 260)

In this section, I will show how to accomplish the purpose served by
'ordered pair' in logic through other channels using other and less troublesome forms of expression, and resolving the old perplexity of where in
the world to find such ordered pairs.[17] Languageless animals don't have
printed pages to rely on. What is needed is some way of representing
who-did-what-to-whom that does not implicitly rely on sequencing. The
baboon who sees one baboon grooming another sees them both at the
same time; the referents of both arguments are simultaneously present.

Linguistic semanticists, more interested in the meanings of particular
lexical items than logicians, have developed ways of making finer
distinctions than are made by the logician's simple device of ordering
the arguments of a predicate. In the examples above (consider the true
instances, rather than their reversed pairs), both BRUTUS and SCARLETT
were predicated of the first arguments of their respective two-place
predicates; and CAESAR and TARA were predicated of the second
arguments of those predicates, respectively. The simple ordering notation
makes no distinction between the two very different kinds of relation
involved with STAB and OWN. One proposition, with STAB, describes an
action, with an animate Agent and an animate Patient; the proposition
with OWN describes a state of affairs, with no action taking place, no
movement, involving one animate participant (Scarlett) and one
inanimate (Tara, the plantation). Notational conventions vary, but one
variant is to augment the logical formulae with extra labels indicating the
roles played by the participants in the events. For example:

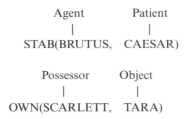

Recasting these in our revision of the traditional notation, without individual constants, they would be:

[17] The claim I will make only applies to logical representation in the context of the
evolution of language, and not to other applications, for example in theorizing about the
foundations of mathematics.

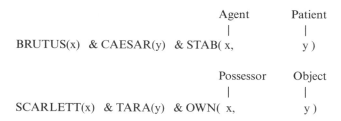

Note that this labelling with participant roles makes the logician's ordering of the arguments redundant. And the participant role labels give more specific information about the nature of the event depicted than is possible by ordering. So we can eliminate the commas from the notation and deal instead with **unordered sets**[18] of arguments labelled with participant roles.

With the arguments labelled, the ordering on the page of the arguments of a two-place predicate is immaterial; they are logically unordered, just as the conjuncts joined by '&' are unordered.

Thus far, the notation has eliminated ordering at the expense of introducing a new kind of term, namely participant role labels. They are certainly useful, giving specific information about the ways in which the participants of the depicted event are involved. Nothing is lost, however, and ontological parsimony is gained, if we simply regard these participant role markers as predicates. Thus 'Agent' and 'Patient', and all other roles that have been invented by linguists, are just one-place predicates, and we'll write them AGENT and PATIENT henceforth. Having made this move, our examples are now conjunctions of simple propositions, like this:

$$\text{BRUTUS}(x)$$
$$\&\ \text{CAESAR}(y)$$
$$\&\ \text{AGENT}(x)$$
$$\&\ \text{PATIENT}(y)$$
$$\&\ \text{STAB}(x\ y)$$

---

[18] Hence the curly brackets below replacing the earlier round parentheses.

Exactly the same information would be given if we had written the components out in any other order, for example as follows:

$$\text{STAB}(y\ x)$$
$$\&\ \text{PATIENT}(y)$$
$$\&\ \text{CAESAR}(y)$$
$$\&\ \text{BRUTUS}(x)$$
$$\&\ \text{AGENT}(x)$$

This notational juggling has a point. It significantly reduces the number of different types of term in our representations, which are aimed at meshing eventually with different types of brain mechanism. To summarize, we now have only the following:

one-place predicates
individual variables as arguments of the one-place predicates
two- and three-place predicates taking unordered sets of arguments
logical conjunction '&'.

(In the next section, when we return to the proposed box notation, I will claim that two- and three-place predicates can be eliminated, and replaced by one-place predicates applying to whole scenes, thus reducing everything to conjunctions of one-place predicates.)

Treating participant roles (a.k.a. thematic roles, theta-roles) as predicates is an idea that has shown up often, but sporadically, in the semantics literature. It has become particularly widespread in work in the tradition of Event Semantics. Borer (2005, p. 218) represents the meaning of *The cat climbed the tree* as

∃e [originator (cat, e) & default participant (the tree, e) & climb(e)]

In the usual way of paraphrasing in terms of event theory, this can be read as *There was a climbing event, e, in which the originator was the cat and the default participant was the tree.* (Clearly, Borer's notation still recognizes the semantic equivalent of proper names, unlike me.) Here are two more examples: Higginbotham (2000, p. 57) renders *John walked slowly* as

walk(e) ∧ Actor(John, e) ∧ slow(e)

and Parsons (2000, p. 81) gives *Brutus stabbed Caesar violently with a knife* as

∃e(Stabbing(e) ∧ Cul(e, past) ∧ Agent(e, Brutus) ∧ Object(e, Caesar) ∧ Violent(e) ∧ With(e, knife))

Treating participant roles as predicates, as in these examples, has not been the topic of any grand debate, which may indicate that it has been seen as a matter more of terminological convenience than of significant content. But ideally our terminology should reflect our ontology. If we think participant roles are really nothing more than a kind of predicate, we should not continue to speak and write of them as if they were something else.

In the particular case of the Agent role, the criteria used for diagnosing it include all those used to diagnose animacy (a.k.a. agency) in an individual object. Animacy is the **potential** to act as an Agent. A bird is animate, but not always acting in the Agent role, as when a cat eats a bird; but when a bird eats a worm, it is acting in the Agent role. If we had never known objects from a particular category to be able to participate in events in the Agent role, we would never classify them as animate. ANIMATE is a predicate that applies to objects; AGENT is a predicate that applies to ANIMATE objects temporarily when certain further criteria are met, such as wilful action having a causal effect on other objects. See Cruse (1973) and Dowty (1991) for extended discussion of such criteria.

It might be argued against the treatment of participant roles as predicates that participant roles are subject to a 'one-per-event' restriction that does not apply to predicates. Higginbotham (1999, p. 837), for instance, illustrates this putative restriction with the example *The prisoner escaped with a bribe with a machine gun*. This example is odd because it is a case of zeugma, like *He escaped with one bound and a million dollars*. 'Double-occupancy' of participant roles does happen in cases of reciprocal action, as in the situation described by *John and Bill fought each other*, where both Bill and John are simultaneously both Agents and Patients in a single fighting event. Double-occupancy of participant roles is admittedly rare, and this constitutes a difference between participant roles and some predicates. But, I shall argue in the next section, role predicates like AGENT and PATIENT are not the only predicates to be typically affected by a one-per-event (or one-per-scene) restriction, which also often applies to relative concepts like BIG.

Cases expressed by a conjunction of phrases in languages, as in *I fished it out with a stick and a magnet*, or *Brutus and Cassius stabbed Caesar*, are not clearly cases of double-occupancy of a participant role. In the latter case, it cannot be argued that the group referred to by the conjunction of noun phrases *Brutus and Cassius* collectively fulfils the relevant role, because it was **both** Brutus and Cassius, as separate individuals, who did the stabbing. This is not a case of a plural entity constituted by Brutus and

Cassius doing the stabbing; each of them did it, with his own sword. But against double-occupancy in this case it could possibly be argued that the sentence describes two separate events, one in which Brutus is the Agent and another in which Cassius is the Agent. A case such as is expressed by *Brutus and Cassius lifted the piano*, where we assume that they both individually did some lifting, but the resulting movement of the piano was still a single event, could be a better candidate for double-occupancy of the AGENT role in a single event.

Most discussions of participant roles (thematic roles, theta-roles) in linguistics concentrate on sentences with (non-copular) verbs, such as *Franny slept* or *Floyd broke the glass with a hammer*. They do not bring copular sentences, such as *This is a knife* or *Philip is Anne's father*, into discussion of these roles. This is understandable, because the roles most frequently discussed, Agent and Patient, are obviously missing from the situations described by such sentences. Indeed, it is difficult to apply the idea of a 'role' to anything mentioned in such sentences: to be a knife is not, in any ordinary sense, to take any particular role in a situation of 'knife-being'. Familiar participant roles do not figure in the meanings of all sentences. This fits well with the idea of participant roles being predicates. Just as not every sentence is about knives, or about people, or about beer, or about being happy or female, so not every sentence is about events with Agents, or with Patients. The representations of most copular sentences simply don't happen to use the predicates AGENT or PATIENT.[19] *This is a knife* can simply be represented as KNIFE(x), where the variable x stands for whatever is deictically referred to by *this* on the occasion of use. This view has the advantage of unifying the analysis of all sentences. We don't need to think of two different types of sentence, those which involve special entities called participant roles and those which don't. Certainly, sentences involving the predicate AGENT are more frequent than sentences involving KNIFE or HAPPY, but this is just a matter of frequency. It has often been stressed that the Agent role has a privileged function in determining the choice of grammatical subject. This is a topic relating to the externalization of meanings in public messages, and so I will not go into it here, but will reserve discussion of it for Volume 2, on the emergence of linguistic form.

The representations that I propose are similar, though not identical, to those of Pietroski (2002, 2005), who argues for a 'Conjunctivist' form

---

[19] Some copular sentences do encode AGENT and PATIENT roles, as in *Smith is the killer of Jones*.

of semantic representation. 'Conjunctivism is a thesis about semantic composition in natural language: when expressions are concatenated, they are interpreted as (conjoinable) monadic predicates; and the resulting phrase is interpreted as a predicate satisfied by whatever satisfies both constituents' (Pietroski 2005, p. 28). Pietroski, unlike me, still uses individual constants, but, like me, treats participant roles such as AGENT as predicates. Our goals differ; Pietroski's proposals are about interpreting human language sentences, whereas mine are about plausible prelinguistic representations of the world in the minds of animals. But it is surely significant that there should be this beginning of a convergence. The message I take from it is that the appropriate semantic representations for mapping onto modern sentences were present in our ancestors before language came on the scene. The sentences of human languages, and their semantic interrelationships, moulded themselves to the pre-existing semantic forms. But let's not overcook this incipient convergence. As I mentioned, even Pietroski's representations still differ in detail from what I wish to propose. Pietroski's representations are conjunctions of mainly monadic (one-place) predications. He still keeps a few relations (two-place predicates). I will go a step further, again in the interests of a parsimonious account that has some hope of being mapped relatively directly onto brain mechanisms.

5.4 ONE-PLACE PREDICATES OVER SCENES AND OBJECTS

The earlier representation

$$
\begin{aligned}
&\text{STAB}(y\ x) \\
&\&\ \text{PATIENT}(y) \\
&\&\ \text{CAESAR}(y) \\
&\&\ \text{BRUTUS}(x) \\
&\&\ \text{AGENT}(x)
\end{aligned}
$$

can be translated into box notation as follows:

(Within boxes, order is immaterial, so there are many other equivalent diagrams.) This can be paraphrased as *There was a stabbing scene involving Caesar as patient and Brutus as agent.* Note that the box notation allows us to treat STAB, AGENT, and PATIENT as one-place predicates. Treating

STAB as a one-place predicate over events or scenes is already in line with Event Semantics, as cited earlier, and so is relatively uncontroversial.

Implicit in the box notation is a **relativizing** function, so that the terms within a box are interpreted as dependent on, or relative to, the context established by the scene itself. Placing $\boxed{\text{BRUTUS, AGENT}}$ inside an outer box labelled STAB implies that Brutus is the Agent **in a scene** characterized by stabbing. It is not necessary to see AGENT as a two-place relation between the participant and the event. Barry Schein, a philosopher, discusses the issue of the context-dependence of thematic roles, such as AGENT and PATIENT. 'As for the thematic roles themselves, I assume that one can ask whether or not they are relativized to the event concepts or semantic fields in the same spirit that one asks whether an attributive predicate such as *slow* is similarly relativized' (Schein 2002, p. 267). Schein compares *Brutus stabbed Caesar* with *Brutus insulted Caesar*, and asks, 'does Caesar succumb in the same way, "Patient(e, Caesar)" to both insult and injury, or by different cuts, "Patient(e, Caesar, 'stab')" and "Patient(e, Caesar, 'insult')"?' (p. 267). I maintain that roles are partly interpreted relative to context, like gradable adjectives such as *slow, big*, and *hot*, but do also contribute some inherent content of their own to the proposition. This is in line with Dowty (1991)'s analysis whereby a participant in different kinds of events, such as a stabbing event or an insulting event, can play the same (proto-)role, even if their exact manner of participation is somewhat different, for example, involving physical action or not.

With two-place predications (if they are asymmetric, as most are), there is always some property distinguishing one participant from the other. If there were no feature distinguishing between the relata of a two-place relation, it would be a symmetric relation. The very term *asymmetric* implies this difference between the properties of the participants. The box notation exploits this aspect of (asymmetric) predicates. In the STAB example above, the information given in standard logical notation by making BRUTUS the first argument of STAB is given here by associating the property AGENT with BRUTUS. The box notation, where a box contains several sub-boxes, **implicitly** represents the fact that there is **some unspecified relation** between the participants, and **some unspecified relation** between the parts and the whole. The outer box establishes a relevant context in which the contents of the inner boxes are interpreted.

The box notation allows us to eliminate apparent (but not genuine) two-place predicates. It is standard practice in Event Semantics to treat Agent, Patient, and other participant roles as two-place predicates taking the event variable e as one argument and the relevant object as the other.

An example cited earlier is Higginbotham (2000)'s rendering of *John walked slowly* as

$$\text{walk}(e) \wedge \text{Actor}(\text{John}, e) \wedge \text{slow}(e)$$

Here, Actor takes two arguments. In a box notation, this can be avoided, in either of two ways, thus:

The left-hand diagram here is a somewhat mechanical translation of Higginbotham's event-theoretic formula. The right-hand diagram, I maintain, is a more direct representation of a visual scene, in which there is one object, in which the properties of walking, slowness, and 'Johnness' are apparent.

The view advocated here treats terms such as AGENT and PATIENT as designating monadic properties and **not** as implicitly (or explicitly) relational. Recall the discussion, in Chapter 1.4, of biological motion and agency, where biological motion and potential agency were diagnosed in single objects, not necessarily participating in actions with other objects. Not every distinguishing property of a participant in a scene is discerned relative to the whole scene in the same way as AGENT. For example, to represent a scene of which the judgement is made that Fred, who is singing, and Mary, who is dancing, are acting in rhythmic synchrony with each other, we might use:

This diagram is formally the same shape as that used to represent Brutus stabbing Caesar, earlier. Clearly, we don't want to claim that any of the judgements MARY, FRED, SING, and DANCE are so contextually relative as AGENT. All mental pre-linguistic predicates are, I claim, monadic, but some predicates are **more contextually relativized** than others. MARY, FRED, TREE, and LION can all be assigned to objects with little or no interference from the overall scene in which they appear. Others, such as AGENT, PATIENT, PART, and BIG, are mentally assigned to an object with much more consideration of the overall properties assigned to the scene in which they appear.

The very same visual stimuli emanating from an object can be assigned different properties depending on what property is assigned to the whole containing scene. Consider a puppet show, in which Punch whacks Judy. Suspending our disbelief, we assign the predicate WHACK to the whole event; this is a whacking event, in which Punch is the Agent. But to reassure our kids that such domestic violence is just make-believe, we point out that Punch is really 'not doing it', hence not an Agent, and that the real Agent is a person behind the scenes manipulating a Punch-glove; with this different perspective on the same scene, Punch and Judy are inanimate objects in a PLAY event. I'm not suggesting that animals can indulge in such radical 'what-iffery', but animals do play-fight, and can tell the difference between play-fighting and real fighting. It may take an animal a few seconds to judge whether a particular interaction between two others is a real fight or just play. For alternative verdicts, it will presumably then assign somewhat different roles to the actors, depending on its overall categorization of the interaction. Assignment of certain properties, such as Agent-hood, to objects in a scene is influenced by the properties assigned to the whole scene.

As far as attention is concerned, objects which are the **parts** of larger objects can be treated similarly to objects which are contained in a scene, with one extra item of information. For genuine subparts of larger objects, the proto-predicate PART expresses the role that a smaller object can play with respect to a larger object. Thus PART, traditionally regarded as a relational concept, can be treated in the same way as AGENT. An object is understood as a part relative to some larger whole, just as an object is understood as an agent relative to some encompassing event. An example illustrating this in the box notation is:

	PART BULBOUS	PART BLUE	PART BLUE
FACE	NOSE	EYE	EYE

Not all linguistically two-place relations need be represented with a 'scene-describing' predicate at the top scene level. Given the context-sensitivity of size judgements, it seems reasonable to claim that attributions of bigness and smallness, for example, can be made relative to the other objects in the scene. So the following diagram would correspond to the judgement that one cat is bigger than another.

CAT BIG	CAT SMALL

On its own, a box such as  CAT, BIG would represent a single object, an unusually big cat (i.e. big-for-a-cat). Recall Sarris (1998)'s experiments showing that chickens can be trained to make such perceptual judgements as small-for-a-red-cube and big-for-a-green-cube (of same-sized cubes). I imagine that there would be some cognitive dissonance experienced in trying simultaneously to grasp the complex idea of a small-for-a-horse horse being bigger than a big-for-a-dog dog.

To take another comparative example, suppose that a captive chimp remembers from experience that, when it comes to tickling, Laura is better at it than Herb, but when it comes to feeding, Herb is a much more satisfactory or generous feeder than Laura. We might represent these two stored experiences as:

More directly sensory examples might be:

 versus

You get the idea, suggesting that, possibly, a single relativized concept applies to judgements of both size and weight. Nothing hangs on this specific claim; we are just exploring the territory here.

In human languages, relational words which are usually interpreted as asymmetric, like *stab*, can be made symmetric by the addition of some particle indicating reciprocity, as with English *each other*. If Caesar and Brutus stab each other in the same event, they both have the AGENT property, and neither participant can be distinguished as the sole animate wilfully moving participant in the event.

As noted earlier, the perceptual distinction between global and local attention shows a kind of doublethink that is alien to standard logic. The box notation captures in one diagram the blended representation produced jointly by the parallel global process and the serial local processes. By allowing the terms in inner boxes to be **implicitly** relativized to the predicates in the outer box, it does not need to be stated explicitly that, to use the classic example, Brutus is the Agent with respect to a particular occasion of stabbing, notated as:

$$\text{STAB}(e) \land \text{AGENT}(\text{BRUTUS},e)$$

The global/local point can also be made by recalling Luria's simul-tanagnosic patient (Farah 1990, pp. 22–23), who could recognize a rectangle formed by six dots, but not count the dots; if he focused on one of the dots, he lost sight of the rectangle. We need, for normal higher animals, a way of representing the fact that a scene is **both** one rectangle **and** some number (up to four) of dots. The box notation does this straightforwardly:

The box notation captures this natural perceptual 'doublethink', using an iconic analogue of a scene and its participants, simultaneously por-trayed. (Remember that the spatial arrangement of boxes at the same level is entirely arbitrary; the only iconic feature is the containment relation between outer and inner boxes.) A simultanagnosic patient could only hold one box and its predicates at a time. Relating these diagrams to the details of global and local attention, consider, for example, a scene consisting of meat and potatoes on a plate. The predicates that come to mind on making a quick global scan of this scene may be some, all or none of the following: PLATE, POTATOES, MEAT, BROWN, STEAMING. If only the last four come to mind (i.e. if the plate is not salient), we get, on a quick global scan:

MEAT
POTATOES
STEAMING
BROWN

Result of quick global scan

On focal attention to the individual objects in meal scene, the representa-tion resolves to:

Results of focal attention to objects in scene

Simultanagnosic patients cannot handle both levels at once. Hence their typical inability to diagnose the who-did-what-to-whom information in a scene, as reported by Luria (1959) and Boutsen and Humphreys (1999).

The claimed elimination of two- and three-place predicates is not as radical as may be thought. Some animals can make SAME/DIFFERENT judgements of an array of objects. I suggest that this can be analysed as the animal perceiving a sameness situation, predicated of a whole single scene, but with a requirement that such a scene contain more than one object. An animal can only arrive at a SAME judgement on the basis of more than one object. We might represent a judgement of Alex the parrot's as:

Spatial relationships between a large background and a foregrounded object, typically expressed in English by prepositions, such as *in* and *on*, can be naturally analysed as having the nature of the background delivered by global attention and the foreground object as the object of local attention, as in these examples:

Other spatial relationships, between roughly equally foregrounded objects, can be analysed as kinds of static event, with the participants taking different roles, as below:

Thus relationships such as are conveyed by English propositions like *on, under, over*, and *below* can be analysed as applying to whole scenes, with the requirement that such scenes contain two relevant objects. As with other cases discussed earlier, the asymmetry of such relations can be captured by showing some monadic property of one of the participants not shared by the other. Dyadic relational concepts such as ON and IN can only be attributed to a scene containing two objects.

The proposal for this box notation is programmatic. The programme stretches in two directions: backwards to animal representations, and forwards to the formalisms best suited for representing the meanings of human sentences. It should be clear that not all meanings expressible in human languages ought to be representable in this notation. In particular, we should make no attempt to represent any rhetorical aspect of meaning pertinent only to the **communicative presentation** of information, rather than to the bare **content** of a scene or event. The following are instances of sets of English expressions which would all be assigned the same representations in the proposed notation, assuming the relevant scenes are observed by an ape:

- Active/passive pairs:
  - *Kanzi gave Matata a banana*
  - *Matata was given a banana by Kanzi*
  - *A banana was given to Matata by Kanzi*
- Various Topicalization devices:
  - *Kanzi bit Matata*
  - *Matata, Kanzi bit her*
  - *It was Matata that Kanzi bit*
- Some relative clause or modifying structures:
  - *Kanzi bit the chimp that was screaming*
  - *Kanzi bit the screaming chimp*
  - *The chimp that Kanzi bit was screaming*
  - *The screaming one that Kanzi bit was a chimp*

In classical semantic terms, the members of these sets of sentences have the same truth conditions, although their communicative effects vary. At this stage, we are only concerned with animals, pre-communicative mental representations. For the same reason, no difference corresponding to that between definite and indefinite noun phrases (e.g. *the* bird versus *a* bird) is necessary, as this is a difference arising out of communicative discourse.

Logical notation is designed to be unambiguous, unlike natural language expressions, which are notoriously ambiguous. The representations attributed to animals observing scenes should be similarly unambiguous, although they may well be vague. Ambiguity arises when an expression can be paraphrased in several different ways which are not themselves paraphrases of each other. For example, *ripe bananas and grapes* is ambiguous, because it can be paraphrased by both *grapes and ripe bananas* and *ripe bananas and ripe grapes*, and these two do not mean the same thing (the former includes more fruit, even unripe grapes, than the latter). In contrast, all predicates are at least somewhat vague, or fuzzy, in their denotation—the range of things, scenes, and events that they can apply to in the world. A well-known English example is the respective denotations of TREE and BUSH, which blend into each other.

Animals' mental representations of scenes and events are rooted in perception. It follows that concepts that are not rather directly based on perception (or proprioception) will have no terms for them. Thus I assume that animals have no access to human concepts such as 342, UNICORN, THURSDAY, and BACHELOR. Perhaps the furthest that animals manage to get from purely perceptual concepts is concepts of social relations, such as DOMINANT or SUBORDINATE, and even these are based on observation of concrete events, such as fights.

In both directions, that of human meaning, and that of animal representations, empirical work is called for. On the animal side, relevant questions include: which species make any distinction at all between global and local attention? What degree of nesting (zooming-in) from more global to more local levels are closely related primates capable of? In what sensory modalities is the global/local distinction found in various species? What range of concepts can animals of various species apply at the global level? And so on.

On the side of human language, the main question is obviously how far this box notation, with its implicit claim that meanings can be conceived as conjunctions of monadic predicates, is adequate to represent all the complex types of meaning that humans are capable of expressing in language. As mentioned earlier, Pietroski (2005) has made a start on the linguistic side, suggesting a programme to explore the possibility that **in general** 'when expressions are concatenated, they are interpreted as (conjoinable) monadic predicates' (p. 28). It is not my purpose here to delve deeper into human linguistic semantics, and I will restrict myself to a few more illustrative examples, aiming to show that the notational proposal is not prima facie obviously untenable for some simple examples that might at first blush appear to be problematic.

The two representations below are equivalent.

TORN-RIGHT-EAR(x) & SWEATY-SMELLING(x) & STRUTS(x)

TORN-RIGHT-EAR
SWEATY-SMELLING
STRUTS

Inclusion of predicates in the same box gives the same information as applying predicates to the same individual variable. These are alternative notational representations of a scene with one individual. But the new box notation is more appropriate for representation of offline stored knowledge than the more traditional representation with variables as arguments of predicates. In section 4.2 a correspondence was claimed between the logical individual variables (w, x, y, z) and the indices used by the visual system in tracking a limited number of objects in a scene. But when the objects are no longer present, the visual indices are no longer correlated with them. All that is left, after perceiving an object and taking in some of its properties, is the **content** of the information taken in, namely the properties, plus the information that they all came from the same object. This latter information is captured by grouping the predicates from one object in the same box. One box, one object. Santos et al. (2002) show how macaques store contentful information about the properties of objects to maintain them as separate known individuals when they are no longer in view. The representation of known, but not currently perceived, objects is as bundles of features.

This last example might seem to raise the problem that we have lost the distinction between **truth** and **reference**. That is, the same box notation, it is claimed, can be translated either by the sentence *There's someone with a torn right ear, sweaty-smelling and strutting* or by the noun phrase contained in this sentence, after *There's*. Traditionally, sentences are true and noun phrases refer. It is important to recall here that we are not (yet) discussing language. Carstairs-McCarthy (1999) argues at length that this traditional philosophical distinction has no basis outside public language. The truth/reference relation to the world, he argues, is all the same thing. The terms have just been selectively applied according to which kind of grammatical expression they apply to: the sentence-to-world relation is called 'truth', and the NP-to-world relation is called reference. Concurring arguments are given in Stainton (2004a, 2004b), and Hurford (2007). The box diagrams used here represent scenes that an animal can in some sense comprehend. Take a human analogy. When you see, and register, Peter coming into view, what thought passes through your mind, a sentence-thought (*There's Peter*) or a NP-thought (*Peter*)? To the extent that humans actually verbalize when thinking, this can be answered by observation, and in my experience, both sentences and NPs are uttered in such circumstances. But animals, of course, do not verbalize their thoughts, and it makes no sense to ask such a question in the case of a languageless animal. Put the same question in terms of retrieved memories: do you bring to mind Peter entering (NP), Peter's entrance (NP), or that Peter entered (sentence)? Surely you can't tell the difference. The importance of the truth/reference distinction is also called into question by the kind of data that Chomsky (1970) cites, data such as *The enemy destroyed the city* versus *the enemy's destruction of the city*. The fact that any sentence can be freely nominalized for purposes of embedding into a higher clause, without substantial effect on the propositional content, indicates a commonality between sentences and NPs.

If desired, we can still dissect our box diagrams in a way that fits an intuitive distinction between a referring component and a truth-claiming component. A box, devoid of its predicate contents, may be said to refer to whatever object in the world is being attended to in the represented scene. A box, remember, corresponds to a logical individual variable, such as x or y. These variables have no predicative content. **Pure** reference, as in deictic pointing, is descriptively uninformative. The predicates inside a box can then be said to make truth claims about the object referred to.

5.5 ARMCHAIR ONTOLOGY OF OBJECTS, EVENTS, AND SCENES

The notation developed in the preceding sections exploited the psychological difference between the quick and parallel taking in of a scene with several participants, as opposed to the serial detailed local attention to the individual participants in the scene, registering relevant conjunctions of their features. I also emphasized that attention could zoom in on a single object in a scene, so that, in effect, that object becomes the new scene, and its parts, or participants, can be subject to local attention at a 'deeper' level. Thus the assumed ontology makes no essential distinction between some traditional ontological categories, such as objects, events, and scenes.

There are various ways of interpreting the business of ontology, reflected in the following two rather different questions. What different kinds of entities does the world really contain? What different kinds of entities do languages (typically, alas, meaning just English) seem to treat the world as containing? I have tried to avoid these approaches, and to ask, guided by Occam's razor: What kinds of entities do our perceptual attentional systems seem to treat the world as containing? And the answer, as expressed in the box notation, has been that there are only two basic kinds of entities: (1) objects/events/scenes—all the same kind of thing; and (2) properties, which can be variously static or dynamic and can impose constraints on the objects/events/scenes that they are properties of. Static and dynamic features of an object are treated alike by these attention mechanisms (Nakayama and Silverman 1986). The quick global view can register either colour, or shape, or motion as individual features, but cannot accurately register how these features are conjoined in any one object. Thus motion, a dynamic feature, behaves in this respect like colour or shape, which are static features. Many examples were given in the preceding sections.

We humans have strong intuitions about the difference between objects and events, and this distinction rests primarily on the static/dynamic dimension. Long interweaving traditions in philosophy have variously emphasized dynamic **processes** (starting as far as we know with Heraclitus) or static **things** and **substances**. A fascination with static things and their enduring relations belies a deep, and wholly understandable, insecurity in the face of change. We like things to be reliably there. But time passes inexorably, and life is caught up in inevitable change, as things perish and are replaced by other things, of different kinds. Many sciences are host to a tension between a bold embrace of the inevitability of process, and instincts to construct worlds (material or theoretical) which are at least tolerably static. In linguistics Humboldt (1836, p. 150) emphasized process: 'Language is not a product (Ergon), but an activity (Energeia).'[20] Modern generative grammar, by contrast, has strongly emphasized grammars as (mental) objects. In physics the contrast is seen in the puzzling apparent alternatives of light being composed of waves or particles, and in the recognition of the relation between energy and matter.

In a scientific sense, we know that objects are nothing but slow events, some slower than others. Mesons are extremely fast events, existing apparently for less than a millionth of a second; adult mayflies are slower events, living for only a day; and we individual humans are objects that will with luck exist for as much as a hundred years, making us even slower events. Less loftily, ordinary folk and their animals live in a world in which some things last for so long (like the rocks of Greenland or my father's bathrobe) that we need not worry about them changing, while the fabric of our lives—breathing, moving, eating, and getting hungry again—involves continuous negotiation of change. It seems natural and practical to distinguish between objects and events, while recognizing that there are a few borderline cases, like flames, ocean waves, and shooting stars. Where we humans naturally draw the line between objects and events is entirely relative to our size, our lifespan and life rhythms, and our perceptual mechanisms (and to a limited extent to our particular cultures). There is no absolute non-relative fact of the matter distinguishing objects from events. Psychological experiments on object permanence, discussed in Chapter 3, are in fact testing the extent to which natural adult human concepts of objecthood are shared by other animals and infants.

Metaphysical discussion by philosophers and logicians usually starts from the human intuition of a basic ontological difference between objects and events. Some philosophers end up holding fast to the distinction, at the expense of possibly absurd reinterpretations of what events and objects 'really' are. Whitehead (1919), for example, retained a firm distinction. 'Objects convey the permanences recognised in events, and are

---

[20] In German: 'Sie selbst (die Sprache) ist kein Werk (Ergon), sondern eine Thätigkeit (Energeia).'

recognised as self-identical amid different circumstances; that is to say, the same object is related to diverse events' (pp. 62–63). Whitehead's position, however, is maintained at the expense of a counterintuitive view of events: 'Events never change. Nature develops, in the sense that an event *e* becomes part of an event *e'* ... Thus we say that events pass but do not change. The passage of an event is its passing into some other event which is not it' (p. 62). This robs the idea of an event of its dynamic nature, which many would consider essential. To most people, including philosophical ontologists, what Whitehead calls 'passing' between events **is** itself an event. Compare Link (1997, p. 305): 'Changes are events'. Whitehead also ends up with a counterintuitive view of objects. For example: 'It is an error to ascribe parts to objects. ... [I]t is natural to think of various parts of a stone, simultaneously existing. Such a conception confuses the stone as an object with the event which exhibits the actual relations of the stone within nature' (Whitehead 1919, p. 65). Again, 'The fundamental rule is that events have parts and that—except in a derivative sense, from their relations to events,—objects have no parts' (p. 66).

Whitehead was attempting to find a 'real' ontology, and not a scheme related to human perception.

Objects and events are only waveringly discriminated in common thought.... The struggle to make precise the concept of these objects [of common life] either forces us back to the sense-objects or forward to the scientific objects. The difficulty is chiefly one of making thought clear. That there is a perception of an object with self-identity, is shown by the common usage of mankind. Indeed these perceptual objects forced upon mankind—and seemingly also on animals, unless it be those of the lowest type—their knowledge of the objectified character of nature. But the confusion of the object, which is a unity, with the events, which have parts, is always imminent.

(Whitehead 1919, pp. 64–66)

So, for 'common thought' at least, the object/event distinction is not so hard and fast. Whitehead's concept of an event, essentially static, with objects as parts, is more like a 'state of affairs' or situation, a set of relations between objects. He appeared not to consider 'events' involving single objects.

More recently, Link (1997) has argued for a more graded view. 'Once we admit temporal parts of individuals the dividing line between individuals and events is already somewhat obscured' (p. 281).

The thrust of my line of reasoning is really that our regular objects are more 'abstract' than it is usually assumed. While it is often granted that events are particulars in space and time and yet abstract ... regular objects are said to be concrete, not abstract particulars. What I am saying here is that if that is the only difference between objects and events then that is not much of a difference after all. ... [A] meteor is an object and then again an event, viz. the phenomenon of its incandescence, just depending on the way we look at it.

(Link 1997, p. 283)

Link proceeds to articulate a view of '*processes* as the one category that I like to think of as underlying both individuals and events' (p. 284). The ensuing discussion is technical and algebraic, but clearly here is a modern ontologist who rejects a sharp distinction between objects and events. Schein (2002, p. 279), a philosopher and formal semanticist, concurs: 'it is with respect to medium-grained events that we appear to talk about objects and events in roughly the same way with roughly the same precision'.

Dynamic events have preoccupied ontologists, but remarkably little attention has been paid to their static counterpart, which we may call 'situations' or 'states'. Brutus stabbing Caesar is a prototypical event, but Caesar lying dead on the floor is a situation. In a situation, nothing (relevant) changes. In a situation with several participants, the relation between the participants persists. Just as the object/event distinction is a graded continuum, so too is the event/state distinction. Kamp and Reyle (1993, p. 507) agree: 'we are led to conclude (i) that not every sentence can be treated as the description of an event; (ii) that some sentences must rather be seen as descriptions of states; and (iii) that the division between event-describing and state-describing sentences appears to be graded rather than sharp.'

Davidson (1967) seminally proposed mapping sentences describing actions onto representations invoking a distinct ontological category of events. A whole stream of formal semantics, kicked off by Parsons (1990), has built on this idea. But the idea is centrally about language, and the arguments are based upon the particular ways in which sentences in human languages put their parts together. Thus the apparent distinctness of events as an ontological category may not necessarily hold of pre-linguistic cognition. There are significant philosophical counterarguments that, even for language, 'any philosophical theory of events should be extended to cover states as well, because the differences between them are of the superficial kind that would seem significant only to someone doing the kind of "conceptual analysis" that shades of into mere lexicography' (Bennett 1988, p. 7). An alternative to the Davidsonian ontology has been proposed by Kim (1969, 1976). The sometimes assumed ubiquity of event variables in the semantics of sentences has been criticized by Maienborn (2005). There is no space to go into the hairy details of these philosophico-semantic debates here. Suffice it to say that enough doubt has been cast on ontologies that distinguish objects from events, or events from states, or states from objects, to keep open the possibility of the much more reduced ontology that I have proposed.

To summarize, I envisage a single type of fact, whose internal properties may vary, depending on the way we look at them, between relatively dynamic and relatively static, and according to the number of objects they involve. This is illustrated by the examples below

Participant objects	Static scenes	Dynamic events
0	It's cold	It's raining
	freezing weather	It's snowing
1	(This is) a knife	Something twinkles
		The knife falls
2	(There's) a knife on the floor	Brutus picks up the knife
	The knife is on the floor	Brutus strikes Caesar
3	(There's) a knife on the floor	Brutus stabs Caesar with a
	near Caesar	knife

A concomitant of the possibility of shifting back and forth between local and global attention is that some properties or predicates can sometimes be attributed to a whole scene and sometimes to one of its partipants. In the case of Brutus violently killing Caesar, it may be said that the whole event was violent or that Brutus was violent. Both are true. Poor old Caesar was not violent on that occasion, as far as this description tells us. In the case of a twinkling star, one may say that there is a twinkling event involving a star, or that it is not the event, but its participant object, the star, that twinkles. In the case of a man walking, one may say that there is a walking event involving a man, or that it is not the event but its participant object, the man, who is walking. In such cases of one-participant events, the distinction seems to be without content. The changing object **is** the event.

Let me forestall a possible linguistic objection here. The two English phrases *the changing object* and *the changing of the object* (or *the object's changing*) are not synonymous. In the former, the noun *object* is the grammatical head of the phrase, and the phrase denotes the object; in the latter, the grammatical head is the nominalized verb *changing* and the phrase denotes what happens to the object. Given language, it is possible to make such distinctions. And such distinctions can in principle be useful when embedded in other expressions, although in fact English speakers, at least, do not often avail themselves of this possibility. Thus, for example, if I use *The changing weather annoyed me*, this is most naturally taken as saying the same as *The changing of the weather annoyed me*. Now try to picture a visual scene to which one of the two phrases, *the changing object* and *the changing of the object*, but not the other, applies. You can't see the changing of an object without seeing the object changing, and vice versa. It is just a difference of focus of attention, which can be reflected in language, as it is in these two English phrases. The point is eloquently made by Derek Bickerton:

> The subject–predicate distinction in language is so fundamental, and so much taken for granted, that it is perhaps worth emphasizing that it corresponds to nothing in nature. There is no sense in which we can perceive a creature without simultaneously perceiving that it is doing something—sleeping, grazing, walking, flying—and no way in which we can see a behavior like grazing, flying, sleeping, or walking without simultaneously seeing the creature that performs it. (Bickerton 1990, p. 39)

In this part of the book, I am concerned with the representations of the world formed by pre-linguistic creatures, on the basis of their perceptions. The properties picked out by attention are to some extent primed by the animal's phylogeny and previous experience. But depending on local and temporal circumstances, an animal is still 'free' to allow different properties of an observed object to be selected for attention. To reuse a previous example, when Fred the chimpanzee sees his conspecific whom he knows well (and whom we have dubbed Mary) scratching, what may come to his mind is one, or both, or even neither, of the following two conjuncts:

> MARY
> SCRATCH

In language, the relative salience of one or the other of the two properties mentioned can be conveyed by expressions such as *Mary, who happens to be scratching* versus *a scratching event, which happened to involve Mary*. Using sentences, rather than NPs, the event/scene/object could be variously described, with different emphases, as *Mary was scratching* or *The one scratching was Mary*. Obviously there will be other properties of Mary that simply do not come to attention on some particular occasion.

Similar comments also apply when more than one object is involved. A disinterested observer of events in the Roman senate might, for example, only be interested in the fact that both Brutus and Caesar are present, and not care about what they are doing to each other. If we observe two people together, because of our overwhelming interest in social relations, we are typically very interested in what, if anything, they are doing to each other. But take away the factor of social empathy, and it is possible to view a scene with several objects (which may be dynamically interacting) and only be interested in their individual properties. A socially unempathic person fascinated by cataloguing and counting animal species may see a lion attacking a zebra and find the most salient features of the scene to be the lionhood of one participant and the zebrahood of the other, with scarce regard for the action, because it doesn't add to his score of species collected. A ruthless prison jailer checking on inmates late at night may only note who is present in a cell and pay no attention to what, if anything, they are doing to each other. Normal people find it hard to be so detached from significant activities, and thus two-place action predicates tend to spring easily to mind. But with inanimate objects, among which there cannot be wilful activity, like the meat and potatoes on a dinner plate, a scene which can be taken in at a glance, no two-place predicate springs to mind, although both the meat and the potatoes are participants in the scene.

We can't just end on meat and potatoes. Remember, this chapter was a linguistic semanticist tidying house so that neighbouring psychologists and neuroscientists won't be shocked or baffled when they pay a visit, as they ought, if they have any interest in the evolution of language. The technical jargon and formulae of linguistic semantics can be formidable to an outsider, and I know of distinguished and serious neuroscientists who have given up on linguistic theory because of its impenetrability. One aim of this chapter was to reduce this impenetrability. No one can say that the box diagrams that I have proposed aren't simple, even though arguing towards them, and away from the ontologically richer representations used by linguists, necessarily got to grips with some of the old complexity. The simplification is not mere dumbing-down for non-linguists. The simple box diagrams are proposed seriously as sufficient to capture representations of scenes in the world in the minds of language-less creatures, near the brink of language, like apes. The notation bears a recognizable relation to the shape of simple propositions as conceived by logic, in particular incorporating the pre-linguistic counterparts of predicates and their arguments, and conjunctions of propositions. Thus, evolutionary continuity between non-humans and humans becomes easier to envisage.

As I wrote before, consider these proposals on their merits. If they don't deserve to be torn down, build on them. There is plenty more to do. I have not discussed such important questions as negation, quantification, and inference in the minds of pre-linguistic animals. In tackling such questions, start your thinking, if possible, where the animals are, by imagining yourself in a non-linguistic state, but otherwise cognitively pretty much as you are. José Luis Bermúdez, in his philosophical monograph *Thinking without Words* (Bermúdez 2003), has begun to tackle some of these problems in a way broadly, but not wholly, consistent with my own thinking. He makes some interesting suggestions, such as analysing negation in non-linguistic thought as the use of unitary negative predicates, like UN-SQUARE or UN-RED, rather than negation being an operator on whole propositions. In his account, this kind of 'proto-negation' can combine with a grasp of 'proto-causation' to implement at least three inferential rules: modus ponens, modus tollens, and disjunctive syllogism. The research programme is under way. Join in, or at least watch with interest.

These five chapters are as much proto-semantics as there is space for, here. We have seen that animals lead quite rich cognitive lives, with signs of the beginnings of much of what has often been taken to be distinctively human. But mostly they keep this rich content to themselves. A flip subtitle for this book might have been *What animals know, and why they don't tell*. We've seen what they know; in Part II, on proto-pragmatics, we'll examine why they don't tell.

PART TWO

Communication: What and Why?

In Part II, we go public. The topic of Part I was animals' internal representations of an external world, with little or no consideration of any possibility for public expression of these representations. But animals are seldom alone, and most higher animals live in social groups, involving interaction with others. Here, in Part II, we will explore the evolutionary basis of publicly expressed meaning. Much of this involves what linguists call 'Pragmatics', the study of interpersonal communication. The evolution of social behaviour ran in parallel with the evolution of private representations of the world. Books necessarily have linear structure, and the separation into private and public evolutionary developments is an expository convenience, not implying that the evolution of private conceptions and of social behaviour were not intertwined; they certainly were.

CHAPTER SIX

Communication by Dyadic Acts

In this chapter, I will explore the most basic precursors of human communication, **dyadic** interactions between animals. I use *dyadic* as synonymous with *non-referring*. In a very basic sense, I can communicate with you without referring to anything, as when I greet you with a cheery 'Hi!' The idea is to exclude, for the moment, consideration of communication which brings in (by referring to it) some third person, object, or event other than the sender or receiver(s) of a signal. It seems intuitively obvious that dyadic communication preceded triadic communication. The subsequent chapter will move on to triadic communication, and the origins of reference. Dyadic communication is not restricted to interactions between only two animals. *Dyadic* alludes to two **roles**: those of sender and receiver(s) of a message. Mostly, only two animals are involved, but we will see cases where an animal sends a signal intended for several others. First, a little section on what is meant by *communication*.

6.1 ROUGHLY AND READILY DEFINING 'COMMUNICATION'

We want to cast an evolutionary light on human language, so we'll start by restricting the scope of the term *communication* to interactions between animals of the same species. Starting with flowers attracting insects would be starting too far back, and possibly on the wrong track. The restriction to conspecifics is motivated because two-way human communication has not evolved in any symbiotic or parasitic relationship with other species. Adversarial 'communication' between species does happen, as for example when a plover diverts a predator away from its nest by trailing a wing as if it were broken, or when an angler fish lures prey near to it by waving the inbuilt fishing rod on its nose. Cooperative communication between humans and other species also occurs, as with a shepherd whistling commands to a sheepdog, or a rider giving verbal commands to a horse. But the animals don't answer back in the same code; it is not a reciprocal business like human language. It is characteristic of human language that anyone can act as either producer or recipient of a message. Human language shows no vestiges of traits that might have been involved in communication with other species. But we can take an important general message about communication from all these non-precursors to human language. **A form of communication exists because the producer of a signal normally gets some benefit from it.**[1] So we should look for the precursors of human-to-human communication in behaviours that benefit the signaller.

Defining communication precisely is problematic, as I will briefly show (but we can draw a useful moral from this very difficulty, as we will also see). For any proposed definition of communication, we can think of some action fitting the definition that we would not want, intuitively, to characterize as communication, and certainly not as any kind of communication that could be an evolutionary precursor to human language. And conversely we can think of some other kind of action that is, counterintuitively, excluded. Within the animal kingdom, communication is sometimes defined as any behaviour by one organism that influences the state of another. This definition makes communication necessarily **dyadic**, ruling out any idea of an animal communicating with itself. In the case of human language, people certainly do talk usefully to themselves, and we ought not to exclude the possibility that this can reasonably be seen as a kind of communication. Clearly, however, communication between two different organisms is the prototypical norm, and a good place to start. It seems reasonable to regard talking to oneself in language as an evolutionary derivative of talking to other people. So we will stick with the idea of dyadic interaction as the evolutionary basis for human communication in language.

Defining communication as behaviour that influences the state of another is still too broad for our purposes. It stretches the idea of communication to say that the chimpanzee that has killed a chimpanzee from a rival group has 'communicated' with the doomed chimp. A reasonable way to narrow the term down might then be to exclude direct physiological causes. The killer chimp's behaviour directly causes the other chimp's death, by cutting off the blood supply to its brain, a physiological effect. *Physiological* is a term denoting one end of a spectrum of bodily

---

[1] In a later chapter, we will return to the much more specific, and intricate, question of the evolutionary cost–benefit of multi-functional human language.

processes, and is conveniently opposed to *mental* or *cognitive*, denoting processes at the other end of the spectrum. Ultimately, however, defining communication as non-physiological causation also becomes problematic, as, for example, loud noises may affect the distribution of certain neurotransmitters in a hearer's brain, and therefore change the mood of an animal hearing loud noises. The action of neurotransmitters is a physiological process. But I do want to say that the fact of shouting loudly, as opposed to whispering, can communicate something to the hearer. So 'non-physiological' is problematic. We could enter another definitional quagmire by linking communication to properties such as **deliberate** or **voluntary**. A man who doesn't realize how loudly he is talking (so he's not deliberately talking loudly) nevertheless communicates something to us just by the loudness of his talk. Sometimes it seems reasonable to say that someone has 'unintentionally communicated' something to us. So deliberateness won't help us define communication. Finally, I won't even attempt to wade through the bog that flourishes around the idea of **information** (Shannon and Weaver 1963; Dretske 1981). Alan Grafen (1990a, Section 7) also surveys difficulties in defining *signal*, with similar lack of success: 'I am unable to offer a formal definition of signals in terms of game theory' (p. 536).

Our definitional problems vindicate Wittgenstein (1953)'s point that the best we can do is to find family resemblances between different instances of things described by the same word. But, more importantly here, the difficulty of arriving at a completely satisfactory definition of communication makes a central evolutionary point. The point is that so-called communicative acts intimately share a landscape with allegedly non-communicative acts. Communicative acts evolved out of non-communicative acts. There was, in the evolutionary process, no abrupt phase-change where one could say that communication started. And many of the physical devices and actions clearly used nowadays for communication are the same physical devices and actions that in slightly different situations and contexts are not obviously communicative. A cough can be used diplomatically to communicate one's presence to someone engrossed in a book. Virtually the same cough can be given simply to ease a tickle. Communicative acts are made of the same stuff as non-communicative acts.

So we will look for precursors to human-to-human communication in non-communicative acts to a member of the same species that would have benefited the producer. It will be useful first to sketch some elements of the first target of our evolutionary story: modern human speech acts.

6.2 PRAGMATIC ORIGINS

This section outlines some basic linguistic pragmatics, especially the theory of speech acts, so that we can get an idea of where we are going, what kinds of facts about human use of language we are aiming to account for in evolutionary terms. The key idea is that language is used by people to **do things to each other**.

'Actions speak louder than words' is a popular proverb. A 'man of action' is often thought to be a man of few words. In the popular imagination, actions and words are exclusive alternatives. 'Stop talking and DO something', people often say. But in fact many modern human actions can be carried out in words, and some only in words. The American Declaration of Independence, though consisting only of words, was a significant historical **act**. Words and sentences are not merely **descriptive**, but can be used to carry out **actions**. Among the most significant events in history are a few which in themselves have no linguistic content at all, such as floods, droughts, and volcanic eruptions, which are not caused by human agency. Some other great events, such as battles, executions, and discoveries, which are not themselves verbal events, mainly derive their historic significance from the linguistic acts which surround or follow them, such as surrender, defiant declarations from the scaffold, or territorial claims. Linguistic acts shape history. At a more mundane level, they shape the lives of individuals, in the form of marriage vows, contracts, or merely agreements to meet for lunch. The point was nicely expressed in the title of the seminal book on speech acts, J. L. Austin's *How to Do Things with Words* (with the emphasis on *Do*) (Austin 1962). There is a large set of conventional acts which we normally carry out with words, acts such as thanking, apologizing, complaining, congratulating, greeting, taking leave, challenging, and warning. Human life is clearly lifted a level above animal life by the possibility of such verbal acts. Austin tried for a while to separate sentences out into two sorts: those that perform acts, and those that simply describe events or situations. But it is generally agreed now that almost all sentences carry both sorts of meaning simultaneously. If I say to a store manager 'The eggs I bought here yesterday were all stale', I am simultaneously carrying out the act of complaining and describing a state of affairs.

There are just a few expressions (one cannot really call them sentences) in all languages which are purely act-performing. Short colloquial greetings such as *Hello!* and *Hi!* are just act-performing words; they don't describe anything, and they can't be said to be true or false, as a description can. Here is a table of some such expressions used in English-speaking communities.

Expression	Function
Hello	Greeting
Bye!	Taking leave
Hey!	Loudly attracting attention
pssst!	Discretely attracting attention
Ta (British English)	Thanking
Sorry	Apologizing

scram   mwah   shush

These expressions all carry out social acts, that is they involve interaction with another person. (In cultures where people routinely deal with animals, such a list can be extended to include 'words' used to give commands to animals.) In addition to these necessarily social act-words, there are some which do not absolutely require the involvement of another person; they can be said to oneself. Examples are:

Expression	Function
'tut tut' (alveolar click, sometimes repeated)	Expressing disapproval or disappointment
Mmmm	Expressing sensual pleasure
Hmmmm	Expressing thoughtfulness or doubt
Pah!	Expressing contempt
Aha!	Expressing surprise at a discovery
Ouch!	Expressing pain
Phew!	Expressing relief

Expressions such as these can be taken to indicate an internal state of the speaker. As such they are intermediate between purely 'doing' words like *Hello* and obviously descriptive expressions like *It's raining*. Usually, however, one does not use such 'expressive' words without some purpose of affecting a hearer somehow—what would be the point of uttering them otherwise? In fact, there are **no** expressions in any language which can **only** be used descriptively, that is without the possibility of any socially significant act being carried out when they are uttered. If one says 'It's

Figure 6.1 Large open-ended area = All meaningful expressions in a language. Small shaded area = Expressions such as *Hello* and *Hey!* with purely illocutionary, non-propositional, meaning.

raining' certainly one is describing a situation, but one typically has some purpose in mind, such as indirectly warning someone or advising them, or indeed jokingly complaining. We thus find an asymmetric situation. The great majority, but not all, of the expressions in a language have meaningful content which is descriptive of some state of affairs; all expressions in a language can be used to carry out acts of some sort; and a tiny minority of expressions are used **only** for carrying out acts, and have no descriptive content. To introduce some terminology, the great majority of complete expressions in a language have **propositional content**; all sentences in a language have potential **illocutionary force**; and a tiny minority of expressions have no propositional content, but only conventional illocutionary force. In Figure 6.1 above this asymmetric situation is shown as a tiny finite pool of purely illocutionary expressions located in an open-ended ocean of expressions which, besides having illocutionary potential, also have descriptive, propositional content.

It is strongly typical of modern human utterances that they involve an intended effect on a hearer. Even an utterance like 'Mmmm' expressing sensual pleasure, which may sometimes be uttered to nobody but oneself, is conventionally used to inform someone else of one's pleasure. We are naturally starting our investigation into human communication with an implicit definition of *utterance* which rules out signals not typically intended to have an effect on a hearer. In modern human life, there are borderline cases, such as belches and farts, which are mostly involuntary and uncommunicative, but which can be put to communicative use in atypical circumstances. Thus **intended effect on a hearer** is a core ingredient of modern human communication, and I will take it to be an evolutionary foundation.

By contrast, while the vast majority of modern human utterances do have some propositional, or descriptive, content, there is a small nucleus of clear cases which do not, such as 'Hello', 'Hey!', and 'Bye'. The descriptive or propositional content of utterances is based on the internal representations of the world which was the subject of Part I of this book, 'Meaning before Communication'. Animals have well-developed internal representations of objects, scenes, and events in the world, without ever communicating these representations to other animals. The aboutness, or Intentionality,[2] of modern human utterances derives from the aboutness or Intentionality of pre-linguistic mental representations. As an independent and parallel evolutionary development, I shall suggest, animals used controlled gestures and noises to have an effect on each other, but these first signals, like modern 'Hello', were not **about** any object, event, or scene in the outside world. These first signals were purely dyadic, involving only the signaller and the recipient, and not **referring** to any third object, and not being **true** of any situation. In short, I advance the following hypothesis:

Communicative Act Foundation hypothesis: Primitive other-directed acts descriptive of nothing outside the signaller formed the original communicative component of the foundation upon which grew later complex utterance types combining illocutionary force with descriptive content.

In this view, there might be an evolutionary progression that we can mimic in modern terms as follows:

Aha! simply expressing surprise (to an addressee),
Aha, blackberries! expressing surprise, and identifying the topic or cause of surprise,
Aha, John's coming! describing a situation and simultaneously conveying surprise about it.

or

Hey! attracting attention,
Hey, John! attracting attention and simultaneously identifying the addressee,
Hey, John, your shoelace is undone describing a situation and simultaneously attracting the attention of the addressee.

There is nothing logically compelling about the Communicative Act Foundation hypothesis. Nothing inherent to either speech acts or descriptive language makes it necessarily true that pure speech acts had to precede descriptive language. An alternative hypothesis is conceivable:

Independent Description hypothesis: Utterances with descriptive content arose independently of any illocutionary expressions with intended effects on receivers.

---

[2] Recall the use of *Intentionality* with a capital *I* for aboutness. The word *intentionality*, derived from the verb *intend*, meaning an animal's capacity to intend to do things, is spelt with a small *i*.

It is perhaps conceivable that propositional descriptive language arose separately from speech acts, as a way of externalizing our thoughts about the world, but not communicating them to any other person. One might notice that a certain tree has good fruit and for some reason mutter to oneself, 'That tree has good fruit'. One might perhaps do this to help one remember where the good fruit is, using the utterance as a private memory-reinforcer. Or one might find that thinking aloud helped one's mental calculations about the best way to get around the foraging ground. There need be no interaction with another person, hence no kind of social act. Although Chomsky is generally reluctant to engage in evolutionary speculation, the above Independent Description hypothesis is more in line with his views on the function of language, as expressed, for example, in:

Suppose that in the quiet of my study I think about a problem, using language, and even write down what I think. Suppose that someone speaks honestly, merely out of a sense of integrity, fully aware that his audience will refuse to comprehend or even consider what he is saying. Consider informal conversation conducted for the sole purpose of maintaining casual friendly relations, with no particular concern as to its content. Are these examples of 'communication'? If so, what do we mean by 'communication' in the absence of an audience, or with an audience assumed to be completely unresponsive, or with no intention to convey information or modify belief or attitude?

It seems that either we must deprive the notion 'communication' of all significance, or else we must reject the view that the purpose of language is communication.   (Chomsky 1980, p. 230)

In the real world, a person would not be successful in 'maintaining casual friendly relations' if he had 'no particular concern as to the content' of his utterances. The quality of honesty and the 'sense of integrity' that Chomsky mentions are arguably (some would say obviously) social in origin. Indeed, people do occasionally utter descriptive sentences for non-social reasons, without any intended effect on a hearer, as when talking to oneself. It is **logically** conceivable that this was the first use of such sentences. There is no logical need to assume that the descriptive language arose on the back of calls with originally purely illocutionary (speech act, social coinage) force. But a powerful argument telling against such non-social origin is the fact that in a whole society, the **same** words are used by all people, even for talking to oneself. Talking to oneself goes a step beyond solipsistic thinking. Much thought is not in words. Talking to oneself involves putting publicly available arbitrary labels on the elements of the thoughts. Here I envisage the elements of thoughts to be such as the pre-linguistic predicates discussed extensively in Part I of this book. If the first case of attaching arbitrary labels to elements of thought were for some private non-social purpose, there would have been no reason for all members of a social group to use the same labels. If the external labels were not intended to have any effect on another creature, why would such standardized labels arise?

Accordingly I shall pursue the idea that the first communicative acts between the remote ancestors of modern humans were of the purely illocutionary variety, like 'Hey!' and 'Hello!' Nowadays purely illocutionary expressions occupy a very marginal status in modern languages. They are mostly, syntactically, interjections, which means that they have no place within the system of multi-word expressions defined by the grammar of the language concerned. The only way most such expressions can be integrated into an English sentence is by quoting them. *Hello*, *Bye*, and *Hey* can be followed by a person's name, as in *Hey, John!*, but that is the extent of the possible integration of these expressions into the English syntactic system. Many of these expressions also lie outside the normal English phonological system for forming words: many contain no vowel sound, and some contain consonantal sounds, such as clicks, not found in any regular English word. A slightly more integrated, but still marginal, use of purely illocutionary expressions in English is the insertion of taboo words into angry discourse, as for example 'Get your fucking hands off my car'. The insertion of such words certainly adds no descriptive content to utterances, and is surely a marker of the speaker's momentary stance towards the hearer, be it anger or non-conformist solidarity. Similarly, inserting words like *Sweetie*, *Honey*, and *Darling* into discourse between intimates adds no descriptive content but reinforces a social relation between speaker and hearer. In more public discourse, the English word *please* inserted into a sentence carries no descriptive content, but marks the social act carried out as a request. In many languages a question is formed from a corresponding statement by adding a particle at the front or the back of the sentence. Thus in Japanese, interrogative sentences are formed by adding *ka* at the end of a sentence. Likewise in Mandarin Chinese, a question can be formed by adding *ma* to the corresponding statement. The difference between questions and statements is purely illocutionary; they require different responses from the hearer, but they deal with the same propositional (descriptive) content. The relative marginality of pure illocution markers is typical of languages in general, but they are not wholly unintegrated, as Burling (2005) claims.

Purely illocutionary expressions clearly do not provide a basis for the grammatical complexity and descriptive power of modern human language. But the absolute centrality of illocution in human language, the fact that every human linguistic expression can be, and most often is, used to **do something**, makes simple dyadic non-descriptive communicative acts a good place to look at the origins of human public language. The idea will be that grammatical complexity and descriptive power grew on top of such basic acts, vastly transforming the communicative capacity of individuals, and eventually also transforming individuals' private mental capacities, as well. But that is to look a long way ahead in our story.

In the literature on speech acts, one sometimes finds **asserting, referring**, and **predicating** mentioned as speech acts. But it is clear that asserting, referring, and predicating are different in nature from the inherently social speech acts such as promising, insulting, congratulating, and greeting. The latter are all 'coins' in a currency of conventional social interaction. Certain situations demand certain speech acts, and if they are not given, group coherence is weakened. Greeting, apologizing, thanking, and congratulating on appropriate occasions are expected and their performance strengthens social ties. Insulting deliberately changes social relations, and sets up expectations of further social acts. But asserting, referring, and predicating are like none of these. If, while speaking to you, I happen to refer to a particular apple, that act of referring is not itself a coin in the same social currency. If I say 'I promise to give you this apple', the act of promising is indeed a coin in the social currency, but the embedded act of referring is not inherently social in the same way. Likewise, to predicate some property of a referent object, as in saying, for example, 'This apple is unripe', is not itself to pass a coin in the social currency of speech acts, even though the whole utterance may carry out the speech act of warning. And I have argued in Part I that reference, predication, and truth are originally and basically not features of public acts, but relationships between private mental representations and the experienced world.

The argument in this section relates to a long-standing issue about the function and evolution of language. Far too often, the debate has been presented as an all-or-nothing choice between communication and internal mental representation. An example is: 'We should search for the ancestry of language not in prior systems of animal communication but in prior representational systems' (Bickerton 1990, p. 23). This is in keeping with Chomsky, who in several of his writings has consistently asserted that the function of language is more to do with mental representation than with communication (e.g. Chomsky 1980). Pinker and Bloom (1990, p. 714) reject this view, but, sensibly, without dismissing the idea of a 'language-like representational medium', while pointing out that in their surface structure 'Natural languages are hopeless for this function'. The issue is explored in detail in Hurford (2002). In the present work, an emphatically more eclectic stance is taken, with Part I 'Meaning before Communication' exploring prior representational systems in relation to human semantics, and this part exploring the communicative abilities of animals.

6.3 THINGS ANIMALS DO TO EACH OTHER

The previous section outlined the ways in which human use of language involves people doing things to each other. Here we will look at animal precursors: communicative ways in which animals do things to each other.

In the most basic form of unlearned instinctive behaviour between conspecifics, animals simply act on each other as physical objects, for example shoving each other out of the way to get at food. In social species, however, virtually all significant interactions show a 'causal gap' between an action and its effect on the recipient. An animal need not always physically push another out of the way, but can obtain the same effect, if the other animal is smaller or less dominant, simply by growling. Krebs and Dawkins (1984) introduced the ideas of **manipulation** and **mind-reading** to begin to explain such facts. In fact 'mind-reading' can be taken to attribute unnecessarily telepathic powers to an animal, and we can start with a weaker version: **prediction**. This weaker capacity does not involve any mental ability to imagine oneself in the position of another, as in full-blown Theory of Mind (to which we will return later). Animals can take suitable action in response to the movements of inanimate objects, such as falling rocks. An animal dodging a falling rock acts **as if it knows** where the rock will be in a few milliseconds' time. Such instinctive behaviour has been hardwired into the animal's reflexes by natural selection. Animals that didn't dodge falling rocks quickly enough had fewer offspring.

The evolutionary environment of social species includes danger from conspecifics as well as from inanimate objects. Animals attack each other, and wounded animals are generally less fit to survive and reproduce. If an animal can predict an attack (not necessarily in any way consciously) and take evasive action, its fitness is improved. Movements preparatory to an attack can trigger an evolved evasive response. The classic exponent of these ideas is Tinbergen (1952, 1964).

Many signaling movements resemble incomplete versions of movements which themselves have another function. For instance, many threat postures involve the first stages of fighting in which the weapons are brought into a position of readiness; birds point the bill at an opponent or lift the carpal joints; fish may open their mouths; many mammals bare their teeth.

(Tinbergen 1964)

Animals evolve reflex evasive actions against the most common dangers in their environment, including dangers from conspecifics.

Danger is an impersonal term; *threat* (in careful usage) adds an intentional act component. Once an evasive response to an impending attack has evolved, the evolutionary environment of would-be attackers has changed. Now, mere preparatory actions, such as teeth-baring, can have the same effect as a full-blooded attack—the victim gets out of the way. Preparatory movements are less costly of energy than full attacks, and in response to the evolved evasive action, a **ritualized** threat gesture evolves, by which the actor can often get the same result as from an attack but with much less effort. Given this evolutionary chain of mutual adaptations, an instinctive routine has emerged between threat-giver and threat-receiver. An animal halfway up the dominance hierarchy can act in either role, depending on who she is interacting with. It looks as if the beginnings of a simple code—**teeth-baring = threat**—has evolved in the species. To work effectively, such ritual moves must be clearly distinct from other similar moves not associated with the implicit message, and so a certain degree of stylization often takes place. The teeth-baring of a threat display to a conspecific may be a bit more obvious to an observer than the teeth-baring preparatory to an attack on prey of another species. In adversarial situations, the threat-giver must also be prepared occasionally to follow up his threat if necessary, or else receivers might evolve to ignore it.

Conspecifics may often be in fierce rivalry, especially males competing for sexual partners in some social setups. In some species and some circumstances rival males actually kill each other, if that is how self-interest works out. But it is not easy to kill a similar-sized conspecific without risk of injury to oneself, and alternative ritualized behaviours have often evolved. This is not a case of 'species-selection' where the (relative) kid-gloves behaviour might be thought to have evolved for the purpose of preserving the species. It is not a case of 'I had better not kill him, because that might endanger the species'. It is rather that behaviours have evolved by which clear enough evidence is given of both protagonists' respective strengths, in time for the one who perceives himself to be the weaker to withdraw without paying the ultimate price, thus saving his genes for a more auspicious occasion; if the stronger chose to give chase and fight on, he too would be wasting energy better spent on mating.[3]

Conspecifics need to find mates, and potential mates need to advertise themselves. In the many species where males and females differ in appearance, much of the variation is due to clues telling the opposite sex of that particular species that an individual is appropriate. Domb and Pagel (2002, p. 204) found thats

> sexual swellings in wild baboons reliably advertise a female's reproductive value over her lifetime, in accordance with a theoretical model of honest signalling. Females with larger swellings attained sexual maturity earlier, produced both more offspring and more surviving offspring per year than females with smaller swellings, and had a higher overall proportion of their offspring survive. Male baboons use the size of the sexual swelling to determine their mating effort, fighting more aggressively to consort females with larger swellings, and spending more time grooming these females.

Male sexual ornament is in fact more common than such female sexual ornament—witness the peacock's splendid tail.

Behavioural signalling by males to attract females is very common. Examples are birdsong (which also has a territorial component), frog calls, and the elaborate bower-building by bower birds. In species where females are choosy about their partners, a permanent marking or difference in shape will not do. Actions to repel or attract suitable partners and to coordinate sexual activity have evolved. Semple et al. (2002) studied how female baboons vocalize before, during, and after copulation and the effect of such calls on males. Hauser (1996, pp. 404–405) gives a list of primate signals used to manage copulation in various ways:

1. Females call to synchronize orgasm with the male (Hamilton and Arrowood 1978) or to facilitate proper endocrinological exchanges required for mating (Cheng 1992). The idea here is that orgasm aids fertilization via an increase in sperm transfer up the reproductive tract. This hypothesis would require coordination between between the male and the female, such that the female would signal that she is close to orgasm and the male would call just prior to ejaculation.
2. Females call to announce their reproductive state. Variation in call structure may covary with different stages of the reproductive cycle (Aich et al. 1990; Gust et al. 1990).

---

[3] An influential paper by Enquist and Leimar (1983), modelling the kinds of cost–benefit relations involved in deciding whether to fight, initiated a line of research under the heading of 'self-assessment games'.

3. Females call to announce the presence of a male consort and to recruit aid from other females as a mechanism to reduce harassment (O'Connell and Cowlishaw 1994)
4. Females call when mating with low-ranking males as a mechanism for promoting male-male competition. As a result of generating a competitive arena, females can make more informed choices about male viability or physical condition (Cox and LeBoeuf 1977).

In Hauser's first example above, there is evidence of coordination between two signallers, a kind of brief duet during sex. Duetting is quite common in a range of distantly related species. Deputte (1982) gives a detailed description of duetting in gibbons.

To summarize, in a mated pair, when the female sings, the male starts to sing. During each buildup phase of the female song, the male stops singing. After the climax of the female song, he resumes his song by uttering a response. This response is characterized by its structural complexity, loudness, and associated locomotory displays. Therefore, in the white-cheeked gibbons, duets are antiphonal.   (Deputte 1982, p. 80)

Deputte also briefly surveys duetting behaviour in other primates and some bird species. It arises as an adaptation in monogamous territorial species in environments where visual contact is restricted, such as dense jungle. In duetting, one can see similarities with the turn-taking in human conversations, but the resemblance is very limited:

I investigated whether wild chimpanzee vocal exchanges exhibit uniquely human conversational attributes. The results indicate that wild chimpanzees vocalize at low rates, tend not to respond to calls that they hear, and, when they do respond, tend to give calls that are similar to the ones they have heard. Thus, chimpanzee vocal interactions resemble those of other primate species, and show no special similarity to human conversations.
                                             (Arcadi 2000, p. 205)

Many animal communications are not addressed to single addressees, but to all and sundry who may be in the vicinity. One simple message may be paraphrased as 'Here I am', communicating more or less exactly the location of the caller. What this does to the hearers varies. In territorial species, a 'Here I am' call may warn others away. In species that forage in groups, such a call helps to keep group-members in loose contact with each other.

The cohesion-spacing vocal system of *C[ebus] nigrivittatus* operates to maintain the characteristic spacing. The huh, a highly repetitive call, appears to elicit little response from neighbors. Animals deliver these calls when in auditory and often visual contact with neighbors. The circumstances of their use indicate that huh calls discourage neighbors from approaching and encourage them to move away. The continual production of these calls counteracts a tendency of animals to bunch together, especially around resources. Arrawhs and hehs are given following more extreme perturbations. Arrawhs bring animals together and hehs space them out.

(Robinson 1982, pp. 112–114)

In gray-cheeked mangabeys 'the whoopgobble vocalization probably mediates both intergroup spacing and intragroup cohesion (Chalmers 1968; Waser 1975, 1976, 1977), and it typically elicits rapid approach by specific dominant adult males' (Brown 1982).

The mention of signals for intragroup cohesion here implicitly takes us beyond discussion of **unlearned** signals. Signals that are distinctive of social subgroups within a breeding species must be passed on through learning, rather than in the DNA characteristic of the whole species.

Similarities in the spectrotemporal properties of vocalizations within primate social groups have been shown in a variety of species: chimpanzees, Barbary macaques, pigtail macaques (*M. nemestrina*), rhesus macaques, cotton-top tamarins, and mouse lemurs (*Microcebus murinus*). These acoustic similarities are called different things by different authors: dialects, vocal signatures or vocal accommodation (Fischer, 2002). However, they all may serve the purpose of signaling current group membership.   (Egnor et al. 2006, p. 665)

Crockford et al. (2004, p. 221) describe how, in wild chimpanzees from several groups, 'neither habitat nor genetic differences accounted for the observation that there were acoustic differences in the pant hoot structure of males living in neighbouring communities, but not in those of males from a distant community. This suggests that chimpanzees may actively modify pant hoots to be different from their neighbours.' (See also Arcadi 1996 for interpopulation variability of the chimpanzee pant-hoot.) Thus we have behaviour 'designed' not just to be similar to the members of one's own group, but also to be different from the behaviour of other groups. Egnor et al. (2006) give a number of other examples of possible 'group-signals', but sound an important note of caution: 'However, all studies on group-specific signatures to date have been observational. It is still an open question whether these signatures are meaningful to receivers, though it seems likely, given that the tendency to produce such signatures appears to be widespread among primates' (Egnor et al. 2006, p. 665). In other words, it may be the case that the animals are disposed to imitate the characteristics of other animals in their groups, but do not respond in any significant way to perception of this group similarity. Thus such characteristics may not be (intentional) signals at all, but rather just behavioural similarities observable by a human researcher. A human analogy might be 'body language', which is often unconsciously imitated. When you cross your legs, I cross mine; when you smile, I smile too. But there are no conventionalized leg-crossing or smiling signals identifying the specific social group that you and I belong to (whatever that may be). In language, priming is a well-recognized phenomenon; here the form (e.g. choice of vocabulary, choice of syntactic construction) of one person's utterance has been shown to be influenced, in the direction of similarity, by the form of the previous speaker's utterance (see e.g. Cleland and Pickering 2003).

Likewise, if a 'Here I am' call can be interpreted as indicating the location of a **particular** animal known to the other group-members, then again we are dealing with features of a signal that are learned, because an association between a specific call and a specific individual cannot have been coded for in the species' genes. There is no advantage in a territorial call (that warns others to keep away) to identify the particular individual signaller, although it would be advantageous to include clues to one's fighting potential, as a backup to the signal, should an intruder call the signaller's bluff. But individual identification, involving learning, could be adaptive for intragroup cohesion. 'Cotton-top tamarins produce a species-specific vocalization called a combination long call (CLC) when separated from group members. This long distance, multi-syllabic vocalization typically elicits antiphonal calls and approach behavior from conspecifics' (Egnor et al. 2006, p. 665). It might be tempting to paraphrase such a call as 'Here I am, and I'm lost'. But if the recipients of the call do not specifically recognize the individual caller, then a better paraphrase would be 'Mayday, mayday, cotton-top tamarin here lost contact'. In fact, such calls incorporate both an innate and a learned component. Tamarins give an innately specified 'Mayday, lost contact' call, which other tamarins interpret instinctively, but fellow group members learn the particular voice qualities of individuals. A human analogy would be the sound of spontaneous laughter, with no communicative intent. Because of inherited human physiology, laughter always has certain features, to which hearers often instinctively react by laughing themselves. But we can also learn to recognize **which** person is laughing, when we hear laughter. The analogy is quite close.

In some cases, the evolutionary origins of ritualized moves, such as teeth-baring preparatory to attack, can still be seen, but in other cases the origins of signals are not so transparent. For our purposes, the important things to note about all these types of signal are (1) they are all still dyadic (non-referential), just influencing the behaviour of others without being about, or referring to, any third object or event; (2) they are probably (though we don't know for sure) mostly the result of innate dispositions rather than learned behaviours; (3) they are social acts, whereby animals do things to each other; (4) the relationship between the signal and its function is largely **arbitrary**, although there may be some iconic components such as extra loudness to convey extra urgency; and (5) in some species, turn-taking weakly resembling conversational exchanges, as in duetting, has evolved.

In the last of these three properties, namely the illocutionary doing-things-to-each-other property, the arbitrariness of the signal–function relationship, and the beginning of 'conversational' turn-taking, we see some similarity with human language. The other features of human language, Intentionality or **aboutness**, and **learned** signal–meaning pairings, are absent. At the stage of the animal signals summarized here, the animals are performing pragmatic acts on each other, sometimes coordinated in pairs, getting each other to do things by mostly arbitrary signals, which they are largely innately disposed to produce and to respond to.

I take a different view from Burling (2005) on the relevance of primate communication to the origins of human language. I share with his stimulating book the emphasis on the enormous gap between any kind of animal communication and human language, and the view that elements of primate-like communication still exist in parallel with, but barely integrated into, human language. He writes:

Language, however, is organized in such utterly different ways from primate or mammalian calls and it conveys such utterly different kinds of meanings, that I find it impossible to imagine a realistic sequence by which natural or sexual selection could have converted a call system into a language. Human beings, moreover, still have a fine set of primate calls that remains quite separate from language. Primate calls have much less in common with human language than with human screams, sighs, sobs, and laughter. Our own audible cries, howls, giggles and snorts, along with our visible scowls, smiles, and stares, all belong securely to our primate heritage. They form the primate communication of the human primate. . . . We will understand more about the origins of language by considering the ways in which language differs from the cries and gestures of human and non-human primates than by looking for ways in which they are alike.   (Burling 2005, p. 16)

I agree with a lot of this, but not with the conclusion. Burling's book neglects the vital illocutionary doing-things-to-each-other property that is common to primate calls and all human utterances, and the concomitant dyadic nature of primate signalling interactions. In fact, the whole field of pragmatics, at least as linguists understand it, is neglected in Burling's book; there are no mentions of pragmatics or of speech acts, or of authors such as Austin, Searle, and Grice who pioneered the central importance of interpersonal meaning in human language. The book also tends strongly, with a few incidental reservations, to relegate primate calls to purely analogue signals. Burling writes, 'Language is digital, gesture-calls are analog' (p. 27), but qualifies this at the beginning of the next paragraph by 'Immediately, complications need to be acknowledged'. In short, I share Burling's emphasis on the huge difference in complexity between primate calls and human language, and agree that human language has some totally new kinds of component, in particular aboutness and learning of signal–meaning pairs (and of course complex syntax). But I see enough common ground between primate calls and human utterances not to give up the idea that the evolution of human language built upon the pre-existing use of arbitrary signals by animals to do things to each other. As an analogy, modern complex technology far outstrips Stone Age tools; they are about as different as modern human language is from primate calls, and there is hardly a place for stone tools of any kind in modern life. Yet modern technology could not have evolved if there had been no Stone Age. Paleolithic tools were an essential stepping stone on the way to computers, spaceships, and nanotechnology.

Human language is a unique naturally occurring case of **learned** and **arbitrary symbolic** communication, **about** objects and events in a shared external world.[4] Alongside modern human language, and accompanying it in utterances, we find elements of the kind of non-referring communication that we have just surveyed in animals. Some aspects of speech, such as speed, loudness, and pitch range, are iconically connected with the affective mood of the speaker, and these correlations are found across all languages with little variation. You can tell when a speaker is excited, even if you can't understand a word he is saying. These aspects of human language behaviour are largely unlearned, and come instinctively. They have been called 'paralanguage', implying that they do not belong to a language system proper. But this ancient paralinguistic behaviour is interwoven with the more complex language unique to humans. When

---

[4] Human language is further unique in having complex syntax; we will put the evolution of complex syntax aside until Volume 2.

humans converse, they are undeniably doing things to each other, as well as often commenting on the outside world. Some of the purely dyadic social moves made in language are signalled by learned words, such as *please*, *Hello*, and *Cheers*. The connections between these words and their functions are arbitrary. In the learning, but not in the arbitrariness, of such forms we have evolved away from the ritualized signals of animals. Defining 'language proper' as what is unique to humans, it is correct to exclude paralanguage, as we share this kind of communication with many animals, but it is probable that uniquely complex human language could not have evolved without the social ritualized doing-things-to-each-other scaffolding found in many other social species, including our nearest relatives, the primates.

6.4 GETTING THE RIGHT ENVIRONMENTAL CONDITIONS

Animals who live solitary lives don't need, and don't have the opportunity, to communicate very much. Living constantly in a group is obviously a prerequisite for developed communication. The ancestors of humans presumably lived in the right kind of groups for a rich communication system to emerge. What features of social organization favour the emergence of lively and frequent communication? From what is known about communication in other species, group size and (lack of) hierarchical structure make a contribution. Furthermore, the environmental conditions in which a species lives make a difference to their communicative habits. We'll take a brief look at each of these factors. Note that we are still just considering a dyadic, non-referring, purely illocutionary (doing-things-to-each-other) kind of communication at this stage.

6.4.1 The Physical Environment and the Communication Medium

Sound carries in the dark and through thick forest. Visual signals are no good in the dark and less effective than acoustic signals in dense jungle. Even in open savannah, visual signals require the receiver to be looking at the signaller, a requirement not imposed on vocal signals. It is not my purpose here to delve into the debate over whether the forerunners of human language were vocal or gestural.[5] The literature on animal communication is stronger on vocal signalling than on gestural signalling, although Hewes (1973) does mention some primate gestural signalling, and see a 2005 special issue on gesture in primates (Gómez 2005b; Leavens

---

[5] For some of literature on the gestural origins of human language, see Hewes (1973); Armstrong et al. (1995); Corballis (2002); Arbib (2005); MacNeilage and Davis (2005).

and Hopkins 2005; Maestripieri 2005; Pika et al. 2005). It would bolster the argument for gestural origins of human language if further widespread examples of gestural communication in animals could be found. But the literature is relatively thin on this topic, compared to that on vocal communication, due at least in part, one suspects, to the paucity of good examples from the field. Egnor et al. (2006, p. 660) attribute this relative neglect of non-vocal communication in primates to the fact that 'the analytical techniques for analyzing the [vocal] signal and testing its perceptual significance in primates are far more sophisticated than for the visual, tactile or olfactory channels'. Gesture, as opposed to vocal signals, has (at least) one great advantage: that it can be used very transparently for **pointing** at things. Pointing is the beginning of communicative referring, and I will return to this major step towards human language in the next chapter. For the present, our concern is the principled idea that ecological and social conditions correlate with the modality, amount, and quality of doing-things-to-each-other (i.e. illocutionary) communicative signals.

Facial expressions play a role in the social life of primates, and only work effectively at close range, in good light, and with the communicators facing each other. This immediately highlights a principled relationship between the medium and the typical message of a signal. Facial expressions cannot be broadcast so widely as vocal signals, and are therefore particularly appropriate to close-range communication between pairs of animals. Primate, and especially ape, faces are more complexly muscled and mobile than those of other animals, allowing considerable versatility in signalling (Huber 1931; Gómez 2004). Signalling by facial expression is common among primates; for a good survey discussion, see Hauser (1996, pp. 245–251).

6.4.2 Social Conditions

Our main interest here is to establish the principle that ecological and social conditions affect the amount and quality of social communication. Many animals give territorial calls. These, by definition, are 'antisocial', deterring further contact. Territorial calls are not a good place to look for highly developed or complex communication. We are also interested here only in the function or meaning end of communication, so details of the selection of vocal calls with different acoustic properties according to a species' typical habitat are of less interest to us here.[6]

---

[6] See Alcock (1984, pp. 453–463) for a brief survey of ecological conditions affecting characteristics of animal signals.

Ecological conditions, including availability of food and frequency of predation, strongly affect the sizes of social groups. Vast herds of herbivores graze open plains, while the carnivores that prey on them go in small packs or even alone. Sawaguchi (1992) found a correlation between the diet and social structure of anthropoid primates and their relative neocortex size (RSN), a factor playing a part in complexity of communication. '[F]rugivorous anthropoids had higher values of RSNs than folivorous anthropoids, and polygynous anthropoids had significantly higher values of RSNs than monogynous anthropoids. Furthermore, RSNs were positively correlated with the size of the troop' (p. 130). Dunbar (1996a) presents a general model of determinants of group size in primates. Neocortex size co-varies with social network size. This truth is complicated by the fact that 'in respect of neocortex size, there are as many as four statistically distinct grades within the primates (including humans).' (Kudo and Dunbar 2001, p. 711); this means that the general formula for calculating the relation between neocortex size and group size contains four different constants for the four different suborders of primates considered. In its turn, the size of groups is a factor playing a role in the evolution of communication. Dunbar (1996b) is well known for making a plausible case that group size contributes to the kind of communication that could eventually lead to language. One central inter-personal activity among primates is physical grooming. Grooming each other acts as a calming influence, defuses strife, and strengthens bonds between individuals. Primates, who typically live in smallish groups of less than 100, spend a lot of time grooming. Dunbar argues that in a group larger than this there simply would not be enough spare time for an individual to manage to physically groom all the individuals in the group with whom it is necessary to keep up a social relationship. The suggestion is that vocal communication took the place of physical grooming. Whispering 'sweet nothings' can be done to several individuals at a time. Dunbar found a correlation, across a range of species, between the size of a social group and the size of an individual's neocortex. Byrne and Corp (2004) also found a correlation between neocortex size and rate of tactical deception among primates. Taken together with Dunbar's results, this suggests that increased brain size served the function of keeping a record of an increased number of social relationships and their increased complexity.

Dunbar's theory does not actually correlate group size with complexity of a communication system, but a positive correlation exists. An early suggestion was as follows:

The structural complexity of primate vocal systems is likely to parallel inter-specific differences in the size, organization, and distribution of the social unit. For example, species with small social units, consisting of three to six individuals, as is characteristic of de Brazza's monkey (*Cercopithecus neglectus*), may require a less sophisticated vocal system for the mediation of vocal exchanges than species with large social units of a hundred or more individuals, as exhibited by talapoin monkeys (*Miopithecus talapoin*).

(Snowdon et al. 1982, p. 63)

This conjecture has now been emphatically confirmed by McComb and Semple (2005), who surveyed data on forty-two primate species, to see what correlation could be found between group size and size of vocal repertoire. For twenty species for which data was available on amount of time spent grooming, they also looked for correlations between grooming time and group size and vocal repertoire. They conclude:

[C]lear and strong relationships between social group size, grooming time and vocal repertoire size have emerged in our analyses. Independent contrast analyses revealed that evolutionary changes in repertoire are a strong predictor of both changes in group size and changes in grooming time among non-human primates. Simple cross-species comparisons also indicate strong present-day relationships between repertoire size and the two measures of sociality. It is important to note that the direction of causality cannot be inferred from correlational analyses, therefore it is not possible to say whether evolutionary increases in vocal repertoire sizes directly preceded or followed increases in levels of sociality. However, our findings are consistent with the hypothesis that the vocal communication system may facilitate (or constrain) increases in group size and levels of social bonding within primate social groups.   (McComb and Semple 2005, p. 3)[7]

These data suggest that, rather than vocal communication taking over from grooming, as Dunbar suggests, increased grooming and vocal communication co-evolved along with group size.

It is also noteworthy that of the forty-two species surveyed, the species with both the largest typical group size (125) and the largest vocal repertoire (38 calls) was the bonobos (*Pan paniscus*), the species to which Kanzi, the most successfully language-trained primate, belongs.[8] One must be cautious, however, of accepting such counts as final and definitive of

[7] Alan Grafen (personal communication) has expressed some technical statistical reservations about these conclusions, to do with an incompatibility between independent contrast analyses and simple cross-species comparisons.

[8] Data from Bermejo and Omedes (1999); data on bonobo grooming time was not available.

all bonobo signalling. Pika et al. (2005), in a study of seven subadult bonobos, captive-born and naturally raised in a zoo, found some gestures that had not been observed before, and did not find some gestures which had been observed before; and they also noted some idiosyncratic gestures used by just one animal.

A different kind of clue to the social conditions most favourable to the emergence of a language comes from a study of the rise of new modern sign languages, such as Nicaraguan Sign Language and Al-Sayyid Bedouin Sign Language (Senghas 2005). Senghas lists high group size and frequent close contact, older individuals to younger, among the 'minimal environmental social factors required to generate a language'. Although these modern sign languages arose embedded in a modern human context, these particular required factors would probably also have had a facilitating effect in the rise of the first proto-human signalling systems.

The pre-linguistic ancestors of humans probably had highly developed repertoires of vocal calls and lived in relatively large groups. Primate vocal calls (apart from the complex songs of gibbons) are all atomic, like mini-vocabularies, with each individual call paired to its social function, and with (apparently) no possibility of analysing a call into reusable constituents, as the syllables of human languages can be analysed into consonants and vowels. As the size of the vocal repertoire grows, the load on memory increases, and it becomes more advantageous to compose calls productively out of a smaller inventory of subunits. This (apart from the duetting of gibbons) has not happened in non-human primates.[9] But it is possible that the bonobo repertoire of thirty-eight calls is getting near the limit beyond which it becomes advantageous to have some kind of combinatory system to generate a larger number of calls.

Larger group size is conducive to a larger communicative repertoire, but size is not all. The nature and complexity of the social organization within a group is also important. There are nineteen species of macaque (genus *Macaca*). Maestripieri (1999) studied three species: Rhesus (*M. mulatta*), pigtail (*M. nemestrina*), and stumptail (*M. arctoides*). He investigated a possible correlation between the typical social arrangements of each species and their communicative repertoires, as shown in the observation period, and the frequency with which they communicated. He counted only gestural (non-vocal) communicative acts, although he states that 'it

---

[9] 'Duetting' is sometimes mentioned in chimpanzees, but I have not been able to find any detailed study of its structure. The chimpanzee 'pant-hoot' is sometimes said to be composed of several components (Arcadi 1996) and sometimes treated as a single unit.

seems likely that differences in vocal communication among macaque species are parallel rather than complementary to those found for their gestural communication' (p. 73). There are interesting differences in the social structures of these species, which Maestripieri located on

a continuum, with 'despotic-nepotistic' societies at one extreme and 'egalitarian-individualistic' societies at the other (Thierry, 1990). In despotic-nepotistic primate societies, the distribution of affiliative interactions (e.g. grooming) and agonistic interactions (aggression and coalition support) is strongly influenced by a linear dominance hierarchy and by kinship. In contrast, in egalitarian-individualistic societies, a strict dominance hierarchy is usually absent, strong bonds between kin are limited to those between mothers and their immature offspring, and physical and social skills play an important role in defining the individual's position in the social group.

(Maestripieri 1999, p. 57).

Rhesus macaques are near the despotic-nepotistic end of this continuum, pigtail macaques are in the middle, and stumptail macaques are near the egalitarian-individualistic end.[10]

In rhesus macaques, only 4 gestures (Bared-Teeth, Present, Mount, and Lip-Smack) were displayed with a frequency equal to or greater than one event per individual, compared with 8 gestures in pigtail macaques and 12 in stump-tail macaques. The frequency of gestures per individual was significantly different in the three species...and was higher for pigtails and stumptails than for rhesus (p < .05) Thus, pigtail macaques and especially stumptail macaques have a wider repertoire of gestures of dominance–submission and affiliation than do rhesus macaques, and they use these gestures with higher frequency.

(Maestripieri 1999, pp. 63–64)

The article is fascinating enough to quote some of its discussion even further.

The differences found in the size of the gestural repertoire and in the communication dynamics of rhesus, pigtail, and stumptail macaques are generally consistent with the characteristics of their social organization. The despotic and nepotistic features of rhesus society leave little room for complex patterns of affiliative communication and bonding. Intense affiliation and bonding

[10] Though these differences between macaque species are well known in the wild, they are not immutable. De Waal and Johanowicz (1993) put groups of rhesus and stumptail macaques together in the same living space for five months. At the end of the period, the rhesus, who had hitherto engaged in rather little reconciliation behaviour, did so as frequently as the stumptails.

patterns in pigtail macaques appear to have coevolved with complex dynamics of intragroup cooperation and with considerable social tolerance. . . .

Dominance hierarchies and nepotistic behavior have probably been a constant presence in human evolution and are still conspicuous in most contemporary human societies. In the initial stages of hominid evolution, however, an increase in group size resulting from direct intergroup competition might have intensified intragroup competition and in turn increased the need to recruit allies from beyond the boundaries of an individual's kin group or dominance class (Alexander, 1974). . . .

Interestingly, it has recently been suggested that the long hunter-gatherer phase in human evolution might have been characterized by a relatively individualistic and egalitarian lifestyle (Knauft, 1991; Boehm, 1993; Erdal and Whiten, 1994). The psychological dispositions underlying this lifestyle, including the tendencies both to dominate and to resist domination, to share and to be opportunistically selfish, and to pursue flexible and short-term strategies of cooperation with different individuals according to the circumstances, could have been important factors in molding the early human mind.
(Maestripieri 1999, pp. 72, 74)

Coussi-Korbel and Fragaszy (1995) have also argued for a correlation between egalitarian social arrangements in animals and relatively fluent communication within a group leading to cooperation and group cohesion.

The correlation between increased communication and egalitarian-individualistic social arrangements is at first heartening to liberal-minded intellectuals, but if it is assumed that the main function of communication in primate groups is negotiation of social relationships, the correlation is almost tautologous. In a society where everyone has a fixed place and knows it, no negotiation is necessary. In a looser society in which people's places can change, negotiation of social place by communication is to be expected. Nevertheless, Maestripieri's results do reinforce a widely held belief that negotiation of social life in primates is the central function of communication among primates, rather than the giving and receiving of practical information about the world, for purposes, say, of cooperation. (Liberal-minded intellectuals may be less happy to know that a large part of the brain power devoted to negotiation of social relationships among primates is used for purposes of deception—see p. 187.)

Sometimes a dichotomy is implied between explanations appealing to genetic factors affecting the phenotypes of individuals and social facts about the organization of groups. Cultural traditions and learning can indeed add information to the complex of dispositions determining an individual's behaviour. But it all happens within a biological envelope. And genetic heredity plays a role in animals' dispositions to various kinds of behaviour. This has recently been strikingly shown in experiments with transgenic voles. Alteration of a single gene transforms a vole of a naturally promiscuous species into a monogamously inclined vole.

> Prairie voles (*Microtus ochrogaster*) exhibit a monogamous social structure in nature, whereas closely related meadow voles (*Microtus pennsylvanicus*) are solitary and polygamous.... We show that a change in the expression of a single gene in the larger context of pre-existing genetic and neural circuits can profoundly alter social behaviour, providing a potential molecular mechanism for the rapid evolution of complex social behaviour.
>
> (Lim et al. 2004, p. 754)

The overall frameworks of our primate ancestors' social arrangements were largely determined by their genetic dispositions, in the environments in which they had evolved. This is not to deny that non-genetic factors, especially when learning and plasticity are increasingly involved, also determine the social arrangements of different species. In fact we will see in the next chapter that apes of the same species have very different dispositions to point to things, depending on whether they are in captivity or living in the wild, a difference entirely due to their ecological conditions, rather than to their genes.

Monogamy and polygamy are features of social organization that could conceivably be relevant to the evolution of enhanced communication. The social and mating arrangements of great ape species vary markedly.[11] Orangutans live mostly solitary lives; the longest contact is between mothers and immature offspring. This is hardly fruitful terrain for a rich communication system to develop. Gorillas live in male-dominated harem groups. There is a well-known correlation between harem-polygamous species and sexual dimorphism. In species with male-dominated harems, such as sea-lions and gorillas, the male is typically much larger than the female. In polygamous (polygynous) species, the activities of mate attraction and mate defence are often similar, if not identical. The male is at least as much concerned with scaring off the male competition as impressing an onlooking female. Beside the well-known ground-slapping behaviour, gorillas near water (Parnell and Buchanan-Smith 2001) splash violently as a display. Gorilla courtship is not elaborate, and typically consists of the female making it manifest that she is in oestrous. Harem

---

[11] See Vehrencamp and Bradbury (1984) for a detailed discussion of the theory of relationships between mating systems and ecology.

polygny does not seem conducive to enhanced communication, at least for purposes of courtship.

Just as modern great apes differ widely in their social arrangements, especially with regard to monogamy or polygamy, it seems likely that there has been an evolutionary shift from harem-polygyny in australopithecines towards the more symmetric sex roles seen among modern humans. 'Bones of australopithecines, *Australopithecus afarensis*, were unearthed near Hadar, Ethiopia. The males of some of these ancestors were nearly twice as large as the females' (Margulis and Sagan 1991, p. 14).

Male *afarensis* are much larger than females. One thing we know with confidence from other primates is that differences in body size between the sexes indicates a polygynous mating system (Clutton-Brock and Harvey, 1976). Males evolve larger because big bodies help them in male–male competition. Male and female members of monogamous primate systems, in which there is little male–male competition, tend to be about the same size. Thus Lucy was probably not living in a monogamous social system. She may have been in a harem situation, but it's equally possible that she had access to several males and that they had access to her.   (Small 1993, p. 190)

Several remains at Laetoli and Hadar exhibit notable size differences—for example, the footprints at Laetoli and the upper jaws of AL200 and AL199 at Hadar. The differences in size can be interpreted as due to sexual dimorphism (Johanson and White 1979). These size differences appear greater than those between sexes for humans today. However, the canine teeth do not appear to exhibit as pronounced dimorphism as among most living primates (Johanson and White 1979). Quite possibly, then, *A. afarensis* had already undergone some reduction of sexual dimorphism, and its descendants were to undergo even more.   (Tanner 1981, p. 190)

It is possible, given the uncertainty surounding all such ancient fossils, that the large and small specimens were not male and female members of the same species, but belonged to different species. McHenry (1996) has made a detailed study of all extant data relevant to this problem and concluded that *Australopithecus arafensis* were indeed sexually dimorphic, to a far greater degree than modern humans, but less so than gorillas; he also concludes that they were polygynous. Later in hominid evolution,

Homo erectus males were not much larger than *Homo erectus* females. *Homo erectus* was a communal species who not only gathered edible plants but hunted mammoths and used fire. Eating and sleeping together in groups— the sort of cooperative groups needed to hunt—may have made them far more social, more talkative, and better barterers than their sexually dimorphic australopithecine ancestors.   (Margulis and Sagan 1991, p. 51)

In their sexual arrangements, humans most closely resemble bonobos, mating frequently and all the year round. But humans are more monogamous, less promiscuous, than bonobos. The most commonly favoured explanation for the loss of a marked period of oestrus (high female sexual appetite) in humans involves a division of labour and increased cooperation between the sexes, co-evolving with a pressure to keep strong monogamous pair-bonds, leading to enhanced paternal investment in caring for offspring (Alcock 1984, pp. 526–527; Jolly 1985, pp. 288–298).

Both bonobos and chimpanzees live in fission–fusion societies. Migration between primate groups is rare but bonobos and chimpanzees migrate from one group to another more frequently than other primates. Whereas other primate species tend strongly to gather in groups that do not mix with others, bonobo groups occasionally get together with animals from both groups mixing freely in a party atmosphere, and females sometimes go off at the end of the 'party' with a new group. This would be a mechanism for communicative behaviours to spread, either by the spread of genetically based dispositions, or by copying and learning. Bonobo and chimpanzee group membership is more labile than that of other primate species. Bonobos and chimpanzees, more than other apes, frequently face the need to negotiate new social relationships, including sexual relationships. Bonobos, in particular, are well known for their frequent heterosexual and homosexual copulations, which act as a peace-keeping and reconciliation mechanism. Chimpanzee and bonobo society is less strictly hierarchical than, for instance, macaque society; subordinate chimpanzees sometimes take revenge on a dominant, but this is extremely rare in macaques (de Waal 1996, p. 157). The fluidity of bonobo society means that there is a relatively high amount of interpersonal communication, including a lot of communication around sex acts. It was noted earlier that bonobos have the largest number of vocal calls of all primates.

Ujhelyi (1996) proposes that it was territorial monogamy, as in gibbons, that provided the original impetus for varied vocalizations in primates. There is certainly a correlation between duetting behaviour and territorial monogamy in birds: 'Vocal duetting is a well-known and well-documented phenomenon, especially in tropical birds where males and females establish long-lasting bonds, live in forest habitats and show territorial behavior' (Deputte 1982, p. 68). (Deputte gives eleven references to back up this assertion.) Ujhelyi's suggestion is that this ability to control complex vocalizations persisted after the change in bonobos and chimpanzees to a fission–fusion society. The connection to monogamy was investigated by Geissmann (1999, p. 1005), who analysed

the changes in duet structure in two pairs of siamangs during a forced partner exchange. The duet songs of the siamangs underwent many notable changes during partner exchange. . . . After the partner exchange, new pair-specific traits occurred, some of them obviously achieved through a partner-directed effort of one or both individual(s). Moreover, the pair-bonding hypothesis appears to be one of the few biological functions suggested so far which could explain a high degree of duet-complexity as adaptive.

We are looking for possible precursors of group-wide reciprocal communicative behaviour, used by all individuals in roles of both sender and receiver. To repeat an analogy, such signals are more likely to represent the 'Stone Age' precursor[12] out of which later much more sophisticated systems of communication could have developed, by integration with non-communicative mental representational capacities, such as were discussed in Part I of this book. Social relations giving opportunity for reciprocal communication, with either party able to be sender or receiver of the same signal, are not common in ape society (though probably more common in some apes than in any other communicative species). Signals associated with mating involve individuals in different roles; the male–female relationship is not symmetric. A signal given by a male during courtship or mating may be responded to by the female, but her signal is typically not a close repeat or imitation of the male signal. Likewise, in parent–offspring interaction, the relationship is asymmetric. Male–female sexual relations and parent–infant relations are likely to be more stereotyped than the set of possible other relations between all individuals in a group. Bonobos, with their versatile hetero/homosexual behaviour, are the exception to this generalization. Play behaviour among young apes in the same group is the most symmetric, and is likely to involve genuinely shared signals. In signals used to negotiate social position (other than stereotyped sexual partnership) there is more likelihood of finding the (tiny) seeds of the kind of flexible creative ad hoc communication that we see in humans. This introduces the topic of the learning of communicative signals, which will be discussed just below, and again more extensively in the next section.

---

[12] Remember, this is just a metaphor; obviously non-human primates have not even reached the level of the human Stone Age.

6.4.3 Birth and Ontogeny

A notable bio-social feature of humans is the long period of dependency of the young on their parents, typically their mothers. Humans, more than any other primates, are born immature, and rely for much longer on support and protection from adult kin. Humans have reached 25% of their final adult brain size at birth, compared with rhesus monkeys, which have reached 50–60% of their final adult brain size at birth. Immature traits at birth are known as 'altricial', as opposed to 'precocial'. In nature there is a loose correlation (complex and with exceptions) between altriciality and a prolonged period of post-natal dependence. It is usually assumed that this altriciality of humans is related to bipedalism, with the narrowing of the pelvis, and the consequent adaptation to be born with a smaller head. Brain development was postponed in human evolution to a post-natal stage, opening the door to a far greater influence from the environment, i.e. to learning. Prolonged post-natal dependence in humans most probably led to intensified communication between mother and infant, but the more significant contribution to the evolution of language is the extended opportunity for learning communicative skills afforded to young pre-humans.

Locke and Bogin (2005) have proposed that humans evolved a distinctive four-stage ontogeny, consisting of infancy, childhood, juvenility, and adolescence, where childhood and adolescence are evolutionary innovations not seen in the life histories of apes. They speculate on the possible consequences of this evolved ontogeny, favouring the evolution of language. The new, and human-specific, stage of childhood is defined as a period after weaning (freeing the mother to have more offspring), but before the child is able to forage for itself. This entails a greater degree of child support from related adults, accompanied, it is suggested, by enhanced engagement by the child in the social life of the group. The adolescence stage is also new and human-specific, marked by a growth spurt after a period in juvenility when growth was slowing down. Adolescence affords humans a period in which to practise communication skills relating to courtship. These ideas are new and stimulating, but remain (as of 2007) fairly speculative.

Related to the evolutionary narrowing of the birth canal in human ancestors, it has been plausibly suggested by Trevathan (1987) that the added difficulties of human childbirth would have made the help of others in the role of midwives adaptive, especially in cases of breech presentation. All in all, to the extent that social consequences can be plausibly predicted from the narrowing of the birth canal, these would have been in the direction of increased social cooperation.

To summarize this section, the conditions that seem most likely to have given rise to the group-wide reciprocal social purposes for which humans use language include: large group size, relatively egalitarian-individualistic social structure, and a long period of infant (or child) dependency. There is some tension in this regard between fission–fusion structure, which is likely to spread learned behaviour between groups, and long-term monogamy, which involves long-term cooperation between non-kin and doubled parental investment in dependent offspring. The evolutionary trajectory of modern humans has probably led us from gorilla-like harem social arrangements of australopithecines to social arrangements which fluctuate between chimpanzee-like fission–fusion and gibbon-like[13] monogamy. Among primates, captive bonobos have shown the greatest disposition towards human-like communicative behaviour, and gibbons exhibit the most complex vocal displays, associated with duetting by male–female pairs. Both species, of course, are still far from humans in their communicative capacities.

6.5 FROM INNATE TO LEARNED

In the preceding sections, the shadow of learned behaviour has been looming. It is an oversimplification to classify **any** behaviour as 100% innate or 100% learned. All behaviour is the outcome of the interaction of the genes and the environment. A clear example comes from the learned songs of songbirds:

The developing avian brain is *not* an acoustic sponge that accepts all song material for use in subsequent production. Rather, there appears to be a blueprint (Thorpe 1959) that guides young birds to select the conspecific song from among different songs in the environment. The innate template, in contrast, appears to provide a reference for the feedback control of song development in the absence of an external model (Konishi, 1965b; Konishi, 1965a; Konishi, 1985).   (Hauser 1996 p. 278)

The communicative acts we have surveyed, by which animals do things to each other socially, are largely instinctive, that is automatic responses

---

[13] Kathleen Gibson has pointed out to me that gibbon monogamy is actually quite different from human monogamy in that adult gibbons forcibly evict their own offspring when they reach sexual maturity, and gibbons have nothing like the extended family structure found in modern humans.

to circumstances, not obviously the outcome of any formative experience. But recognition of individuals was also mentioned, as was recognition of group membership, which cannot have been completely coded in the genes. Nevertheless, even with individual and group-specific signals, many of their properties are also characteristic of the species as a whole, and beyond variation by individuals or groups. Learning takes place within a biological envelope.

Communicative signals specific to one social group, as opposed to a whole species, and widely used within that group, are indicative of learning. Tomasello (1990 p. 299) surveyed signals from two wild and three captive groups of chimpanzees, identifying as many as nine signals in two of the groups that were not observed in any of the other groups. (These two groups did not overlap in their unique signals, either.) An example is the 'head tip' gesture used in the Gombe, and only in that group (of the five surveyed), to convey aggression. The functions of these signals were all of the doing-things-to-each-other sort that we are concerned with in this chapter: aggression, sex, submission, feeding another, grooming, care-giving, and play. Clearly, quite a lot of learning of such signals happens in these groups. 'Learning', however, is a broad label, and only certain kinds of learning are conducive to the spread of arbitrary, reciprocally used signals that are characteristic of human language. Let's have a closer look at non-human primate learning of communicative acts.

Within learning, a two-way distinction is common, between individual (or associative) learning and social (or observational) learning. As we are concerned with the possible learning of elements of communication, the learning we are interested in is necessarily social, because communication is social. It will be useful to distinguish also among **ontogenetic ritualiza-tion** and **imitation** and **emulation**. The classification shapes up like this:

Individual/associative learning: learning what action brings what effect, as when a pigeon learns from its own experience that pressing the left-hand bar brings a food reward. A social example would be learning by experience that a particular facial grimace (not copied from someone else) tends to elicit laughter.

Ontogenetic ritualization (often equated with conventionalization): here the learned action, and the reaction of another animal to it, both become stereotyped. A classic example is the 'nursing poke' where a baby chimpanzee starts by pushing his mother's arm aside to get at the nipple; after a while, the mother learns to raise her arm when he goes to move it, and the baby learns that he only has to touch her side to get the required effect. This kind of learning shares with (second-person) imitation the social feature of interaction with another person. Both parties learn, but the roles are asymmetric, as in the baby/mother example given. A well-known human example is the two-arm-raising action of a human toddler asking to be picked up, arising from raising the arms earlier in life to help a parent lift it (Lock 1978). I cannot resist mentioning a nineteenth century experimental replication of this effect, called *schematization of action* by J. C. Gómez:

> Thorndike (1898) found that cats that were released from a puzzle-box upon performance of an arbitrarily chosen action (e.g., licking their paw), instead of by the accidental activation of the releasing device, tended to develop an abridged, sketched-out version of the relevant behaviour—something like a 'gesture' of paw-licking.' (Gómez 2005b, p. 93)

Emulation (to be distinguished from imitation): an animal observes the actions of another, and the typical effects, then carries out some action which achieves the same goal as the observed action, but is not necessarily a close imitation of the observed action. Example: seeing your mother cut paper into strips with scissors, which you emulate by tearing the paper into strips.

Imitation learning: imitating more or less precisely the action of another animal. Example: you stick out your tongue and a human baby sticks out her tongue too. (Meltzoff 1988).

Second-person imitation: imitating an act performed at you, as the addressee.

Third-person imitation: imitating an act performed by someone else to someone else.

Both types of imitation are less 'intelligent' than emulation, involving no calculation of cause and effect.[14]

The term 'emulation' is due to Wood (1988) and I believe the term 'ontogenetic ritualization' is due to Michael Tomasello. Whiten et al. (2004) survey the literature on 'aping' by apes. They argue that there are intermediate cases between imitation and emulation, and indeed different types of emulation. Among apes, there is more emulation than pure imitation, and both kinds of copying occur much more readily when the demonstrator is a human trainer than spontaneously among apes

---

[14] If you can't immediately see a cause–effect relationship, then often doing the dumb thing (imitating others) is the rational thing to do (Andy Whiten, personal communication).

themselves. None of the work surveyed, however, involves the copying of clearly communicative behaviours.

Our target is to find the seeds in animals' learning of communication of the kind of learned behaviour seen in human language. What kind of learning, within the above classification, is involved when humans learn vocabulary?[15] To the extent that, for example, submission gestures in animals are still iconic, they could be learned by emulation. That is, a young animal might see that cowering deflects an imminent attack, conjecture that rolling over could achieve the same effect, and try rolling over as a submissive gesture. This is unlikely, as submission gestures are largely innately determined. However, we are looking for the emergence of signals with an **arbitrary**, non-iconic, non-indexical, and not physically causal, relationship to their function. This eliminates learning by emulation as a candidate precursor to the human ability to acquire vocabulary. If you observe someone successfully open a door by saying 'Open, Sesame', you cannot figure out any other way of getting the same effect, because the relationship between the utterance and its effect is arbitrary.

We are, furthermore, looking for the potential origins of **reciprocal** signals, that can be used by any individual either as sender or as receiver. This tends to eliminate ontogenetic ritualization, as the classic cases of this kind of learning are in socially asymmetric situations, such as mother–infant interactions. Tomasello (1990, p. 297), in an excellently careful and informative article on the possibility of cultural transmission in chimpanzees, reports a study in which '8 out of 28 signal types were one-way signals; that is, they involved social functions that were solicited by youngsters from adults, but not vice versa. For example, adults never begged food or tickling from a youngster (nor did youngsters use these with each other).' Tomasello also notes that signals used at one stage in a chimpanzee's life, for example, in infancy, are often not used at another stage, for example, because the animal has grown up, and no longer needs specific infant-to-mother signals. The very process of ontogenetic ritualization involves a somewhat protracted history of interaction between two individuals, during the course of which both actors gradually adjust and abbreviate or stereotype their respective actions to accommodate each other. It would not be possible, in a large social group, for each individual to participate in such a history of interaction with all the others, so ontogenetic ritualization as a direct source of group-wide arbitrary

---

[15] I put aside the acquisition of syntax for the moment, it being too far away from the animal examples we have so far discussed.

learned illocutionary signals, like English *Hello* and *Bye*, is unlikely. Chris Knight agrees:

> The nursing poke has no prospect of becoming circulated beyond the specific mother–infant relationship in which it first emerges. Each mother–infant dyad must re-invent the wheel, as it were, arriving independently at its own idiosyncratic version of the poke. Destined to survive only until that particular infant is weaned, each such token, correspondingly, has no prospect of becoming a cultural replicator or meme. . . .
>
> [Such] conventional signals will be confined within isolated, restricted pockets of social space where sufficient trust momentarily prevails. In their capacity as incipient memes, therefore, such signals lack prospects of achieving immortality. They may evolve, but without leaving any descendants. Consequently, neither linguistic nor more general symbolic cultural evolution can get under way.   (Knight 2002, p. 148)

(We will return to Knight's important emphasis on mutual trust in later chapters.)

This leaves imitation. Tomasello (1990)'s only candidate for this kind of learning among chimpanzees is the 'throw stuff' gesture used to attract attention to the signaller. He reports a longitudinal study (Tomasello et al. 1989) in which all seven juvenile chimpanzees in a group had acquired a 'throw stuff' behaviour as a way of attracting attention to themselves. In the early phase of the study, this behaviour was absent; it seems to have been invented after the introduction of woodchips into the compound, and then generalized by the chimpanzees to throwing any loose material, using any action: overarm, underarm, or backhand. After discussion, Tomasello concludes that this is more likely to have been a case of emulation, rather than imitation, although the restriction to throwing stuff does indicate an imitative element.

Myowa-Yamakoshi et al. (2004) have shown that newborn chimpanzees do imitate some facial expressions (tongue protrusion and mouth opening), just as Meltzoff and Moore (1977, 1983) showed that newborn human babies do. They conclude that 'the capacity for neonatal imitation is a characteristic that is common to humans and chimpanzees. However, the ability to imitate a broad range of whole-body actions or facial expressions is probably an attribute that evolved after the human lineage separated from that of chimpanzees' (p. 441). The instinct to imitate is shared by humans and chimpanzees, but humans have developed it further. It is also evident that latent imitative dispositions in chimpanzees are drawn out more readily in captivity than in the wild. The imitation of facial gestures is communicative only in a basic sense. The infant (human or chimp) communicates some empathy with the imitatee. But nothing more than this is communicated. Imitation of facial gestures can be said to show that a channel for communication is open, but no actual messages pass through the channel.

The overall conclusion is that there is some learning of communicative signals in wild chimpanzees, but not of the kind, as Tomasello and Knight rightly point out, that could lead to the kind of group-wide reciprocal signalling characteristic of humans.[16] Knight also introduces the theme of trust and motivation, to which we will return.

So, have we reached yet another dead end in our search for precursors of human language? I don't think so; here's why. Learning, of whatever kind, is **one small step** in the human direction from largely genetically determined signals. Apes, and especially chimpanzees and bonobos, exhibit greater plasticity of behaviour, including communicative behaviour, than other primates. Apes, compared to other non-human primates, are ace learners.

Just being able to learn communicative behaviours is not the single step that takes us from pre-human to human. There is no such single step. A lot of elements of behaviour had to come together to give us human language. Richard Shillcock (personal communication) said, 'Chimps have a motivation problem'. Note that emulation, as opposed to imitation, as characterized above, is well motivated. The emulator can see what he is likely to get out of an action. But why imitate? What does the baby, in sticking out its tongue in imitation of an adult, get out of it? A reassuring smile at best, but that doesn't compare in stark evolutionary terms with the practical nourishing result that a chimpanzee gets from emulating its parent fishing for termites. Imitation is in a clear sense less 'intelligent' than emulation, which involves some calculation of specific causes and effects. Humans with autistic spectrum disorder are well known to perform poorly in imitating actions (see Williams et al. 2004 for a review).

Interestingly, Horner and Whiten (2005) have shown that children deploy a less 'intelligent' strategy than chimpanzees in solving a problem involving retrieving an object from a box. The subjects were shown how to get the object in a demonstration which included some causally irrelevant actions. Where it was clear how to retrieve the object, the chimpanzees cut straight to the chase, and extracted it without repeating the causally irrelevant actions. The children, on the other hand, imitatively went through

[16] Pika et al. (2003, p. 95) reach a similar conclusion for gorillas: 'Ontogenetic ritualization is the main process involved, but some form of social learning may also be responsible for the acquisition of special gestures.'

all the motions of the original demonstration, including the causally irrelevant ones. The authors suggest 'the difference in performance of chimpanzees and children may be due to a greater susceptibility of children to cultural conventions' (p. 164). A language, of course, is the paramount instance of a set of cultural conventions. But we are constantly reminded that the chimpanzee/human difference is a matter of degree, for Whiten et al. (2005) have shown that some chimpanzees who had discovered their own method of solving a practical problem 'nevertheless went on to match the predominant approach of their companions, showing a conformity bias that is regarded as a hallmark of human culture' (p. 737).

Chimpanzees, sensibly enough, can't see as much point as children in pure imitation for its own sake, with no immediate reward. We can safely assume, however, that human infants, with their strong instinctive urge to imitate (Meltzoff and Moore 1977, 1983), are not wasting their energy. The energy used in imitation by infants is a kind of long-term investment, or, in an alternative metaphor, the price of an entry ticket into a game played with arbitrary symbols. Children do not, of course, make any conscious calculation about the ultimate benefits of imitation. If there is a goal at all (and it is surely not conscious), it is to achieve some kind of immediate empathic bonding with the adult who is being imitated. Human children are nature's first, and so far only, beneficiaries of the 'discovery' by genetic evolution of an imitative behaviour leading to the building of learned conventional arbitrary symbolic codes.   How?

It is easy to see what chimpanzees get out of the kind of learning they are good at. Monkeys and apes, and especially chimpanzees, live in highly political societies, as emphasized in much recent work (e.g. Byrne and Whiten Byrne and Whiten 1988; de Waal de Waal 1998). The phrase 'Machiavellian intelligence' has been aptly applied to primate social life.   )
Here are some examples:

Ten years of observation by Toshisada Nishida and his colleagues, of Ntologi, the alpha male of Mahale, shows that the patterns of sharing can be complex (Nishida et al. 1992). Ntologi did not share with young males rising in the dominance hierarchy, nor with the beta-male; in other words, he avoided sharing with any animal who presented a threat to his high status. It was not a matter of personalities or grudges: when one beta-male dropped in rank, then Ntologi began to share meat with him.'   (Byrne 1995, p. 200)

Beside the well-recognized importance of dominance hierarchies in primate societies, de Waal (1998, p. 207) emphasizes the importance of a second layer: a network of positions of influence. . . . [I]ndividuals losing a top rank certainly do not fall into oblivion: they are still able to pull many strings. In the same way, an individual rising in rank and at first sight appearing to be the big boss does not automatically have the greatest say in all matters.

Neocortex size is directly related to the Machiavellian aspects of primate social life: 'We show that the use of deception within the primates is well predicted by the neocortical volume' (Byrne and Corp 2004, p. 1). Picking up the theme of deception, one further quotation gives the flavour of monkey and ape politics, and mentions a factor, namely the directing of attention, that we will pick up in the next chapter:

Although the insight necessary to *plan* or *understand* deception seems to be restricted to great apes, monkeys *use* deception often, apparently learning the tactics from lucky coincidences by the trial and error of conditioning [i.e. individual/associative learning, JRH]. . . . The tricks are many and various. Most concern the manipulation of attention (Whiten and Byrne, 1988), where an animal's focus of attention is shifted towards or away from just what will most profit the agent of the deceit.   (Byrne 1995, p. 203)

All the studies cited above were of colonies of wild or semi-wild chimpanzees. In these circumstances, genuine cases of learning by imitation are certainly extremely rare, compared to humans. Yet captive bonobos, including the famous Kanzi, can learn by third-person imitation. Kanzi observed his mother being taught lexigrams (without success). Later he showed that he had mastered many of the form-meaning pairings that his mother had failed to learn, and began, to his keepers' surprise, to use them. Kanzi was not a member of a large colony of conspecifics. Many of his social fellows were humans.

Monkeys and apes in their natural groups are wily, scheming, competitive creatures, constantly on the lookout for their own advantage. In their natural habitats, they learn large inventories of contingent facts about the particular individuals in their group, regularly updating these mental databases to keep track of shifting alliances, the rise and fall of rivals, and who mates with whom. They deploy this learned knowledge productively in social manipulation that is directly advantageous to them. This manipulation involves a lot of communication, but of a kind that falls short of what would be required to get human-like language up and running. The very move from largely innate signals to learned signals is a step in the human direction, but at least one ingredient is missing, and I have suggested, following Chris Knight, that this has to do with **trust**, a topic that will be taken up in Chapter 9.

CHAPTER SEVEN

Going Triadic: Precursors of Reference

Dyadic communication involves only two creatures: a sender and a receiver of a message. Such communication is not **about** anything external to the sender and the receiver. It is just a matter of one animal or person doing something to another, like greeting it, or threatening it, or submitting to it. This kind of communication is widespread in the animal kingdom. We now turn to **triadic** communication, where the message-sender communicates to a receiver about some third entity, an object or event in the outside world. This chapter, therefore, will start to discuss the origins of **reference** in communication.

The qualification 'in communication' is necessary, because, as I argued in Part I of this book, reference in its most basic, original form exists before communication. When an animal contemplates in solitude some object, scene, or event, the animal's brain is in a certain state characteristic of attention to that particular object, scene, or event. This brain state, I argued, refers (in a non-communicative way) to whatever in the outside world is being attended to. Thus the key psychological factor relating to reference is **attention**. We have seen in the previous chapter how animals manipulate each other. Here we get more specific, and investigate the ways in which animals manipulate each other's attention to things in the world outside them.

7.1 EARLY MANIPULATION OF ATTENTION

As mentioned briefly in the last chapter, apes can track and manipulate the attention of others. On gaze-following in apes, there is unanimity among researchers. All great ape species follow gaze to distant locations and around barriers (Bräuer et al. 2005; see also Povinelli et al. 2003; Povinelli and Eddy 1997). Bräuer et al. (2005)'s experiments were with apes following human gaze. Tomasello et al. (1998) also showed that five species of primates (chimpanzees, sooty mangabeys, and three species of macaques) follow the gaze of conspecifics. 'Individuals from all species reliably followed the gaze of conspecifics, looking to the food about 80% of the time in experimental trials, compared with about 20% of the time in control trials' (Tomasello et al. 1998, p. 1063). Anderson and Mitchell (1999, p. 17) 'compared the propensity of lemurs (*Eulemur macaco*) and macaques (*Macaca arctoides*) to engage in VCO [visual co-orientation], defined as turning to look in the same direction as another individual whose focus of attention changes. The macaques consistently showed VCO whereas the lemurs showed no such response.' This study used humans as the 'other' individuals. Perhaps lemurs are more responsive to their own species. Scerif et al. (2004) have shown that Diana monkeys can follow the gaze of familiar conspecifics, even from such artificial stimuli as photographs of the conspecific gazer. Domestic goats also follow the gaze of humans and conspecifics (Kaminski et al. 2005), but goats have not been tested for gaze-following around barriers. (These last authors found that goats, besides being good at following eyegaze, were also quite good at detecting the location of a desired object by following human pointing, like other domesticated species. Locating an object after seeing pointing is a separate topic from following eyegaze, and is taken up in the next section.)

It is sometimes suggested that the prominence of the selera (white of the eye) in humans, as opposed to other species, helps in gaze-following. Clearly there is some truth in this; see Kobayashi and Kohshima (1997); Emery (2000); Ricciardelli et al. (2000); Symons et al. (2004) for some recent work on human sclerae in relation to gaze-following. But animals with less prominent sclerae[1] can use head orientation as a clue to gaze direction. The subject is complicated by the fact that animals of some species, such as orangutans, avoid looking each other directly in the face, and so must usually do gaze-following covertly (see Kaplan and Rogers 2002).

Is gaze-following 'merely' an automatic response, or does it involve some calculation of the gazer's reasons for looking where he is looking? Both. Bräuer et al. (2005) compare an 'orienting-response' model with a 'perspective-taking' model. It is important to notice that these are not strict alternatives. The perspective-taking model **includes** an initial step of an orienting response. Emery (2000) discusses the hypothesis that

[1] See http://www.sciences.une.edu.au/zoology/docs/orangposter.pdf for some good pictures of orangutans looking sideways, and showing some eye-white. (This website was still active on 23/08/2006.)

gaze-following is 'hardwired' in the brain, and may be localized within a circuit linking the superior temporal sulcus, amygdala, and orbitofrontal cortex.

There are regions in the monkey and human brain which contain neurons that respond selectively to faces, bodies and eye gaze. The ability to follow another individual's gaze direction is affected in individuals with autism and other psychopathological disorders, and after particular localized brain lesions.

(Emery 2000, p. 581)

This situation is very reminiscent of the dorsal/ventral separation, discussed in Part I of this book (Chapter 4.2). One mechanism in the brain delivers a fast orienting response, allowing other mechanisms in the brain to carry out other, more 'calculating' operations, which are also, in humans, more accessible to conscious report. Bräuer et al. (2005) argue convincingly in favour of a perspective-taking mechanism in primate gaze-following. That is, the animals not only instinctively follow eyegaze, but are also able to behave in calculating ways, depending on what they find on following gaze. Evidence includes facts such as the following:

Call, Hare, and Tomasello (1998) found in their study that when a chimpanzee tracked the gaze of a human to a location and found nothing interesting there, they quite often looked back to the individual's face and tracked their gaze direction a second time (the so-called *double looks*). . . .

On observing a human experimenter repeatedly looking up into empty space, adult chimpanzees, but not infant chimpanzees, habituated and stopped responding. This may suggest that adults can overwrite the orienting response because they know that there is actually nothing unusual to look at, whereas infants are more tightly controlled by the orienting response.

(Bräuer et al. 2005, pp. 145–146)

Active manipulation of attention happens in at least two ways, positively or negatively, and as a cross-cutting dimension, the attention of the other animal can relate to the actor itself, or to some strategic third object or place.

As for examples of 'positive' attention-drawing to oneself, Whiten et al. (1999) list five attention-getting actions observed in various wild chimpanzee colonies: knuckle-knocking, sapling branch-bending and releasing, branch-slapping, noisy stem-pulling, and squashing shrub stems underfoot. In captivity, chimpanzees show awareness of the target individual's state. Thus, they use sounds to attract the attention of someone (human or chimpanzee) facing away from them, and visual gestures to draw the attention of someone already facing them (Bodamer and Gardner 2002; Leavens et al. 2004). The purpose of such attention-getting is usually to initiate some activity like play ('Come on, let's play'), to be included in some activity such as feeding ('Hey, let me in, too'), or to issue a warning. Gómez (2005a) describes experiments with captive chimpanzees, in which three out of six initiated attention-getting behaviours when ignored by a normally attentive human. The three chimps who did not show attention-getting behaviour 'were those with less experience of humans in their early years' (p. 71). Despite these mixed results, Gómez concludes that 'available evidence suggests that chimpanzees can not only detect attention contact but also actively provoke it in a strategic way' (p. 71). We have already mentioned sexual advertisement signals, which can also be counted as attention-getting signals.

As for negative manipulation of attention, distracting or keeping attention away from oneself, the most obvious case is hiding, or hiding what one is doing.

As an illustrative example of the use of such tactical deception by primates, consider the predicament of a female prevented by a dominant male from contact with a younger male. This may not be in her interests, and she has various options. She may carefully manage to become separated from the bulk of the group, alone with the younger male. . . . Sound can still reveal what is happening, and she additionally may travel especially quietly . . . or inhibit loud copulation calls that are usually a reliable indicator of mating in some species.   (Byrne and Whiten 1992, p. 613)

This is manipulation of attention, but not by signalling; rather it is by lack of any attention-drawing action.

7.2 INDEXICAL/DEICTIC POINTING

So far, this kind of signalling, or non-signalling, is still dyadic, not involving any third entity besides, the signaller (or non-signaller) and the addressee. But it shows an essential ingredient of one kind of triadic communication, namely the manipulation of an addressee's attention. Negative examples of triadic attention manipulation, away from strategic objects, again come from the literature on tactical deception. A common type of example is an animal, on noticing food in the presence of others, acting nonchalantly as if they have not noticed it, so that the attention of the other animals will not be attracted to it. Byrne and Whiten (1992) classify this as 'concealment by inhibiting interest in object'. Another class is 'concealment by hiding an object'. A much-cited case involving both these types of concealment is described by Menzel (1974): here Belle, a female chimpanzee, tired of losing food to a dominant male, Rock, would sit on the food, hiding it, until Rock left. The case is further interesting, because Rock realized what was going on after a few episodes, and developed a counterdeception strategy of shoving her aside, when he suspected that she was hiding food. Thereupon, Belle negatively manipulated his attention in a different way, by not approaching the food so closely, whereupon Rock started to search the area around her.[2]

Of course, the kind of attention manipulation that eventually paves the way for reference in language is **positive**, drawing the attention of another creature to some object, scene, or event in the surroundings. This typically requires some cooperative relationship between the animals, and interestingly such cooperative positive manipulation of another's attention **to** a third entity is rare, if even found at all in non-human primates in the wild. Wild primates, being at least as often competitive rather than cooperative with each other, frequently act to draw other creatures' attention **away** from objects. The most common cooperative triadic act is food-sharing. Not all food-sharing is active giving; sometimes it is more a case of just not defending the food, so that others can 'share' it. In other cases, when an ape or monkey more deliberately gives a piece of meat to another, the giver is in some sense simultaneously attending to both the recipient and the meat-lump. But such giving is very rare in primates, even from mothers to infants, and in any case it is barely communication 'about' the food.

7.2.1 Begging and Pointing in Animals

A more communicative triadic act than food-giving is begging for food. This needs to be distinguished from simply reaching for food, which is not communicative. A criterion for begging is simultaneous management of attention to the giver and to the desired object. Diagnosing such dual attention in the animal involves seeing where it is looking. If the animal looks back and forth between the object and the face of the other animal, while gesturing towards the object, this 'gaze alternation' is taken as a sign that it is monitoring the attention of the other animal to the object of shared attention, and therefore begging, rather than merely reaching. Chimpanzees sometimes beg for objects other than food, such as a tool, paying the same kind of attention to the attitude of the human with the tool (Russell et al. 2005).

---

[2] This example of a deception/counterdeception arms race is also quoted in full in Byrne (1995).

Gómez (2005b) gives a thorough survey of begging and requesting gestures in monkeys and apes, addressing the question of the extent to which such gestures can be considered referential. Apes seem on the whole to beg more than monkeys. Such begging behaviour has been observed in a captive hand-reared gorilla (Gómez 1990, 1991, 1992), in captive chimpanzees (Leavens and Hopkins 1998), and in captive orangutans and bonobos (Gómez 1996). As in the case of dyadic attention-drawing, begging apes in particular are sensitive to the attentive posture of a human giver. Liebal et al. (2004) found that apes requesting food from a human would move around to the front of the person if he or she were facing away from the ape. Chimpanzees and bonobos were better at this than gorillas and orangutans. But Povinelli et al. (2003) present careful experimental evidence that begging chimpanzees do not do a careful calculation of whether the relevant human can see them or not. For instance, in the presence of two human experimenters, one with her back to the chimp but looking over her shoulder with open eyes towards him, and the other facing the chimp but with eyes shut, the chimp begged towards the experimenter with eyes shut. Povinelli et al. (2003)'s other experiments showed that begging chimpanzees have a clear preference for begging from someone whose body is facing them, but this does not extend to a more detailed consideration of whether that person can in fact see them; for instance, chimps begged as much from experimenters facing them with their hands over their eyes as from experimenters facing them with eyes open and uncovered.

The results of this extended series of studies suggested that despite their natural use of the begging gesture, and despite their interest in the eyes and gaze direction of others, chimpanzees do not, in fact, understand a key aspect of these gestures—namely, that the gestures must be seen by the recipients in order for the gesture to function. In contrast, by 2 years of age, young children seem to understand this aspect of seeing (Lempers et al. 1977; Povinelli and Eddy 1996). (Povinelli et al. 2003, pp. 58–59)

Note that all these observations involved captive animals. Captive animals address begging gestures to humans much more than wild animals do to each other in their free state. This indicates that the animals have learnt certain characteristic human, and uncharacteristically ape- or monkey-like, ways in captivity. Life in the zoo mostly involves being fed by a human, rather than foraging on your own. Captive animals expect humans to feed them. Such generosity is much less common in wild troops, occurring most frequently from mothers to their infants. And the relationship between a captive adult primate and its human keeper is not unlike the wild infant–mother relationship. So adult monkeys and apes in captivity can **learn** begging gestures, or resurrect their natural infantile begging gestures.

Begging is communicative, whereas mere reaching is not. We now need to make another distinction, between 'imperative' begging and 'declarative' pointing.[3] Imperative begging involves trying to get something for oneself, by enlisting the help of someone else—'Give me that!' Declarative pointing involves drawing someone's attention to an object with no desire to get it—'Look at that!' Pointing is in many circumstances more disinterested than begging, and perhaps even altruistic or cooperative. A reasonable operational criterion to tell whether an animal is begging for something or pointing to it is the practical availability of the object involved. If the object is within reach of the addressee, but not the gesturer, and the addressee could easily get the object and pass it to the gesturer, the gesturer could well be begging (though we can't know for certain). If, on the other hand, the object is practically out of reach of the addressee, and furthermore if the addressee had not been previously attending to it, it seems likely that the gesturer is pointing. (Note, linguists, how these criteria closely match the felicity conditions on speech acts, such as requesting (Austin 1962; Searle 1969, 1979). Possibly in the act of pointing, less monitoring of the other animal's gaze is involved than in an act of begging.

The distinction between begging and pointing is not always carefully respected, and furthermore we enter here an area in which there is some factual disagreement among researchers. I will try to separate out the nuggets of agreement. Three parameters (in part already mentioned) are important:

- a dimension with different species ranged along it,[4] from monkeys through apes, with chimpanzees and bonobos near the end of the axis, and humans at the extreme;

---

[3] The imperative/declarative terminology is common in the literature on pointing, and I will keep to it here for convenience. But these terms invoke certain incorrect presuppositions which I will explain towards the end of this section, when we get to the relation between ape pointing and human baby pointing.

[4] This 'species dimension' is not intended to portray the idea, outdated since Darwin, of a *scala naturae*, or ladder of nature, with each successive species 'improving' on the previous one. As our interest is in specifically human capacities, this dimension reflects nothing more than similarity to humans in species' pointing-like behaviour, which happens to correlate approximately with genetic closeness to humans. See Donald (2001, pp. 113–117) for a discussion of the *scala naturae* in the light of modern knowledge and a quest for what makes us human.

- an environmental dimension from wild, through non-home-reared captive, to home-reared captive animals;
  - in a captive environment, whether the animal is interacting with a human or with a conspecific.

Reporting on Blaschke and Ettlinger (1987)'s experiments with rhesus macaques, Gómez writes, 'on the one hand the monkeys needed a lot of training [an average of 428 trials] to point; on the other, some spontaneously produced joint attention behaviours, and the training was transferred to comprehension' (Gómez, 2005b, p. 95). By contrast, Leavens et al. (2005, p. 185) write that 'pointing emerges spontaneously, without explicit training, in captive chimpanzees. Because pointing is so commonplace in captive chimpanzees and virtually absent in wild chimpanzees, and because both captive and wild chimpanzees are sampled from the same gene pool, pointing by captive apes is attributable to environmental influences on communicative development.' Leavens (2004, p. 388) gives a helpful table, which is worth reproducing in full (Table 7.1. on p. 213).

The 'insufficient data' reported in Table 7.1 for chimpanzees in the wild is in dispute:

There is no convincing evidence that natural populations of chimpanzees (i.e. chimpanzees with only marginal contact with humans) display the pointing gesture. Plooij (1978) conducted an analysis of the communicative gestures of young chimpanzees at Gombe and reported no evidence for the appearance of the gesture. Furthermore, neither of the two major long-term studies of the natural history of chimpanzees (which have each spanned nearly 40 years) have reported the presence of the pointing gesture in chimpanzees (Goodall, 1986; Nishida, 1970).   (Povinelli et al. 2003, p. 41).

Despite some disagreements in the literature, it is fairly clear that, as we move along the feral→home-reared scale, and also along the species dimension from monkeys through great apes to humans, declarative[5] pointing increases. Obviously more data need to be collected in the wild, though that will not be easy. Apes do point, in captivity, as Leavens et al. (2005) demonstrate. It is clear that the pointing in captivity is not just 'reaching', because it is sensitive to the presence of people who could help the chimpanzees get the food, and therefore is at least somewhat

---

[5] I stick to the term *declarative*, since it is used by Leavens and other authors, but an act of pointing in order to attract the attention of an onlooker to some object does not have the force of a human declarative sentence. The adoption of terminology from one discipline by another can cause misunderstanding.

Table 7.1 Phylogenetic patterns in manual deixis.

	Characteristics of pointing	
	Imperative?	Declarative?
Humans		
Western civilization, Japan (*Homo sapiens*)[a]	Yes	Yes
Autism[b]	Yes	Rare
Great apes (captive, language-trained or home-reared)		
Chimpanzees (*Pan troglodytes*)[c]	Yes	Yes
Bonobos (*Pan paniscus*)[d]	Yes	Yes
Gorillas (*Gorilla gorilla*)[e]	Yes	Yes
Orangutans (*Pongo pygmaeus*)[f]	Yes	Yes
Great apes (captive, neither language-trained nor home-reared)		
Chimpanzees (*Pan troglodytes*)[g]	Yes	No
Bonobos (*Pan paniscus*)[h]	Yes	No
Gorillas (*Gorilla gorilla*)[i]	No	No
Orangutans (*Pongo pygmaeus*)[j]	Yes	N/A
Great apes (feral, in natural habitats)		
Chimpanzees (*Pan troglodytes*)[k]	N/A	N/A
Bonobos (*Pan paniscus*)[l]	N/A	Yes
Gorillas (*Gorilla gorilla*)	N/A	N/A
Orangutans (*Pongo pygmaeus*)	N/A	N/A
Monkeys (captive)		
Rhesus macaque (*Macaca mulatta*)[m]	Yes	N/A
Capuchin (*Cebus apella*)[n]	Yes	N/A
Monkeys (feral, in natural habitats)	No reports of pointing to date	

Notes: N/A = insufficient data. Representative references: [a](Bates et al. 1987); [b](Baron-Cohen et al. 1996); [c](Gardner and Gardner 1971; Kellogg and Kellogg 1933; Savage-Rumbaugh 1986); [d](Savage-Rumbaugh et al. 1998); [e](Bonvillian and Patterson 1999); [f](Call and Tomasello 1994; Furness 1916; Miles 1990); [g](Leavens and Hopkins 1998; Leavens et al. 1996; Leavens et al. 2004); [h](Savage-Rumbaugh et al. 1977); [i](Pika et al. 2003; Tanner and Byrne 1999); [j](Call and Tomasello 1994); [k](Inoue-Nakamura and Matsuzawa 1997); [l](Veá and Sabater-Pi 1998); [m](Hess et al. 1993); [n](Mitchell and Anderson 1997).
Source: Leavens (2004, p. 388).

calculating of the attention of other creatures. Leavens et al. (2005, p. 185) report that 'Between 41% and 71% of chimpanzees in our studies point to unreachable food, with sample sizes ranging from 29 to 115 subjects.' (So between 59% and 29% of the chimpanzees didn't point, or weren't observed pointing.)

The important parameter missing from these summaries is whether the addressees are ever **conspecifics**. Tomasello et al. (2005, p. 685) write: 'Apes do not point, show or even actively offer things to conspecifics.' Butterworth comes the same conclusion: 'on the evidence to date, only humans use the pointing gesture declaratively to share attention with conspecifics' (2003, p. 29) Contrast these statements with:

Savage-Rumbaugh (1986) reported 37 instances in which Sherman and Austin, two language-trained chimpanzees, pointed in communication between themselves. What distinguishes Sherman and Austin from most other captive apes is that they were explicitly raised in a food-sharing culture; that is, they were trained to share and to take turns from an early age. Hence, they were often placed in experimental circumstances in which their training required them to await the actions of the other. In these circumstances, they frequently pointed, apparently to draw the attention of the other to the correct response, or to items of fallen food'.   (Leavens, 2004, p. 399).

The only evidence of chimpanzees pointing in the wild comes from a very limited domain. During grooming, they point to those bodyparts that they want the groomer to groom, and these pointing gestures are acted upon by the groomers significantly often. The researchers who discovered this write: 'Our observations suggest that the recipient of the signal has an understanding of the intended meaning of the gesture and that wild chimpanzees use gestures to specify an area of the body to be groomed and to depict a desired future action' (Pika and Mitani 2006, p. 192). This limited and closely interpersonal use of referential pointing has not been generalized by wild chimpanzees to pointing to objects outside the pointer's body.

It is accepted that captive apes often point to things while addressing humans. Some of the most impressive examples are reported by Menzel (2005). His chimpanzee Panzee pointed very regularly, accurately, and spontaneously to locations of food she had seen hidden outside her enclosure, sometimes days before. She was also adept at pointing to a place on a video screen showing the food location, if she could not actually point outside. More impressively (and bizarrely) she could operate a joy-stick to manoeuvre a laser pointer device (mounted beyond her reach) to place a laser dot on the location of food hidden outside her enclosure, with the same function as hand-finger pointing, successfully guiding a naive human helper to find the food.

Although the broad factual outlines are pretty clear, there is disagreement among researchers on matters of detail regarding pointing by primates in the wild, partly arising from differences in research methods and traditions. Some of the differences over matters of fact arise between field observers and laboratory experimenters. In Leavens' table (Table 7.1 above), a 'Yes' is given for declarative pointing in the wild for bonobos, drawing on a study by Veá and Sabater-Pi (1998). It needs to be mentioned that this response is based on only one individual animal; the report should be regarded with caution, because the exact conditions under which it was observed were not clearly controlled. There is a methodological problem of contamination with trying to get data on wild animals. In trying to do controlled experiments, especially when trying to elicit deliberate behaviour such as pointing, the situation can easily become artificial, and not of the kind that animals are likely to encounter in their normal wild lives. (This is not to say that experiments in the wild cannot be very useful; they can, as is shown, for example, by the experiments on wild vervets by Cheney and Seyfarth 1990 and on Diana monkeys by Zuberbühler et al. 1999.)

The value of field observations, collected without controlled experiment, has been defended by Byrne (1997). Interestingly, experimentalists took about a decade to agree with the conclusions on apes' knowing the intentions of others put forward by Byrne and Whiten (1992) on the basis of field observations systematically analysed. And still not all experimentalists agree. Here is a taste of the movement in the field:

With regard to the understanding of goal-directed action, there is currently a good bit of controversy. Povinelli and Vonk (2003) consider the understanding of goals and perceptions to be an instance of understanding mental states, and their view is that apes understand only behavior not mental states. In contrast, Tomasello, Call, and Hare (2003) (revising the view expressed in Tomasello and Call (1997)), argue that there are now new data which compel us to attribute to great apes the ability to understand intentional action in terms of goals and perceptions.   (Tomasello et al. 2005, p. 684)

I conclude that the state of knowledge at the moment is that bonobos and other apes in the wild point declaratively with conspecifics extremely rarely at most, and quite probably never, except in the limited domain of pointing to the pointer's own bodyparts during grooming; in captivity they point declaratively much more, to external objects, mostly with humans, but occasionally, depending on how they have been raised, with conspecifics.

Now what are we to make of all this information on pointing? We are trying to discern the relevant differences between apes and humans, and to see, if we can, the beginning of a route that could culminate (once joined by other evolutionary tributary pathways) in human language. For the sake of some concreteness in the arguments, I will describe three hypotheses (two adopted from Leavens et al. (2005) and one of my own) and then see how they fit the facts.

Promethean hypothesis: 'Through continued close association with human caregivers, captive apes achieve an insight that their caregivers have independent agency (i.e. are intentional beings). . . . [E]xposure to humans invests captive apes with a novel cognitive capacity, the capacity to recognize and manipulate intentional states in others.' (Leavens et al. 2005, pp. 303–304)

Social tool use hypothesis: 'According to this hypothesis, captive apes will have had long experience with humans as 'food-delivery machines'; that is, they will have experienced so many instances in which caregivers have delivered food that when faced with a situation in which both desirable, but unreachable, food and a human are present, pointing emerges as a simple solution to a common problem faced in captivity (but not in the wild).' (Leavens et al. 2005, p. 304)

Cooperative environment hypothesis: Wild apes already have the insight that other apes are intentional beings; this does not just dawn on them only in captivity. But in the wild environment, apes are so seldom cooperative with each other that a helpful response to a pointing gesture is not expected. In captivity, they readily attribute intentionality to humans, who are physically similar to them; they know the difference between a human and a food-delivery machine. They monitor human eyegaze. They learn in the captive environment that humans are likely to respond helpfully to pointing gestures, and deploy their native manipulative skills to achieve their ends by pointing.

This last hypothesis foreshadows a theme of (non-)cooperativeness in apes that will pervade much of the next chapter, and will be explicitly discussed in Chapter 9. It should be evident that I favour the last hypothesis, mostly on the grounds that apes in the wild seem to display intense and subtle attention to the attentional states of others, and to manipulate them. Philosophically speaking, however, it must be admitted that the issue is not so clear-cut. All the apes' behaviour **could** be accounted for on the hypothesis that they have learned to manipulate their human keepers in the same way that humans learn to drive a car, without attribution of intentions and desires to what is clearly a machine. Individual apes and people are variably helpful and less predictable than cars, and what apes evidently learn in captivity is not simply a set of rules for 'driving a human', **any** human. Just as they register in the wild who is dominant and who is subordinate, they register in captivity which humans are considerate towards them and which are not, and adjust their behaviour accordingly. This suggests an economical theory in the ape's mind, making use of such explanatory constructs as 'goals' and 'intentions' in terms of which the dispositions of others can be represented. I certainly wouldn't want to espouse a Cartesian position according to which apes do not reason about others in anything like the same way that humans do. The difference between humans and apes lies partly in the degree of subtlety with which we and they can carry out social calculations, just as expert chess-players can calculate more moves ahead than beginners. This difference in calculating power can be conceived as a quantitative difference, but it is almost certainly affected by a qualitative difference between species, namely our ability sometimes to reason about problems explicitly in language. We will come to how that works in a subsequent book.

There is another qualitative difference between apes and humans that helps us to understand why wild apes don't point and captive apes do. This is the fact that in their native wild state, apes are competitive, and not cooperative, with each other. The crucial difference between competition and cooperation is explored by Tomasello and his colleagues and largely summarized in Tomasello et al. (2005). In competitive tasks, primates are good at tracking the attention of others to objects, for their own selfish ends. They have what it takes to know whether another animal is attending to some desired object, and to manipulate the object, or the other animal, to their own advantage. And they appear to act on the reasonable assumption that other animals will have similar selfish motivations. When humans manipulate the attention of others to objects, it is often for a cooperative purpose, as for example in saying 'There's an apple for you on the table'. By contrast, even for such a humanized ape as Kanzi, 96% of his utterances were requests (Savage-Rumbaugh et al. 1985).

More evidence of this lack of cooperative motivation in non-humans will be given in Chapter 9. It explains why apes in the wild don't point. It may also explain why apes are not very good, in certain conditions, at proceeding from deliberate indicating actions by humans to the locations indicated. A test of this is the 'object-choice' task, where a particular object, such as a cup or a bucket, is baited with food invisible to the animal, while a similar object nearby is not baited; the animal subject has to detect, on the basis of human signals, which receptacle contains the food. Some of the research on this task, for various species, suggests an interesting hypothesis about a difference between domesticated species, such as dogs and goats, and non-domesticated species. Unfortunately, however, the jury is still out, as there is disagreement about the comparability of the results under different experimental metaconditions. I will explain, starting with the interesting hypothesis (which may be wrong).

Some experiments with chimpanzees, goats, domestic dogs, and wolves have indicated that goats and domestic dogs are good at following human signals in the object-choice paradigm, while wolves and chimpanzees are much less good. The idea is encapsulated in the following abstract:

Dogs are more skillful than great apes at a number of tasks in which they must read human communicative signals indicating the location of hidden food. In this study, we found that wolves who were raised by humans do not show these same skills, whereas domestic dog puppies only a few weeks old, even those that have had little human contact, do show these skills. These findings suggest that during the process of domestication, dogs have been selected for a set of social-cognitive abilities that enable them to communicate with humans in unique ways.

(Hare et al. 2002, p. 1634)[6]

Some of the relevant experiments are: on chimpanzees—Tomasello et al. (1997); Call et al. (1998); Itakura et al. (1999); Call et al. (2000); on domestic dogs—Miklosi et al. (1998); Hare and Tomasello (1999); Agnetta et al. (2000); Soproni et al. (2001); Hare et al. (2002); on wolves—Hare et al. (2002); Miklosi et al. (2003); and on goats—Kaminski et al. (2005); there are also results for other animals.[7]

If dogs and goats have been selected, during the 10,000 or so years of domestication, for their ability to follow human indications, and chimpanzees and wolves, species not subject to selection by domestication, can't follow these indications (so well), it is tempting to include humans

---

[6] Freedman (1958) compared four different breeds of dogs, including Shetland sheepdogs and Basenjis. He found that Shetland sheepdogs had absorbed more human 'morality' than Basenjis. The sheepdogs stayed away from forbidden food even in the absence of a punishing human, whereas the Basenjis ate the forbidden food as soon as the human's back was turned. Basenjis were domesticated in Africa, and preserve certain wild-like characteristics, such as coming into heat only once a year.

[7] 'Dolphins, *Tursiops truncatus* (Herman et al. 1999; Tschudin et al. 2001), fur seals, *Arctocephalus pusillus* (Scheumann and Call 2004) and a grey seal, *Halichoerus grypus* (Shapiro et al. 2003) were also skilful at using some human communicative cues in the task (for example pointing and head orientation), but these were individuals reared and extensively trained for other tasks by humans (e.g. for public shows in an aquarium). Of four horses, *Equus caballus*, tested, only one was skilful (McKinley and Sambrook 2000)' (Kaminski et al. 2005, p. 12). My student Karinna Hurley has shown that Exmoor ponies, a primitive breed of horse, do not follow human pointing, unless perhaps those extensively familiarized with humans (Hurley 2006).

themselves, who can follow human indications excellently, among the domesticated species. Humans have **domesticated themselves**! Furthermore, if the social abilities of dogs can have been bred into them in such a short period (10,000 years is a very short time for biological evolution), it is quite plausible to suggest that over the 150,000 years of anatomically modern *Homo sapiens'* existence, a similar form of socio-genetic evolution has taken place. (Putting it like this, there is room for the social evolutionary step(s) to have followed the anatomical evolutionary step that gave us *Homo sapiens*.) Of course, why our species should have 'domesticated itself' when others didn't remains a puzzle.

Under artificial selection, a very humanized tame subspecies can emerge in remarkably few generations. Trut (1999) describes a forty-year experiment, in which Siberian foxes, usually bred for their fur, were selected each generation for their friendliness, or lack of fear, towards humans. After only six generations, a strain had emerged which followed humans round like dogs, and responded to human attention by licking and tail-wagging—all traits very far removed from the wild, fearful, aggressive behaviour of their great-great-great-great-grandparents. After twenty generations, further traits not directly associated with tameness emerged, including floppy ears and some piebald or mottled colouring and shorter or curlier tails. Interestingly, some of these traits are also characteristic of very young wild, unselected Siberian foxes. The artificial selection process seems to have bred into the emergent strain a property of prolonged juvenility. Humans, too, are notable for their long period of childhood dependency. Neurochemical properties also evolved in the foxes, including a lower basal level of corticosteroids and a higher level of serotonin.

A process of human self-domestication can be envisaged like this. In human prehistory, it is possible that mate selection involved selection for friendliness, trustingness, and cooperativeness. Experiments by Melis et al. (2006a, 2006b) show that, in a mutualistic setup, where cooperation is beneficial to both parties, chimpanzees, given a choice of cooperative partner, will recruit a helper who is known to them to be more helpful, in preference over an animal known to be less effective as a collaborator. Alternatively, there could have been infanticide, or parental neglect, of offspring who were not friendly, trusting or cooperative enough. Given the evidence of the Siberian foxes, it would only take a little pressure in this direction to produce the relatively amiable species that we are today.

A slight shadow has been cast over the hypothesis that domestication correlates with better untrained ability to follow human signals. Barth et al. (2005) distinguish between two experimental metaconditions in object-choice experiments: in the LEAVE condition, the subject animal enters the room after the food has been placed and leaves afterwards prior to the next test; and in the STAY condition, the animal is in the room for all tests, including while the food is hidden, but out of its sight. In experiments of their own, Barth et al. (2005) showed that chimpanzees performed better in the LEAVE condition than in the STAY condition, and pointed out a possible source of bias in all the experiments on which the interesting hypothesis described above was based. For instance, in Hare et al. (2002)'s experiments, 'the dogs were tested using the LEAVE method, whereas the wolves were tested using the STAY method' (Barth et al. 2005, p. 91).

Ah, well, back to the lab. For my money, however, I bet there is some viability in the domestication hypothesis. Watch this space.

7.2.2 Human Pointing and Linguistic Deixis

Whatever the relative abilities of domesticated and non-domesticated animals are, it is clear that human babies are a step up from all of them in their natural pointing behaviour. Butterworth et al. (2002) describe a number of ways in which pointing by human babies is species-specific.

[T]he function of pointing is referential and declarative from the outset (differently from indicating in chimpanzees, which is exclusively requestive; e.g. see (Gómez 1991) and (Leavens and Hopkins 1998)). Franco and Butterworth (1996), for example, compared the incidence of pointing and reaching in 10-18-month-old babies in different communicative contexts in order to establish whether pointing might develop out of failed reaching, as Vygotsky (1988) argued, and therefore be associated with a request function. Pointing and reaching gestures were never used interchangeably by babies who had recently begun to point. From the outset, pointing was directed to distal targets and was accompanied by vocalizations, positive affect and visual checking with a social partner, thus revealing communicative intent. Checking may also help establish that the partner has comprehended the referent for the gesture. Thus, pointing was used with the declarative function...of sharing attention on a referent with someone.   (Butterworth et al. 2002, p. 2)

Furthermore, there is a close link in human babies between pointing and language:

A link between pointing and speech development appears evident. Two studies have shown that the age of onset of pointing and its frequency at

12 months predicts the amount of speech in production at 15 months and also at 24 months (Butterworth and Morissette 1996; Camaioni et al. 1991). For speech comprehension, babies depend on the adult's referential acts, including pointing (Baldwin 1991; Baldwin 1993) and they comprehend their first categorical nominals in the same week that they begin to point (Harris et al. 1995).   (Butterworth et al. 2002, p. 2)

Butterworth took as the title of a further article (Butterworth 2003) 'Pointing is the Royal Road to Language for Babies'. His conclusions are that human index-finger pointing is 'biologically based and species spe-cific [and]. . . intimately connected with species-typical handedness, preci-sion grip, and acquisition of language' (pp. 28–29). If not taken on their strongest possible interpretation, these conclusions are justified on the evi-dence to date. But it must be noted that the biological bias is not so strong that it cannot be overridden by culture. We have seen that apes' behaviour can be strongly influenced by their social environment: wild apes don't point, captive apes point. A more subtle example is the difference between index-finger pointing and whole-hand pointing, which in apes varies with whether they have been language-trained. Leavens and Hopkins (1999, p. 421) present a clear graph showing that captive but language-naive chimpanzees point most with the whole hand; human babies between 8 and 12 months point mostly with the whole hand, but are beginning to use the index finger; human babies from 13 to 18 months mainly use the index finger, but still sometimes point with the whole hand; and finally language-trained chimpanzees (presumably adult) use the index finger most of all the creatures here compared. These results for humans relate to Western babies. We should not be surprised to find that some innate biases in humans can also be affected by cultural environment. Indeed, index-finger pointing is not a human cultural universal. Wilkins (2003) uses data from Arrernte, a central Australian (Pama-Nyungan) language, to challenge two widely held views: '(a) that pointing with the index finger is a universal human behavior, and (b) that pointing with the index finger is not socially transmitted but is a basic (natural) form of reference' (Wilkins 2003, p. 171). Wilkins states: 'Lip pointing . . . can be found in indigenous communities on all inhabited continents, which strongly indicates independent development' (p. 175). The communities Wilkins mentions include the Kuna Indians of Panama,[8] and cultures in the North American Southwest, Guatemala, parts of South America,

---

[8] For the Kuna, Wilkins cites Sherzer (1973, 1983, 1993).

central and northern Australia, and Papua New Guinea. Most tellingly, Wilkins reports:

> Mike Olson (personal communication) contended that there is no conventional index-finger pointing among the Barai of Papua New Guinea. Lip pointing, in contrast, is the ubiquitous deictic behavior and is highly conventionalized. Certainly the Barai were confounded when Olson used index-finger points with respect to objects as a means for getting names for them. It was not apparently a matter of reading the behavior as impolite, but merely not understanding the referential intent. Lip pointing is the primary means of drawing a person's attention to something for naming, and his attempts at index-finger pointing could not engage the same dialogic interaction.
>
> (Wilkins, 2003, p. 176)

Similar behaviour was confirmed for the Yimas and Watam groups of Papua New Guinea by the linguist Bill Foley. Importantly, however, Wilkins does conclude: 'pointing (i.e. the use of some part of the body to make deictic gestural reference) appears to be [a human] universal' (p. 212).

There are both genetic and environmental differences between apes and human babies. And the genetic differences contribute to the environmental differences. Apes genes do not dispose them, in a community of conspecifics, to participate in shared goals, so they don't point, or only do so very rarely, in the wild. In home-reared circumstances, especially when trained by humans to be somewhat cooperative with each other, they can learn to point, as Sherman and Austin did. The difference could be quite small. Let me illustrate from game theory. In the Iterated Prisoner's Dilemma, a favourite topic in Reciprocal Altruism theory (Trivers 1971; Axelrod 1984), a successful strategy is 'Tit-for-Tat'. This strategy says: on meeting someone for the first time, act cooperatively with them; on subsequent meetings, act cooperatively with them if last time they acted cooperatively with you, otherwise do not cooperate. Note the condition for the first meeting. It is crucial to the emergence of populations in which reciprocal cooperation is the norm. If that condition on the first meeting starts set the other way (i.e. on meeting someone for the first time, don't cooperate with them), what you get is a population in which non-cooperation is the norm. Even a mutant with a 'cooperate on first meeting' disposition born into such a population would end up as a lifelong non-cooperator, because all the people he meets would do him down on the first meeting, after which he would apply the second condition—'do as they did to you'. Of course, a saintly mutant, cooperating with everyone no matter how they act to him, would have poor survival chances. The point is that a slight difference in inbuilt disposition can make a big difference to the prevalent norms of the community, which then combine with the inbuilt dispositions to determine a creature's long-term behaviour. Home-reared apes have no doubt been forgiven by their adult keepers for early uncooperative acts, and so these keepers are not marked as targets for non-cooperation by the main clause of the Tit-for-Tat rule. Thus such home-reared apes are able to act somewhat cooperatively with their human keepers, in this environment where cooperation is the norm. We can bring the point closer to home by considering the effect of a brutal environment (e.g. some prisons) on people who would act more unselfishly in a more congenial environment, and conversely the possible redeeming effect of a persistently congenial environment on a naturally fairly sociable person raised in brutal conditions. But let's not get too Pollyanna-ish— some dispositions, whether genetic or environmentally conditioned, or a bit of both, are hard to modify in adulthood.

Note on terminology: Butterworth et al. (2002) above, like Leavens (2004) and others, use the term 'declarative' to distinguish the function of 'purely informative' pointing from begging. The imperative/declarative terminology is in danger of jumping too far towards language, being borrowed from a grammatical tradition used to describe the structure of **sentences**. The literature on pointing is only concerned with whether a non-linguistic **act** is communicative. For this reason, we might consider switching instead to Searle (1969)'s classificatory terms for speech acts, using 'directive' (for requests and the like) and 'assertive' (for purely informative utterances). But in fact this would also not be satisfactory, because pointing is not informative in the same way as a linguistic declarative utterance, which, crucially, attributes some property to something, using a word corresponding to a predicate. For example, utterances like 'It's dead' or 'It's a leopard' or 'It's running' tell a hearer something about the object being referred to. Pointing, on its own, does not give such information. Pointing merely draws attention. Pointing **refers** but does not assert anything of the object referred to. The most appropriate term for pointing, I believe, is **deictic**.[9]

The importance of all this for linguistic reference is that the most basic form of reference is **deixis**, literally pointing. An early argument locating deixis as the source of reference is in Lyons (1975). Deixis, or indexicality,

---

[9] *Deictic* is a term favoured by linguists; *indexical* is the corrresponding term favoured by philosophers. I will use them more or less interchangeably.

as the philosophers call it, is the kind of reference achieved by words such as *this* and *here*, whose referent objects can only be identified by observing the situation in which they are uttered. If I say 'Here' now, it means somewhere in Edinburgh, whereas if my elder daughter says it now, it means somewhere in Berlin, and if my younger daughter says it now, it means somewhere in San Diego. Of course *now* is also deictic, pointing to the time of utterance (or writing), so by the time you read this, the places referred to may have changed again. Pointing with the finger is the same. Believe it or not, I am pointing to something with my finger as I write this, but you haven't a clue what I am referring to, because you are not here. The most basic kind of reference is of this portable, deictic kind. Pointing is a useful device that can be used anywhere in face-to-face conversation, to refer to anything where you are, just like the words *this* and *here*.

I'll now relate deixis by finger-pointing to the discussion of predicate-argument structure in Chapters 4 and 5 of Part I. When a creature's attention is drawn to an object, the dorsal stream mechanism directs the eyes and head so that the object comes into focal attention. At this point, before the ventral stream mechanisms can attribute properties to the object, there is a fleeting 'bare-object', propertyless representation in the brain, which I have identified with a logical individual variable, such as x, y, or z. In the notation proposed in Chapter 5, the bare object of attention is represented as an empty box, ⬛ –something's there! Filling the box with predicate terms corresponds to assigning properties to the variable argument. When a creature merely points to an object, she directs the attention of an addressee to an object, without expressing any properties of the object. If the pointing gesture is successful, the addressee also attends to the same object, and a similar fleeting bare-object representation, ⬛, is formed in her brain, as her dorsal stream locates the object. Of course, both parties in the exchange may bring to mind certain selected predicates applying to the object, but all that is actually **communicated** by the pointing gesture is the presence, and relevance, of the object. Something's there! Nothing is expressed **about** it.

With both manual pointing and the use of deictic words, joint attention to the object pointed to is involved. We have seen that many species closely related to humans, and in particular chimpanzees, are fully capable of attending to the same object as another animal, and checking that the other animal is attending to it as well, but that, especially in the wild, they lack the motivation to participate actively in this kind of cooperative pointing behaviour. This raises a very general issue of the sources of cooperativeness in humans, an issue central to linguistic pragmatics, and to which we will return in a later chapter.

Something is now known about the neural basis of joint (as opposed to non-joint) attention. Williams et al. (2005) have shown, using fMRI scanning, that 'Joint attention was associated with activity in the ventro-medial frontal cortex, the left superior frontal gyrus (BA10), cingulate cortex, and caudate nuclei. The ventromedial frontal cortex has been consistently shown to be activated during mental state attribution tasks' (p. 133). In other words, the same brain area is involved in joint attention as is involved when people attribute mental states, such as knowing and wanting, to other people. Moreover this brain area overlaps with an area which some of the same authors have shown to be abnormal in autistic spectrum disorder (Waiter et al. 2004, 2005).

Pointing with a hand or finger is different in an important way from linguistic deixis, in that it is largely indexical. The reservation implicit in 'largely' here is due to the difficulty of imposing Peirce (1897/1955)'s trichotomy icon/index/symbol in a completely watertight way. The connection between a pointing gesture and the object pointed to is still somewhat conventional and arbitrary (thus like a symbol), even though it is obvious to us (if not to the Arrernte or the Kuna), whereas deictic words such as *this* and *here* are, besides being indexical, also **symbolic**, having only an **arbitrary** relationship with their meanings, and needing to be learned in each separate language. These words straddle the gap between purely indexical finger-pointing to some object in the immediate situation of communication and the use of learned arbitrary symbols. Deictic words such as *this* and *here* also draw a hearer's attention to some object in the immediate situation of communication, but to achieve this effect both participants have to have learned the same arbitrary symbols.

Positive attention-drawing to important things in the environment, but by arbitrary symbolic means, expressing predicates, rather than by deictic pointing, does occur in primates and indeed in a wide range of other animals. But the typical circumstances are rather different, in ways to be discussed in the next section.

7.3 STANDARDIZED ALARM AND FOOD CALLS

The communicative behaviours surveyed in the previous section (1) were indexical, often transparent in meaning, as with pointing; (2) involved quite subtle calculation of the attentive states of other animals; and (3) involved learning. In this section, by contrast, we will look at a very different evolutionary route that some species have taken, apparently in the approximate direction of referential meaning as seen in human language. This kind of behaviour (1) involves an arbitrary, non-indexical, relation between the signal and what is meant; (2) involves little or no calculation of the attentive state of other animals; and (3) is largely innate.

Animals of several different classes within the chordate phylum, and especially certain species of mammals and birds, have characteristic calls warning of predators and announcing the discovery of food. But with these calls, there is seldom such a discernible element of calculation on the part of the signaller, and it is not so clear that the animals are so deliberately manipulating the outcome as in the cases of tactical deception mentioned above.

The best-known example is that of the vervet monkeys, who have distinct alarm calls for different predators: a 'bark' to warn of leopard, a 'cough' to warn of an eagle, and a 'chutter' to warn of a snake (Cheney and Seyfarth 1990). Vervets make these sounds on noticing a predator of the relevant type, and they take the appropriate evasive action when they hear such a sound. They run up a tree on hearing the leopard call, dive under the bushes on hearing the eagle call, and stand on tiptoe looking at the ground on hearing the snake call.

In fact, there are many species with a very short inventory of alarm calls. Digweed et al. (2005) describe two such calls in white-faced capuchin monkeys: one call for bird predators, and one more general call for a range of snakes and mammals. Writing of the pale-winged trumpeter, an Amazonian bird, Seddon et al. (2002, p. 1331) write: 'On detection of danger, trumpeters gave two acoustically different calls, one for aerial predators, and another for terrestrial predators or conspecific intruders. They also produced distinct calls on detection of large prey items such as snakes. These (alarm and snake-finding) call types seemed to evoke different responses by receivers and therefore appeared to be functionally referent.' Domestic chickens also have alarm calls differentiated for aerial and ground predators (Karakashian et al. 1988; Evans et al. 1993).

These are just a few of many examples. The judgement by Seddon et al. (2002) that the calls are 'functionally referent' touches on a key issue. Different scholars have different criteria for deciding whether such calls are 'really' referential. An ingenious experiment by Klaus Zuberbühler and colleagues sheds light on this question. What does a specific alarm call mean to the animal that hears it? Are the calls merely triggers for the appropriate evasive activity, not in any sense bringing the concepts of the specific predators to mind? Or are they at least somewhat more like human words,[10] which evoke concepts that are kept in the mind for some time?

In order to answer this question, Zuberbühler and colleagues (Zuber- bühler et al. 1999) worked with Diana monkeys of the African forest who have distinct calls for leopards and eagles. Female monkeys both give spontaneous alarm calls on sensing a predator and respond to alarm calls from males by repeating the call. Besides recording the alarm calls, the researchers also recorded characteristic noises associated with the two predators, such as the growl of a leopard and an eagle's shriek. Next, they played back three different kinds of pairs of stimuli, where the stimuli in each pair were separated by an interval of five minutes' silence. On hearing first an eagle alarm call, then (after five minutes) the shriek of an eagle, female monkeys showed less sign of alarm (giving fewer repeat calls) than after hearing, for example, an eagle alarm call followed by the growl of a leopard. The logic is this. If, on hearing an eagle alarm call you are prepared to be wary of an eagle in the area, you are less disturbed by hearing the actual eagle shriek. The eagle shriek merely confirms what the earlier alarm call told you. But if you hear an eagle alarm and then hear a leopard growl, the growl is new information, telling you about a kind of predator that you hadn't been made aware of by the previous call. The researchers did of course try out all the necessary control conditions to consolidate this conclusion. The conclusion is that the alarm calls do not merely trigger the relevant evasive action, with no representation of the specific source of danger being kept in the head: the Diana monkeys, on hearing a leopard alarm call, keep the idea of a leopard in their minds for at least five minutes; and likewise with the eagle alarm call. This behaviour meets the criteria set by Marler et al. (1992) for calls being 'functionally referential'. It seems likely that similar results would be obtained with all species with small inventories of predator-specific alarm calls.

In the terms and notation of Part I of this book, the mind of the Diana monkey alarm-caller who spots an eagle first momentarily represents the bare object of attention as ⬚ ; then, rapidly recognizing the attended object as an eagle, the monkey brain forms a representation that we

---

[10] Here and whenever I use the term *word* in a comparison of animal calls with human language, I use it in the informal, natural, and familiar sense in which human babies' first utterances are counted as 'words', even though at that holophrastic stage babies don't form sentences. Within the framework of a description of the grammar of a human language, the term *word* takes on more baggage. There is, of course, no claim that animal calls fit into any more complex hierarchy of communicative units, such as the word–phrase–clause–sentence hierarchy used by human languages.

notate[11] as EAGLE . The alarm caller is attending to an eagle. According to Zuberbühler et al. (1999)'s experiments, a Diana monkey receiver of an eagle alarm call also brings to her mind the presence of an eagle. She is not necessarily attending to an actually perceived eagle, so her representation can be thought of as a (proto-)predicate EAGLE without an argument, raw information that something is eagle-ish round here, like a weather predicate RAIN. Possibly top-down information to the effect that eagles are objects (unlike rain) then causes an argument to be supplied, in our terms placing a box around the predicate. The relevant part of the call-receiver's state of mind at the time can also be represented, for our purposes, as EAGLE .

The terms *refer* and *referential* are not used with optimal precision in much of the literature in this area. Some linguists (but regrettably not all) are careful to observe an important distinction between **reference** and **extension** or **denotation**.[12] This parallels the distinction between what a speaker means on any given occasion, and what expressions in a language mean in any and all contexts of use. Here is an example: imagine that I point, rather vaguely, in the direction of two men, and say, 'That man was at Jane's party last night'. You might well ask, 'Which man?', in which case you are asking **what I meant** when I said 'That man'; you are asking which man I was **referring to** just then. You are not asking what the words *that man* mean—you know that perfectly well. A French schoolchild might be given the exercise of translating the sentence *That man was at Jane's party last night* into French. In this case, nobody in particular used the sentence; it is just an example taken out of context; but it still means something. The French child would learn that *that man* means (is a translation of) *cet homme là*. And she would not ask which particular man was meant. Going back to the reference/denotation distinction, we linguists (when we are careful) say that a speaker uttering 'That man' on a particular occasion is (probably) **referring** to a **particular** person nearby. By contrast the English phrase *that man* considered in any and all of its contexts of use **denotes** the same **class** of entities as the French phrase *cet homme là* (give or take a few slight differences in what might count as a *man* in English and an *homme* in French).[13] Here in the context of animal calls with very simple

---

[11] Remember all the caveats from Part I about the impossibility (or at least the uncertainty) of perfect translation of animal proto-predicates into human categories.

[12] See Lyons (1977, Vol. 1, Sections 7.2 and 7.4).

[13] In case you have been wondering about my notational conventions, they are designed to respect the difference between **utterances** and **linguistic expressions**. Utterances are

semantics I make no distinction between *extension* and *denotation*. Thus, for example, the extension of French *homme* is (give or take, etc.) the same as the extension of English *man*, namely the class of entities to which these words can be applied. In Part I, I emphasized that private concepts (as opposed to public words or calls) have extensions. An adult vervet monkey seems to have some concept, a pattern of activation potentials in its brain, that is activated on attending to pretty much anything that we would call a leopard. The extension of this concept is the class of leopards (give or take a bit).

The relationship between reference and extension/denotation is a difference between actual and potential. On an actual occasion of use, a speaker using a definite noun phrase refers to, i.e. picks out for the benefit of a hearer, some entity (object or event) in the context. In the abstract, theoretically discounting context, the same phrase, considered as a part of the system of the language, denotes all the possible entities that it could possibly be used to refer to on particular occasions of use. In short, speakers refer, on particular occasions; expressions in a language denote, timelessly.

Now applying this careful linguist's terminology to the topics of this section and the last, the finger-pointing human or ape **refers** to the particular thing indicated. The vervet's bark, considered as a type of call that vervets can make, may be considered to **denote** the class of leopards. Equivalently put, that call expresses a concept whose **extension** is the class of leopards. Remember that we have seen from Zuberbühler's experiments that the Diana monkey's eagle alarm call probably brings the concept of an eagle to the mind of a Diana monkey hearer. When a vervet barks, it does not have the same effect as finger-pointing towards a particular predator. The bark is not aptly paraphrased in English as the single demonstrative word *that*. A better paraphrase (remembering always that such paraphrases are rough and ready, and the vervet's representation of the world is only partially similar to ours) would be 'There's a leopard

spoken on particular occasions, and typically involve the speaker referring to particular things. Linguistic expressions include words, phrases, and sentences, considered in the abstract, as when learning a language in some (rather old-fashioned) schools. Utterances are represented in quotation marks, so you might right now say to yourself 'Does it matter?' By contrast, linguistic expressions are written in italics, so, resulting from your question, you and I could proceed to discuss the various denotations of the English word *matter*, sometimes used as a concrete noun, sometimes as an abstract noun, and sometimes as a verb. See Hurford and Heasley (1983, Unit 2) for some textbook exercises to practise this distinction.

round here!' I am prepared to say that vervet, chicken, and Diana monkey alarm calls and the like do **denote**, in the sense that they systematically bring to mind representations of quite specific categories of predators.

For each alarm-calling species, the researcher's labelling of the relevant classes of predators is a matter of ad hoc convenience. In glossing the vervet's bark as a 'leopard call', we need to keep in mind that a vervet's concept of what makes it give the 'leopard call' is almost certainly not exactly coextensive with our concept of a leopard. Indeed, I bet that even you and I have slightly different ideas about what counts as a leopard. Can you tell a leopard from a jaguar, or a cheetah, or a panther, or a puma? It's just that LEOPARD is the closest human category to the class of stimuli that prompts a vervet to bark. For other species, we might find that some label like MIDDLE-SIZED QUADRUPEDAL GROUND ANIMAL was a better approximation.

The sending and receiving of alarm calls are not necessarily under the same degree of genetic control. For vervets, at least, the evidence about call-production is that very young vervets give the right call for the right broad class of predator. That is, they do not give the eagle call on seeing a leopard, or vice versa. To this extent, the link between the meaning and the form of the call seems to be genetically determined. It would be interesting, but difficult, to try to condition vervets to give the opposite calls. While the production of each call seems to be innately tied to a particular broad class of predator, there is good evidence of fine-tuning of these broad classes by learning in young vervets. Seyfarth and Cheney (1982) give a clear diagram showing the progressive refinement, from infancy, through juvenility to adulthood, of production of the vervet predator calls.

In marked contrast to adults, infants (monkeys under 1 year of age) and juveniles (monkeys older than 1 year but not yet adult size) gave alarm calls to a significantly wider variety of species and were significantly more likely to give alarms to nonpredators like warthogs, pigeons and falling leaves that posed no danger to them.... Intriguingly, however, although infants gave alarm calls to a wider variety of species than did adults, infant alarm-calling behavior was not entirely random. Infants gave leopard alarm calls primarily to terrestrial mammals, eagle alarms to birds, and snake alarms to snakes or long thin objects. In other words, from a very early age infants distinguished between general predator *classes* (e.g. terrestrial mammal vs. flying bird), whereas adults distinguished between particular predator species within such classes (e.g. leopards vs. other terrestrial mammals and martial eagles vs. other birds).   (Seyfarth and Cheney 1982, pp. 244–245)

On the reception side of vervet signals, there is also evidence of fine-tuning by learning.

[P]layback experiments showed that infant responses were more generalized than those of adults and that infants were significantly more likely than adults to respond in ways that were potentially maladaptive (Seyfarth and Cheney 1980). Given that adultlike, alarm-specific responses develop only after experience, it is of interest that infants differed from adults in two further respects. First, infants in playback experiments were significantly more likely than adults to respond in a given way only after first looking at another animal who had already begun that same response; and second, infants near their mothers were more likely to show adultlike responses than infants whose mothers had temporarily wandered more than 5 m away.

(Seyfarth and Cheney 1982, pp. 246–247)

Then there is a higher-level question of to what extent the alarm-giving animal is deliberately giving the signal in anything like the same calculating kind of way as Machiavellian apes manipulating the attention of others. It is less likely that this is the case, although there is some evidence of context-sensitivity in these alarm calls.

The male domestic chicken (*Gallus gallus*) has been found to modulate the production of vocal signals in response to the presence or absence of a suitable audience. We investigated effects on alarm calling by presenting overhead predator models to cockerels in the presence of a variety of social companions. The production of aerial predator calls in response to hawk silhouettes varied with the presence or absence of a member of the same species. The kinds of audience investigated included the mate, unfamiliar females, other females and males with which subjects had had prior visual and auditory contact, and broody hens with and without young. Domestic chicks, unrelated to the subjects, were almost as effective an audience as conspecific adults. A member of another species, however, failed to potentiate alarm-call production. The subjects gave more alarm calls when they were in the presence of either a male or a female audience than when they were alone.

(Karakashian et al. 1988, p. 129)

Similarly, vervets are less likely to give their alarm calls when they are alone than when other vervets, especially offspring or kin, are nearby (Cheney and Seyfarth 1990). It is tempting to see this as a somewhat deliberate decision on the part of the caller. He might be thought to calculate 'No point in giving the alarm call, as there's nobody here to hear it'.

On the other hand, it could be the case that presence or absence of conspecifics is part of the complex of stimuli to which an innate automatic alarm-calling mechanism responds. If experiments can show that the circumstances under which calls are given are too implausibly complex to be hardwired into the genes we can surmise that the alarm caller is under some kind of non-automatic control. Here some leverage can perhaps be gained by arguments and predictions from theoretical models of individual and kin selection. For instance, vervet females stay with their native troop all their lives, and so are in the company of kin, whereas male vervets migrate out of their native troops, and so spend their adult lives with less closely related individuals. Abstract Kin Selection theory, if it were to predict a sex difference in alarm calling behaviour, would predict that females, especially those with offspring, would give alarm calls more often than males. To some extent, this is true, as Hauser (1996, p. 429) succinctly summarizes: 'high-ranking females with kin tended to produce more first alarms than high-ranking females without close kin'. Of course, we don't know how much information can be coded into the genes, so at present, we don't know for sure to what extent there is any calculating deliberateness in an animal's alarm-calling behaviour.

A case cited in favour of animals being in some kind of deliberate control of their alarm calls is their use for deception. Munn (1986a, 1986b) reports birds of one species giving 'false' alarm calls to distract birds of another species away from food.[14] This can be described in terms of deliberate calculating behaviour, but, again, there is no very clear way to resolve the issue of the degree of automaticity or instinctiveness of such behaviour. Cheney and Seyfarth (1990) describe an episode, now often retold, of a vervet who, during a skirmish with another troop of vervets, gave the leopard alarm call, when no leopard was present. The vervets ran up the trees, abandoning the fight, which the caller's group might otherwise have lost. Robert Seyfarth (personal communication) regrets the frequency and certitude with which this one episode is cited as a clear example of deliberate tactical deception. Who knows? Until further evidence comes in, the jury is out.

---

[14] This way of putting it should not be taken to imply that the species is the unit of natural selection. There are two possibilities. One is that the 'false' alarm calls (given when no predator is around) deceive any listening individual, of whatever species, and the individual deceiver grabs the food and reaps an individual fitness benefit. A slight variant of this, still compatible with individual-level selection, is that the false alarm calls have evolved in one species to be targeted specifically at members of another species in their environment.

Animals not only have specific, to some extent innately specified, alarm calls for predators; many species also give different calls on discovering different broad categories of food. Both rhesus macaques and chimpanzees signal differently for high-quality food and low-quality food. So far, this is like distinguishing between different types of predators. But here there is some additional evidence bearing on the question of how deliberate and calculating (as opposed to instinctive and automatic) such calls are. Brosnan and de Waal (2002) found that chimpanzees signalled differentially depending on the presence of an audience, and furthermore '[a] visible audience increased the rate of food calling for a large, sharable quantity of food, yet decreased the rate for a small, non-sharable quantity' (p. 211). A chimp might calculate that he would get some social credit without loss of food for announcing sharable food, but that he would lose food by announcing non-sharable food.

More persuasive evidence of deliberation and calculation in food calling comes from a study by Hauser (1992). He watched rhesus macaques in Puerto Rico, and noticed that monkeys who first discovered food but did not announce their discovery were significantly more likely to get beaten up by other monkeys arriving at the scene than monkeys who announced their discovery. The animal discovering food has a choice: to tell or not to tell. Not telling brings the potential reward of getting all the food, but also the potential punishment of getting beaten up if other members of your troop find that you have not told them.

Now, how plausible is it that all the following information is somehow coded in the rhesus macaque genes: (a) when to signal food discovery, and (b) which animals found near food to attack and which not, depending on whether they had announced their first discovery of the food? At least as plausible is a higher-level theory that attributes some degree of flexible control to the animals. According to such a theory, a rhesus macaque knows enough to calculate that attacking a troop member who has not broadcast the discovery of food will deter that animal from keeping silent about it in the future. And this theory also then requires a degree of control over food-signalling behaviour, enough to be affected by punishment. As I say, the jury is still out, and it is too early to assume 'monkeys' lack of a "theory of mind"' (Fitch 2005, p. 205— and see Chapter 9.1, of this book, pp. 307–313). Ability to discern what others are thinking is many-faceted, no doubt partly genetically given, but also subject to facilitation or inhibition depending on environmental conditions.

Alarm calls and food calls seem, on the face of it, to be unselfish, altruistic, or cooperative. The (apparent) altruism or cooperativeness of animal calls is a topic to be discussed in the next chapter.

This concern with whether a behaviour is automatic or calculated/deliberate is one that evolutionary theory shies away from, as Alan Grafen (personal communication) has pointed out to me. As he puts it, 'we [biologists] try not to peer into men's souls', and he wonders whether the question arises here just because I am making a link between linguistics and biology. Yes, that is indeed why it arises, and I want also to link biology with philosophy and psychology, disciplines which (mostly) do not shy away from such questions. I suspect that biologists' wariness here arises, very naturally, because the light around such issues is so dim; there are plenty more brightly lit questions for biologists to work on. (I confess to a shyness of my own, about consciousness.)

Finally and parenthetically, here is a puzzle about some of these arbitrary signals.

Rhesus macaques not only produce acoustically distinct vocalizations for low and high quality food items, they also appear to recognize these categories. In a habituation-discrimination experiment (Hauser, 1996), habituation was shown to transfer between two high quality food call types ('warbles' and 'harmonic arches') despite the fact that they are acoustically distinctive; this suggests that both calls are classified as falling within the same functional category.   (Egnor et al. 2006, p. 661)

What this means is that animals treated a warble as synonymous with a harmonic arch. Soon after hearing one, they did not react to the other as if it conveyed new information. This raises a puzzle: why would rhesus macaques have two different calls for the same meaning? So far, the question is not answered.

This section has discussed calls with specific categorial content, unlike the deictic pointing gestures discussed in the previous section. In the categorial calls there is a strong, but not complete, element of **innateness** to the **arbitrary symbolic** link between a specific call and what it conveys. Apes don't point in the wild, but readily **learn** this indexical behaviour in captivity, when it suits them, typically to human keepers. Both types of communication, pointing and alarm/food calling, have been, rather loosely, lumped together as 'referential' in the literature. It is important to note the differences between them, and to ask how these two types of communication might somehow combine to produce a more human-like kind of communication. I will speculate on this in the next section.

7.4 BEYOND INNATE SYMBOLS AND LEARNED DEIXIS

An ordinary speaker of a human language has learned tens of thousands of arbitrary form–meaning pairs, the vocabulary of the language, going far beyond the minimal, largely innate, vocabularies of vervets, Diana monkeys, and chickens. In addition, humans can readily combine these learned symbols with deictic devices for referring to specific objects. How might these unique abilities in humans have evolved? I will suggest a route in later chapters. First, we'll see just how much apes can be said to have accumulated, and what is needed to achieve the breakthrough to group-wide learned arbitrary Communicative conventions. It will be convenient here to repeat briefly some of the conclusions of Part I, on 'Meaning before Communication'. Here's an inventory of what we've got so far, in primates (and to some extent in other branches of the animal kingdom).

Proposition-like internal representations of perceived scenes, and some ability to imagine scenes (for planning and requesting)

- Objects: indices (traces) of up to four discrete objects at a time in a mentally represented scene
- Proto-predicates: categorizations of whole scenes and of objects within scenes

Communicative behaviour

- Deliberate and calculating social action on others, to a significant degree under voluntary control
- Monitoring and manipulation of the attention of others
   * to oneself and
   * to 'third-person' objects, by indexical/deictic pointing (in captivity)
   * exclusively for selfish ends (e.g. not purely informative)
- Arbitrary symbolic signals for different 'third-person' categories

   * in the wild
     . for categories of objects (quality of food and specific predators)
     . present in small numbers
     . partly innate, partly learned
     . occasionally, in some cases, under voluntary control, and
     . apparently for unselfish ends
   * in captivity, with language training
     . for a range of categories of objects and actions
     . all learned, up to a maximum of about 1,000 (Kanzi)
     . almost exclusively under voluntary control
     . almost exclusively for selfish ends, e.g. requests

Question: which elements in the above summary need to be boosted to produce a creature that learns vocabulary as fast as a human child, and engages spontaneously in communicative informative acts (i.e. not only requests), using one-unit signals? I assume for the purpose of this question that the first steps towards human language by hominids involved single-unit signals, meaning that the signals were not composed of any smaller units that could be used communicatively on their own. This assumption seems natural to me, but is not the only possibility. Other possibilities will be discussed later. As for the semantic content conveyed by these first signals, let us assume, as also seems natural, that they were of the same sort as the alarm and food calls discussed in the previous section, with content like LEOPARD and GOOD-FOOD.

Now back to our question: what needs to be boosted in order to give a group of creatures learning largish inventories (say 50-100 items as a starting stage) and using them freely to give each other useful information? The big difference between chimpanzee and bonobo behaviour in the wild, and in captivity, especially with home-rearing, shows that given a suitable environment, the learning gap is easily bridged. In the wild, these animals have no learned arbitrary communicative symbols[15] and do not use indexical pointing. Put them in a protective human environment, where the dominant animals (humans) are not repressive or competitive for resources, and moreover directly or indirectly reinforce the use of learned symbols, and then a qualitative shift in the behavioural phenotype occurs. They can learn modest vocabularies of symbols, numbering hundreds of items, and they point. They engage in these behaviours almost exclusively with humans. An ability to learn arbitrary symbols, and an understanding of the effects of pointing are within the reach of the chimpanzee genome, given a suitable environment.

Sure, chimpanzee vocabulary learning is nowhere near as impressive as a human child's, but this is certainly a quantitative, not a qualitative difference. Let me show you a rough and relevant calculation. For this purpose, we'll quantify vocabulary-learning ability in terms of the maximum number of learnable items, and attribute to some remote human ancestor the ability to learn 30 items, as against the 50,000 (at least) items that a modern human can learn. Assuming twenty-five years per generation,

---

[15] Chimpanzees do vary from group to group in their dyadic attention-getting methods, such as knuckle-knocking or branch-slapping, so presumably these behaviours are learned, but they are non-arbitrary, as noisy activity naturally attracts attention, and they do not denote external categories of object or event.

there are 6,000 generations between 150,000 years ago and the present. An increase of roughly 0.13% (0.0013) per generation in size of learnable vocabulary would bridge that gap. Progress at first would be very slow; it would take about twenty-five generations to push the learnable vocabulary up from 30 to 31. This is obviously an over-simple calculation, but it puts our remote ancestors within plausible reach of modern capacities. If this change started further back, say a million years ago, which is certainly possible, the necessary average increment per generation would be much less.

The common dismissal of vervet-like calls as irrelevant to the origins of human symbolic behaviour is too hasty. A strict dichotomy between innate and learned symbols is wrong. As we have seen above, there are learned components to the vervet calls in both production and reception. Under certain conditions, it is possible for specific aspects of the genome in a group to drift relatively freely and de-differentiate, with an increase in learning taking up the slack caused by a degradation of innate dispositions. This rather new but very promising idea is propounded by Deacon (2003), and is applied by Ritchie and Kirby (2007) to the learning of complex songs by finches. Learning, even when not artificially selected for, can flourish in domesticated situations. I have already mentioned the possible relevance of **self-domestication** to the emergence of language in humans. Wilkins and Wakefield (1995, p. 179) envisage a transition from largely innate calls to the beginnings of a learned vocabulary as early as *Homo habilis*.

It is not unreasonable to assume that *H. habilis* too was a noisy animal, that she had a systematic repertoire of calls. It seems not unreasonable also to think that a habiline child might have recruited from this call repertoire to create a linguistic sign.... These acoustic signals, simply part of the primate call system for the adult vocalizer, might have taken the form of linguistic signs in the mind of the child.

Even when apes can learn arbitrary symbolic connections, they cannot necessarily always invoke them in use. Call (2006) gives evidence that

Apes (and possibly other animals) are actually quite good at understanding and reasoning about certain physical properties of their world while at the same time they are quite bad at associating arbitrary stimuli and responses. In other words, if two stimuli have a causal connection (as when food inside a shaken cup makes noises) apes perform better than if stimuli hold an arbitrary relation (as when an unrelated noise indicates food), even if the contingencies of reinforcement are the same.   (p. 219)

A striking example of real-world reasoning repressing symbolic reasoning in chimpanzees is found in experiments by Sarah Boysen and colleagues (Boysen and Berntson 1995; Boysen et al. 1996). In these experiments, chimpanzees were trained to interpret 'Arabic' symbols for numbers, and had to perform a counterintuitive task in which selection of a lower-valued symbol from a presented pair of symbols resulted in being given a food reward proportional to the higher-valued symbol presented. For example, given two symbols, '2' and '6', if you choose the 6 you are given two bits of candy, but if you choose the 2, you are given six bits of candy. Chimpanzees learned to perform this task maximizing the food reward; they tended significantly to choose the lower-valued symbol. This shows an ability to think with symbols to advantage. The animals had all been successfully trained in the meanings of the symbols 1-6, so they knew that 2 signifies a smaller number than 6. But, interestingly, when the presented stimuli were not symbols, but actual heaps of candy, despite constant frustration, the chimpanzees could not overcome their urge to select the **larger** pile, which always resulted in their receiving the smaller, less desirable, pile of candy. Thinking in symbols can be used to advantage, but in these chimpanzees, the immediate prospect of real food overrides the symbolic thinking. Here we see the interaction of **ability** to use symbols, which chimpanzees are clearly capable of, with **motivation** to use symbols, which in chimpanzees can be easily overridden by immediate drives.

As many ape language-training studies have shown, apes can learn arbitrary symbols, given the right environment. To reach human levels, chimpanzee word-learning would need to be qualitatively boosted by several orders of magnitude. It is quite conceivable that this degree of improvement in memory and learning was accomplished by human ancestors in the 3 or 4 million years since australopithecines. Still today, there is individual variation among humans in size of vocabulary, significantly correlated with genetic factors. Stromswold (2001) surveyed a large range of individual variation in language influenced by genetic factors, including vocabulary size. In a meta-analysis of one set of twin studies, she concluded that 'genetic factors accounted for the majority of the variance in older children's vocabulary (53%) with shared environmental factors accounting for only 18% of the variance and nonshared environmental factors accounting for 29% of the variance' (p. 669). Indeed, it seems very plausible that the growth of lexical capacity is a significant contributor to the spectacular tripling in brain size since the australopithecines.[16] Such continuous growth implies a constant selection pressure in one direction.

In the above, the key phrase is 'given the right environment'. In captivity, modest latent symbol-learning abilities come to the surface in apes. But somehow, our ancestors had to **give themselves** the right social environment. The hypothesis is that the social arrangements of our ancestors changed so that their reciprocal relations with each other became more like the (one-way) relations between home-reared apes and their human keepers, whereby the keepers routinely provide aid and succour. In human societies, members of the same social group routinely provide each other with aid and succour, and even sometimes help strangers. How this happened is more of a puzzle than the steady quantitative incrementation of arbitrary symbol-learning capacity. The social environment we are looking for is one in which individual animals can reap some advantage from enhanced symbol-learning capacity and from pointing indexically to things. I will suggest in the next chapter that the crucial change was one affecting the interpersonal relationships characteristic of early hominid communities.

Standardized alarm and food calls are quite situation-specific, as Jackendoff (2002, p. 239) notes, by contrast with children's one-word utterances. 'A food call is used when food is discovered (or imminently anticipated) but not to suggest that food be sought. A leopard alarm call can be used to report the sighting of a leopard, but cannot be used to ask if anyone has seen a leopard lately' (p. 239). By contrast, humans, even children at the one-word stage, use words to convey a range of different situations, so that, for example, *Daddy* can be used to call Daddy into the room, to announce Daddy's arrival outside, to say that a shoe belongs to (or is somehow associated with) Daddy, and so on. Just as the relatively harsh exigencies of life in the wild do not bring out the latent ability to learn symbols and to point, they also severely narrow the range of interpretations that can usefully by be assigned to signals. In the wild, chimpanzees do not have the individual dispositions, or the communal social relations, that promote behaviour in relation to food other than finding it, eating it, and occasionally sharing it with those nearby. Getting food is an almost constant pressure. When bellies are

---

[16] However, the relationship between brain size in individuals and their intellectual performance is very variable, as studies of microcephalics show. Some small-brained people have high IQs. For a brief and lively survey, see Skoyles and Sagan (2002, p. 237–240); see also Sells (1977); Sassaman and Zartler (1982); Rossi et al. (1987); Giedd et al. (1996).

full, the pressure is temporarily off, but hunger soon comes again, and the animals are adapted to having a largely one-dimensional relationship with food, confined to its immediate presence. Likewise, even more strongly, with predators. It is highly adaptive, in a wild environment, to have a one-dimensional relationship with predators—you simply escape from them. With both food and predators, the calls signify an immediately present situation.

Captive apes, such as Kanzi, can acquire less situation-specific uses of symbols, for example with meanings like HURT and VISIT, showing that there is not a qualitative gap between bonobo and human abilities, but rather a difference in degree. Even captive apes are very preoccupied with the here and now, but they do have some capacity to communicate about things which are not so immediate. This capacity is brought out in the captive environment, where survival pressures are less severe. Humans have evolved an ability to detach their overt physical responses to signals from direct action responding to the referents of the signals. We can discuss the difference between a leopard's spots and a tiger's stripes without being scared up the nearest tree. It is intriguing to speculate on the possible change in conditions which enabled this degree of detachment. There could have been a co-evolutionary feedback cycle between an enhancement of ability to plan for predator-avoidance and food-getting and a decrease in the immediacy of survival pressures. If you can plan your hunting a day ahead and be more confident that you will not go hungry, your response to the mention of food will not necessarily be to look for it immediately. This speculation poses the twin questions of how such a co-evolutionary cycle could have been initiated, and why it has only affected humans.

I have emphasized in previous sections the important differences in animal behaviours that have often all been lumped together under the heading of 'referential'. As noted, deictic pointing is referential in a quite different way from the standardized alarm calls of animals such as vervets. In deictic pointing there is no implicit semantic content: you can point at anything, be it a leopard, an eagle, a python, a rock, your mother, your baby, or whatever object you want to draw someone's attention to. Deictic pointing is bound by the here and now of the pointing act. But standardized alarm calls mean what they mean consistently across situations, and do not necessarily involve drawing the attention of recipients to the actual object that stimulated them. On hearing a leopard alarm, don't waste time gazing at the leopard, even if you have seen it—just get up a tree!

In human languages, both standardized (i.e. conventional) semantically contentful signals (in the human case learned, not innate) and deictic devices dependent on the place and time of the utterance (like the words *here* and *now*) are indispensable, and combine productively. No working language can manage without deictic devices, nor of course without semantically contentful expressions. An increasing capacity to learn vocabularies of arbitrary symbols is not enough to give the beginnings of human-like communication. It is necessary to link the use of these symbols to specific contexts of use, by means of deictic devices. So, in the evolution of language, we need to look for signs of the **integration** of deictic devices, such as pointing, with semantically contentful standardized symbols. As Kanzi's behaviour shows, bonobos in human settings can readily combine deictic gestures with the use of contentful symbols. The most common type of meaningful two-element combination used by Kanzi, listed by Greenfield and Savage-Rumbaugh (1990, p. 557), is one in which he names a category, such as PEANUT, with a lexigram, and points to an object of the relevant sort, for example, a peanut. Combinations of this type account for 182 of the 723 examples collected. The next most frequent two-element combination (119 occurrences) is also a combination of a lexigram and a pointing gesture; the example given by Greenfield and Savage-Rumbaugh (1990) is the lexigram for CARRY accompanied by a gesture to the researcher Phil, whom Kanzi wanted to carry him. So once symbols have been learned and deictic pointing has become habitual in apes, productive two-unit deictic+symbol combinations come naturally.

Human babies instinctively point and in their second year readily combine pointing gestures and contentful symbols For example, a baby will point to a dog and say something interpretable as 'dog'; or, a bit later in development, a baby will point to a drawer and say 'open'. These examples, strikingly like the Kanzi examples above, are from Goldin-Meadow and Butcher (2003). There are no quantitative comparisons of the frequency and fluency of deictic/symbolic combination by apes and human babies, but the impressionistic and anecdotal evidence indicates that human babies are more naturally disposed to combining pointing gestures with symbols than apes. In the ontogeny of language, this disposition to combine deictic pointing with symbol use is a stepping stone to the first combinatorial use of symbols: two-word utterances. This is shown convincingly by Goldin-Meadow and Butcher (2003).

For the moment the point is that the difference between apes and human infants in deictic/semantic integration is a matter of degree. So again, **given the right environment**, the disposition to integrate deixis with symbols can be hypothesized to have increased gradually by natural selection during the few million years since the australopithecines, in parallel with the increase in vocabulary-learning capacity. Indeed, the growth of vocabulary would provide an increased pressure to integrate symbols with deictic devices. As an informal example, say the vocabulary has grown to a stage where there is a conventionalized symbol for RUNNING, and a creature utters this symbol. The recipients are likely to want to know, in some circumstances, who or what is running, since joint attention to the same object cannot be expected in all circumstances.

The integration of deixis and symbols is the basis of declarative information-giving. The growth of symbolic vocabulary, and the increase in deictic/symbolic integration, can only take off if the animals concerned are disposed to give each other information. The quantitative dispositional differences (admittedly great) between humans and apes in these areas can be accounted for by gradual change under pressure from social arrangements conducive to free exchange of information. So it looks as if a crucial change preceding these increases is to be sought in the social dispositions of our remote ancestors.

Go to p304

CHAPTER EIGHT

Why Communicate? Squaring with Evolutionary Theory

I have suggested a couple of evolutionary changes that led to the first nearly language-like communication: gradual enhancement of the capacity for learning arbitrary symbols, and of the disposition to combine symbols with deictic gestures to convey elementary propositional meanings such as are expressed in English by *This is a peanut*. But why should these evolutionary changes have affected only one species? Why would such abilities be favoured by natural selection? They are only advantageous in very unusual (for the animal world) social circumstances, in which there is a willingness to share information with others, without too much risk of being taken advantage of. I suggest, then, that a crucial precursor to the appearance of these proto-linguistic abilities was not in itself a specifically linguistic change, but rather a shift in the normal social relationships between individuals in a group. How plausible are such changes from the viewpoint of evolutionary theory?

Before we start, here is a story that I think runs parallel to the concerns of this chapter. Antoine Magnan (1934, p. 8) concluded that, according to aerodynamical laws of air resistance, insect flight is impossible. The story somehow got narrowed down to bumblebees, which are big and heavy, relative to the size of their wings.[1] But insects can fly. The problem is now pretty well cracked, with some very heavy-duty aerodynamic theory (Ellington et al. 1996; Dickinson et al. 1999). Likewise, it seemed to early evolutionary theorists that altruism and cooperation shouldn't exist in nature; but they do. Read on.

---

[1] McMasters (1989) summarized this scientific urban myth entertainingly.

8.1 BRIDGES, BULLETS, MONSTERS, AND NICHES

In trying to answer any question about a unique phenomenon, we are necessarily out on a scientific limb. Scientific explanations are the better the more different kinds of data they account for. Newtonian mechanics was so impressive because it accounted for falling objects, and the movements of the moon, the planets, and the tides, all in a few simple formulae. Any general theory of why humans evolved the special ability to learn large numbers of arbitrary form–meaning pairings raises the question 'Yes, but why **only** humans?' If there can be a set of principles predicting the emergence of this phenomenon, we should expect to see it more often in the natural world. I plan to tell a story of how the ape abilities that we have so far seen could have combined to give the human ability. This, then, is a story of a coincidence, a coincidence with far-reaching consequences. There are no ape data that we can call upon to argue for, or against, the coincidental productive combination that I will suggest. There cannot be, because it has only happened once.[2] The quality of the story will have to be judged on how far it stretches what we know about the existing elements that, somehow, got combined.

It is common to emphasize the enormous gap that exists between human language and anything that animals are capable of. It is true that the difference between our cultural achievements and those of animals, to the extent that they have any, is extremely impressive. But small changes can have huge effects. Proverbs and folk wisdom are replete with recognition of small changes having (or preventing) large effects, from the last straw which breaks the camel's back, through 'tipping the balance', to the Dutch boy with his finger in the dyke. Consider an analogy with building a bridge across a river, or a thousand-mile pipeline across a desert. While the ends are not connected, the bridge or the pipeline is as good as non-existent; no traffic, or no oil, can flow. As soon as the last connection is made, however, there is a massive qualitative leap. Traffic or oil flows, and the surrounding ecology is changed for ever. New communities arise, to trade with and feed off the new traffic. Old roads and old communities fall into new uses, or disuse. If the bridge is almost built, needing just the last metre to join the ends, but some external catastrophe, like a war, intervenes, none of this happens. It is the final joining up of the ends, one small step, that makes the crucial difference.

---

[2] Well, it may have happened more than once, for example in related (sub-)species such as Neanderthals, but we don't know. If the Neanderthals did have something like language, it didn't save them from extinction.

The bridge analogy is not entirely apt because humans **plan** to build bridges, and their effects have usually been intended. But there are natural small events with sweeping, sometimes catastrophic, effects. River capture is one example. Here gradual erosion culminates in a relatively sudden breakthrough between river systems, with significant shifts in the drainage arrangements, and hence the ecology, of large land areas. Another example is the small temperature change needed to cause the phase transition from ice to liquid water, essential to life. We have already seen a genetic example in the case of normally monogamous prairie voles, in whom 'a change in the expression of a single gene in the larger context of pre-existing genetic and neural circuits can profoundly alter social behaviour, providing a potential molecular mechanism for the rapid evolution of complex social behaviour' (Lim et al. 2004, p. 754).

We are looking for a small change that made a big difference. But we must beware of some notorious traps in evolutionary theorizing, the traps of postulating magic bullets or hopeful monsters. These are in fact two faces of the same problem. The most common kind of magic bullet in this area is an unspecified genetic mutation that, somehow, we know not how, generated the desired phenotype, that, for example, changed animals with only chimpanzee-like capacities into modern humans with fully fledged linguistic capacities. In the very early days of generative linguistics, the 1950s and 1960s, when the structure of DNA had only recently been discovered, linguists, in common with most people outside the specialist field of genetics, had naive ideas about mutations. The idea of a 'macromutation' that is solely responsible for language is now largely discredited. Indeed the macromutation idea may always have been a straw man, because there are few serious proposals for it, and no genetically well-informed ones. The best known is by Richard Klein, suggesting a single far-reaching mutation within the last 100,000 years, initiating a cascade of neurological changes that led to modern human language Klein (1991, 2003). In a reply to this proposal, Wolpoff et al. (2004) put the counterargument succinctly:

There is no single silver bullet that will pin down language chronologically through either genetics or anatomy. . . . Language is a highly polygenic trait, and scores of selective sweeps must have occurred as the trait evolved during the Pleistocene. No single genetic change was sufficient for language, and it is a mistake to assume that the evolution of this highly complex trait was primarily saltational (Hauser et al. 2002). Rather, we must understand language in its fullest cognitive and social senses as involving a cluster of related features.   (Wolpoff et al. 2004, p. 536)

In this connection, the specifically human version of the FOXP2 gene (Enard et al. 2002), which appears to have arisen some time during the last 200,000 years, though relevant to language, is certainly not the single 'grammar gene' responsible for all our complex modern language capacity. Knight et al. (2000, p. 5) describe Bickerton (1990)'s proposal for 'the crucial mutation' as a macromutation, although that was not the term used by Bickerton. But the idea certainly had some informal currency. 'People at dinner last night kept asking me what Chomsky's innate grammar is all about. Where is this language macromutation in the brain, and all that? . . . Wrong question, of course' (Calvin and Bickerton 2000, p. 1). And Pinker (2003, p. 25) devotes a paragraph to arguing why the macromutation theory of language evolution is wrong. One biological objection to macromutations is that most, if not all, mutations are tiny copying errors, typically affecting a single nucleotide base, and massive changes to the whole DNA sequence seldom happen all at once. However, the macromutation idea does not necessarily refer to the actual DNA, but rather to the phenotype, being understood as a (possibly small) mutation that made a big change in the phenotype. Here, given our very limited knowledge of the relationship between genes and phenotype, especially when it comes to language, the objection to macromutations is not so well founded, because we do know that very small differences in the DNA can sometimes lead to major differences in the phenotype.

But if we're talking about big changes in the phenotype, as opposed to changes in DNA, then the trap labelled 'hopeful monsters' opens up. Evolution does not plan. It works by random experiments. Given an already well-adapted animal, changing its phenotype in some tiny way may possibly lead to an improvement in its fitness, its adaptedness to its environment. Many such changes, of course, are deleterious, and don't survive. But tiny changes to the design of a well-adapted animal do stand a fighting chance of making some improvement. By contrast, changes which affect a whole lot of things at once are much less likely than tiny changes to come up with any overall improvement. Anyone who has designed a complex machine or computer program knows that you need to test each individual small change before proceeding to the next. If you change a lot of things at once, almost certainly it won't work.

It is not possible at this stage in our knowledge completely to avoid appealing to an evolutionary step not yet fully understood. We must limit the damage as far as possible by making the step as small as possible. In terms of the earlier bridge analogy, we must show that the ends of the bridge waiting to be joined up are really not very far apart—and here we have in mind the behavioural phenotype, not the genotype. This has been the strategy so far in this book: to explore the full range of cognitive and communicative pre-adaptations in animals, especially those closely related to humans, that could together have formed a platform for a unique human small step towards language. The word *towards* here is chosen deliberately. We must not expect the effect of the small step to transform the surrounding ecology **instantaneously**. Going back to the bridge metaphor, after the ends were joined up, the surrounding ecology was indeed changed, and faster than any changes in the preceding centuries, but the changes took some time, perhaps many generations.

Another metaphor, now standard in evolutionary theory, is **niche**. The world provides a vast complex range of possible environments, not all parts or features of them exploited by living organisms. In the early history of life on Earth, there was light, but it was an unexploited niche. The appearance of photosynthesis allowed light energy to be exploited by transforming it into chemical energy, stored in carbohydrates. Photosynthesis opened up a huge range of possibilities for new types of organisms. The ecological landscape changed. Primitive plants and oxygen accumulated, and the abundance of plants and oxygen constituted a new niche, unexploited (indeed toxic) until aerobic metabolism evolved. This in turn led to an avalanche of new lifeforms capable of breathing the oxygen and feeding off the plants. Much later, the land was a niche unexploited by animals. It took some quite special changes to allow the first animals to begin to exploit the terrestrial niche. They were arthropods, already equipped with exoskeletons, giving the possibility of protection against dessication and support for their increased bodyweight out of water. No doubt their first steps on land were faltering, but they clung onto their new environment well enough to breed and give natural selection a whole new set of adaptive possibilities to explore.

Maynard Smith and Szathmáry (1995, p. 6) identify eight major transitions in evolution, including the transition from replicating molecules to populations of molecules in compartments, the transition from RNA to DNA, the appearance of multicellular organisms, the evolution of sex, the emergence of cooperation and animal social groups, and finally the evolution of human societies with language. Each major transition involves a new level of information transmission, which is exploited by selection over new types of information-processing devices. In an abstract way, each new level of information transmission is a new niche, which gets colonized by new kinds of entities.

Evolution typically goes faster after a move into a new, previously unexploited, niche. Some mutations and recombinations that would have led to dead ends in the old environment have new scope. The new environment determines new channels guiding the evolutionary trajectory of the lineage. For example, changes enabling fast running are of no use to an animal living in water, but once it moves onto land, that particular kind of locomotion can be very advantageous. Correspondingly, some of the old restrictive channels dictated by the previous environment, now left behind, no longer apply, and the genome of the lineage is free to become more varied in certain respects. For instance, some of the body-streamlining adaptations from an aquatic life can be abandoned without disadvantage on land, and old streamlining adaptations are under less pressure to be maintained. So entry into a new niche tends to speed evolution in some directions and in other areas to permit more variation to accumulate, providing more fodder for later selection.

In introducing the idea of an evolutionary niche, we need to keep two of the component ideas separate. There is adaptation to a previously unexploited niche, and there is **niche-construction**. This latter idea is relatively new, though well supported (see Laland et al. 2000). In an older, simpler theory, the environment provides niches, like liquid water, or light, or land, that can be occupied by the first opportunist organism to evolve the capacity for exploiting what they offer. The niches are always there in the environment, waiting to be filled. It is now recognized that evolving organisms also change their environment. Plants breathing out oxygen is an example. Before plants, there wasn't all that free oxygen in the atmosphere. Beavers building dams is a much more recent example.

This small, but growing, body of theory suggests that niche construction and ecological inheritance may be of greater evolutionary importance than generally conceived. In our view, the capacity of populations of organisms to modify their selective environment through niche construction, and the fact that many of these changes persist for multiple generations, demand an adjustment in understanding of the evolutionary dynamic, because they suggest that a description of evolutionary change relative only to independent environments is rather restrictive. In the presence of niche construction, adaptation ceases to be a one-way process, exclusively a response to environmentally imposed problems: instead it becomes a two-way process, with populations of organisms setting as well as solving problems (Lewontin 1983; Odling-Smee et al. 1996). Evolution consists of mutual and simultaneous processes of natural selection and niche construction.

(Laland et al. 2000, p. 135)

The most spectacular example of niche construction is, of course, humans, who have transformed their natural environment, adding many artificial features. The environment into which a child is born on an impoverished housing estate in a Western country is full of challenges—traffic, balconies of tower blocks, discarded needles, household chemicals of all sorts, junk food, school—completely different from the challenges which faced the first human babies 150,000 years ago; for these latter, finding water and hunting or gathering their own food were the highest priorities, occupying most of their time. This human example involves the evolution of rich socially transmitted, learning-mediated cultures, a factor not present in oxygen-emitting plants or dam-building beavers.

The addition of learning and culture to the picture constitutes a phase shift in the concept of 'environment'. The environment is no longer just the physical potentials and challenges, the food and the pitfalls. Surviving among foreigners is a totally different problem from surviving alone in the desert or the jungle. The trick is to learn not to be foreign. You can't change your skin colour or your eye-shape, but the better you can learn what these people around you had, in their turn, to learn, the better your prospects of thriving. Their ancestors gradually created a culture, partly physically by building special buildings such as temples and churches, inventing clothing of certain styles, and so on, but the crucial ingredient for survival in any culture is to learn the **significance** of these physical artefacts. A church is not just any building; it is linked to a set of learned behaviours defining it as a church. These behaviours, though manifest in flesh-and-blood activities of human bodies, are not physically causally related to survival and reproduction in the same way as picking berries, running from predators, or fecundating a sexual partner. Cultural environments can change very fast, much faster than typical physical environments, so an ability to learn whatever their characteristics are is the key to survival.

As soon as culturally transmitted, learning-mediated traditions start to get established, pressure to be able to learn arbitrary associations increases. Cultural invention is cheap, given some disposition to innovative behaviour and some likelihood of being learned from. With these two 'givens', we can expect a positive feedback loop, pushing the capacity for learning, and expanding the body of what needs to be learned.

If, as seems likely, the rate of change of cultural niche construction is rapid relative to independent changes in the environment, biological evolutionary rates may be accelerated. A number of gene-culture coevolutionary models have found that, as cultural transmission may homogenise a population's behaviour, and because culturally transmitted traits can spread through populations rapidly compared with genetic variants, culture can generate atypically strong selection (Feldman and Laland 1996).

(Laland et al. 2000, p. 140)

Beltman et al. (2004) investigated the relation between niche-construction and the emergence of new species. In their theoretical model they established a relationship between learning and speciation: 'when colonization without genetic adaptation [i.e. by learning, JRH] is successful, a stronger mating preference makes genetic divergence easier' (p. 35).

Is the evolution of learned behaviour a case of adaptation to an independently existing niche, or a case of niche-construction? It is usually both, in varying strengths. A case where the learning adapts to an existing niche, but only minimally creates a new niche, is the case of the 'nursing poke', where, by ontogenetic ritualization, a ritual develops between an infant chimpanzee and its mother, allowing the baby to get to the nipple with little hassle to both parties (as discussed in Chapter 6.5). The independently given environment to which the baby's learning is an adaptation is the mother chimp's body shape, with the arm often blocking access to the nipple. The mother and infant together learn a behaviour that makes access easier. So the infant's learning changes his mother's behaviour, at first uncooperative, later cooperative, when she moves her arm as soon as he pokes her side. But it stops there. The ritual only involves the mother and her baby, not the whole troop.[3] There is no general effect on the environment of other members of the population, so no general niche is constructed to which other animals have to adapt. Knight (2002, p. 148), as mentioned earlier, wrote that such ontogenetic ritualization of 'conventional signals will be confined within isolated, restricted pockets of social space where sufficient trust momentarily prevails'. In the case of the 'nursing poke' the restriction is due not least to the topic of the communication, namely the mother's nipple, which only she can provide.

But note in the nursing-poke case the special cooperative nature of the mother–infant relationship. This mother–infant-specific ritualized behaviour can only develop within this cooperative framework. If cooperation

[3] Things might possibly be different where a mother is nursing several young, or where several mothers nurse each other's offspring, as with lions. In such cases it is possible that ontogenetically ritualized behaviours could arise involving a whole family group. There are no reports of this, that I know of.

were more general and routine within a group, one would expect further learned conventional communicative routines to develop, adapted to other tasks faced by the group. If such conventional learned communicative behaviour were to develop, even in a very simple form not yet like full human language, infants newly born into the group would enter a niche created for them by previous generations, and there would be evolutionary advantage in their being genetically disposed to learn the conventions of the group.

In many fields, fast incremental changes are the product of feedback mechanisms giving rise to runaway processes. In evolution, sexual selection (such as is often held responsible for the peacock's spectacular tail) and predator–prey arms races are examples of such runaway processes fuelled by feedback mechanisms. Hurford and Kirby (1999) construct a model in which there is an 'arms race' between speed and proficiency in learning the established communicative code of a community and the actual size of the code to be learned. As the conventional code is augmented near its biologically given limits on learnability by occasional cultural innovations, there is more for the child to learn. This creates pressure for more efficient learning, which in turn creates spare biological capacity for the invention and absorption of further cultural innovations. 'Our model depicts a self-feeding spiral of language size responding to increases in speed of acquisition, and speed of acquisition in turn responding to increased language size' (p. 63). This is an example, in the domain of language evolution, of feedback between a culturally created environmental niche and the evolving biological ability to adapt to, and augment, that niche. Something like it may actually have happened. The model is predicated on an assumption that there is an evolutionary advantage in being able to produce and interpret communicative signals.

What we are looking for, because this is the human case, is the establishment, facilitated by a cooperative social environment, of group-wide learned arbitrary communicative conventions, whose very establishment constructs a social niche that all new members of the group must adapt to, by learning. The 'magic bullet' and 'hopeful monster' jibes warn us to try to find an evolutionary step that is as plausible as possible, minimizing the gap between the 'before' and 'after' situations. On the other hand, the notions of niche, and particularly niche-construction, give cause to believe that relatively fast and sweeping changes are provided for by evolutionary theory, provided the conditions can be set out adequately.

8.2 EVOLUTIONARY THEORIES OF ALTRUISM AND COOPERATION

8.2.1 Cooperation in Language

In linguistic pragmatics, it is taken for granted that much human communication is based on a Principle of Cooperation, introduced by Paul Grice (Grice 1967, 1975), which has been a cornerstone of theories and courses in pragmatics for three decades. The Gricean Principle of Cooperation is a convenient place to start, being relatively concrete and perspicuous, and because cooperation is characteristic of much, if not all, human use of language. Grice bridged a gap between formal logical studies and the facts of ordinary conversation. He thereby solved a puzzle which had often caused enormous unease to students of logic who also had an interest in the ordinary use of language. The problem is that we modern humans can readily communicate by saying things that are patently false, or apparently irrelevant to the matter in hand, or apparently less than ideally informative.

One of Grice's examples was the flowery, and now old-fashioned, compliment 'You're the cream in my coffee'. In the days of its currency, this communicated something like 'You make my day perfect'. But no person is literally cream or sits in a coffee cup, so the utterance must always be literally false. But it can be made sense of if the hearer believes that the speaker, though technically uttering a falsehood, is nevertheless trying to convey something informative. The hearer, in other words, looks behind the obvious falsehood for some interpretation related to its literal meaning, on the assumption that some related truth **is** being intended. Take another example. If on a lonely road I tell a stranger that my car has broken down, and he replies 'There's a garage down the road', I am normally safe in inferring that the garage is probably open. This is because I presume that the speaker is trying to help me. If he knew the garage was closed, it would be unhelpful to tell me about it, but since he did choose to tell me about it, I can infer, based on the premiss that he is being cooperative, that the garage is indeed likely to be open. Everyday conversation is laden with examples like this. Typically, people just don't deliberately say unhelpful things to each other. You infer a speaker's intended message, couched in an apparently 'illogical' utterance, using the assumed helpfulness of the speaker as a major premiss in the inferential process.

Grice's theory has been technically superseded by Relevance Theory (Sperber and Wilson 1986). 'Relevance-theoretic pragmatics differs from other Gricean approaches.... It does not treat communication as

necessarily cooperative in Grice's sense; for communication to be successful, the only goal that speaker and hearer need to share is that of
understanding and being understood' (Wilson 1999, p. 720). Certainly,
not all communication is cooperative. Deliberate deception is the obvious counterexample. Think also of cross-examination of a defendant in
court, where the defendant may well not wish to cooperate fully with
the barrister. Some politicans and evangelical preachers are adept at
communication, but in what sense could their speeches be said to be
'cooperating' with their audience? Nevertheless, even with examples such
as these, and assuming Relevance Theory, there is is still a crucial sense
in which cooperation between speaker and hearer is involved in all truly
communicative exchanges. Even in an act of deliberate deception, the
deceiving speaker at least cooperates to the extent that he couches his message in a code which the hearer understands; there is momentary cooperation in the very transmission of the message, even if the longer-term
goal of the speaker is not helpful to the hearer. Momentarily, during the
production and parsing of the deceiving utterance, speaker and hearer are
playing the same game together. Deception is 'the exception that proves
the rule'. Most human conversation is not deliberately deceptive, and
speakers mostly adhere to the Gricean maxim of telling the truth. If language were not used most of the time for honest purposes, deception using
language would not be possible. Confidence tricksters exploit the existence
of a generally high level of honesty, on which people come to depend.

Figuring out the intentions of others is not a uniquely human attribute.
As we have seen, apes are very calculating creatures, and can plot the
intentions of other apes, or at least their future actions, from their movements. A hungry chimpanzee seeing another making a move towards food
will accelerate its own movement in that direction, to get the food first. A
junior male chimpanzee will copulate behind a rock, to avoid being seen
at it by a dominant male. So a variety of mind-reading is well attested
in apes. Mind-reading is inference about the intentions, or at least the
impending actions, of others. Inference is always partly based on given
premises brought to the situation, and not evident in the situation itself.
The ape racing another for food makes an assumption (i.e. takes as a
premiss) that apes of his kind typically go for food of that kind. In the
human case, we routinely bring to the interpretation of conversation the
premiss that others are likely to be being helpful, even if it takes a bit of
work in inferring the intended message from what they actually say.

Grice's Cooperative Principle is usually presented as a basic fact about
human use of language, accounting for much that would otherwise not

make sense. The linguist interested in evolution is bound to ask how any such general principle of cooperative behaviour came to exist. Why are humans generally so cooperative with each other in their everyday conversation? This question plugs into an area that has been of intense interest to theoretical biologists. From the viewpoint of Darwinian theory, which emphasizes selection of traits benefiting individuals, it is a prima facie puzzle why any creature should help another, unless the helping is also to its own benefit, which often it is not.

Besides the term *cooperation*, the term *altruism* is often used in this area of theory, and sometimes the two terms are used interchangeably. Moore (1984) points out important differences between altruism and cooperation (and also between helping and sharing). Altruism is defined as action which **does not** benefit the actor, but only some other creature. Cooperation, as its prefix *co-* indicates, requires joint action, and the problem here is that other people can't be relied upon to cooperate. This contrasts with altruism, which can be done by a single actor without relying on cooperation by the beneficiary. Cooperation is usefully defined as bringing greater rewards to a pair of cooperators than either could expect if they acted individually. Limited examples of altruism exist in nature. Intentional cooperation[4] in non-human nature is rare, if it exists at all. Perhaps surprisingly, humans are among the most altruistic and cooperative of species. We will have a look at some theories of altruism and cooperation in the natural world, concentrating first on two prominent theories: Kin Selection (and the related idea of Inclusive Fitness) and Reciprocal Altruism (whose best-known example is the Tit-for-Tat strategy).[5] Kin Selection is a theory of altruism; Reciprocal Altruism, despite its name, is rather a theory of cooperation.

Both Kin Selection theory and Reciprocal Altruism theory postulate idealized and simplified conditions. The great advantage of such idealized theories is that they can be treated with precise mathematical analysis or, failing that, by computer simulation. Theorists acknowledge that the real world is messier than the simple conditions studied by the theory, but assume that the messiness merely contributes random noise to the clean mathematical or computational results. Such a theory, if the idealized

---

[4] The qualification 'intentional' will be explained later.

[5] The first section, entitled 'Benselfishness', of Chapter 7 of Dan Dennett's *Freedom Evolves* (Dennett 2003b) is a brilliant dashing gallop through this area, ending up with a view like my own, but I feel you have to know the work he's writing about to understand how he gets there. My own treatment here will be more pedestrian and pedagogical in flavour.

conditions succeed in capturing essential properties of the real systems
we are interested in, gives us an insight into how these properties interact
with each other in reality. It is the familiar story of idealization in science,
such as postulating frictionless surfaces, or perfectly rigid rods or a perfect
vacuum, in physics. In physics, such idealizations have been fruitful. The
idealizations involved in theories of Kin Selection and Reciprocal Altruism have also been fruitful.

The purpose of discussing these theories is to explore what explanations there can be for humans' great willingness to give each other useful
information in language, altruistically and/or cooperatively. Seeing what
these theories can offer presupposes that the use of language is altruistic
and/or cooperative, which it clearly often is. We will see in these theories a substantial, though still partial, contribution to an explanation of
why humans have evolved a communication system capable of imparting
enormously rich and detailed information. Reciprocal Altruism is usually
discussed within the general framework of Evolutionary Game Theory,
which compares the prospects of alternative behavioural strategies win-
ning or losing in specified circumstances. A common feature of Kin Selection and Reciprocal Altruism is that they show how, despite appearances
of pure altruism, the apparent altruists (or their genes) actually benefit
from such behaviour. Other theories, to be discussed in the following
section, focus less on action apparently to the benefit of others, and
explore the ways in which communication benefits the sender, rather than
the recipient, of a message. The central question surrounding all these
theories is *cui bono?*—who gets any benefit from communication? I will
adopt an eclectic answer. We do not need to suppose that the use of
language must always be either wholly for the benefit of the hearer, or
alternatively wholly for the benefit of the speaker. Certainly, some uses of
language are mostly altruistic, just for the benefit of the hearer, but also in
many cases the speaker gets a lot out of it too. We will start by looking at
theories explaining altruistic and cooperative behaviour.

8.2.2 Kin Selection and Inclusive Fitness

Kin Selection theory (and its relative, Inclusive Fitness theory) accounts
for a disposition to behave altruistically towards kin in proportion to
the closeness of their biological relationship to the behaver. The theory
is emphatically not a theory about 'the survival of the species'; it is a
theory about the continuation across successive generations of the genetic
dispositions of individuals. In vertebrates, the most selflessly altruistic

behaviour is that of a mother to her infants. This is the formative idea in Kin Selection theory, as propounded by Dawkins (1976) in his version of Hamilton (1964)'s theory of Inclusive Fitness. If a mother is genetically disposed to look after her babies, her babies are likely (a) to survive, and (b) to carry into the next generation the disposition to look after their own young. We have to express it in terms of likelihood because a mammal mother gives birth to a baby that has at least a 50% chance of inheriting some specific gene of hers. Given some probability that the father also carries that gene, the probability of the baby having it is greater than 50%. If a mother with the look-after-your-babies gene has several babies, the chances are very high that that gene will be present among them. Since she will (inevitably, barring accidents) look after her babies, then the chances of this gene propagating into the next generation are high. Thus any such gene has a built-in nature tending strongly to ensure its own continuing propagation.

Kin Selection theory generalizes beyond mother–infant relationships to all biological relationships. The general formula, known as Hamilton's Rule, predicting the conditions under which altruistic behaviour will occur is:

$$BENEFIT \times RELATEDNESS > COST.$$

In other words, it is worth acting altruistically to someone else if the benefit to them, diluted by their degree of genetic closeness to you, outweighs the cost to you.

Let us say that, statistically in general for any other-directed action, *BENEFIT* to the recipient of some action is any increase in the average number of offspring after the act in question, and that *COST* to the actor is any decrease in the average number of offspring after the act. *RELATEDNESS* is reckoned in the theory in the following terms[6]: a parent is 50% related to its child; siblings with the same parents are also 50% related to each other; a grandparent is 25% related to its grandchild; a great-grandparent is 12.5% related to its great-grandchild; a blood uncle or aunt is 25% related to his or her nephew or niece. This is the commonest statement of relatedness, consistent with the principle that the relatedness between a pair of individuals is the probability that by recent common descent they will share the same allele at a given locus. The technical literature on Kin Selection theory develops other definitions of relatedness:

---

[6] In species where all individuals are diploid, bearing two sets of genes, each set inherited from one parent.

'Later, (Hamilton 1970, 1972) redefined relatedness in a more general way as a statistical measure of genetic similarity regardless of its source. The coefficient of relatedness (r) was redefined as the regression slope of recipient genotype on actor genotype' (Pepper 2000, p. 356). A regression slope can be either positive or negative, which a probability cannot. Allowing for negative relatedness generalizes the theory to account for spiteful behaviour as well as altruistic behaviour. Relatedness is not, of course, the overall percentage of genes shared by two individuals, an interpretation which would make a human about 98% related to a chimpanzee! For simplicity, as far as we need to evaluate Kin Selection theory here, it will be suitable to stick with the percentage characterizations of relatedness given at the beginning of this paragraph.

Putting this concretely, say the cost to a mother of sacrificing food to her child during a famine is that, in her weakened state and at her age, she can expect to have one less further child than if she did not make that sacrifice: so *COST* here is 1. Say the extra nourishment given to the child saves its life and makes it likely to have one child of its own, rather than none: so here *BENEFIT* is also 1. Now, it is **not** the case that $1 \times 0.5 > 1$, so in these circumstances an altruistic act is not advantageous.

But change the scenario, so that the mother, at her age, cannot expect to have further children anyway; now the cost to her is zero, and if the benefit to the child is the same as before, the conditions in the formula are satisfied, and an altruistic sacrifice would ensure the continuation of the gene into the next generation. Or say that the child recipient of the action might expect to have one or two offspring, expressed as an expectation of 1.5, while the mother can expect to have at most one further child, expressed as 0.5. In this case again, Hamilton's condition for altruism from mother to child is met, as $1.5 \times 0.5 > 0.5$.

There is undoubtedly something right about this theory; it does seem to explain some things about the world. Some instinct tells animals 'Protect your own kin'. The strength and manner of realization of this instinct varies from species to species. It accounts for the care given by parents to their offspring, most conspicuously a mother's care for her babies. McGrew (1975) reports that of 457 instances of banana-giving among chimpanzees observed at Gombe, 391 (86%) were between mother and offspring. Female ground squirrels tend to live near to close relatives, whereas males move out of the kin group, and females give alarm calls significantly more often than males; this is interpreted as natural selection favouring a disposition specifically to warn genetic kin of danger (Sherman 1977).

A male lion courting a lioness with cubs that are not his will often ruthlessly kill them to gain sexual access to the female (Packer and Pusey 1983). But male lions do not kill their own cubs. So a cub-killing behaviour distinguishes between kin and non-kin. This pattern extends to humans as well. It is more common for stepfathers to kill their stepchildren than it is for them to kill their own children. Daly and Wilson (1982) studied 508 homicides successfully investigated in Detroit in 1972: 'consanguineal kin were relatively rarely killed in comparison to spouses and other non-relatives (chi-square, 1df = 161, p < .0001). . . . This analysis suggests that unrelated cohabitants are at dramatically higher risk than related cohabitants' (Daly and Wilson 1982, p. 373).

It is still controversial whether Kin Selection theory works well to explain the self-sacrificing behaviour of many eusocial[7] insects, with haplodiploid genetic systems. A diploid organism has two parallel sets of chromosomes and passes half of its genes to its offspring, the rest coming from the other parent; a haploid organism has only one set of chromosomes and passes all of its genes to its immediate offspring.[8] Eusocial ants, bees, and wasps have a mixture of haploid and diploid arrangements. 100% of a haploid father's genes are passed on to his diploid daughters, which get another 50% of their own genes from their mothers; thus sisters from the same parents are 75% related to each other. Hamilton (1964) originally suggested that haplodiploidy and Kin Selection account for greater self-sacrificial behaviour between sisters in these species. This suggestion has gained wide currency but is still controversial. Sceptical or opposing arguments are found in Lin and Michener (1972); Evans (1977); Wilson (2005); Wilson and Hölldobler (2005). Many haplodiploid species are not social, and examples of eusociality are found, if rarely, among diploid species, such as naked mole rats. To the contrary, Foster et al. (2006) argue that 'kin selection remains the key explanation for the evolution of altruism in eusocial insects' (p. 57). An excellently informative overview of the evolution of insect social behaviour can be found in Brockmann (1984).

---

[7] Eusociality is usually defined as satisfying three conditions: (1) animals cooperate in the rearing of each other's young—there are no nuclear, or even extended, families within the colony; (2) the generations overlap, so that there is continuity of the colony; (3) some individuals do not reproduce, whereas others bear the brunt of the reproductive labour. Eusociality is most common in hymenoptera (ants, bees, and wasps) but is found in other phyla too.

[8] Which, to complicate matters, could be diploid, through sexual reproduction by two haploid parents.

Fortunately, we can steer clear of this controversy, as humans and their close relatives are diploid. In uniformly diploid animals such as vertebrates, the reach of Kin Selection theory quickly runs thin as genetic relatedness decreases.[9] The theory predicts a somewhat high distribution of altruistic acts between parents and children, and between siblings, but predicts a much sparser distribution of altruism beyond the outskirts of a nuclear family; the circumstances have to be unusual to predict an altruistic act towards a second cousin. In bonobo groups of about 125 (McComb and Semple 2005), for example, the relatedness between most pairs of individuals is 12.5% or less. Bertram (1976) 'calculated an average coefficient of relatedness between females in a typical pride as 0.15 (little more than between cousins) and argued that suckling another female's cub should evolve through kin selection if the benefit of the other cub exceeds seven times the cost to the altruistic female's own cub' (Kawecki 1991, p. 496).[10] Empirical research confirms the point. Mitani et al. (2000) studied the formation of alliances in wild chimpanzees, comparing genetic relatedness between individuals with the frequency of alliance-formation between the same animals. Contrary to expectations based on the success of Kin Selection theories, they concluded: '[t]hus far, current evidence suggests that genetic relatedness does not structure these within-community, "second-order" relationships' (p. 891). The authors make the reservation that their study relates to within-group alliances. The hostility between males from different groups can still probably be predicted on the basis of their lesser genetic relatedness.

In humans, an oft-cited example in support of Kin Selection is a study of Maine lobster fishermen (Palmer 1991). In two rather different groups of fishermen, one small and somewhat isolated, the other larger and in contact with tourist outsiders, it was found that fishermen of both groups preferentially gave information on the whereabouts of lobsters to their close relatives. The effect was stronger in the larger group; in the smaller group, non-kin individuals were nevertheless familiar and presumably trustworthy.

In the human case, however, a note of caution is advisable, as the possible role of learned and culturally transmitted ethical prescriptions against harming kin must also be considered. Evidence from animals tells us that

---

[9] A lack of migration over time tends to increase the degree of interrelatedness of individuals in a group, but also, of course, increases inbreeding.

[10] Kawecki's own argument, on the basis of simulations, is that 'sex-linkage [of an altruistic gene, as opposed to its autosomal inheritance] seems to enhance the probability of the evolution of altruism' (Kawecki 1991, p. 494), but the effect is not large.

any such cultural prescription is not against nature. It seems likely that cultural prescriptions have built on and strengthened a natural instinct, and extended the principle to all members of a group, kin or non-kin. But such prescriptions are passed through the medium of language, and our present goal is to seek factors existing in pre-linguistic species which might lead to the altruistic and cooperative exchange of information via an embryonic proto-linguistic system.

Empirical testing of Hamilton's Rule is difficult because of the problems inherent in estimating cost and benefit. The most precise study on humans in this respect is Bowles and Posel (2005).

Data on remittances sent by South African migrant workers to their rural households of origin allow an explicit test, to our knowledge the first of its kind for humans. Using estimates of the fitness benefits and costs associated with the remittance, the genetic relatedness of the migrant to the beneficiaries of the transfer, and their age- and sex-specific reproductive values, we estimate the level of remittance that maximizes the migrant worker's inclusive fitness. ... [T]he effect is modest: less than a third of the observed level of remittances can be explained by our kin-altruism model.

(Bowles and Posel 2005, p. 380)

To explain the emergence of altruistic communication across a whole social group, a notion of relatedness other than strict genetic relatedness could work, if, say, the relatedness of all individuals within a social group were to be defined as 100% (or close). But this would be counter to the spirit of Hamilton's theory, which stands solidly within the Selfish Gene tradition (Dawkins 1976) of accounting for behaviour in terms of Darwinian natural selection on the genes of individuals, passed on by biological replication. If, somehow, the hormonal basis of altruistic dispositions towards close kin could be 'beefed up' by some genetic change, we would expect more altruism to more distant kin, and perhaps even to non-kin, but such a possibility is outside Hamilton's Kin Selection framework, the impressive ingenuity of which relies solidly on a specifically genetic vision of relatedness. (See pp. 328–329 for actual data on such hormonal influence on trust among non-kin.)

Kin Selection theory is obviously highly idealized, with the basic model dealing in terms of single 'kin-altruism-genes' (of which there may be many). No behaviour is determined by a single gene. Altruistic acts in reality form a varied class, with little or no common core of motor components. What characterizes a class of actions as altruistic relies on complex knowledge and calculations of the circumstances. Sharing food and defending from aggression are both altruistic, but the physical actions involved are very different. If we are talking about a genetic disposition to altruism in any form (to kin or others), the mechanism has to involve higher cognitive faculties. It is much easier to see how evolution can engineer a mother's instinct to give her baby a nipple, than to see how evolution could engineer such an abstractly defined class of acts as all those lumped under the heading 'altruism'.

Of course, fathers are just as much parents of their offspring as mothers. Fathers and mothers make equal contributions to the genetic dispositions of their progeny. But paternity is much more difficult to be certain of than maternity. A mother knows that the baby she gives birth to is hers. A father seldom knows for certain whether the baby a female gives birth to is his. So it is much harder for evolution to engineer an altruistic disposition to his offspring in a male. A problem facing the implementation of Kin Selection theory in nature is the difficulty of knowing exactly who one's relatives are. The kin-identification problem is addressed by Axelrod et al. (2004), who develop a model of the co-evolution of innate traits (called 'tags', e.g. distinctive smell) indicative of relatedness. 'A remarkable result of the simulation model is that discrimination based on an unreliable and potentially deceptive indicator of kinship can actually increase the total amount of cooperation in the population' (p. 1835). This result is strongly facilitated by the local spatial organization of the agents in Axelrod et al. (2004)'s simulation. Individuals interacted very locally, with neighbours. It is well known that restricting interactions to neighbours or near-neighbours is a factor that facilitates the emergence of cooperation (see, for example, Sober 1992; Skyrms 1996; Dessalles 1999; Di Paolo 2000; Grim et al. 2006).

The possibility that a potentially deceptive indicator of kinship can help to promote cooperation leads the way to mechanisms that extend altruism beyond kin. It is appropriate at this point to elaborate on the difference between Kin Selection theory and its more general relative, Inclusive Fitness, pioneered by Hamilton (1964). The two ideas are often conflated, because common descent (i.e. kinship) is by far the most significant cause of genetic similarity between individuals. Hamilton's Inclusive Fitness theory operates with genetic similarity whatever its cause, common ancestry or otherwise (e.g. mere chance). Under the broad heading of Inclusive Fitness, altruism could in principle evolve between unrelated individuals. But the problem of identification remains. How do you tell whether someone is genetically similar to you, even if not through heredity? A theoretical solution to this problem was described by Hamilton (1964), and was later dubbed the 'Green Beard Effect' by Dawkins (1976). Hypothetically, any phenotypic trait (such as the whimsical green beard) that helps one to identify genetically similar individuals, correlated with a disposition to act altruistically towards carriers of that trait, could facilitate the evolution of altruism. In short, recognition of fellow altruists is distinct from recognition of kin. Jansen and van Baalen (2006) have shown through modelling that if the Green Beard Effect is caused by loosely coupled genes, 'this allows altruism to persist even in weakly structured populations and . . . can be expected to be much more prevalent than hitherto assumed' (p. 663). Keller and Ross (1998) claim to have found a green beard gene in the red ant; red ants with a particular gene combination kill queens that do not have it, and this gene combination is manifested in a characteristic odour; in this case the green beard is a specific smell. If killing certain ants entails sparing some other ants, this may be seen as altruism towards the lucky spared ones, but it is not a great example of the evolution of altruism.

In humans, an empirically attested example like a Green Beard Effect is the greater trust placed in people with similar faces to the truster (DeBruine 2002, 2005). Trust is not exactly altruism, but it presupposes altruism. If you trust someone, you assume that they will act altruistically towards you. Facial resemblance can be a cue to genetic relatedness, but facial resemblance to oneself would have been difficult for our remote ancestors to judge, before the advent of mirrors. A non-genetic factor can also be involved, as Buckingham et al. (2006) have shown that faces resembling those to which one has recently been exposed also tend to be judged as more trustworthy. This is a foot in the door for theories that account for altruism in terms of non-genetic relationships between the actors, such as membership of the same social group—a topic to be discussed just below and later in this chapter.

Biological kinship clearly plays a role in the apparently altruistic behaviour of animals. Human cultures have built cooperative structures on the model of biological kinship, but significantly transforming it. Chris Knight expresses it well: 'Humans do not just accept the facts of biology. Instead, they collectively reconstruct those facts' (Knight 2006, p. 1). Alan Barnard (1978), in a seminal article, defines 'universal kinship systems' as those in which every member of the social group is said to be the kin, in some relationship or other, with everyone else. Such nominal ties of kinship bring obligations to cooperate. And such universal kinship systems are widespread, especially among hunter-gatherers, being found in Australia, Asia, South America, and Africa.

A classic example of the cultural stretching of biological kinship, from Australian aboriginal tribal organization, is:

A man is always classed with his brother and a woman with her sister. If I apply a given term of relationship to a man, I apply the same term to his brother. Thus I call my father's brother by the same term that I apply to my father, and similarly, I call my mother's sister 'mother'. The consequential relationships are followed out. The children of any man I call 'father' or of any woman I call 'mother' are my 'brothers' and 'sisters'. The children of any man I call 'brother', if I am a male, call me 'father', and I call them 'son' and 'daughter'.   (Radcliffe-Brown 1931, p. 13)

Another example comes from the Hopi Pueblo Indians:

The position of the mother's sister is practically identical with that of the mother. She normally lives in the same household and aids in the training of her sister's daughter for adult life. . . . They co-operate in all the tasks of the household, grinding corn together, plastering the house, cooking and the like. . . . Their children are reared together and cared for as their own.
                                        (Eggan 1950, pp. 33, 35, 36)

Treating nephews and nieces like one's own sons and daughters replaces a biological relatedness of 25% by a 'virtual relatedness'[11] of 50%. This is a cultural strategy which seems to recognize the importance of biological kin, in the vocabulary typically used by the tribal peoples, and artificially (culturally) stretches the reach of kin selection. That this cultural stretch is so widespread testifies to its effectiveness and confirms our view of the limited reach of purely biological kin selection. This cultural adaptation provides a link between purely biological selection and cultural group selection, to be discussed in Section 4 of this chapter (pp. 293–305).

In summary, in our quest for an evolutionary theory that would provide a setting for the emergence of freely used communication across a whole group, kin selection may play some role, but it does not take us far enough. It is implausible that the genetic kin selection mechanism alone gave pre-humans a sufficient basis for establishing a group-wide set of learned conventional signals (assumed to be mostly altruistic or at least cooperative). But kin selection may have provided some part of the genetic impetus leading to cooperative behaviour extending beyond kin. Some evolutionary tinkering with altruistic dispositions towards kin could possibly have extended the scope of such dispositions beyond kin. Fitch (2005, p. 114) sees kin selection as an evolutionary foot in the door,

---

[11] The phrase 'virtual relatedness' is from Poulshock (2006).

paving the way for a mechanism of reciprocal altruism (to be discussed in the next subsection). 'The logical benefits of reciprocal altruism become almost unavoidable once a low-cost, unlimited communication system with the potential for honest information transfer has evolved via kin selection. . . . Crucially, a kin-selected communication system could pave the way to a reciprocally-altruistic information transfer among non-kin without any further genetic change, but the converse is not true' (Fitch 2005, p. 214). This seems right, and the idea will come up again in the following sections.

8.2.3 Reciprocal Altruism—Tit-for-Tat

We will look next at the other classic theory of cooperative behaviour, the theory of Reciprocal Altruism, due to Trivers (1971) and substantially backed up by work by Robert Axelrod (Axelrod and Hamilton 1981; Axelrod 1984, 1997). This theory takes as its starting point a kind of situation where people (typically just two) can enjoy great benefit if they cooperate with each other, but cannot predict whether the partner will cooperate or not. Furthermore if one party tries to cooperate and it turns out that the other one doesn't, the party who tries to cooperate suffers a cost, and the uncooperative party gets a small reward, but not as great a reward as if he had actually cooperated. A concrete example, originally due to Rousseau (1755) and made a bit more precise here, would be two strangers who together could catch a small deer, but could not do it alone, whereas each alone could manage to catch a hare. Importantly, neither stranger knows how the other will act. Struggling alone to catch a deer is a waste of time, and potentially dangerous. The meat from a small deer is worth the meat from three hares. This example is more natural than the usual example, called the Prisoner's Dilemma, but the formal nature of the dilemma facing both parties is the same: 'Is it worth my while to cooperate, given the uncertainty of the other person's action?':

Taking the deer/hare example, we can set out the rewards to one party in all the possible different circumstances in a table, like this:

	C	D
C	1.5	0
D	1	1

Here 'C' stands for 'cooperate' and 'D' stands for 'defect', the rows indicate possible choices for the actor, and the columns indicate the possible actions of the other person. In other words, if I join with you and you join with me in hunting a small deer (top left cell), I'll get half the deer (1.5 units of meat); if I think you'll help me catch a deer, but you defect (top right cell), I'll get nothing; if I don't join you in deer-hunting, whatever you do (bottom row), I'll get a hare (1 unit of meat). At this point you may object to the numbers—surely they have been set up in a deliberately, and artificially, dilemma-posing way?[12]

Yes, they have, but a prolific academic industry has grown around this kind of scenario, with interesting results, so it is worth pursuing a little further. Alternative numbers could define a different 'mutualistic' scenario, in which mutual cooperation was always more beneficial to both parties than if either defected. We'll come back to mutualism later.

For the moment, let's stay with the hare/deer example, and the particular numbers in the diagram above. Now, given that I can't know in advance whether you'll join me in a small deer hunt, what game should I decide to go after? Assuming that there is a 50-50 chance that you'll cooperate, half the time I'll get nothing if I try deer hunting, and half the time I'll get 1.5 worth of meat, so my average reward will be 0.75. On the same assumption, if I never bother going after deer, but go my own solitary way after hare, I can be assured of getting 1 unit of meat. Obviously, rationally, in this idealized setting of uncertain interaction between strangers, it makes sense for each to 'defect' and not to join in the cooperative activity. Not a promising start for a theory accounting for cooperation.

But things get much better when more realistic assumptions about social groups are made. It is true of humans, even, that they don't cooperate as readily with strangers as they do with people in their own social group. If a complete stranger asks you for money to invest in a money-making scheme, with a promised split of the profits, what do you do? But if a person with a known track record of not defecting on others makes the same offer, you consider it much more seriously. This is the basis of the development of this theory known as the Iterated Prisoner's Dilemma. Here, the participants meet each other repeatedly and are faced with the same kinds of choice as in the deer/hare example above, but, in various versions of the game, with different quantifications of the payoffs. Players can remember the behaviour of other individuals from previous episodes.

---

[12] In the 'classic' Prisoner's Dilemma scenario, as discussed in the literature, the numbers are more artificial than those I have assigned here to Rousseau's deer/hare example, with a requirement that the number in the bottom left cell be greater than that in the bottom right cell.

In the Iterated Prisoner's Dilemma scenario, a Tit-for-Tat strategy is often the most successful. This is a strategy that says: 'On first meeting someone, cooperate, and remember whether that person cooperates with you or defects; on subsequent meetings with that person, cooperate if he cooperated last time, and defect if he defected on you last time.' The success of this strategy was strikingly demonstrated in a public computer tournament devised by Axelrod (1984). Axelrod defined the Iterated Prisoner's Dilemma game, setting the exact payoff parameters for his version, and invited all and sundry to send in computer programs, in a standard format, to play against each other, in an all-play-all league setup. Many different strategies were implemented in the entries of these computer programs, some very simple, and some of Byzantine complexity. The simplest strategy of all, Tit-for-Tat, as defined above, submitted by Anatol Rapoport, beat all comers. That is, over all encounters, pitted against all other strategies, the Tit-for-Tat strategy accumulated more rewards than all the others. Axelrod publicized this outcome, and challenged the interested academic community to devise a strategy that could beat Tit-for-Tat. Now the entrants to the competition had an advantage: they knew what they were up against. Still, no entry was sent in that could outcompete Tit-for-Tat.

In the years that followed, of course, various sophisticated versions of basic Tit-for-Tat have been proposed, some of which perform marginally better than the basic version defined above. One such variant is O'Riordan (2000), called 'Forgiving Tit-for-Tat'. This strategy is essentially like the basic version, but 'forgives' one or two instances of defection by another person, by still cooperating with them, despite the treacherous behaviour on the last occasion. The strategy is only forgiving to a certain extent, and will not indefinitely cooperate with a consistent defector. O'Riordan writes of this strategy that 'the above modifications do not violate the first three recommendations (generally accepted) forwarded by Axelrod— never defect first, be retaliatory, be forgiving'. And O'Riordan shows in computer simulations how Forgiving Tit-for-Tat outperforms a range of other realistically chosen strategies.

More generally, 'recent models have shown that TFT is not always evolutionarily stable (Nowak and Sigmund 1993): indeed one can always find a mixed strategy capable of invading any pure strategy, including TFT (Dugatkin 1997)' (Palameta and Brown 1999, p. F1). The most obvious argument that Tit-for-Tat is not an evolutionarily stable strategy is that in a population wholly composed of Tit-for-Tatters, all encounters will be reciprocally cooperative—there will never be any occasion to use the retaliatory 'defect' option. Given this constantly cooperative society, a mutant who follows an 'always cooperate' strategy will be behaviourally indistinguishable from the innate Tit-for-Tatters, and so will suffer no disadvantage. The genetic make-up of the population can then drift randomly, so that it eventually consists of a mixture of the mutant unconditional cooperators and the original Tit-for-Tatters. Now in this society, a new mutant 'never cooperate' strategy can arise, and can prosper at the expense of the unconditional cooperators (while still being relatiated against by the remaining Tit-for-Tatters). But if by this time the remaining Tit-for-Tatters are a small proportion of the population, the mutant 'never-cooperators' can take over. (A good survey of a range of strategies, and their relative success against other strategies, can be found in Pusey and Packer 1997.)

All this computer simulation is artificial, of course, but it contains a serious element of applicability to nature. In an environment where cooperation for mutual reward is possible, creatures following a Tit-for-Tat strategy will prosper. Not all environments provide the opportunity. Rather few species, apes among them, meet the conditions under which reciprocal altruism works. Solitary creatures, who do not encounter the same individuals over and over again, will not be able to take advantage of this pattern of behaviour. So the theory applies particularly to species living in social groups. But the groups must be quite small for a recip-rocally altruistic strategy to be maintained (Boyd and Richerson 1988). Furthermore, animals whose 'choices' of behaviour are limited (e.g. zebras who just eat grass and follow the herd) have little or no scope for either cooperation or defection. It is only in animals with varied and versatile behavioural repertoires that such a strategy has a chance of taking off. And for the theory to apply in a general way, explaining a large range of physically different types of cooperative behaviour, having in common only their cooperative character, the animals concerned must have enough cognitive brainpower to be able to foresee the consequences of cooperative acts. For example, an animal must be able to calculate the effects of collaborating with another in a range of activities.

Finally, of course, Reciprocal Altruism theory relies on animals having a capacity for remembering, in detail, the past behaviour of others, a variety of episodic memory of the kind discussed earlier, in Chapter 3. Language itself can short-circuit this requirement. With language, an individual can know about the previous behaviour of another, not from its own experience, but at second hand from the reports of others (always providing these reports are reliable). A communication system enabling people to gossip about the reciprocal cooperativeness of others effectively expands the community of potential reciprocal cooperators. One can adjust one's behaviour towards another, not only from previous experience of that person, but on the basis of what one has heard about him. Enquist and Leimar (1993) modelled a population and showed this result. Under certain conditions, when coalitions between individuals were not very brief, and when it took a somewhat long time to find any new 'naive' (or sucker) individual to take advantage of, freeriders (non-cooperators) were eliminated even without the exchange of gossipy information about likely cooperators. But with the addition of gossip to the model, whereby information was circulated about who had recently cooperated and who had recently defected in some episode, the space of conditions under which freeriders were eliminated was expanded.

How far can the theories of Kin Selection and Reciprocal Altruism help us in explaining the rise of language? We have already noted the limited reach of Kin Selection—only to the outskirts of the nuclear family. Now we consider whether there is really any connection at all, as is often assumed in discussions of language evolution, between the use of language and altruism or cooperation. In what ways is human conversation anything like cooperative behaviours such as helping another person out of a difficult situation (say, stuck in mud, or in a fight) or truly collaborative hunting (as opposed to everyone happening to chase the same prey)? The basic use of imperative utterances is typically for the benefit of the speaker. Declarative utterances give information, but they don't give information **away**, because information is infinitely divisible without loss, unlike food. Giving information can be genuinely altruistic, as when an animal informs others of discovered food that is only enough to feed one animal. Indeed, as we have seen with Hauser (1992)'s study of rhesus macaques, there already seems to be some expectation among these animals that discoverers of food 'should' announce it. They get punished if they don't.

Oliphant (1997) makes an interesting attempt to apply Reciprocal Altruism to the evolution of successful communication. In his simulations, the communicative codes were innate, rather than learned, but that is not an important factor here. Consistent with the two choices assumed in the Prisoner's Dilemma, Oliphant envisaged two separate kinds of communicative act that an individual could perform: a cooperative act and a 'retaliatory' act (corresponding to the 'Defect' option). His simulated organisms had encoded in their genes a single system for interpreting signals, but two different production systems: a cooperative one and a retaliatory one. The cooperative production system meshed well with the reception system, in the sense that it encoded each particular meaning with the very same signal associated with that meaning by the receptive system. In other words, in cooperative mode, if you would understand *ovis* to mean SHEEP when someone says it to you, then in your turn, say *ovis* when you want to convey the idea of SHEEP to them. The retaliatory production system perversely encoded meanings with signals that were not those associated with them by the given reception system. In other words, in this perverse mode, if you have SHEEP in mind and think your hearer is interested in knowing what you have in mind, say **anything but** *ovis*, even though you yourself would understand *ovis* to mean SHEEP. All these innate systems were subject to random mutation, so that they could evolve and drift. In running the simulation, the simulated organisms were prompted with random meanings, which they signalled to an interlocutor, either cooperatively or retaliatorily, depending on how their interlocutor had treated them on the last encounter, i.e. following a Tit-for-Tat strategy. Organisms that successfully interpreted the meaning with which the sender had been prompted gained in fitness, and were more likely to pass their genes on to the next generation in the simulation. Oliphant's ingenious translation of the 'Defect' option of the Prisoner's Dilemma as 'retaliatory communication', i.e. a signal designed **not** to be interpreted, may sound inherently contradictory. But we see aspects of this behaviour in modern life. Some people, especially proverbial politicians, use the strategy 'If asked a difficult question, give an obfuscating answer'. In other words, go through the motions of communicating in the conventionally accepted manner, but in fact make your answer difficult to interpret clearly. This, in many modern circumstances, is more acceptable than a stony silence.

In Oliphant's simulations, modelling Reciprocal Altruism, populations converge on overall systems achieving high communicative accuracy, and also having a 'gene' prescribing cooperative behaviour on a first encounter. The central reason for this result is that 'if a mutant that does not transmit accurately enters the population, they will be responded to through the use of a less accurate transmission system. This maintains pressure on accurate transmission, even though it is not directly enforced by the fitness function' (Oliphant 1997, p. 45). In other words, a common communicative code evolves[13] in the particular setup of these simulations. In this setup, individuals are prompted with a given meaning, and **obliged**

---

[13] Interestingly, Oliphant also shows that such successful communicative codes are not stable. Drift occurs, so that occasionally the population lapses into a situation in which communication is less than perfect. In Oliphant's model, there are clear reasons for this.

to emit some signal to an interlocutor, who gains in fitness when he manages to interpret the signal as signifying the original meaning. Sure, given an obligation to say something, and facing a penalty if what you say cannot be interpreted, you and your descendants will tend to evolve towards saying things that can be interpreted. What such simulations do not explain is the origin of the obligation to communicate.

Besides using language to achieve some non-linguistic goal that individuals could not reach on their own (e.g. 'Help me move this rock'), there is a deeper sense in which the normal use of language is cooperative. Everday conversation contains many instances of cooperation, as the great success of Grice's theory testifies. And, as has been noted, the very act of conversing, even sometimes deceptively, presupposes some kind of shared cooperative enterprise. We humans use language so effortlessly that we tend to overlook the fact that an understanding of the other person's intentions is involved in the productive planning of an utterance and in its receptive interpretation. When using language, we are **thereby cooperating** in a communicative exchange. An analogy is with structured competitive games such as tennis or football. Although tennis players try their hardest to make things difficult for each other, they are nevertheless cooperating in playing a game of tennis. Genuinely uncooperative behaviour in relation to tennis would be just not showing up for the game. Oliphant's simulated organisms show up for the communication game, and duly evolve a common conventional code mapping meanings onto signals and faithfully back again. But what is not yet explained is why they are willing to participate in the communication game.

It is useful to make a distinction between what I shall call **communicative cooperation**, and **material cooperation**. Simply speaking a language that your interlocutor understands is communicative cooperation. This is like sticking to the rules while playing tennis. Beyond communicative cooperation, the issue of material cooperation arises. Honest communication of information helpful to your interlocutor (e.g. 'Hey, there's food here') is materially cooperative. Deceptive or obfuscatory communication in a code known to your interlocutor is not materially cooperative, but it is communicatively cooperative. This is in line with the dictum of Relevance Theory, noted earlier: 'for communication to be successful, the only goal that speaker and hearer need to share is that of understanding and being understood' (Wilson 1999, p. 720).[14]

---

[14] I wryly suggest that Relevance Theory stands in the same relationship to its predecessor Gricean theory as Einsteinian relativity does to Newtonian physics; the earlier theory

As soon as any tiny meaning-to-signal code is established, the option exists, either for genetic evolution or for a learning organism, to give or not to give a signal from that code, and in a way appropriate or inappropriate to the occasion. Only the appropriate giving of a signal benefits the receiver. The other cases, silence, obfuscation, or downright deception, do not benefit the recipient. A Tit-for-Tat mechanism will ensure that a recipient who detects that a helpful signal has not been given when it could have been will retaliate against the non-helpful signaller.[15] In this way, if the seed of a set of communicative conventions has been sown in a group of animals, a Tit-for-Tat strategy will tend to push them either to communicate more helpfully or to disguise the evidence that they have anything to communicate. Probably in a close social group the latter option is harder to bring off, as the punishment of macaques who do not announce discovery of food indicates.

Reciprocal Altruism's Tit-for-Tat strategy, with its 'cooperate on first encounter' clause, guarantees that it will reach beyond acquaintances one has already dealt with. The burden of remembering who cooperated with you and who didn't on their last encounter could be alleviated if there were some fairly reliable observable characteristic of one's interlocutor identifying him as likely to be a cooperator. In Axelrod et al. (2004)'s model, such traits, or 'tags', are indicators of genetic relatedness. But if they were indicators of group membership, a modification of the Tit-for-Tat strategy saying 'Cooperate with fellow group members, don't cooperate with others' could evolve. In the case of material cooperation on physical tasks, this would require adequate policing mechanisms to detect and punish cheating out-groupers masquerading as in-groupers, benefiting from cooperation but not reciprocating. But communication is a special case. An out-grouper, by learning to use the code of the in-group, would **thereby** begin to engage in playing the sort of cooperative game that is constituted by a conventional communicative code. Recall the analogy of the tennis players, doing their damnedest to beat each other, but cooperating nevertheless in both playing by the rules of the game. If use of the arbitrary communicative code itself were a reliable signal of group membership and of disposition to cooperate (in this special sense of communicative cooperation), then a feedback loop is formed. If you use the code, others will use it to you, and the number of code-using and

is more concrete and easier to apply to everyday examples, while the latter is more all-embracing and abstract.

[15] Scope of negation is deliberately ambiguous here—either giver of a non-helpful signal or non-signaller.

code-sharing individuals expands to the limits of the social group. This does not mean that the messages conveyed will necessarily be materially helpful. Deception and obfuscation between code-users is still possible, though it is not the norm between conspecifics of any species. Analytically, **given a shared code**, this must be true, as the accepted meaning of a signal is created only by usage, so the most common use cannot be deception.

Unlike Kin Selection, there is much less evidence in nature for Reciprocal Altruism. Food-sharing among non-kin by chimpanzees is the most frequently suggested possible example. But in this case, a 'tolerated scrounging' model has been suggested, in which a chimpanzee in control of a dead monkey only gives bits away to distract possible challengers for the whole carcass, in other words for purely selfish reasons. If the chimp gave nothing away, he could expect a fight for the whole carcass; he might lose the booty and be wounded. If he gives pieces away, the others are kept reasonably happy, and he gets to eat enough (Wrangham 1975; Moore 1984).

De Waal (1996) rejects the 'tolerated scrounging' explanation, and gives data on nearly 5,000 interactions between chimpanzees in the Yerkes colony (from de Waal 1989), supporting a Reciprocal Altruism interpretation of food sharing.

Food transfers in the colony were analyzed in all possible directions among adults. As predicted by the reciprocity hypothesis, the number of transfers in each direction was related to the number in the opposite direction; that is, if A shared a lot with B, B generally shared a lot with A, and if A shared little with C, C also shared little with A. The reciprocity hypothesis was further supported by the finding that grooming affected subsequent sharing: A's chances for getting food from B improved if A had groomed B earlier that day.   (de Waal 1996, p. 153)

Cotton-top tamarin monkeys have notably egalitarian social arrangements, and in this species Hauser et al. (2003) observed preferential reciprocating food-sharing to animals who altruistically also gave food.

Further, but more negatively, on the empirical evidence for Tit-for-Tat in nature:

Observations consistent with TFT have been reported for various animal species (Lombardo 1985; Milinski 1987; Dugatkin 1988; Milinski et al. 1990; Huntingford et al. 1994). Recently, Clements and Stephens (1995) disputed such claims on the grounds that (1) the payoff structures of the behaviours in question did not necessarily conform to PD [Prisoner's Dilemma], and (2) alternative explanations were not considered. Clements and Stephens (1995) recorded the behaviour of blue jays playing carefully controlled PD and mutualism games, and found stable cooperation only in the latter situation. Because the payoff structure of mutualism games ensures that cooperation is the best choice regardless of what your partner/opponent does, the occurrence of cooperation in such games is simply a by-product of individual animals maximizing their own immediate rewards without reacting to each other's behaviour at all (Roberts, 1997). Thus there is no need to invoke reciprocity or TFT as a necessary route to cooperation.

(Palameta and Brown 1999, p. F1)

The experimental results of Clements and Stephens (1995), cited above, are so clear that they are worth describing in more detail. They compared the behaviour of pairs of blue jays in a typical Prisoner's Dilemma (PD) scenario and in a mutualistic scenario. The difference between the scenarios is in the numbers chosen for the different combinations of behaviours, as shown in the diagrams below, which may be compared with the hare/deer payoff table used above (p. 264).

	C	D
C	3	0
D	5	1

A Prisoner's Dilemma scenario

	C	D
C	4	1
D	1	0

A mutualistic scenario

These exact numbers correspond to the numbers of food pellets given as rewards by Clements and Stephens (1995) to their blue jays in the following experimental setup. Two blue jays in adjacent cages each had two keys, a 'C(ooperate)' key and a 'D(efect)' key. The combined (but not coordinated) key-pressing actions of the birds resulted in them getting the numbers of food pellets as shown in the tables above. Blue jays are smart, and they figured out very quickly what was to their own individual advantage. In the Prisoner's Dilemma scenario they quickly learned always to press the Defect key, and in the mutualistic scenario they quickly learned to press the Cooperate key. It made no difference whether one blue jay could see the other's action.

Even in mutualistic scenarios, however, animals need a certain degree of foresight to appreciate the mutual benefits of cooperation. Many animals seem unable to appreciate such benefits. Cronin et al. (2005) survey a number of experiments on primates in many of which experimenters failed to get animals to cooperate in a mutually beneficial task. The more obvious the connection between action and result (e.g. with transparent experimental apparatus) the more likely animals are to be induced to cooperate with each other. And animals with more egalitarian social arrangements, such as cotton-top tamarins, seem to have an advantage here too. This makes sense, as in more despotic societies, it can be anticipated that a dominant animal will take all or most of the reward, thus making it a one-sided, rather than genuinely mutualistic, situation.

Reciprocal Altruism theory, based on a Prisoner's Dilemma scenario, arbitrarily chooses the cost and benefit values in the payoff matrix, and the degree of generosity in the initial altruistic act and the reciprocator's response. Clements and Stephens (1995, p. 533) allege that 'there is no empirical evidence of nonkin cooperation in a situation, natural or contrived, where the payoffs are known to conform to a Prisoner's Dilemma'. Given their results with blue jays in the mutualistic scenario, we may well ask how often a Prisoner's Dilemma scenario is relevant to real-world situations. If in fact the environment in which animals live often presents them with mutualistic scenarios, in which it is always immediately advantageous to cooperate, then it is much less of a puzzle why cooperative behaviour should exist. And if this is the case, all the theorizing of Reciprocal Altruism, based on PD-type payoff tables, becomes less relevant to the problem of cooperation by animals in nature.

There is some possibility of relating cooperation in mutualistic scenarios to Brown and Levinson (1987)'s theory of conversational politeness and 'Face'. Cooperation could be related to mutually face-saving behaviour, with the potential cost to one's own face, and defection to mutually face-threatening behaviour. If the cumulative benefit of saving an interlocutor's face and having one's own face saved outweighs the benefits of saving one's own face by failing to engage, then we could have an example of linguistic mutualism. Brown and Levinson do not discuss this explicitly, but their analysis of 'assessment of payoff and weighting of risk' (p. 83) is highly reminiscent of discussions of Prisoner's Dilemma and mutualistic setups.[16]

A difficulty with Reciprocal Altruism theory, pointed out by Dessalles (1999) and Moore (1984), among others, is that the initial emergence of a genetically determined Tit-for-Tat strategy, which is quite complex as innate behaviours go, is hard to explain. '[C]ooperative altruism can only occur under very specific circumstances, in which some highly profitable trade is possible between two individuals' (Dessalles 1999, p.155). Another idealized (and idealistic) aspect of Reciprocal Altruism theory is that it paints a picture of equal-status individuals floating freely in a

---

[16] This connection with Brown and Levinson's theory of 'Face' was suggested to me by Emma Healey.

social structure, and sorting their (un)cooperative behaviour towards others purely on grounds of previous encounters. The hierarchical political nature of primate social groups does not come into the picture. Again, we shall see later that the picture can be fruitfully developed once the hierarchical status of individuals is taken into account.

A further difficulty with Reciprocal Altruism is that it does not work when times are hard. In dire emergencies, such as famine, the future of individuals becomes uncertain, so the probability of dealing repeatedly with the same person diminishes. If you think you won't see this person again, the conditions revert to one-off, non-iterated episodes, in which it pays each individual to act for short-term advantage, because the threat of retaliation is minimal. A later theoretical development, Strong Reciprocity (Gintis 2000), to be discussed in Section 4 of this chapter, overcomes this limitation.

Finally, the Tit-for-Tat strategy corresponds partly, but not wholly, to modern human conversational behaviour. There are big cultural differences in behaviour on first meeting a stranger with whom one is destined to spend some time. On British trains, until recently, strangers seldom, if ever, spoke. In other cultures, people are more forthcoming, more in accordance with the 'Cooperate on first encounter' rule. Generally, if you receive no reply in a conversation, you also stop speaking—Tit-for-Tat. (But some people don't care whether they are getting a reply or not, and talk on regardless.) Likewise, if a person speaks to you and then stops, it is conventional to speak back—Tit-for-Tat (subject to various constraints such as social rank—'Speak when you're spoken to'). However, there are no clear conversational equivalents of the payoff scores in a Prisoner's Dilemma scenario.

In summary, there is some positive, but limited, prospect that Reciprocal Altruism, under Prisoner's Dilemma assumptions about cost and benefit to the players, can help to explain the rise of cooperative human language. The Prisoner's Dilemma assumption of this theory may be unnecessarily biased against the possibility of cooperation in the real world, as mutualistic scenarios, in which there is no real problem, may be more common. The theories discussed in this section, Kin Selection and Reciprocal Altruism, have been taken to be relevant to the emergence of language because of the widespread assumption that language use is altruistic or at least cooperative. In both theories the immediate benefit from a single act is to the receiver, and the actor bears the immediate cost; hence the emphasis on altruism in descriptions of these theories. Both theories are ways of showing that this is **apparent** altruism or cooperation, and is actually of benefit later to the signaller or to his genes (and so in some sense not genuine selfless altruism), in full conformity with Darwinian thought. Kin Selection and Reciprocal Altruism probably had some role to play in the evolution of language. Geoff Miller (2000b) notes some pointers that those theories cannot be the whole story. His argument rests on the fact that in both these theories, the cost falls upon the producer of a message and the benefit accrues to the receiver.

> As long as language is viewed purely in terms of information transmission, it will be seen as bringing more benefits to the listener than to the speaker. The speaker already knows the information being conveyed, and learns nothing new by sharing it, but the listener does gain information by listening.... This leads to an interesting prediction: we should be a species of extremely good listeners and very reluctant talkers.
>
> This does not describe the human species as I know it.... People compete to say things. They strive to be heard.... [T]hose who fail to yield the floor are considered selfish, not altruistic.
>
> Nor do the kinship and reciprocity theories predict our anatomy very accurately.... Our hearing apparatus remains evolutionarily conservative, very similar to that of other apes, while our speaking apparatus has been dramatically re-engineered.   (Miller 2000b, pp. 350–351)

Miller's argument is only half right. Kin Selection shows why it is in the interests of an animal's genes to give alarm calls for close kin, so we can expect some selection for efficient alarm-calling. Likewise Reciprocal Altruism puts animals in the roles of both giver and receiver of (apparent) altruism; if the quality of your giving is poor, then you cannot expect to receive much in reciprocation, so Reciprocal Altruism predicts some selection on the quality of the (apparently altruistic) giving. This applies equally to the giving of goods and the giving of information. And the prediction that we should be a species of extremely good listeners is not entirely false. While it is true that our hearing apparatus is more evolutionarily conservative than our speaking apparatus, nevertheless human hearing, and especially perception, differs significantly from other primate hearing in a number of ways; this will be dealt with in detail in Volume 2 of this work, but some relevant references are Kuhl (1991); Sinnott and Williamson (1999); Coleman and Ross (2004).

I also do not share Miller's picture of 'the human species as [he] know[s] it'. In some American subcultures (Miller is an American) the use of language is indeed very competitive. In my university it is well known that in mixed tutorial groups, Americans tend to talk most, followed closely by Southern English types from richer backgrounds, while most Scots and Japanese tend to keep politely quiet.[17] Individual exceptions exist, but there is some truth in cultural stereotypes. In many societies, 'showing off' and 'blethering' are discouraged. In all societies, there is great variation among individuals in their talkativeness and urge to hold forth. This is behavioural polymorphism; any theory which predicts a distribution of different behaviours, or different degrees of engagement in a particular behaviour, where this matches the facts, is on the right track. Miller's theory, to the contrary, predicts that we all join the competition to be outstanding talkers.

Miller's argument, however, draws our attention to the possibility of more patently selfish motivations for communication. In the next section, we will look at evolutionary theories that assume no necessary benefit to the hearer and take communication to be inherently beneficial to the speaker.

8.3 EVOLUTIONARY THEORIES OF SELFISH COMMUNICATION

8.3.1 Communication for Display of Form

Language evolved as much to display our fitness as to communicate useful information. To many language researchers and philosophers, this is a scandalous idea. They regard altruistic communication as the norm, from which our self-serving fantasies might sometimes deviate. But to biologists, fitness advertisement is the norm, and language is an exceptional form of it. We are the only species in the evolutionary history of our planet to have discovered a system of fitness indicators and sexual ornaments that also happens to transmit ideas from one head to another.   (Miller 2000b, pp. 390–391)

Note the separation of two functions implicit here, an 'ornamental' function indicating fitness to a mate, and another function of transmitting ideas from one head to another. In this subsection, we shall be concerned with the first, sexual attraction, rather than the second, propositionally informative, function.

Many animals engage in elaborate or conspicuous courtship displays. These can be very spectacular, and include both bodily morphology (e.g. long tail feathers, antlers, outsize claws, and elaborately varied and patterned colouring) and behaviour (e.g. dancing, turning somersaults, calling very loudly, and building complicated structures). Mostly these

---

[17] Alan Grafen, a Scot, points out that these same Scots are probably very voluble in the pub, where mate attraction is higher up the agenda than in my linguistics tutorials.

displays result from innate dispositions. But in many songbirds, there is also an element of learning of the characteristic courtship song (often combined with a territorial signal). In discussing the evolution of language, and the possible relevance of display as a driving force, we need to focus on elaborate, rather than merely conspicuous, displays. A display feature can evolve to be conspicuous, but not elaborate, simply by exaggeration of one dimension, such as size of genitalia in chimpanzees, size of one claw in some lobsters, lowness of pitch in frog croaks, loudness of call in some birds. Human language is extremely finely articulated; this fine articulation has not evolved just by saying one thing more loudly, or on a lower pitch. Displays that are articulated into several parts are more likely candidates as possible precursors of articulated language.

At this stage in our story of language evolution, still very close to apes, we are only dealing with the very first learned shared symbols, which it is reasonable to suppose had unitary meanings. There are several different views ('synthetic' versus 'analytic') on the exact nature of the earliest learned public signal-to-meaning mappings, and the route from them to modern syntax. Here it is sufficient to say that we are dealing with the possible advantages for display of multi-parted signals in which the parts had no separate meanings, only the whole signal having a meaning— typically something simple, such as 'Come and be my mate' or 'Look how strong I am'. These two examples illustrate two prominent, and rather similar, evolutionary theories to account for costly displays. One is Sexual Selection, started by Darwin (1871) and developed by Fisher (1930). The other theory is Zahavi's 'Handicap Principle' (Zahavi 1975, 1977).

Sexual selection can work through male–male contests for access to females. But signals evolved for this purpose tend to be one-dimensional exaggerations of a particular trait, such as loudness or low pitch, and so are of less interest as possible precursors of complex articulated language. In the context of language, the mechanism more frequently mentioned is female mate choice, on the basis of a particularly attractive signal by the male.

The central idea of the mate-choice version of Sexual Selection theory is that males and females co-evolve complementary traits (typically in the male) and preferences (typically in the female). For example, male birds who dance more vigorously than others are preferred by females. This leads to selection of vigorous male dancers. As the average vigour of dancing by males increases, females still prefer the most vigorous dancers, leading to further increases in the vigour of male dances. If the females were always satisfied with dancing vigour above some constant threshold, this effect would not happen. For sexual selection to happen in this example, vigorous male dancing and a female preference for vigorous male dancers must have a common genetic basis. More generally, one or more genes exert pleiotropic effects on male courtship behaviour and female preferences.

There are some empirical reports of such a common genetic basis for a trait and a preference for it in the other sex. One way of discovering such a correlation is to use closely related species, in each of which there is a distinctive male mating call, and a female preference for that call. The key step is to cross (hybridize) these species and see whether the mating calls of the hybrid males are preferred by the hybrid females over the calls of the original species. If the hybridization process produces both a hybrid male call, distinct from (but usually intermediate between) the calls of the original species, and a female preference for that hybrid call, a strong hypothesis is that both the call and the preference for it are under the control of the same genes. Reports of such facts can be found in Kyriacou and Hall (1986) for drosophila, in Hoy and Paul (1973) and Hoy et al. (1977) for crickets, and in Doherty and Gerhardt (1983) for tree frogs. Simmons (2004) expresses doubt about the conclusions regarding crickets.

The mechanism of sexual selection provides for unusually fast runaway evolution of genetically determined traits. The runaway mechanism is an elaboration of Darwin's original idea by the great statistician and evolutionary biologist, R. A. Fisher (Fisher 1915, 1930).

Several authors have argued that sexual selection played a role in the evolution of human language. Darwin started it:

When we treat of sexual selection we shall see that primeval man, or rather some early progenitor of man, probably first used his voice in producing true musical cadences, that is in singing, as do some of the gibbon-apes at the present day; and we may conclude from a widely-spread analogy, that this power would have been especially exerted during the courtship of the sexes,— would have expressed various emotions, such as love, jealousy, triumph,—and would have served as a challenge to rivals.   (Darwin 1871)

Otto Jespersen, a renowned linguist, waxed even more romantic: 'Language was born in the courting days of mankind; the first utterances of speech I fancy to myself like something between the nightly love-lyrics of puss upon the tiles and the melodious love-songs of the nightingale' (Jespersen 1922, p. 484).[18]

---

[18] I have spared the reader the rest of Jespersen's rosy vision of primitive love-making.

Darwin clearly thought that sexual selection for musical properties in communication **preceded** articulate language: 'it appears probable that the progenitors of man, either the males or females or both sexes, before acquiring the power of expressing their mutual love in articulate language, endeavoured to charm each other with musical notes and rhythm' (Darwin 1871, p. 880).

A prominent modern example of the Sexual Selection theory is Miller (2000b). The idea is that the use of more fancy language attracted more mates. Miller appeals to a variety of ways in which pre-modern human communication might have been sexually attractive, including range of vocabulary, melodic patterning, syntactic complexity, and informativeness. Miller's discussion of sexual selection in language evolution is not pitched precisely at any particular stage of evolution. Some of the examples he gives clearly involve the conveying of elaborate meanings by elaborate compositional syntax, using whole complex sentences with individually meaningful words. 'There are some hints of sexual ornamentation in the human voice's pitch and timbre, the size of our vocabularies, the complexity of our grammar, and the narrative conventions of storytelling' (p. 358). Most of this is language at an advanced, even modern stage. And other examples that Miller gives rely on the propositional informativeness of the language used. In this case the verbal displayer is demonstrating how much he knows (that is novel and interesting) as well as how good he is at expressing it. Unitary signals can convey propositional information, and compound signals can convey even richer propositional information. Later below, I will discuss the possible role of informative propositional content in the very early stage when the first ape-like creatures began using the very first learned symbols among themselves. Here, I am just concerned with whether sexual selection played a role in shaping an elaborate attractive **form** for the first learned symbols used in the wild. In another paper, Miller (2000a) expresses a lack of interest in such questions:

Identifying an adaptation and its function does not require telling the phylogenetic story of how the adaptation first arose at a particular time and place in prehistory . . . Adaptationist analysis does not worry very much about origins, precursors, or stages of evolutionary development. . . . It is just not very important whether music evolved two hundred thousand years ago or two million years ago, or whether language evolved as a precursor to music.

(Miller 2000a, pp. 336–337)

The best examples in the animal world of semantically unitary but formally complex signals used for sexual display are birdsong and the songs of gibbons. Gibbon song is undoubtedly very complex, in its 'phono-logical syntax'. Ujhelyi (1998) classifies gibbon songs as having 'lexical syntax', on the basis that the subunits of which they are composed have separate meanings outside the context of the long call songs, for example as alarm or contact calls. However, the meanings of the long calls are not, as far as we know, a compositional function of the meanings of these subunits. The long calls serve to identify individuals, like signature tunes. In this sense, a gibbon long call may be likened to a human mantra, or a certain sort of nursery rhyme, composed of words, where the words have referential meanings outside the context of the mantra or rhyme, but within the mantra or rhyme these meanings make no contribution to its function. A nursery rhyme example would be *Hey diddle dumpling*, which is not about diddling or about dumplings, nor really **about** anything. According to Mitani and Marler (1989), thirteen basic subunits—'note types'—can be distinguished in gibbon long calls. Gibbon long calls also undoubtedly have a sexual function, as they are often performed in duets by mated pairs.

Interestingly, one of the most detailed studies of gibbon song (Geissmann 2000, p. 103) states: 'Structural and behavioral similarities suggest that, of all vocalizations produced by non-human primates, loud calls of Old World monkeys and apes are the most likely candidates for models of a precursor of human singing and, thus, human music.' The article makes no mention of such songs being a precursor of human **language**. But, in line with Darwin and Jespersen, possibly our ape ancestors also had such complex songs, sexually selected, and used them much like modern gibbons.[19] And the capacity to control such 'musical' out-puts may have given rise to the human capacity to combine **prosodic** structure[20] with articulated, semantically compositional language which arose later (as Darwin suggested). There is plenty of evidence suggest-ing a dissociation in modern humans between control of emotionally affective prosody (both productive and receptive) and control over artic-ulated propositional/referential language. For example: 'Following right hemisphere lesions, adults' speech can become copious and inappropri-ate, with abnormal prosody, and they may be unable to comprehend metaphor or humour. Their symptoms resemble those of children with

---

[19] Rousseau (1781) also saw the origin of language in song, but had no theory of sexual selection.

[20] In linguistics, prosodic structure is structure associated with correlated facts about the rhythm, pitch, and amplitude of speech, along with the duration of segments (consonants and vowels).

semantic-pragmatic language disorder, who use fluent, grammatically complex language, but with poor sensitivity to the communicative situation' (Shields 1991, p. 383). Another relevant early work connecting prosody, affective content, and the right hemisphere is Ross (1981). It is also highly relevant that '[a]ffective prosody is strikingly similar in humans and other primates, so that human subjects having no previous experience with monkeys correctly identify the emotional content of their screams (Linnankoski et al. 1994)' (Kotchoubey 2005, p. 136). Sexual selection may have played a role in the evolution of the prosodic, affective, 'musical' features of language, onto which the semantically compositional referential/propositional systems were later grafted. However, the story cannot be simply that all prosodic aspects of language have a separate origin from syntactic devices used to convey propositional meaning. The intonation patterns of languages are intricately interwoven with their syntactic structure. If early sexual selection for musical properties of calls had a role to play in the evolution of language, the role was likely to be in the evolution of a capacity for learning to produce and interpret intonationally elaborate strings, somewhat voluntarily. Mithen (2005) is an extensive speculative work arguing, based on both the similarities and the differences between music and language, and especially on the prosodic, affective, musical features of language, that they both evolved from the same ancient precursor capacities. Like Darwin, Jespersen, and Miller, Mithen is sympathetic to a sexual selection explanation of these proto-musical and proto-linguistic capacities. Mithen puts the divergence between music and language some time after the first *Homo*, around 2 million years ago.

Any connection between human language and birdsong would be a matter of analogy (independent evolution), rather than homology (common descent). It is widely asserted that complex birdsong results from sexual selection, and there is loads of positive evidence. One example, from a study of European starlings, is:

Males with more complex song acquired mates faster. This relationship remained significant when nest-site preference was statistically controlled, indicating that female starlings chose males with complex song rather than those that defended preferred nest sites.

(Mountjoy and Lemon 1996, p. 65)

As another example, Price and Lanyon (2004) used mitochondrial DNA to reconstruct vocal evolution in the oropendolas and caciques (a group of oscine birds), and concluded: 'sexual selection has had important influences on song evolution in these birds, but has targeted different components of song in different taxa' (p. 485). But the data are not unanimously in favour of sexual selection as the source of articulated complexity in birdsong. Some complex birdsong involves inserting mimicked calls of other species into the song. Reed warblers do this. 'Male Warblers incorporated the mimetic sounds into their songs, and each male mimicked 2-5 species. We found no evidence that females preferred males with large mimetic repertoires. This suggests that vocal mimicry has not evolved in response to selection by females in this species' (Hamao and Eda-Fujiwara 2004, p. 61).

One common objection to a hypothesis of sexual selection in the evolution of language is that sexual selection commonly results in marked sexual dimorphism—big differences between males and females—with males typically having the more elaborate form or behaviour (Dessalles 1999, p. 157; Fitch 2005, p. 212). In humans, however, there is not much difference between the sexes in their command of language, and some tests show females to be better language users than males. Miller pointedly puts the relevant question: 'Why do women have higher verbal ability than men, if language was sexually selected?' (2000b, p. 375). And he has a satisfactory answer. Men do indeed talk more, especially in public, and women are marginally better at comprehension tasks. This is consistent with sexual selection. Furthermore, 'the male-display, female-choice system is not an accurate model of human conversation anyway' (p. 376). At the time when Miller was writing, other theorists and empirical observers were beginning to unpick a long-standing assumption of sexual selection theory: that mate-choice is one-sided.

Mate choice is seldom structured so that one side is entirely passive (Cunningham and Birkhead 1998). Instead, males and females are actively engaged in mutual choice where each can potentially accept or reject the other.

Mutual mate choice may be much more common than we think, and mate choice models must be constructed that incorporate this important feature of sexual selection.   (Bergstrom and Real 2000, p. 494)

The model proposed by Bergstrom and Real (2000) shows strategies for arriving at pairings as satisfactory as possible to individuals of both sexes, given that there may be popular favourites, and given active choice by both sexes. No prediction of sexual dimorphism arises from such a model, but it is not inconsistent with the evolved elaboration of displays. So this objection to sexual selection as a possible motivating force in the evolution of complex articulate language is not sustained. One would predict that mutual mate choice correlates well with monogamy, equal parental care for the young, and less marked sexual dimorphism. Empirical support for this comes from a comparison of red-winged and red-shouldered blackbirds (native to Cuba). Whittingham et al. (1997, p. 279) write: 'Red-shouldered Blackbirds are socially monogamous and both sexes feed young with equal frequency, unlike Red-winged Blackbirds. In addition, Red-shouldered Blackbirds are less sexually dimorphic in size and plumage than Red-winged Blackbirds (Whittingham et al. 1992; Whittingham et al. 1996).' Interestingly, red-shouldered blackbirds engage in duetting song which seems to have a pair-bonding function.

A more telling objection to sexual selection in language evolution[21] is the fact that language is acquired in infancy and childhood, before puberty. Traits associated with sexual attraction come onstream around puberty, with sexual maturity. To attract sexual partners before one is able to reproduce would be a waste of effort and potentially harmful. The most prominent sexually dimorphic feature in human language, the typical pitch of the voice, comes onstream around puberty, when the male voice 'breaks'. This lowering of pitch in the male signal is well known as a sexually selected feature in a number of animals. But human babies start showing signs of language learning around one year of age, and they are probably busy absorbing a lot well before that age, even in the womb, and language acquisition proceeds rapidly in children during their pre-pubertal years. In normal children, full command of informal spoken language is complete at least a few years before puberty (command of formal and written registers is something else). Clearly the adaptive uses to which babies and children put language do not include the attraction of mates.[22]

To conclude this survey of the likelihood of a role for sexual selection in the evolution of language, it seems to me that Geoff Miller, its most enthusiastic proponent, has not made a fully convincing case, except for the prosodic aspects of language, following Darwin and Jespersen. Counter to Miller's somewhat florid descriptions of human male–female encounters, a typical reaction by many academic commentators has been: 'Being a good articulate talker never got me any good sex.' Maybe academic talk is a peculiarly sexually non-adaptive form of speech, but it is not as obvious as Miller would have us believe that highly articulate language, or brute domination of conversation, attracts mates now. However, we

---

[21] Noted by Fitch (2005, p. 212).

[22] Although, sadly and dysfunctionally, paedophiles may find the language of minors sexually attractive.

would do well to remember that the whimsical objection about the lack of good-sex-generating power of being articulate may hide a deeper misunderstanding by some authors about evolutionary arguments, namely, what matters is the sexual effect that being incipiently articulate may have had in our ancestors at the key moment when language was emerging. Once language and its many consequences are in place, the rules of the game may have completely changed and what once was 'sexy' no longer is now.

In the pre-Minimalism days (roughly before Chomsky 1995) when generative linguists used to emphasize how the language faculty contained many abstract principles, a frequently talked-about principle was 'Subjacency'. This is an allegedly universal grammatical constraint accounting for the ungrammaticality of such sentences as *What do you believe the claim that Mary saw?*, as opposed to the very similar but grammatical *What do you believe Mary saw?* David Lightfoot memorably remarked: 'the Subjacency Condition has many virtues, but I am not sure that it could have increased the chances of having fruitful sex' (Lightfoot 1991, p. 69). A sexual selection argument for the evolution of any of the abstract principles governing articulate language postulated by pre-Minimalism generative grammar is very implausible. The modern Minimalist programme in generative grammar no longer postulates a number of separate abstract innate grammatical principles. The current Chomskyan position is that the only possibly distinctive property of the human language faculty in the narrow sense (i.e. not shared with either animal communication or with human non-linguistic cognition) is recursion (Hauser et al. 2002). Was a command of recursion in language sexually attractive? Henry James wrote in convoluted sentences with much use of recursion; Ernest Hemingway wrote in mainly short sentences with spare use of recursion. Which writing style is the sexier? Would prehistoric conversation have been sexier for incorporating a lot of recursive constructions? We don't know, of course, but it seems unlikely that sexual selection for attractive compositional complexity of form played a major role in the evolution of syntactic language. In the very early single-unit phase of hominid communication, the semantically unitary but phonologically complex signals, like gibbon songs, may have been sexually selected for their musical qualities. But any later exaptation of these calls for referential purposes seems unlikely to have been motivated by sexual selection.

It needs to be noted that such discussion of sexual selection for aspects of language is overly simple, in the absence of good data. Such discussion typically assumes, for example, that a particular trait, if it is attractive, will be permanently and universally attractive. But research on human and non-human sexual attraction shows that different traits are attractive to different females, and, varying independently, at different times in their ovulating cycle. Women in good physical and psychological condition, as defined by objective measures, tend to prefer male faces defined as healthy more than other women (Penton-Voak and Perrett 2000; Jones et al. 2005). And women prefer different male faces at different phases of their cycle (Frost 1994; Penton-Voak and Perrett 2000). A similar result has been obtained for women's preferences for male voices: 'We found women displayed general masculinity preferences for men's voices; masculinity preferences were greater in the fertile (late-follicular) phase of the cycle than the non-fertile (early-follicular and luteal) phase' (Feinberg et al. 2006, p. 215). The attractiveness of the female voice is correlated with other measures of female attractiveness such as body shape and facial characteristics (Collins and Missing 2003; Hughes et al. 2004; Feinberg et al. 2005). The difference between male and female voices is by far the most salient sexually dimorphic feature of language, and, to linguists interested in the general structure of language, is of little interest, probably because of this correlation with non-linguistic features. What would be interesting would be experimental evidence of variation in some specifically linguistic structural feature correlated with variation in sexual attractiveness. Quite possibly, different features of language are also differentially attractive, depending on the chooser and her menstrual state; we just don't know, apart from the studies of voice preference. The absence of relevant studies may indicate a general anticipation that there is nothing to be found by way of sexual selection for interesting structural features of human language.

Moving on from orthodox Sexual Selection theory, another theory, Amotz Zahavi's 'Handicap Principle' (Zahavi 1975, 1977; Grafen 1990a, 1990b) claims to explain the evolution of elaborate form in a similar, but subtly different way. Zahavi's insight is that the sexually selected characteristics are often **costly**. The peacock's tail is a great burden, the bower bird's building of a 'bower' costs it a lot of effort that could be better spent on getting food, and so on. The fact that a male peacock can manage to haul his great tail around without getting caught by predators is a mark of his fitness. It is as if he is saying, 'Look how strong I am, to manage with this handicap'. (But if strength were all, why does the tail also get to be so beautiful?)

The Handicap theory has been applied very widely, by Zahavi and others, to include behaviour between different species. Zahavi and Zahavi (1997), for example, note that Arabian babbler birds bombard predators

with loud and protracted alarm calling. The protractedness of the calling
is a point in favour of this claim, as the birds continue calling long after
all in the flock have become aware of the danger. Zahavi's idea is that the
call signals to a predator 'I've seen you', and to the conspecifics 'Look
how bold I am in carrying on squawking at the predator!' It is not clear
why the loud calling would deter a predator just because it thinks it has
been seen; equally plausible is the idea that the predator finds loud noise
distracting, as humans do. But Zahavi has noticed an important aspect
of risky behaviour in some social species: they compete with each other
to take risks. This cannot be explained by Kin Selection or Reciprocal
Altruism. Zahavi's explanation is:

A babbler who can stand guard longer than its comrades, give them part of
its food, approach a raptor, take the risk of sleeping at the exposed end of the
row—and can also prevent others from doing such deeds—proves daily to its
comrades its superiority over them. By doing so, that individual increases its
prestige.   (Zahavi and Zahavi 1997, p. 144)

The Handicap Principle has even been extended to the red colouring of
trees in autumn (Hamilton and Brown 2001). I take this application with
a sceptical pinch of salt.[23]

But anyway, we are concerned with communication between members
of the same species. We ask whether anything inherent in the elaborate
form of proto-linguistic signals would have conveyed an impression of
above average fitness, because the signaller was bearing an impressive cost
(handicap) in giving these signals. Expressed in this way, the Handicap
idea is only very subtly different from orthodox sexual selection. It seems
to attribute an extra step of interpretation to the choosing sex (typically
the female). Rather than just being disposed to simply finding some male
trait sexually attractive, the male trait is taken as representing the male's
quality in other respects. Reversing the sexes, it is the difference between
'Broad hips are a sign of good childbearing potential, even though they
may hinder mobility' versus 'Broad hips turn me on, especially because
they hinder mobility—this person is fit enough to afford dysfunctional
display'. Dessalles (1999, p. 156) gives a fair objection: 'the handicap

---

[23] A striking instance of the differing basic assumptions of different disciplines is seen
in biologist Alan Grafen's comment on my scepticism here. He writes (personal communication): 'Is there a reason for the scepticism about the handicap principle in this context?
I hope it's not that "trees can't think": evolution proceeds by outcomes not mechanisms
and we aren't concerned with motivations.' Indeed that was my reason. Alan also wrote,
of an earlier passage, that he 'felt excluding plants from having concepts was perhaps too
precipitate'. Clearly more interdisciplinary dialogue is needed.

principle does not predict why the birds should behave altruistically. Any wasteful and conspicuous behavior would be convenient.'

The Handicap Principle is not particularly applicable to the evolution of elaborately articulated linguistic form, for the same reasons as were given above relating to orthodox Sexual Selection theory. Elaborate form of vocal signals is also clearly no way as costly as the peacock's tail or the risk-taking of babbler birds.[24] In the next section, we will come to a development of Zahavi's theory based on valuable informative content, rather than elaborated form.

The Handicap idea does bring out an important aspect of honest signalling. Where mutual trust has not (somehow) been established, a signal that is not costly to its producer is worthless. If I want to convey to you that I am bigger and stronger than I actually am, I can easily do this by lowering the pitch of my voice. But if you know how easy it is to lower one's pitch, you will not be taken in by this pitch-lowering—you will not be deceived. So this cheap signal of size and strength fails. To really convince you, I need to engage in some costly display, to go out of my way to make you believe I am being honest about my size and strength. In adversarial situations, only signals that involve an obvious cost to the sender can be relied upon to be honest. Krebs and Dawkins (1984), in their seminal paper, summarize: 'Co-operative communication, in which manipulator and mind-reader roles share a common interest, should lead to cost-minimizing, muted signals, while non-cooperative signalling should give rise to conspicuous, repetitive signals' (p. 40). This correlation between common interest and low-cost signals, and between conflicting interests and high-cost signals, has become an item of faith in the field: 'The main theoretical results in signalling theory predict that high signal costs will be observed when communication occurs between individuals with conflicting interests' (Lachmann et al. 2002, p. 13189). (But see two paragraphs below for Lachmann et al.'s important contribution, qualifying this widely assumed correlation.)

The conspicuousness or repetitive nature of the best candidates for sexual selection, such as the peacock's tail and much birdsong, bring out the competitive 'battle of the sexes' character implicit in the application of Zahavi's Handicap Principle to sexual selection. Modern human vocal

[24] The large human brain, which enables elaborate human language, is certainly very costly of energy, but I am not aware of any arguments that big brains in themselves are sexually attractive. The human brain is not a handicap in the same sense as the peacock's tail. It is a working organ and compensates for its high energy cost in ways that need no explanation from sexual selection or the Handicap Principle.

signalling is neither as physically effortful as lugging around a heavy tail nor as repetitive as the chaffinch's incessant day-long declaiming of his quite complex song in spring and early summer. In this section, we are considering the possibility of precursors of language being selected for impressive display of form. The apparent cheapness of modern language production might seem to make a Zahavian Handicap explanation largely irrelevant to language evolution. But this is deceptive, as effort, other than pure physical effort, is hard to measure. Compare playing a piano well with repeatedly bashing the keyboard as hard as possible with your fists. The bashing takes more physical effort, but the skilful playing is much harder to do. In favour of a Zahavian explanation, it might be possible to show (some day) what brain power, rather than muscle power, is required for finely and impressively articulated speech. Until that day, the degree to which language is in any way a handicap remains undetermined.

Power (1998) notes the cheapness of vocal signalling as a problem with Dunbar (1996b)'s 'Gossip as Grooming' hypothesis: 'If grooming among primates operates as a "hard to fake" signal of commitment precisely because of its costliness, then the relativeness "cheapness" of vocal grooming undermines its value as an index of commitment' (p. 113). Kin Selection avoids this problem, because the signals to close kin benefit one's own genes, and the situation is therefore not adversarial. Reciprocal Altruism also sets up a non-adversarial environment, in which the cost of a current signal need not be high, because the sender has already invested some cost to himself, by earlier cooperation.

Lachmann et al. (2002) add a significant dimension to the idea of 'cost of a signal'. Hitherto, the cost of a signal has been closely identified with the effort involved in producing it, or living with it, if it is a permanent feature of the body. But consider the situation in which a liar is caught and punished for his lying. Then lying, if detected, is costly to the signaller. This puts a quite different complexion on the prevalent ideas on costly signalling. If cost can be socially imposed, retrospectively, for a deceptive signal (or for lack of a signal when one is appropriate) there is no theoretical need for the cost to be apparent in any effort at the time of producing the signal. As Lachmann et al. (2002) point out, this insight expands the set of social setups in which cheap signalling may be expected to arise, to include those in which individuals are to some extent in competition. The idea only works if there is social imposition of cost of inappropriate code-users, i.e. policing of the conventions. A closely related idea is expressed in Boyd and Richerson (1992)'s title, 'Punishment allows the evolution of cooperation (or anything else) in sizable groups'. Hauser (1992)'s report of macaques who punish non-communicators is an example of this setup being found in nature. We shall see the effectiveness of punishment and policing in the next two sections.

8.3.2 Communication for Impressively Relevant Content

Display can involve informative **content** as well as form. The attractive communicator may be saying 'Look how much I know!' Jean-Louis Dessalles has put forward a hypothesis that the original motivation of human language was **trading relevant information for status** (Dessalles 1998, 1999, 2000). In making status or prestige central, Dessalles' theory is close to Zahavi's Handicap Principle. Dessalles' theory is closely bound to the political nature of primate social life, in which coalitions and alliances are frequently formed, and often shift. In the first paper, Dessalles rightly emphasizes a crucial property of information in conversation, namely **relevance**. A communicator who conveys obvious or unsurprising information, or information that does not relate to the hearer's interests, is not valued by hearers:

The rules of the conversational game . . . may be formulated in this way:

1. Give information that is directly valuable, by pointing at improbable, desirable or undesirable states of affairs.
2. Try to lower the informational value of previous utterances.
3. Point out any logical inconsistency in the state of affairs described or observed.
4. Attribute status to speakers who are successful in the above.

(Dessalles 1998, p. 145)

The first injunction here corresponds to Grice's maxim 'Be relevant'; so far, this promotes cooperation. The difference comes with the second and third injunctions, which are motivated by a competitive urge to minimize the status of other contributors to the conversation. This is very reminiscent of a real game, such as tennis, where the rules are: (1) Play good shots likely to be winners, (2) Try to prevent your opponent playing good shots, (3) Point out any infringement by your opponent of the formal rules of tennis, such as long or wide shots or foot-faults, (4) Concede the match to anyone who beats you at (1-3). As in an earlier section, the question arises: 'Why engage in this cooperative game-playing activity in the first place? Why not just walk away?' Dessalles does not express it in these terms, but he has an answer: this is no game, this is real life. Relevant information is crucial to life. And in primate social life, being a member of an alliance can promote your fitness; being a loner or a member of a weak coalition is not a good recipe for success in primate life. Put the two together, and valuable information becomes the coinage with which entry into a coalition is bought and membership maintained. Dessalles' proposed solution to the cheater problem of an animal who tries to buy his way into an alliance by giving low-quality information (false, obvious, or irrelevant) is the policing mechanism implicit in the second and third injunctions. Every member of the alliance has to be on the alert for the quality of the information used by others to keep them in the alliance. If they fall short, exclude them from the alliance.

Dessalles gives empirically collected examples from conversation confirming his strategies. Some independent support comes from McAndrew and Milenkovic (2002), who did not refer to Dessalles' theory. In an experiment of theirs, '83 college students ranked the interest value and likelihood of spreading gossip about male or female professors, relatives, friends, acquaintances, or strangers based on 12 different gossip scenarios. ... Exploitable information in the form of damaging, negative news about nonallies and positive news about allies was especially prized and likely to be passed on. The findings confirm that gossip can serve as a strategy of status enhancement and function in the interests of individuals' (p. 1).

Dessalles' theory is an advance on earlier content-based theories which naively assumed that there is no problem to cooperatively offering information, and that 'benefit to the group' accounts for the emergence of cooperative behaviour. Uncooperative freeriders can become parasites on cooperative groups, taking the benefits while they last, and contributing nothing, until the success of the group is irreparably sapped. A cooperation-with-policing strategy can ensure the continuing strength of an alliance, and freeriders can be booted out.

Dessalles contrasts his theory with Reciprocal Altruism, but at one level the difference is not so great. Exponents of Reciprocal Altruism theory typically do not specify the coinage in which altruistic acts are manifested. They just deal in the very general terms 'Cooperate' and 'Defect'. These could be anything. If you scratch my back, I'll give you a bit of food. The altruism of Reciprocal Altruism is only deferred self-interest, and so it is with Dessalles' theory of information traded for status. Dessalles claims that the difference is that in his theory the giver of relevant propositional information benefits immediately by being accorded status, so the act is genuinely selfish at the moment of its carrying out. But this seems a false contrast with Reciprocal Altruism. The status accorded to an individual is stored in the heads of others, and is only cashed out in real terms by later behaviour on their part. Dessalles' other objections to Reciprocal Altruism theory, noted earlier, are that the specific cost/benefit payoff conditions typically invoked are not common, and that the high degree of reciprocation assumed by the Tit-for-Tat strategy is unlikely to have sprung from nowhere.

Dessalles' theory makes an important addition to Reciprocal Altruism theory, in giving it a 'political' dimension. Alliances are a feature of primate, and especially chimpanzee, social life. If you belong to a coalition with a strong leader, your own inherent individual fitness is boosted. And the leader and other coalition members also have their own individual fitnesses boosted, relative to what their fitness would be if they were not members of any coalition. Dessalles proposes that membership of a coalition is bought by being able to give highly relevant information (about the neighbours, about imminent danger, about food). This gift of information creates a social bond between giver and receiver. As long as someone is able to provide this rich bounty (relevant information), he is welcome to join our club. Here it becomes clear why playing the communicative game, rather than just opting out, is advantageous. If you don't join in the scramble to impress potential coalition allies by showing how much relevant information you can give, and how much better your info is than others', you'll be left on the sidelines. Those playing the game successfully, and joining strong coalitions, will have more access to mates and get better food. That's the idea.

In Dessalles' theory, relevant honest talk is not cheap. It is easy enough to utter the requisite sounds or make the appropriate manual gestures. That is the cheap part. He argues that coming by a store of information in the first place, remembering it, and being able to impart relevant morsels of it at opportune times, takes some talent. This does not exactly address the problem that honest signals should be costly to be believable, but the social bonding, coalition-forming part of the theory makes the typical communicative situations relatively non-adversarial, so that less cost need be incurred in the giving of honest information. And Dessalles posits a strong policing mechanism to identify those whose contributions are not relevant enough. In fact, given Lachmann et al. (2002)'s insight that effective policing imposes a retrospective cost on the cheating signaller, Dessalles need not have bothered so much to argue that signalling is costly at or before the time of signalling.

Dessalles has identified a potentially important 'political' dimension in the evolution of informative communication. I have the same kind of misgivings about it as I have about Geoff Miller's arguments for sexual selection in the evolution of language. Both theories predict a high level of competition to talk. Undoubtedly, some people are highly competitive talkers, but each society also has its silent types, who do not seem unduly penalized by their non-participation in the competition. (We will see in the next section that this kind of behavioural polymorphism can be explained by one theory.) Both Miller's and Dessalles' theories are rather macho in this respect, projecting a picture of all (pre-)human social life from behaviour typical of a subset. It is good to recognize, as Dessalles does, the competitive, not purely cooperative, aspects of communication.

Dessalles' theory also assumes that the complex cognitive processes for public expression of rich propositional relevant information are in place, as do most of the theories discussed here. There is no evidence at all that apes signal rich propositional information to each other, let alone as a way to join a coalition. Perhaps a story can be told of a runaway evolutionary process fuelled by a feedback mechanism, starting with the provision of relatively simple relevant information. Alarm calls are, after all, highly relevant. And it is easy to imagine the value in terms of status enhancement for an individual capable of transmitting key information (e.g., location of favourite food) with simple informative pointings. Then all (all?!) that is needed is a transition from largely innate to predominantly learned signals, plus enhancement of the symbol-learning ability, followed at some stage by syntactic devices for expressing ever more complex bits of relevant information. Alternatively, perhaps a mechanism such as Dessalles proposes came into play at some stage after a system for conveying rich propositional information had emerged. But this would not answer the question of how such a system emerged in the first place, and only in our species.

8.4 (CULTURAL) GROUP SELECTION

In Dessalles' model, individuals join coalitions. These coalitions remain stable for some time, there is policing to detect non-participation, and individuals enjoy boosted fitness as a result of belonging to successful coalitions. There is competition between coalitions and not all coalitions are equally successful. One may reasonably ask whether this is a model of group selection, for what is the difference between a coalition and a group? Dessalles distances himself from theories of group selection. To explore the issue further, we need a brief survey of what group selection is.

The issue is sometimes conceived as the question of what the true unit of natural selection is, which presupposes that there is a single level at which selection works. After Darwin, who knew nothing about genes, it was naturally assumed that the unit of selection was the individual organism. Darwin concentrated on the phenotypic traits of organisms, discussing their adaptedness, and assuming some unknown mechanism of relatively faithful replication, with minor changes—descent with modification. When the scientific world woke up to Mendel's discovery of genetic factors, genes, a new candidate for the basic unit of selection became available. Dawkins (1976) is the most prominent popular exponent of the view that the basic replicators are genes, and that organisms such as animals and plants are their 'survival vehicles'. So far we appear to have two proposed units of selection, the gene (Dawkins) and the individual (post-Darwin, pre-Mendel), existing at different levels. But we need to be careful not to confuse two distinct ideas: those of **replicator** and **unit of selection**.

Individual selection and gene selection do not logically preclude each other, and there is also a growing number of exponents of **multi-level** selection (e.g. Sober 1993; Wilson and Sober 1994; McAndrew 2002). Multi-level selection theorists typically advocate, following Dawkins' terminology, that the individual organism is a '**vehicle** for selection'. Dawkins, of course, implied as much. Sexually reproducing individuals do not exactly replicate themselves. No two humans, apart from identical twins, are genetically identical. This is what makes identification by DNA so reliable.[25] So the genes, sequences of DNA, are definitely the units of biological **replication**, and individual organisms are not basic units of replication. But the genes need the individual organisms to survive.[26] There are cases where specific genes within an individual propagate themselves successfully, increasing their proportion within the total of the individual's genes, but not migrating out to other individuals. The most obvious case is cancer. Cancer is a successful spread of genes only in the limited sense that cancerous cells invade an individual's body. In most, if not all, such cases, this seriously decreases the fitness of the individual carrier. But the most typical vehicle, or unit, of **selection**, is the individual organism, working as a self-contained entity composed of myriads of phenotypic traits working as a team. It is the teamwork within the separate

[25] Only when proper precautions against contamination of samples are taken, of course.
[26] Read this sentence both possible ways—it's true on both interpretations.

parts of a complex organism that determines its reproductive fitness. The parts must 'co-operate', in the basic etymological sense of 'work together'.

Multi-level selection theorists also typically emphasize that, just as cooperation between the parts of a single organism contributes to its survival, so too, given the right circumstances, the parts of a social entity, such as a swarm of bees, a group of monkeys, or a human tribe, can contribute to the well-being of the group as a whole, and hence to the average survival and reproductive prospects of its individual members. The social group is the survival vehicle of its individual members. Some groups, because of their internal composition and dynamics, are better survival vehicles than others. This is the idea of group selection.

Because in the great majority of cases, genes interact in complex ways to produce the phenotype, one can rarely identify a case where a single gene can be said to have been selected, all on its own, without the cooperation of other genes. What is selected is the whole complex team of interacting genes.[27] When some mutant allele arises which strengthens the working of the whole team in producing a fit phenotype, this is a genuine case of gene selection. There are interesting cases, however, where the fitness contribution of an allele on one chromosome is clearly dependent on the existence of an opposite allele on the matching chromosome. This is known as 'heterozygote advantage'. A well-known case involves sickle-cell anaemia (Allison 1955, 1964). People who carry alleles on both relevant chromosomes disposing them to this disease (call this allele +SCA) will suffer from the disease. People who carry both alleles of the opposite allele (call it −SCA) will be prone to malaria. People with mixed alleles, one +SCA and the other −SCA, are healthier, in malarial regions of the world, than those with uniform alleles. What is preferred by natural selection here is not a single allele of a gene but a two-allele team in which there is division of labour. One allele protects against malaria, while creating a potential vulnerability to sickle-cell anaemia; the other allele keeps that sickle-cell anaemia at bay. Similarly, carriers of a single allele disposing to cystic fibrosis are less vulnerable to dehydrating conditions such as cholera, while people who have two such alleles are, of course, prone to cystic fibrosis (Gabriel et al. 1994). These are neat special cases of the

---

[27] This is shorthand for a somewhat more complex formulation. The complex team of interacting genes does gain advantage, but if the genes are on different chromosomes, the team is broken up during gametogenesis. The success of a gene has to be measured against a complex selective background of which an important part is the other genes around at other loci.

more general phenomenon of alleles being selected in groups, rather than singly.

This division of labour within an individual organism can also be seen in social groups. Indeed such division of labour is a hallmark of complex social groups. The analogy of a team is still relevant. Some members of a group play one role, others play other roles, all for the benefit of the group. This is behavioural polymorphism. Dugatkin (1990) constructed a model of fish behaviour within shoals. Within each evolved shoal, a few daring individuals are disposed to leave the shoal and cautiously check out potential predators. The other members of the shoal are genetically disposed to stay safely within the shoal. Dugatkin's models

are equivalent to intrademic group selection models of evolution in structured populations, in which shoals are trait groups and co-operation evolves by between-shoal selection. While the results are cast in terms of predator inspection, the model itself is general and applies to any multi-group scenario where co-operators benefit entire groups at their own expense. The results presented here add to the mounting theoretical and empirical evidence that co-operation is frequently not a pure evolutionarily stable strategy, and that many metapopulations should be polymorphic for both co-operators and defectors.   (Dugatkin 1990, p. 123)

The prediction of polymorphic populations is an advantage of Group Selection theory. It allows the possibility that not all members of a group will be equally cooperative, or equally competitive to display themselves to advantage. As noted before, with respect to language, human behaviour is somewhat polymorphic: some members of a group dominate conversation, others are more content to be the audience.

'During the 1960's and 70's most biologists rejected group selection as an important evolutionary force, but a positive literature began to grow during the 70's and is rapidly expanding today' (Wilson and Sober 1994, p. 585). Group selection still has a bad name in biology. Biology undergraduates in my university are still taught, so they tell me, that it is a fallacy. The central idea of group selection has been re-worked since Wynne-Edwards (1962)'s original proposal that animals sometimes act 'for the good of the species', a naive idea. Here is a taste of the controversy surrounding the phrase 'group selection'.

Williams (1966) and others argued that group-level adaptations require a process of natural selection at the group level and that this process, though theoretically possible, was unlikely to be important in nature. Their verdict quickly became the majority view and was celebrated as a major scientific advance, similar to the rejection of Lamarkianism. A generation of graduate students learned about group selection as an example of how not to think and it became almost mandatory for the authors of journal articles to assure their readers that group selection was not being invoked.

(Wilson and Sober 1994, p. 586)

I believe that this partly explains why Dessalles distances his coalition theory from Group Selection; he need not protest so much, although, as he has pointed out to me, individuals choose to join coalitions, whereas in the usual sense of Group Selection theory, individuals do not choose their groups. An exponent of 'new group selection' theory, David Sloan Wilson put its claim succinctly:

Group-level adaptations are just as compatible with selfish-gene theory as individual-level adaptations. It would be wrong to claim that groups invariably evolve into adaptive units (the position aptly termed 'naive group selection'), but it would be equally wrong to claim that groups never evolve into adaptive units. The issue must be decided on the basis of where the fitness differences occur—between genes within individuals, between individuals within groups, or between groups within the metapopulation.   (Wilson 1998, p. 92)

The theory of group selection does not insist that groups endure for ever; likewise, of course, individual selection does not require individuals to be immortal. It is only required that groups cohere long enough to confer some reproductive advantage on their members. This makes the difference between the groups of Group Selection theory and Dessalles' coalitions a matter of degree of duration.

Williams admitted the theoretical possibility of group selection, but in fact convincing examples in non-human nature are hard, if not impossible, to find. A central problem is that of forming a 'skin' around a social group that is as impermeable as the skin of an animal. Putting it somewhat figuratively, an animal's skin holds all the parts together and ensures that it functions as a single identifiable entity.[28] For something to be taken seriously as a vehicle of selection, it must copy itself with considerable fidelity through periods of time long enough for the selection process to work, and it must be clear that there is not too much change in the parts of which it is composed. For biological selection, individual organisms generally meet

---

[28] This picture is oversimplified, because animals typically are host to other organisms of different species, some of which may serve functions advantageous to the animal. If this situation perseveres, the guest organisms may eventually evolve to become intrinsic parts of the animal. This is true of mitochondria, now the indispensable powerhouses of animal cells, but once independent bacteria.

these criteria; indeed that is why we call them individual organisms. Social groups rarely have a 'skin' as impermeable as that of an organism. People leave and new people join frequently. For this reason, biological selection of social groups is rare, and possibly nonexistent; whole social groups are not copied by biological means with enough fidelity over the periods of time that it takes for natural selection to work on their shared genotypes. Migration in and out of the group messes up its genetic homogeneity. We will discuss a different version of group selection, in which the selection and copying processes are faster, with a good chance of being fast enough to outpace the effects of frequent migration of individuals in and out of social groups.

Sharing a common learned communicative code can be a strong marker of group membership. As mentioned earlier, in connection with Reciprocal Altruism, a possible descendant of that theory could be one which gives advantage to a strategy prescribing 'Cooperate with fellow group members; don't cooperate with others'. Implementation of such a strategy could involve recognition of group members by their sharing of the common code.[29] In this way, we see a possible complementarity between the evolution of cooperation and the evolution of conventional communicative codes shared within groups.

Human moral codes, learned and transmitted via expression in language, are a force for cohesion within social groups. Moral codes are the basis of policing mechanisms by which non-conforming individuals are punished. Often, such moral codes not only prescribe and proscribe behaviour, but also make statements about group identity. Wilson and Sober (1994) give an example of the Hutterites, a fundamentalist religious sect, whose writings emphasized the virtue of individual selfless behaviour and group identity.

It seems to me that, with an important qualification, Darwin (1871)'s picture of the relationship between groups, moral codes, cheaters, and natural selection was about right. Darwin clearly recognized the cheater problem:

It is extremely doubtful whether the offspring of the more sympathetic and benevolent parents, or of those which were the most faithful to their comrades, would be reared in greater number than the children of selfish and treacherous parents of the same tribe. He who was ready to sacrifice his life,

---

[29] On this topic, see the discussion of Nettle and Dunbar (1997)'s simulations, and Dunbar (1999)'s comments, on p. 301.

as many a savage has been, rather than betray his comrades, would often leave no offspring to inherit his noble nature.   (Darwin 1871, p. 163)

Darwin's solution was high moral standards:[30]

It must not be forgotten that although a high standard of morality gives but a slight or no advantage to each individual man and his children over the other men of the same tribe, yet that an advancement in the standard of morality and an increase in the number of well-endowed men will certainly give an immense advantage to one tribe over another. There can be no doubt that a tribe including many members who, from possessing in a high degree the spirit of patriotism, fidelity, obedience, courage, and sympathy, were always ready to give aid to each other, and to sacrifice themselves for the common good, would be victorious over most other tribes; and this would be natural selection. At all times throughout the world tribes have supplanted other tribes; and as morality is one element in their success, the standard of morality and the number of well-endowed men will thus everywhere tend to rise and increase.   (Darwin 1871, p. 166)

Now, we have a problem here. How can Darwin, of all people, be wrong about natural selection? The situation he describes would only be counted as natural selection by modern biologists if the 'spirit of patriotism, fidelity, obedience, courage and sympathy' were passed on biologically through the genes. What would it mean to say that 'patriotism' was bio-logically inherited? We can read it as a disposition to act in the interests of the group, but this is certainly a weaker concept than patriotism. Similarly, 'obedience' can be read as a biologically inherited disposition to defer to older or dominant members of the group. But chimpanzees, and humans in many cultures, are often willing to challenge dominant individuals. And rigid obedience to dominants may in fact not always be in the best interests of the group, if the leadership is poor.

Let's hypothetically stay with the idea, for the moment, that individual Darwinian virtues promoting group fitness (over other groups) are genet-ically transmitted. In this case, if juveniles do not emigrate out of their birth group, it will be hard to distinguish these virtues from those giving rise to Kin Selection. The group in this case is a collection of genetically related individuals, and acting in the interests of the group is acting in the interests of kin. The two cases are not exactly the same, because close genetic relatedness only applies to very close relatives, and in Kin

---

[30] Darwin was, however, at a loss to explain how particular groups (his example was the Spanish) came to lose their moral standards and begin to lose in competition with other groups (his example was the English).

Selection theory it is only the closest relatives that gain much from the altruism of kin. A distinction could be made if there were some process like imprinting, whereby individuals were genetically disposed to act in the interests of those conspecifics living nearby them while growing up. The invasion of cheaters might be resisted by reciprocally altruistic behaviour.

To make the case that biological group selection can be clearly distinct from kin selection, one would have to envisage a pair of contradictory conditions: (1) a group not defined by kinship relations, and (2) biological transmission of the dispositions to group-preserving virtues. If such a group survives for more than one generation, condition 2 will ensure that condition 1 is violated.

Experience with a range of current human societies makes it clear that the virtues that Darwin identified are largely passed on through **learning**, and not through the genes. Learning solves problems fast, within the lifetime of an individual, whereas natural selection solves problems slowly by sacrificing individuals and experimenting with new variants in successive generations. Different societies have different culturally transmitted moral codes. Compare Britain, Japan, and Saudi Arabia; compare Mormons with Quakers. A modified (some might say 'watered down') version of group selection, **Cultural Group Selection**, is distinguishable from Kin Selection, but such a model has now left the realm of biological models of selection, and so is not closely comparable with, nor a rival to, models such as individual selection or gene selection. In a Cultural Group Selection model, groups are not identified biologically. A group might be an all-male pirate ship crew, or an all-female convent, or all the orphans in an orphanage. If such a group has traditions that are strongly inculcated into members through learning, and if these traditions tend to strengthen the whole group in competition with other groups, the group will thrive and attract new members who also absorb its characteristic values.

In cultural group selection, the genes still have a crucial involvement, as the learning of a group's traditional virtues must be biologically possible. We can envisage a division of labour between genes and culture. The genes provide individuals with a general disposition towards 'groupishness' comprising such traits as seeking companionship, imitation of group members, some disposition to reciprocity, avid learning of arbitrary group norms, and some commitment to enforcing these norms in other group members. This biological envelope is very permissive, and within it many different sets of cultural conventions can thrive, giving rise to the kaleidoscope of languages and cultures that we find among humans today.

In parallel with the linguist's theory of an innate Universal Grammar (UG), a template for any humanly learnable language, we can envisage a characteristically human innate package of dispositions to acquire just the kind of values that contribute to group cohesion.[31]

Axelrod et al. (2004)'s study, discussed earlier, showed the evolution of altruism in groups of individuals living close and sharing observable traits identifying them as appropriate recipients of altruism. This strongly suggests the possibility that altruism could also develop in groups of non-kin living close[32] and sharing some group-identity tag. In Axelrod et al. (2004)'s model, these tags are innate and transmitted genetically, but Nettle and Dunbar (1997) have shown that similar results are obtained with learned tags, or 'badges' of group membership. In their model, Nettle and Dunbar (1997) simulated exchanges of resources among a population of individuals, introducing the restriction that such trade could only occur between individuals who spoke the same dialect, precisely defined in the computer code. It was found that MIMICs, individuals capable of changing their own dialect, chameleon-like, prospered in this scenario, being able to trade with greater numbers of other people, but only when the group's dialect itself was relatively stable. When the group's dialect was less stable, MIMICs did not thrive. Dunbar (1999) insightfully comments on these results:

Although kin selection was not explicitly built into this model, it is not difficult to see that dialect will quickly become important as a badge of relatedness whenever dialect acquisition is based on learning from those individuals with whom you live at an early critical period of development (i.e. well prior to social independence).
The suggestion that dialects are badges of group membership would explain one of the more curious features of language acquisition, namely the fact that while we are capable of learning new languages throughout life, our ability to speak a language as a 'native' seems to be restricted to a very brief period in early childhood.   (Dunbar 1999, p. 203)[33]

---

[31] See Poulshock (2006) for an interesting discussion of these ideas.

[32] 'Nothing propinks like propinquity.'

[33] A reader disagreed with Dunbar's conclusion here, writing: 'On a conventional individual-selection view, the inability to learn later would need to be individually advantageous—but I don't see that it is.' This objection could be countered by a consequence of Hurford (1991)'s model, where the inability to learn after puberty, though not positively advantageous, evolves through the random accumulation of mutations in the population and the lack of any further pressure to learn language once it has already been learned (before puberty).

This gets us close to a scenario of the co-evolution of coopera-
tive/altruistic communication with the learned communicative code itself
as a group identity tag. The function of a language as a marker of group
identity may go some way towards explaining why there are so many
different languages, why the human capacity for language allows so many
different manifestations of language. An identity marker serves simultaneously to bind members of the group and to distance them from members
of other groups.

Dessalles' theory invoked policing within a coalition. Enforcement of
group norms by punishment is also central to an evolutionary model
of altruism developed by Gintis (2000) and Henrich and Boyd (2001)
and explored empirically by Henrich et al. (2001). The model is called
'Strong Reciprocity'. The central idea is that a social group contains
some individuals defined like this: 'A strong reciprocator is predisposed
to cooperate with others and punish non-cooperators, even when this
behavior cannot be justified in terms of extended kinship or reciprocal
altruism' (Gintis 2000, p. 169). Polymorphism is also a feature of this
model. The population need not consist wholly of strong reciprocators.
A problem for Reciprocal Altruism, mentioned earlier, is that it does not
work in hard times, when the likelihood of future reciprocation is low.
A theoretical model of Strong Reciprocity shows how that weakness in
Reciprocal Altruism can be overcome:

[A] small number of strong reciprocators, who punish defectors whether or
not it is in their long-term interest, can dramatically improve the survival
chances of human groups. . . . This is because even if strong reciprocators form
a small fraction of the population, at least occasionally they will form a
sufficient fraction of the group that cooperation can be maintained in bad
times. Such a group will then outcompete other self-interested groups, and
the fraction of strong reciprocators will grow.   (Gintis et al. 2003, p. 163)

What strong reciprocators do is short-circuit the time-gap from one
episode between two people to the next. Under Reciprocal Altruism, after
one episode in which a person has not received due cooperation, the
defector goes on his way, and in hard times may never be seen again. But
if the defector has the bad luck to be dealing with a strong reciprocator,
he will get immediately punished if he doesn't cooperate. So if he knows
who he is dealing with, he cooperates. Even if he thinks there is a chance
he may be dealing with a strong reciprocator, it will be wise to cooperate,
if the likely punishment is severe.

In the next chapter, we will see some empirical evidence that humans and other primates are prepared to ignore their own short-term advantage in order to punish others who, in one way or another, do not conform to group norms of cooperation.

From the point of view of language evolution, we have a chicken-and-egg problem, if we take moral codes, or explicit group norms, to be the crucial glue that holds coherent social groups together. We want to know how language arose from non-language. A degree of social cohesion is a prior condition for the emergence of a group-wide shared communicative system. This degree of cohesion cannot, then, be enforced by a moral code expressed, and propagated to the young, by means of that communicative system. The prescriptions of our moral codes are expressed in quite complex syntactic language. It is possible that the existence of complex language was a factor in maintaining cohesion in groups **after** the human language capacity had evolved to near its present state. But we need to look for other sources of group cohesion if we want to use group cohesion to explain the early rudimentary beginnings of the language faculty.

A relatively simple and obvious group selection model worth exploring would correlate intra-group communication non-linearly with the group's potential for outcompeting other groups. This might be envisaged in the following way. To put it concretely, let's say the main form of inter-group competition is fighting; it could be less violent forms of competition, like deprivation of resources, but fighting makes the example vivid. The idea could be that it's the number of intercommunicating pairs that gives a boost to fighting ability. Then with k fighters, there would be $k(k-1)/2$ possible pairs of communicators. Suppose that each communicating pair effectively adds the equivalent of an extra fighter to the group. Then a group of 10 with no communicating pairs would have the effective fighting capacity of 10. A group with just 2 individuals capable of communicating with each other would have a capacity of 11, and a group in which any individual could communicate with any other would have a capacity of 55. Suppose also, plausibly, that the same code was used for communication in all pairs. Then, given one communicating pair, a third individual joining the communicating pair, would effectively add the strength of 2 to the whole group. A fourth individual joining this communicating trio would effectively add the strength of 3 to the whole group. And a fifth joining individual would add the strength of 4, and so on. This is definitely non-linear in the 'right' direction.

Summarizing this chapter, evolutionary theory provides a large number of tools which might in part solve the mystery of how human communication evolved beyond the stage seen in non-human primates. I have reviewed the most frequently discussed ideas: niche-construction, Kin Selection, Reciprocal Altruism, Sexual Selection, the Handicap Principle, the theory of costly signalling, Dessalles' coalition theory, Group Selection, and Strong Reciprocity. In all cases, the theories are internally coherent, and it is fairly clear what cognitive and social conditions must hold for them to be applicable to the case of human language. No single theory does the trick entirely. One should avoid the tendency in langage evolution studies to advocate any single model, to the exclusion of others that could equally have applied in parallel, or in sequence. On a cross-cultural analysis of human food-giving, Gurven (2004) summarizes: 'Each model can explain some of the variance in sharing patterns within groups, and so generalizations that ignore or deny the importance of any one model may be misleading' (p. 543). In a commentary on Gurven's article, Moore (2004) suggests that human food-sharing can best be accounted for by assuming that 'Rather than distinct alternatives, tolerated scrounging (TS), costly signaling (CS), and reciprocal altruism (RA) are likely to be sequentially evolved components of a single integrated system (and kin selection (KS) important only among very close relatives)' (p. 566). The sequential involvement that Moore has in mind is over the course of phylogenetic evolution. This echoes the thought of Fitch (2005, p. 214) quoted earlier (p. 264), in the specific context of language evolution, suggesting that Kin Selection 'paved the way' for Reciprocal Altruism. As the next evolutionary step, Gintis (2000) has shown that Strong Reciprocity can emerge from Reciprocal Altruism through Group Selection. An evolutionary cascade of selective processes like that shown below can be roughly envisaged from this theorizing:

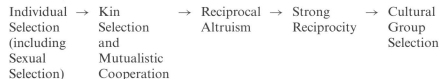

Individual Selection (including Sexual Selection) $\rightarrow$ Kin Selection and Mutualistic Cooperation $\rightarrow$ Reciprocal Altruism $\rightarrow$ Strong Reciprocity $\rightarrow$ Cultural Group Selection

The later a process is in this sequence, the rarer it is in nature, and the more demanding of cognitive resources such as memory and learning. Mutualism requires more than Individual Selection, especially some anticipation of the actions of others, but requires less than Reciprocal Altruism, in that there is no need to keep track of who cooperated in previous encounters. Cultural Group Selection is probably uniquely human, and is still controversial among theorists. Also along this scale, there is progressive enrichment of the type of information conveyed in communication. In Sexual Selection, the information conveyed need not have semantic content about any external object or event; it can have purely illocutionary force, even if the signal itself is somewhat complex, as with some birdsong. In the middle of the scale, with Mutualistic Cooperation and Reciprocal Altruism, communicative forms of altruism and cooperation would be about valuable things in the environment. At the right-hand end of the scale, with Cultural Group Selection, especially as we move towards fully human groups, there is the capacity to formulate explicit public moral codes, which are not only about external objects, but about permitted and forbidden **potential** behaviour.

Taken together, then, there are enough coherent theoretical models to make it not **too** surprising that somewhat cooperative, somewhat competitive, complex human language evolved, and that there are so many different languages. If ever this becomes no surprise at all, we will face the opposite embarrassing question of why language only evolved in one species. This is the state of the field at the moment. A reader has expressed disappointment here: 'This chapter needs a more powerful conclusion that matches the great expectations created in the introductory pages. It doesn't matter if the proposal is then accompanied by qualifications and protests of awareness of its speculative nature. This chapter deserves a better ending.' Well, I'm sorry, but we have to be honest. Work on language evolution is already speculative enough. Humans, especially with the emergence of language, appear to have squeezed through an evolutionary loophole, and it is hard to specify exactly which combination of the factors reviewed in this chapter provided that loophole. But some combination did evidently do the trick. Bumblebees **can** fly, and humans do have extensive cooperative language. To the limited extent that any single factor should be emphasized, I believe it is the rise of a disposition towards **communicative cooperation**, to be discussed at greater length in the next chapter. Almost all the theories surveyed here were not devised with language specifically in mind. Most concentrated on the problem of the evolution of altruism and cooperation. Despite the obvious materially cooperative uses of language for imparting useful information, I wish to emphasize the importance, for language evolution, of a more basic form of cooperation: communicative cooperation. To be communicatively cooperative is simply to use the same communicative code as one's interlocutor. Given communicative cooperation, a speaker is free to decide whether to be materially cooperative (i.e. to give true relevant information in a clear manner) or not (i.e. to lie or obfuscate). Communicative cooperation is 'playing the same language game'. A community of users of the same code can form a cohesive social group, which could be a unit of selection. Use of the common code can serve to distinguish group members from outsiders, for decisions about whether to cooperate or act altruistically. This will arise again in Chapter 9.

CHAPTER NINE

Cooperation, Fair Play, and Trust in Primates

Moving from the theoretical to the empirical, this short chapter will examine the extent to which behaviour reflecting any kind of social contract exists among primates.

9.1 MIND-READING, A PREREQUISITE FOR INTENTIONAL COOPERATION

In Section 5 of Chapter 6 (p. 204), I mentioned the Machiavellian, manipulative nature of life in primate groups. To be able to manipulate others effectively, you need to be able to read their minds. The topic of 'Theory of Mind' in psychology has blossomed in recent years. Put simply, for an animal to have a theory of mind, it has to know that other creatures (usually conspecifics) go through the same mental processes as it does. An animal that can do this can project its own state of mind onto another creature. It can 'say to itself', 'in that situation, I would think in way X, and decide to do Z, so I assume that the other creature is probably also thinking in way X and likely to do Z.'

A theory of mind (ToM) is not something that animals either simply have or do not have. It is multifaceted, or at least its behavioural correlates are, and experimental research necessarily works with a range of different operational tests. Tager-Flusberg and Sullivan (2000), among others, list as components of ToM a capacity for attribution of false beliefs, explanation of the actions of others, and recognition of emotional expressions. Heyes (1998, p. 101), in a critical survey of this area, lists studies of 'imitation, [mirror] self-recognition, social relationships, deception, role-taking (or empathy), and perspective-taking' as the most prominent types claiming to shed light on ToM in non-human primates. In my own brief review here, I will concentrate on experiments which try to test whether apes can recognize or know about different intentional states in others, in particular recognition of cooperative versus competitive intentions, and knowledge of what another animal can see and of what another animal can know.

In the area of ToM research, stark differences in research style also emerge, with experimentalists typically setting the criteria fairly high, i.e. being reluctant to concede any aspect of a theory of mind to non-humans, while ethologists who mainly observe animals in the wild, without experimental intervention, tend to describe their data in more anthropomorphic terms, thus often granting the animals some degree of understanding of other minds. This tension in the field is visible in the following quotation from Celia Heyes, a researcher who is on the 'tough' experimentalist end of the spectrum:

Since the BBS article in which Premack and Woodruff (1978) asked 'Does the chimpanzee have a theory of mind?,' it has been repeatedly claimed that there is observational and experimental evidence that apes have mental state concepts, such as 'want' and 'know'. Unlike research on the development of theory of mind in childhood, however, no substantial progress has been made through this work with non-human primates. A survey of empirical studies of imitation, self-recognition, social relationships, deception, role-taking, and perspective-taking suggests that in every case where non-human primate behavior has been interpreted as a sign of theory of mind, it could instead have occurred by chance or as a product of nonmentalistic processes such as associative learning or inferences based on nonmental categories. Arguments to the effect that, in spite of this, the theory of mind hypothesis should be accepted because it is more parsimonious than alternatives or because it is supported by convergent evidence are not compelling.

(Heyes, 1998, p. 101)

Heyes' article surveys the literature available at the time, and is a textbook exposition of a style of discipline applied in extrapolating from evidence, in controlled experiments. Not surprisingly, it drew protest from highly experienced field ethologists, for example: 'But how often *should* one prefer an implausible, complicated, nonmentalistic account, over a simple mentalistic one?' (Byrne 1998, p. 117). The debate might, wrongly, be taken to reflect a classic historic division in the study of animals, which one could say, with some liberty, pits Cartesians against Darwinians: the former see discontinuity between humans and non-humans, the latter see continuity. What is the appropriate null hypothesis? Is it that humans and apes are so similar that one would expect apes to differ minimally from humans in their mental processes? In this case the onus is on researchers to demonstrate differences in the capacities of humans and apes. This has, of course, been done in great detail for many tasks. The alternative null hypothesis is that humans and apes are so different that one would be surprised to find any similarities in their mental processes, and the onus in this case is on researchers to demonstrate such similarities, which, of course, has also been done in great detail. So the debate cannot be a simple, antiquated dispute between Cartesians and Darwinians. With some exceptions, Darwin has carried the day.

So what **is** this argument about? It is about scientific method. Note how the concept of parsimony is focal. Heyes (1998, p. 135) characterizes a Cartesian approach as based on introspection, which tells the introspecter that her own mental states, at least, are real. This introspectionist approach is eloquently castigated by Provine (2005, p. 713): '[W]e over-estimate the conscious control of behavior and cannot trust its narrative as an explanation of our actions. . . . We are misled by an inner voice that generates a reasonable but often fallacious narrative and explanation of our actions, and we use this account to interpret the actions of others.' But Provine does admit that 'proving this proposition is a challenge' (p. 713). Heyes prefers an alternative 'functionalist view of mental states. I take them to be theoretical entities, characterized by their relationships with sensory inputs, motor outputs, and other (functionally defined) mental states, not by their subjective properties and therefore to afford empirical investigation' (1998, p. 135). Heyes then frankly admits that 'On this issue, we are all to some degree restating dogma' (p. 135). My own a priori commitment does not, unlike Heyes, entirely rule out the evidence of introspection about our own mental states. On the basis of my own awareness of my mental states, and of the evident similarities and differences between humans and apes, I fall somewhere between what Heyes calls the 'chauvinist' and the 'liberal' positions. If I, partly on the basis of introspection, and partly as an elegant way of explaining my own and others' behaviour, believe that I and other humans have mental states that I can, in everyday life, in some way know about, then, since apes are obviously somewhat like us, I regard it as not too improbable that apes also can know about others' mental states. I do not lean over as far as Heyes does in denying a theory of mind to apes, and I grant more plausibility than she does to the conclusions of the 'liberal' field ethologists, like Byrne. Nonetheless, the stiff dose of experimental rigour administered by Heyes keeps one from complacency on this issue. If the whole gamut of ape behaviour can be **easily** explained without appealing to their knowledge of the mental states of others, then so be it.

Chimpanzees can tell the difference between a human who is deliberately teasing them with food and one who is merely clumsy in trying, unsuccessfully, to give them food (Call et al. 2004). In this experiment, a human experimenter sat opposite a chimpanzee on the other side of a plexiglass screen with a hole in it. In the 'teasing' condition, the experimenter offered food to the chimpanzee through the hole, but quickly withdrew it when the chimp was about to take it; the experimenter kept repeating this teasing. In the 'fumbling' condition, the experimenter similarly offers food through the hole, but clumsily drops it, so that it rolls back down a shelf sloping towards the experimenter; the experimenter kept repeating this fumbling. In the teasing condition, the chimpanzees showed significantly more impatience with the situation, angrily banging on the glass and leaving the station early. In the fumbling condition, the chimpanzees waited more patiently for the experimenter to get it right. The visual difference, to the chimpanzee, between the two conditions was minimal. In both cases a hand proferred food through the hole, and at the last minute the food was either pulled back or dropped. This seems to demonstrate an awareness in the chimpanzee of the difference between two intentional attitudes in the experimenter. In a similar experiment with children, Behne et al. (2005) showed that children were able to make a similar discrimination at the age of 9 months, but not at 6 months.

Povinelli and Barth (2005) criticize Call et al. (2004)'s mentalistic interpretation of their experiment: '[W]e note that the experiments they cite in support of the idea that chimpanzees represent intentions are designed in a manner that cannot distinguish between whether they [the chimpanzees] are reasoning about behavior alone, or behavior and mental states' (p. 712). Povinelli and Barth (2005)'s own alternative proposal is a 'reinterpretation hypothesis':

The reinterpretation hypothesis posits that the ancestor of the ape/human group possessed a suite of systems dedicated to representing and reasoning about behavior (detailed in Povinelli & Vonk 2004), but not intentions or other mental states. Further the model posits that, at some point in the evolution of the human lineage (probably coincident with evolution of natural language), a new system for encoding the behavior of self and other in terms of mental states was grafted into these ancestral systems for representing and reasoning about behavior. In modern humans, then, these two systems are now complexly interleaved into each other. (p. 713)

According to Povinelli and Barth (2005), 'only humans represent mental states at all' (p. 713). Provine (2005, p. 713) won't even go this far, or, we might say, goes even further: 'Intention, shared or unshared, is based on the presumption of unknowable and unnecessary motives and mental states in ourselves and others.'

I told you this is a contentious area! My own adopted position is sympathetic to Call et al. (2004)'s mentalistic interpretation of their experiment, according to which chimpanzees can distinguish between different kinds of intentions in an experimenter, between teasing and fumbling. Whatever the interpretation, the experimental results are important. They show something that chimpanzees can do, that we didn't know about before. It is not possible to resolve the intention-reading versus non-intention-reading argument on the basis of one or two experiments. So far, all we know is that chimpanzees can distinguish between the physical manifestations of teasing and fumbling. We need a whole series of experiments to test whether chimpanzees can distinguish between two large, physically heterogeneous, classes of behaviours, to which we humans would give labels such as 'uncooperative' and 'cooperative'. The more such experiments succeed, and the more physically varied are the pairs of stimuli compared, the more compelling it will be to conclude that the chimpanzees have mental categorizations of large and heterogeneous classes of behaviour, which it is convenient for us to label as 'cooperative' and 'uncooperative'. For what it is worth, I expect this is how it will turn out. For all the experiments to be described below, this same methodological issue could be revisited. I will not keep coming back to it. I have stated my preferred position.

'Chimpanzees know what conspecifics do and do not see'. This is the title of an article by Hare et al. (2000). The experimenters kept a dominant chimpanzee in a cage from which it could see one, but not both, of two pieces of food. A subordinate chimpanzee was held in a place from where it could see which of the two pieces the dominant chimpanzee could see. If it was released before the dominant chimp into the food-containing space, it chose to go towards the food which it knew the dominant chimp has not been able to see. This is not surprising, given the results on gaze-following mentioned in Chapter 7.1. In a closely similar experiment with capuchin monkeys, Hare et al. (2003) found that these animals did not systematically choose the food that they had been in a position to see that a dominant animal could not see. 'This series of experiments has demonstrated that when competing for food capuchin monkeys excel at reading the behaviour of conspecifics, but they do not use information about what others do and do not see' (p. 140). Chimpanzees are better than capuchin monkeys at acting in accordance with what others can, or cannot, see.

The same team of experimenters (Hare et al. 2001) followed up with a more complex situation, in which a dominant and a subordinate chimpanzee both saw pieces of food being laid out, and saw each other see it. But then, while the dominant was not looking, but the subordinate **was** looking, one piece was moved to another location. In this situation the subordinate chimpanzee preferentially moved towards the food which it knew the dominant animal had not seen moved. This is the most convincing evidence, to date, that chimpanzees know what others believe.

So far, no experiment has managed to show that any non-human animal can know about the **false** belief of another, as adult humans can. This can be tested for humans by the well-known 'Sally Ann' test used to test autistic people (Baron-Cohen et al. 1985). In this test, a marble is placed in a basket in view of the test subject and an observer (Sally); Sally then leaves the room, and the marble is moved from the basket to a box; the test subject is then asked, 'Where will Sally look for the marble? Most autistics fail to realize that Sally will look in the basket, because that was where the marble was when she last saw it, even though it has been moved since. The Sally Ann test is verbal, as the subject is asked a question. Efforts continue to devise a non-verbal test which can be administered to animals. The Sally Ann test probes the extent to which subjects can ascribe a belief to others which they themselves know to be false. Lohmann and Tomasello (2003) provide evidence that language facilitates this ability in children, and cite a large number of other works reinforcing this conclusion. They note that 'linguistic experience is a strong facilitator, perhaps even necessary condition, in the development of children's false belief understanding' (p. 1139). The findings on (non-language-trained) chimpanzees mentioned above show that they can know what others believe, but it is still not clear whether this extends to specifically **false** beliefs. But exposure to language, especially of the right sort, for example with sentential complement clauses as in *Sally thinks that* . . . , triggers its earlier emergence in normal child development.

In a recent survey of work on 'What chimpanzees know about seeing', Call and Tomasello (2005) admit to some bafflement as to what chimpanzees know about the intentional states of others: 'Chimpanzees' behaviour in many socially complex situations is decidedly mixed. They behave very intelligently in some ways—seeming to understand and reason about others—but they still do not seem to understand some social interactions in the way that humans do' (p. 61). They settle, at this point in the saga of this research, for a middle position on chimpanzees, between the extremes of simple behavioural conditioning and full-blown Theory of Mind.

Knowing what another animal knows sets the scene for cooperation, which we will look at in the next section. Full cooperation requires that the cooperators each know that the other intends to work on the task concerned.

9.2 COOPERATION

Chimpanzees vary in the degree to which they can be rated as helpful to each other. Within an anthropomorphic research tendency, King and Figueredo (1997) analysed the personalities of 100 zoo chimpanzees using the same 'Big Five' personality traits as are commonly used to describe human personality, plus a sixth, 'Dominance' which plays a significant role in chimpanzee social relations.

The Big Five, namely surgency, agreeableness, dependability, emotionality, and openness, emerge across a variety of different Western and non-Western cultures and across different age groups (see (John, 1990; Costa and McCrae, 1992) for reviews). In addition, all five factors have heritabilities approaching .50 (Bouchard, 1994). . . .

The discovery of the human Big Five personality structure in chimpanzees would thus parallel discoveries of advanced social intelligence in this species and would imply that the human pattern of personality organization long antedated the recent emergence of *Homo sapiens*, just as the current research on ape behavior indicates that advanced social intelligence extends far back in our hominid ancestry. . . .

Zoo workers are unquestionably able to rate adjectival personality traits of chimpanzees with reliabilities as great as or possibly greater than comparable peer/peer ratings of humans.

(King and Figueredo 1997, pp. 258, 259, 265)

The factors constituting Agreeableness are +Sympathetic, +Helpful, +Sensitive, +Protective, and +Gentle. This work is significant for our concerns for two reasons. First, it points out the variability within an ape species. One cannot simply generalize to a common uniform chimpanzee personality. This variability, of course, is the fuel of natural selection. Secondly, it appears that one can classify some chimpanzees as in some sense 'sympathetic' and 'helpful' to some degree. Thus these traits are not entirely absent from the chimpanzee population. We can read 'helpful' as roughly synonymous with 'cooperative'. In the questionnaire used for King et al. (2005)'s study, the 'helpful' factor is glossed as 'Subject is willing to assist, accommodate, or cooperate with other chimpanzees'.

The questionnaire did not specify whether the other chimpanzees had to be non-kin. The implication of the study is that chimpanzee helpfulness is sometimes manifested towards non-kin. But the specific manifestations of helpfulness are not classified or quantified, so the study is merely suggestive.

Individual variation among chimpanzees in helpfulness is also demonstrated in experiments by Melis et al. (2006a, 2006b). Here, helpfulness does not mean willingness to volunteer help so much as skill in carrying out a collaborative task effectively. In these experiments, in a setup where a chimpanzee could benefit only by getting another to collaborate, and where it was allowed to choose between two potential collaborators, it learned to choose the animal who, from past experience, it had found to be the more effective collaborator. This shows, not only that there is variation on a dimension related to cooperation, on which natural selection can operate, but also that chimpanzees can act as the agents of this selection. This last assertion is only true if the chosen collaborator gets to share the benefits of the cooperative act. This is often not the case, and a dominant animal will get a subordinate to collaborate, but take most or all of the reward for itself, as reported in experiments on chimpanzees by Chalmeau (1994; Chalmeau and Gallo 1996). In experiments with orangutans (Chalmeau et al. 1997), a dominant animal actually bullied a subordinate into collaboration, and then took 92% of the reward.

Chimpanzees who have been trained to use symbols to request things from humans can also be easily made to transfer this ability to request things from other chimps, and the addressee of such requests usually cooperates by giving the item requested. In the studies which discovered this (Savage-Rumbaugh et al. 1978b; Savage-Rumbaugh 1980), the items requested were tools. The animals would presumably have been less willing to collaborate if the items requested had been food.

Against this picture that chimpanzees can be somewhat helpful to each other, there is a stack of evidence that they are typically selfish, and find it hard to interpret the behaviour of others as helpful, even when it really is. Silk et al. (2005) used an experimental setup in which a chimpanzee could choose between getting food delivered only to itself or to itself and another chimpanzee visible in an adjacent enclosure. There was no advantage or disadvantage to the actor chimp in either case, but there definitely was a possible benefit to the other chimp, if the actor pulled the appropriate handle. So this experiment was not even asking whether chimpanzees would behave altruistically, since there was never any cost to the chooser. All that was sought was 'other-regarding' behaviour, weaker than true altruism. The results showed all the experimental subjects to be indifferent to whether the other animal got any food. Mostly, they chose randomly between the two possible actions. In this setup, chimpanzees are not other-regarding.

Compared to humans, even our closest relatives among the apes, chimpanzees, are more motivated in their natural habitat to act competitively than to act cooperatively. They can to some extent figure out each other's intentions, but their natural expectations seem to be that others will have competitive, rather than cooperative, intentions. This is well shown in an experiment by Hare and Tomasello (2004), who used a novel twist on the object-choice paradigm which was discussed earlier (Chapter 7.2, on pointing and following of pointing). Hare and Tomasello (2004) got the chimpanzee subjects familiar with two human experimenters: one a cooperative person who willingly shared food with the animal and showed pleasure when the animal found food, and another person who acted competitively with the animal, keeping found food for himself and showing annoyance when the chimpanzee got food. The chimpanzees learned these personality traits well. In the actual experiment, in the competitive condition, the competitive experimenter would make a reaching gesture for a container (one of two) containing hidden food. The chimpanzee subjects interpreted this movement relatively well, and tended to grab the food in anticipation of the competitor's getting it. In the cooperative condition, the cooperative experimenter would indicate the position of food by a pointing gesture minimally different from the reaching gesture used by the competitive experimenter; the chimpanzees didn't get it, only choosing the correct container at a near-chance level. The difference between their mainly accurate responses to a human competitor and their apparently random responses to a human cooperator were highly significant ($P = 0.009$). In a similar experiment, comparing a human cooperator with a conspecific (i.e. chimpanzee) competitor, again the chimpanzee subjects responded much more accurately in the face of competition than in a cooperative situation ($P = 0.045$). The message seems to be that though chimpanzees can read the intentions of others, they do not expect those intentions to be cooperative, and so a certain class of others' intentions (the cooperative ones) remains a relatively closed book to them.

In a very stimulating article, Tomasello et al. (2005) introduce the idea of 'shared intentionality'. They postulate that this is what is uniquely distinctive of humans (and therefore found in no other animals):

In general, it is almost unimaginable that two chimpanzees might spontaneously do something as simple as carry something together or help each other make a tool, that is, do something with a commitment to do it together and to help each other with their role if needed. Indeed, in a recent study Hare and Tomasello (2004) found that in a single food finding task structured as either competition or cooperation, chimpanzees performed much more skillfully in the competitive version. Nor does ape communication seem to be collaborative in the same way as human communication. Most basically, there is very little communication about third entities (topics), and there are no signals serving a declarative or informative motive.

(Tomasello et al. 2005, p. 685)

This strong claim is falsified in a weak way by a later study from Tomasello's own lab (Melis et al. 2006b), in which it was found that some pairs of chimpanzees who had in the past been disposed to share food would also spontaneously cooperate by pulling widely separated ropes to draw a food tray within their mutual reach. However, only pairs that, outside the experiment, had showed a degree of tolerance for each other collaborated in this way. Tomasello et al. (2005)'s strong claim also drew criticism on factual grounds from commentators who had obserbed animals in the field. Boesch (2005), for example, decried the lack of mention of many field observations. As we have seen, the experimentalist-versus-field-observer tension is endemic in ethology. Boesch asks what many others have asked in this context: 'Don't lions, and wolves, and chimpanzees hunt **cooperatively**?' Boesch pointed out that chimpanzees, in hunting colobus monkeys, assume various different roles, such as drivers, blockers, chasers, and ambushers. Earlier, Stander (1992) had made a similar observation about lions. He analysed 486 coordinated group hunts and found:

Group hunts generally involved a formation whereby some lionesses (wings) circled prey while others (centres) waited for prey to move towards them. Those lionesses that occupied wing stalking roles frequently initiated an attack on the prey, while lionesses in centre roles moved relatively small distances and most often captured prey in flight from other lionesses. Each lioness in a given pride repeatedly occupied the same position in a hunting formation. Hunts where most lionesses present occupied their preferred positions had a high probability of success.   (Stander 1992, p. 445)

Given descriptions like this, many people naturally ask: 'Is this not cooperative hunting?' Tomasello et al. (2005)'s clear response is that it is not, in the sense of their construct 'shared intentionality'. What happens in such hunts, in their view, is that each animal acts to maximize its own advantage, given its own individual preferences for action and the particular position in the hunting scene that it finds itself in. There is no shared plan. The expression 'shared plan' is ambiguous and needs careful definition in both its senses. Two candidates running for election each have a plan; for each of them, the plan is the same—to get elected. In a sense, they 'share a plan', but of course they do not act cooperatively. Somewhat more relevantly, recall the behaviour of Clements and Stephens (1995)'s blue jays in a mutualistic scenario, described in the previous chapter. Here, the environment in the experiment was set up in such a way that if one blue jay did something that was, incidentally, to the advantage of the other blue jay, the acting blue jay also reaped a benefit. Not so surprisingly, the blue jays, in this mutualistic scenario, acted 'cooperatively'. The blue jays in some sense shared a plan—'maximize **my** reward'. Now, compare this to a lion hunt. If you are a lioness and the other lionesses are setting out in the direction of a wildebeest that you could not catch on your own, and you are hungry, do you join them? And if another lioness goes to the right of the prey, tending to drive it to the left, which way is it advantageous for you to go? Pusey and Packer (1997) note the division of labour in the lion hunts described by Stander, and conclude: 'However, they hunted fleet-footed prey in open habitat, and individual hunting success was close to zero. Thus, their cooperative hunting was highly likely to have been mutualistic' (p. 277). And, in a sense, the lionesses share a plan: they are all after the same prey.

Pack-hunting animals, like wolves, lions, and chimpanzees, are likely to have evolved behavioural dispositions quite specific to the circumstances of their prey and its habitat. Schuster (2005) gives examples from lion and hyena hunting suggesting that these animals occasionally employ a narrowly context-specific form of shared intentionality. The kind of shared intentionality that Tomasello et al. (2005) have in mind is more general-purpose, involving an animal's ability to see in many different circumstances what another animal is trying to do, and to adopt that same intention. Much implementation of shared intentionality in humans is probably learned, and culturally transmitted. Young people have to be taught to help old ladies to cross the road. It is, then, possible to see the difference between humans and non-humans not as a black-or-white matter of one species having shared intentionality and all others simply not having it, but rather as a matter of the large differences of degree and context-boundedness to which various species have shared intentionality.

Other commentators draw attention to the variability of human shared intentionality. Brownell et al. (2005), for example, note that while children show signs of shared intentionality with their caregivers at an early stage, there is 'little evidence of either collaborative understanding or motivation to collaborate with peers until the close of the second year of life or well into the third year' (p. 693). It is also universally acknowledged that, among humans, severe autists do not engage in shared intentionality. Among non-autistic humans it is a matter of willingness as well as of ability. Individual human personalities differ in the degree to which they are moved to help other people. At your next extended family gathering or departmental party, see who volunteers to help prepare the meal or tidy up afterwards, and who doesn't seem to notice what needs to be done.

Tomasello et al. (2005)'s article also drew criticism on grounds of 'alternative magic bullets', as they put it. Bickerton (2005) and Gergely and Csibra (2005), using rather different terms, point to the existence of effective communication as a prerequisite for shared intentionality. Bickerton straightforwardly calls it language, while Gergely and Csibra write of the 'ability to communicate relevant information'. Both commentaries claim that communication must have preceded shared intentionality, to which Tomasello et al. robustly reply that it had to be the other way around. Consider my analogy in the previous chapter (p. 270) with tennis players cooperating insofar as they play tennis together, while all the time trying to gain individual advantage. The very act of using language involves a kind of shared intentionality to play by the rules of the same language game.

There can be shared intentionality without a shared language. I remember a comical twenty minutes trying to gesture to a Greek grocer that I wanted olive oil. He knew that I wanted **something** and attended very sympathetically while I went through a repertoire of picking, pressing, and tasting gestures. Without a common language, we shared for twenty minutes the intention that he would sell me something. Eventually we got there. Having a language in common would have given us a shortcut, achieving the transaction in more businesslike, but less memorable, fashion. On many other occasions, using only the most minimal vocabulary of a host country, I have found that natives pick up fast on my intention of finding some place or thing and willingly give what guidance they can. Learning a language just equips you with a system for quicker and easier intentionality-sharing with its speakers.

Could there be any semblance of language without shared intentionality? It is possible to imagine a couple of advanced robots (say Mars landers), programmed to give each other detailed information about their locations and the terrain where they are. In this way, they can be used to check on each other's work, or, perhaps by taking coordinated readings of the same Martian crater from different positions, they can report interesting facts back to their human controllers. The robots would have been programmed to feed complex information to each other, and to respond to received information with appropriate action. No mention of intentions here yet, let alone shared intentionality. And it is a feasible scenario, in which much detailed information could be exchanged, and appropriate action taken. But this is of course an artificial example; the robots have been programmed by human minds to communicate in this coordinated and cooperative fashion. At a more mundane level, a nut and bolt, or a screw and screwdriver, illustrate pairs of tools fashioned to work together to achieve some goal of their human user. The human programmers might even give the robots heuristic strategies for anticipating each other's movements, and filling in from shared context information not actually coded in the exchanged signals. This is getting to look pretty human-like. It could happen, but **not without a human programmer** inventing it and starting it off.

The case of high-level autistic people and people with Asperger syndrome is relevant here. Many of them have intact language but severe difficulty with many aspects of theory of mind, including some that could qualify as involving shared intentionality (Hobson 2002; Tomasello et al. 2005). This, I would claim, is a borderline case. High-functioning autists have enough awareness of the mental states of others to enable them to participate in conversational exchanges, especially where no metaphor or irony is involved. They have enough shared intentionality to play the language game at a literal, non-metaphorical and non-ironic level, but lack higher levels of mind-reading such as those involved in detecting irony. The most severe autists, on the other hand, have little or no language ability. This confirms the relationship between language and shared intentionality. On the evolutionary question of whether shared intentionality preceded the advent of language or vice versa, one should avoid oversimple hypotheses such as are implicit in the first part of Bickerton (2005)'s title, 'Language first, then shared intentionality, then a beneficent spiral'. The beneficent spiral, with degrees of language ability and disposition to shared intentionality co-evolving, is a good idea, but if such a spiral is traced backwards in time, the tiny beginnings of both co-evolving factors would be so undeveloped in comparison to their modern counterparts that we would not be talking about either in their fully fledged modern sense.

Could a system of learned arbitrary symbols, such as humans use, **evolve** in a community where the individuals were not disposed to participate in shared tasks, having tacitly divined the intentions of others? I think there is a distraction in Tomasello et al.'s example of the improbability 'that two chimpanzees might spontaneously do something as simple as carry something together' (Tomasello et al. 2005, p. 685). There is an easily learnt causal relationship between picking up one end of a log and the subsequent position of the log. The arbitrariness of the symbols by which humans achieve their communicative ends poses a harder problem. When a human infant starts to imitate first words, those words are not used in any practical context like carrying a log with its mother. Only with a great stretch might we say that the infant 'understands' what the mother is trying to do and willingly 'cooperates' with her on that task. We might conceive of the mother's task as initiating the infant into the language game. Do we want to say that the infant **understands** what its mother is trying to do, and then cooperates in achieving the shared goal? I don't think so.

The ambiguity of the term *I/intentionality* rears its head here. For non-philosophers, it most naturally means the capacity to do things intentionally, with a will, and some future goal in mind; it is derived in this sense from *intend* as in *I intend to go straight home*. For philosophers, it has a different meaning, only very indirectly related to the first. In this sense, *Intentionality* is paraphrased by *aboutness*. Words are Intentional insofar as they are **about** things in the world. Mental states are Intentional insofar as they in some sense represent (are about) some situation in the world.

Tomasello et al. conflate these two senses of I/intentionality. They gloss shared intentionality as participating 'in activities involving joint intentions and attention' (Tomasello et al. 2005, p. 675). Sharing future intentions to achieve some goal and sharing present attention to some object are not the same thing. As Tomasello et al. emphasize, and as is well known, normal babies are programmed to want to share experiences, and this strong human infantile disposition leads them to imitate words and to the 'naming insight' that words are **about** things. Human babies clearly are innately disposed to shared Intentionality in the 'aboutness' sense of Intentionality.

Could a human-like disposition to joint attention coupled with an ability to learn names for things be present, while the other sense of shared intentionality (disposition to collaborate in achievement of shared goals) is absent? We could think up hypothetical examples, but in real life Kanzi is a good example of both kinds of shared I/intentionality present in a non-human, but to a lesser degree than in a human. Kanzi was not explicitly taught his first arbitrary symbols, but just picked them up, like a human baby, though not as fast, and not as many. As an adult bonobo, he uses symbols to tell his keepers what he wants, so he does understand that expressing his own goals can get others to bring them about. This is perhaps not quite the same as having a shared goal. And Kanzi can easily follow instructions, like 'put the water in the milk', so in some sense he participates in the achievement of an interlocutor's goal. But there is a great difference in degree between Kanzi's and a human's dispositions to share experiences and goals. And Kanzi is a very humanized ape. Living around humans has allowed him to acquire dispositions that some in earlier generations would never have imagined possible in an ape.

But Kanzi is not human. This most humanized ape is still nowhere near as spontaneously willing to join in social chat with others as humans. Wild bonobos bond by grooming and play. Humans do it largely by using learned codes with tens of thousands of words and complex rules of combination to express propositions describing the world. Even the sentences humans swap in idle chit-chat have descriptive content, like today's weather, or last night's TV. To fully join the club of a human community, without special allowances being made, a growing baby has to learn the large vocabulary and the complex combinations. And human babies are extremely well adapted to this task. Tomasello et al. include several rather different things within the meaning of their term *shared intentionality*, but the key one, as far as the evolution of language is concerned, is the human baby's instinctive desire to join in the community's language game. Recall my distinction in the previous chapter (p. 270) between **communicative cooperation** and **material cooperation**. Just entering into discourse in the same language is communicatively cooperative, even though one's utterances may be all materially uncooperative (like protracted verbal rows in dysfunctional relationships). Tomasello et al. include communicative cooperation within shared intentionality. '[T]he whole point of the Sperber and Wilson analysis is that there are different levels of motivation involved, and that whatever the ultimate goal of the speaker—even if it is for selfish/deceptive reasons in telling someone to do something—the speaker and hearer must cooperate for the message to be received' (Tomasello et al. 2005, p. 724).

It is this component of shared intentionality, an instinctive motivation to join the language-using club and share its purposes, that marks a huge difference in degree between human and non-human communication. Altriciality, coupled with a long period of dependency and plasticity in the social environment, would have promoted this. It is revealed in human babies' apparently 'unintelligent' tendency to imitate where imitation has no other goal than to form a social bond, and to imitate rather than to emulate where some goal exists.

9.3 FAIR PLAY

Animals sometimes act as if they expect certain social rules to apply, consistent with what humans would call fair sharing. And the behaviour from which we infer this is often to the animal's immediate disadvantage, thus posing a challenge for some, but not all, of the evolutionary theories surveyed in the last chapter. The theory most consistent with the phenomena to be briefly surveyed here is Strong Reciprocity (mentioned in the previous chapter), which posits policing and punishment within a group.

In an experiment on punishment and cooperation within human groups, Fehr and Gächter (2002) studied 240 students who, working in groups of four, were each given a chance to 'invest' up to 20 monetary units (MUs) in a group project. The rules were set so that a high individual investment, while costing the individual, benefited the group. Individuals were free to invest however much they liked, making their decisions independently of the simultaneous decisions of the other individuals in the group. In one experimental condition, individuals could also punish each other for low investment by imposing a fine on the low investor. Punishment did not benefit the punisher directly, but in fact was costly to the punisher, so this punishment was altruistic. In another condition, punishment was not permitted. Cooperation in a group was defined as the average of individuals' investments in the group project. Cooperation declined significantly without punishment, and increased significantly with punishment. 'Here we show experimentally that the altruistic punishment of defectors is a key motive for the explanation of cooperation. Altruistic punishment means that individuals punish, although the punishment is costly for them and yields no material gain. We show that cooperation flourishes if altruistic punishment is possible, and breaks down if it is ruled out' (Fehr and Gächter 2002, p. 137).

As a possible non-human precursor to this kind of behaviour, I have already noted Hauser (1992)'s study of macaques who punish discoverers of food who keep their finds to themselves. '[S]ilent discoverers, when detected, were often chased away from the food or aggressively attacked. Similar results have also been observed in white-faced capuchins (*Cebus capucinus*)' (Egnor et al. 2006, p. 661).

Several primate species have been shown to object to another animal getting a better reward than them. Their objection takes the form of refusing to participate in a food-for-token exchange game with the experimenter. For example, an experimenter has trained monkeys to trade a token (which the monkey already has) for an item of food. Then, with two monkeys together, the experimenter rewards one monkey with a grape for each token, and the other monkey with a piece of cucumber. Monkeys prefer grapes to cucumber. After a while the monkey receiving cucumber refuses to play the game any more, sometimes tossing either the token or the cucumber aside in apparent anger. In refusing to participate in the game, the animal actually suffers a loss, in getting no food at all, whereas by continuing to play the game, it could at least have got some cucumber. This experimental paradigm is known as 'Inequity Aversion' (IA). One experiment was with capuchin monkeys, *Cebus apella*.

People judge fairness based both on the distribution of gains and on the possible alternatives to a given outcome. Capuchin monkeys, too, seem to measure reward in relative terms, comparing their own rewards with those available, and their own efforts with those of others. They respond negatively to previously acceptable rewards if a partner gets a better deal.

(Brosnan and de Waal 2003, p. 299)[1]

In similar experiments with chimpanzees, Brosnan et al. (2005) also found inequity aversion. Chimpanzees refused to participate in exchanges when they saw that another animal was getting a better food reward. In refusing to participate, they forfeited food themselves. They would have been better off taking the lower-quality food, even though their partner was receiving higher-quality food. So this behaviour is not simply selfish. One might describe it as petulant. Interestingly, however, this effect was only found among chimpanzees who had not forged long-lasting social relationships. Animals from a more stable and long-lasting social group were tolerant of others receiving better rewards.

---

[1] Henrich (2004) has argued against a close parallel between this capuchin monkey behaviour and human inequity aversion behaviour.

Much of the evolutionary theorizing about altruism discussed in the previous chapter stems from economics, in which a dominant model has assumed that individual agents always act rationally to maximize their own economic benefit. Human altruism clearly presents a problem for this assumption, and this gave rise to the Reciprocal Altruism theory, developed in part by Robert Axelrod, a political scientist. Reciprocal Altruism, as we have seen, meets with mixed success in explaining animal behaviour, and further models, such as Strong Reciprocity (Gintis 2000; Henrich and Boyd 2001), have been developed within the social sciences, but are not yet much taken up by biologists. Strong Reciprocity is developed more with humans in mind than some other theories of altruism, such as Kin Selection.

Gintis et al. (2003) surveyed empirical results on humans showing that they seldom, if ever, conform to the economist's ideal of *Homo economicus*, a rational agent acting purely out of self-interest.[2] Instead, humans, to varying degrees, depending on the culture, act as if they are conforming to some conception of a fair social contract. Of the various experimental games used to achieve these results, one called the 'Ultimatum Game' is relatively easy to describe. Here, there are two players who know of each other's existence, but do not know each other. One player is given a sum of money, say $10, and is told that he can offer as much of it as he likes to the other player. If the other player accepts what he is offered, the first player gets to keep the rest. But (and here's the catch) if the second player chooses not to accept what he is offered, then neither player gets anything. Now a 'fair' offer would be half, say $5, so that the players would split the loot evenly. A purely self-interested offer would be of the minimum, say $1, so that the offerer gets to keep $9. As second player, it always makes (selfish) sense to accept whatever offer you receive, because if you don't, you'll get nothing. The theory of self-interest predicts that the minumim will always be offered, and accepted.

However, when actually played, *the self-interested outcome is never attained and never even approximated*. In fact, as many replications of this experiment have documented, under varying conditions and with varying amounts of money, proposers routinely offer respondents very substantial amounts (50% of the total generally being the modal offer) and respondents frequently reject

---

[2] Alan Grafen makes the point that 'biology actually has a much stronger claim [than economics] to the rational agent model—Darwinian natural selection does the optimising behind the scenes, so that individuals act 'as-if' maximising. In economics, they rely on individual rationality, which is poor' (Grafen, personal communication).

offers below 30% (Camerer and Thaler, 1995; Güth and Tietz, 1990; Roth, Prasnikar, Okuno-Fujiwara, and Zamir, 1991).   (Gintis et al. 2003, p. 157)

Henrich et al. (2001) conducted this Ultimatum Game experiment, and several others, 'with subjects from fifteen hunter gatherer, nomadic herding and other small-scale societies exhibiting a wide variety of economic and cultural conditions' (p. 73). They worked in twelve countries on four continents. The two societies that conformed most closely to the *Homo economicus* ideal were slash-and-burn horticulturalists: the Machiguenga of Peru and the Tsimané of Bolivia. These typically made low offers, and there were virtually no rejections of offers. But even with these people, the mean and modal offers were well above the minimum. The most salient result was that 'group-level differences in the structure of everyday social interactions explain a substantial portion of the behavioral variation across societies: the higher the degree of market integration and the higher the payoffs to cooperation in the production of their livelihood, the greater the level of cooperation in experimental games' (Henrich et al. 2001, p. 73).

In summary, there is evidence of a sense of fair play, of what is an equitable distribution of resources, in primates, including humans. Behaviour conforming to this sense of fair play increases the closer we get to Western everyday norms of commerce, as American undergraduates regularly make the 'fairest' offers in the Ultimatum Game. But humans living in conditions far from Western commerce, such as the Machiguenga, also partly display these tendencies, but without the elements of punishment and rejection of behaviour not conforming to a 'fair' norm. These phenomena are relevant to the evolution of language insofar as they show a common psychosocial thread, from non-human primates to humans, indicating tacit awareness of group norms of cooperative behaviour.

9.4 TRUST(-WORTHINESS), GROUPS, FACES, AND A HORMONE

Linguistic behaviour is typically trusting behaviour. As a speaker, you trust the hearer not to use to your cost what you tell him. And as a hearer, you believe or do what the speaker says. Trust by one party is an inference of trustworthiness in the other. Trusting behaviour and trustworthiness are different, yet obviously interdependent in a working society. How do trust and trustworthiness arise, and what physical phenomena correlate with them? As we will see in this brief section, shared group membership and facial resemblance to the trusting person both enhance the apparent trustworthiness of another, and there are specific hormones which enhance trusting behaviour.

All the research on group membership, facial resemblance, and trust involves humans. Much of the work is done in the context of economic theories. It is difficult to replicate such experiments with animals. This human research plugs into discussions of sexual selection (cf. Chapter 8), since trust is complexly related to sexual attraction, especially for long-term relationships.

Glaeser et al. (2000) played experimental trust games with Harvard undergraduates. In one such game, rather like some of the experimental games described in the previous section, players could choose how much real money to 'invest' in a partner, who might or might not give them a fair return on their investment. One of their main conclusions was:

First, social connection strongly predicts trustworthiness and weakly predicts trust. In particular, national and racial differences between partners strongly predict a tendency to cheat one another.

Second, individual characteristics that relate to family status, social skill, and charisma strongly predict one's total financial returns in the trust experiment. These variables matter because people in our sample are less likely to cheat individuals with these characteristics.   (Glaeser et al. 2000, p. 840)

A similar trusting game was played by DeBruine (2002) with subjects whose game partners were faces on a computer screen, rather than real people. DeBruine computationally morphed the faces so that they resembled or did not resemble the faces of the subjects themselves. Here again one player had to choose whether to trust another player (a morphed face) with money, or, taking the opposite role, whether to reward the face with a decent return on his trusting investment. It was found that

Experimental subjects, who believed that they were playing against pictured opponents while unaware that information from their own faces had been incorporated into the 'morphed' faces of some of those supposed opponents, trusted opponents who resembled themselves significantly more than they trusted other opponents, but did not reward trusting moves by their opponents differentially. These results were replicated in two independent groups of subjects, using two distinct facial morphing procedures.

(DeBruine 2002, p. 1311)

Considering the evolutionary implications of this finding, DeBruine notes that our ancestors, having no mirrors, had little idea what their own faces looked like. So such trusting behaviour is likely to be based on either resemblance to close genetic relatives (complementing Kin Selection theory) or on familiarity (complementing theories associating positive social behaviour with shared group membership). In a later experiment DeBruine (2005) found that

facial resemblance, a putative cue of relatedness, increased judgments of trustworthiness but had no effect on attractiveness in the context of a long-term relationship and decreased attractiveness in the context of a short-term relationship. Perceptions of trustworthiness were increased significantly more than perceptions of attractiveness for long-term or short-term relationships.

(DeBruine 2005, p. 921)

Recently, a discovery was made which is highly suggestive of the neu-rochemical basis of trusting behaviour in social relationships, in both humans and non-humans.

Here we show that intranasal administration of oxytocin, a neuro-peptide that plays a key role in social attachment and affiliation in non-human mammals, causes a substantial increase in trust among humans, thereby greatly increasing the benefits from social interactions. We also show that the effect of oxytocin on trust is not due to a general increase in the readiness to bear risks. On the contrary, oxytocin specifically affects an individual's willingness to accept social risks arising through interpersonal interactions. These results concur with animal research suggesting an essential role for oxytocin as a biological basis of prosocial approach behaviour.

(Kosfeld et al. 2005, p. 673)

The experiment Kosfeld et al. carried out involved an investment game, in which one player (the 'investor') gave a sum of real money to a 'trustee' to invest. When invested by the trustee, the amount was always tripled by the experimenter, simulating a good stock-market profit. Now the trustee was free to return any amount, from zero to the whole increased sum, back to the original investor. The key thing is that the investor has no guarantee that he will get any of his money back; he trusts the trustee to give him a decent return. The trustee is unknown to the investor. In these circumstances, how much would you invest? The amount you invest is an index of your faith, or trust, in the trustee. Kosfeld et al. (2005) ran this game in two conditions. In one condition the investor player had taken oxytocin up his nose; in the other condition a placebo was used. In the oxytocin condition, investors risked significantly more, that is they displayed more trusting behaviour. It was not the case that oxytocin merely decreased risk aversion, as, in a parallel experiment, the amount of money returned by the trustee was determined not by the trustee's decision, but at random. In this random condition, the risk to the investor is the same as before. The difference is that in one case the investor knows he is dealing with another person who will make a decision. In the random condition, there was no difference between the amounts invested by the oxytocin-treated investors and those who had received the placebo. See also Zak et al. (2004) for a very similar report.

The significance of this for the evolution of language is that an element of trust is involved in entering into a linguistic exchange with another person. An element of trust is involved in the baby's instinctive imitation of adult gestures and vocalizations. The strong instinctive desire to conform and to belong that we see in human babies may be physiologically mediated by some hormone such as oxytocin, acting on specific brain areas. A result of this kind has been obtained in rats. Moriceau and Sullivan (2005) found that

hyper-functioning noradrenergic locus coeruleus (LC) enables pups to learn rapid, robust preference for the caregiver. Conversely, a hypo-functional amygdala appears to prevent the infant from learning aversions to the caregiver. Adult LC and amygdala functional emergence correlates with sensitive period termination. This study suggests the neonatal brain is not an immature version of the adult brain but is uniquely designed to optimize attachment to the caregiver. Although human attachment may not rely on identical circuitry, the work reviewed here suggests a new conceptual framework in which to explore human attachments.   (p. 230)

The pro-social effects of oxytocin on experimental animals are well known. I will mention just a few studies. Carter (1998) surveys 'existing behavioral and neuroendocrine perspectives on social attachment and love': 'Central neuropeptides, and especially oxytocin and vasopressin have been implicated ... in social bonding' (p. 779). After experiments on rats, Uvnas-Moberg (1989) concluded: 'Oxytocin released in response to social stimuli may be part of a neuroendocrine substrate which underlies the benefits of positive social experiences' (p. 819).

There are no magic bullets for human language. Chris Knight, while enthusiastic about the oxytocin discoveries, has written (personal communication):

Tracing it all back to a hormone reminds me of Chomsky, who wants to trace the whole of language including even the semantic component to a box of wires somewhere in the head. The wires are probably there in some sense, but that's not the whole story. An evolutionary account has to explain why placing trust in mere words became an evolutionarily stable strategy in the case of our species. To explain this, we have to explain how and why people had the time and energy to punish free-riders who abused that public trust. In short, we have to explain how and why the rule of law became established among our hunter-gatherer ancestors. That means doing everything within a social and anthropological framework, among other frameworks.

To this my reply was that oxytocin came first (e.g. in rats), and the rule of law, undoubtedly related, came second. Human social and anthropological phenomena emerged from animal social behaviour. As should be clear, I don't propose to 'trace it [language] all back to a hormone', though I believe this and other hormones had a role to play. But I share Knight's emphasis on the importance of trust in humans communicating with each other in language, and the enforcement of social norms necessary to keep this an evolutionarily stable strategy, as noted several times in this and the preceding chapter.

9.5 WRAPPING UP

To pull the material in the last two chapters together, here is where I get (even more) speculative. We still have to explain the massive propositional utility, and size, of languages. So far, we have a mutant species, proto-humans, who are innately disposed to bond with each other by imitation of meaningful gestures and vocalizations, and who show a high degree of trust and regard for others. Furthermore, their life-history includes a long period of dependency and cognitive plasticity. They have inherited from their ancestors a largely innate, but partly learned, set of calls, of crucial utility for survival and reproduction. The plasticity of the infants allows the genetic component of these calls to diminish while the learned component can maintain the system. This could be just drift, if the genetic changes were entirely selectively neutral. But equally, it could be selective. If learning picked up the slack or even improved over the rigidity of the genetically determined system, then there could be positive selection to reduce the contribution of the genetic component. This can be expressed as the genetic determination changing from rigid to environmentally flexible.

In time this leads to an enlarged repertoire of learned conventionalized meaningful calls, which simultaneously convey practical information and group membership. The calls are taken seriously (e.g. believed and acted upon) by members of the group because their conventionalized form reliably signals group membership. By the evolution of Strong Reciprocity, misusers or non-users of the group's code are punished, for example by ostracism. This keeps the group together as a cohesive social unit, which can outcompete less cohesive groups because of the practical utility of its communal conventional communicative code. Sustained competition from other groups, playing catch-up in this same process, leads both to enhancement of the code-acquisition mechanisms of infants and to the growth in size, and therefore the referential scope, of the code itself.

These ideas are consistent with some recent models of language evolution, such as those of Hurford and Kirby (1999); Deacon (2003); Ritchie and Kirby (2007), but they clearly need a lot more exploration. One phenomenon that is probably crucially involved at the very beginning of the evolutionary story of an emerging learned repertoire of conventionalized meaningful calls is synaesthesia. The idea is that the earliest users of such a simple repertoire would have exploited certain universal natural synaesthetic connections between aspects of referents in the world, such as shapes, and aspects of human vocal sounds, as suggested by Ramachandran and Hubbard (2001). The standardization of a conventionalized vocabulary across a group is actually now quite well understood, largely due to a wave of computer simulations and experiments with human subjects. Examples of the computer simulations are Hurford (1989); Oliphant (1999); Steels (1999); Smith (2004), approximately implementing the suggestions of an early philosophical study on the origins of convention by Lewis (1969). Examples of experiments with human subjects are Fay et al. (2005); Galantucci (2005). A full consideration of this work is given in the sequel to this book.

CHAPTER TEN

Epilogue and Prologue

We have seen a picture of apes with quite a lot going on their heads. They are host to mental representations, I have argued, with the essential basic structure of human propositions, namely predicate-argument structure. The argument slot is instantiated not as a term with any permanent content, but as a variable, which can be applied to any particular object of attention, whatever the passing show presents that draws the attention of the animal. The animal can attend to up to about four objects at a time, tracking them all and binding their properties to them. These properties are, in the main, categorically distinct, and constitute the proto-predicates of the ape's view of the world. An ape can attend both to the global properties of a scene and to the local properties of the objects participating in it. The global properties can be seen as expressing relationships between the participant objects. Thus the ape's mental representations of the world have two levels, the global and the local, represented in the box notation that I have developed as an outer box and one or more (up to about four) inner boxes. Interpretations of the proto-predicates in the boxes are relative to the context provided by all the other proto-predicates in the representation. Thus what seems big in one scene might seem small in another, and what seems to be the most active participant in one scene, its proto-Agent, may seem more passive in another scene, and be less likely to be judged as a proto-Agent. Some proto-predicates are less susceptible to this contextual relativity than others. Most of the time, a leopard is a leopard is a leopard.

These mental pictures of the world are most vividly triggered by perception and action. While an ape is attending to a scene, its structure is most vividly present to its mind, partially structured top-down by the animal's selective attention to particular objects and particular properties of theirs, in preference to other objects and properties, which are not attended to.

To a limited extent, animals are capable of bringing scenes to mind in the absence of direct perception. Animals can plan and remember, and can make limited inferences over mentally represented scenes. Though made familiar by perception, and instantiated in the brain by sensory-motor 'functional clusters' (Gallese and Lakoff 2005), the mental representations of immediately pre-linguistic creatures can be brought to mind during acts of planning and remembering. To this extent, they are cognitive, as well as perceptual, representations. Some animals show the faint glimmerings of episodic memory, a well-developed faculty in humans, by which non-current scenes and events can be brought to mind. Many animals are capable of entertaining somewhat abstract relations and properties, such as SAME/DIFFERENT and OPPOSITE. Evidence of these can be elicited in experimental situations.

It seems likely that the mental lives of animals in the wild seldom involve such abstract predicates; even more abstractly, properties-of-properties and relations-between-relations, are likely only to be available after some language training, or training with language-like objects, by humans. The semantic predicate-argument structure attributed to animals is emphatically not to be confused with any linguistic structure, such as the Subject-Predicate structure of sentences. It is just unfortunate that the term *predicate* is ambiguous, applying to a structural constituent of a sentence, and to items in the vocabulary of a logical language only indirectly related to language structure.

The pre-linguistic mental representations so far discussed are all activated in individual heads and find no outlet (as yet in the story) in public communication of any kind. Pre-linguistic animals can, in two separate and very limited ways, communicate to others about various states of the world. The largely innate alarm calls of vervet monkeys and many other species are one way.

The limited ability to make and interpret deictic pointing gestures is the other way. Pointing is almost totally absent in the wild, and is brought out mainly in conditions of captivity and interaction with cooperative humans. In these very limited capacities of animals we can see the faint beginnings of communicative reference. Apes have rich mental lives, but keep their pictures of the world to themselves, like all other animals besides humans. Only humans tell each other in detail about events and scenes in the world. And this is something of an evolutionary puzzle, because giving information away would seem prima facie to be against the individual interests of the information-giver.

Evolutionary theory has come up with a number of solutions to the riddle of why humans should, in general, act relatively altruistically, with this (apparent) altruism manifested saliently in language. No one theory on its own, such as Kin Selection, Reciprocal Altruism, or Sexual Selection, can adequately explain the unique human characteristic of freely giving information in such structurally complex ways as we do every day with language. A complex egalitarian social structure with shifting alliances, some degree of monogamy and equality between the sexes, and extended parental care of the young provides the most hospitable environment in which group-wide communicative codes can come to be adopted. Some degree of understanding of other minds is also required; some very limited evidence (Hare et al. 2001) has only recently become available showing that in some circumstances, a chimpanzee can know what another animal knows. But this is not enough, and I have adopted Tomasello et al. (2005)'s concept of shared intentionality as a key ingredient of humans' striking willingness to play complex language games with each other. This involves a degree of trust, a social attitude which is particularly well developed in humans. Our ape cousins have not evolved to exhibit shared intentionality or the appropriate degree of trust paving the evolutionary way for language.

We have reached a watershed. As soon as the breakthrough was made for animals to communicate their thoughts relatively freely to others, a cascade of other innovations was selected, designed to make the transfer of information more effective, and allowing humans to enrich their mental representations by thinking about the representations themselves, in what Quine (1960) has called 'semantic ascent'. This cascade of consequences will be the topic of Volume 2. In it we will see examples of the evolutionary force of self-organization at work. Given creatures with a disposition to transmit messages to each other, there are pressures for these messages to become structured in particular ways, so as to be most easily learned and used by the creatures concerned. In this way, as will be seen in Volume 2, phonological structure and morphosyntactic structure evolved. In a co-evolutionary arms race, human capacities for efficient processing of these structures co-evolved with increasing complexity of the structures themselves.

I hope that when you have read the present volume, Volume 2 will be available or on the way, and that you will have the appetite to read it. For the present, thank you for joining me this far.

Bibliography

Abbott, B. (1995). Thinking without English. *Behavior and Philosophy* 23, 47–52.

—— (2002). Definiteness and proper names: some bad news for the description theory. *Journal of Semantics* 19, 191–201.

Agnetta, B., B. Hare, and M. Tomasello (2000). Cues to food location that domestic dogs (*Canis familiaris*) of different ages do and do not use. *Animal Cognition* 3, 107–112.

Aich, H., R. Moos-Heilen, and E. Zimmerman (1990). Vocalizations of adult gelada baboons (*Theropithecus gelada*): acoustic structure and behavioral context. *Folia Primatologica* 55, 109–132.

Alcock, J. (1984). *Animal Behavior: An Evolutionary Approach*. Sunderland, MA: Sinauer Associates, Inc.

Alexander, R. D. (1974). The evolution of social behavior. *Annual Review of Ecological Systems* 5, 325–383.

Allen, C. (2006). Transitive inference in animals: reasoning or conditioned associations? In S. Hurley and M. Nudds (eds.), *Rational Animals?*, pp. 175–185. Oxford: Oxford University Press.

—— and M. D. Hauser (1991). Concept attribution in nonhuman animals: theoretical and methodological problems in ascribing complex mental processes. *Philosophy of Science* 58, 221–240. (Repr. in *Readings in Animal Cognition*, ed. Marc Bekoff and Dale Jamieson, pp. 47–62, Cambridge, MA: MIT Press (1996).

Allison, A. C. (1955). Aspects of polymorphism in man. *Cold Spring Harbor Symposium on Quantitative Biology* 20, 239–255.

—— (1964). Polymorphism and natural selection in human populations. *Cold Spring Harbor Symposium on Quantitative Biology* 29, 139–149.

Allwood, J. and P. Gärdenfors (eds.) (1999). *Cognitive Semantics: Meaning and Cognition*. Amsterdam: John Benjamins.

Anderson, J. R. and R. W. Mitchell (1999). Macaques but not lemurs co-orient visually with humans. *Folia Primatologica* 70, 17–22.

Arbib, M. A. (2005). From monkey-like action recognition to human language: an evolutionary framework for neurolinguistics. *Behavioral and Brain Sciences* 28(2), 105–125.

Arcadi, A. C. (1996). Phrase structure of wild chimpanzee pant-hoots: patterns of production and interpopulation variability. *American Journal of Primatology* 39, 159–178.

—— (2000). Vocal responsiveness in male wild chimpanzees: implications for the evolution of language. *Journal of Human Evolution* 39(2), 205–223.

Aristotle (c. 350 BC). Categoriae. In R. McKeon (ed.), *The Basic Works of Aristotle*, trans. E. M. Edghill, pp. 7–37. New York: Random House (1941).

Armstrong, D. F., W. C. Stokoe, and S. E. Wilcox (1995). *Gesture and the Nature of Language*. Cambridge: Cambridge University Press.

Armstrong, D. M. (1989). *Universals: An Opinionated Introduction*. Boulder, CO: Westview Press.

Austin, J. L. (1962). *How to Do Things with Words*. Cambridge, MA: Harvard University Press.

Axelrod, R. (1984). *The Evolution of Cooperation*. New York: Basic Books.

—— (1997). *The Complexity of Co-operation*. Princeton, NJ: Princeton University Press.

—— and W. Hamilton (1981). The evolution of cooperation. *Science* 211, 1390–1396.

—— R. A. Hammons, and A. Grafen (2004). Altruism via kin-selection strategies that rely on arbitrary tags with which they co-evolve. *Evolution: International Journal of Organic Evolution* 58(8), 1833–1838.

Baillargeon, R. (1995). Physical reasoning in infancy. In M. Gazzaniga (ed.), *The Cognitive Neurosciences*. Cambridge, MA: MIT Press.

Baldwin, D. (1991). Infants' contribution to the achievement of joint reference. *Child Development* 62, 875–890.

—— (1993). Early referential understanding: infants' ability to recognise referential acts for what they are. *Developmental Psychology* 29(5), 832–843.

Barnard, A. (1978). Universal systems of kin categorization. *African Studies* 37, 69–81.

Baron-Cohen, S., A. Cox, G. Baird, J. Swettenham, N. Nightingale, K. Morgan, A. Drew, and T. Charman (1996). Psychological markers of autism at 18 months of age in a large population. *British Journal of Psychiatry* 168, 158–163.

—— A. M. Leslie, and U. Frith (1985). Does the autistic child have a 'theory of mind'? *Cognition* 21, 37–46.

Barrett, H. C. (2001). On the functional origins of essentialism. *Mind and Society* 3(2), 1–30.

—— (2004). Cognitive development and the understanding of animal behavior. In B. J. Ellis and D. F. Bjorklund (eds.), *Origins of the Social Mind: Evolutionary Psychology and Child Development*, pp. 438–467. New York: Guilford Publications.

—— (2005). Adaptations to predators and prey. In D. M. Buss (ed.), *The Handbook of Evolutionary Psychology*, pp. 200–223. New York: Wiley.

—— and T. Behne (2005). Children's understanding of death as the cessation of agency: a test using sleep versus death. *Cognition* 96(2), 93–108.

Barsalou, L. W. (1999). Perceptual symbol systems. *Behavioral and Brain Sciences* 22(4), 577–660.

Barth, J., J. E. Reaux, and D. J. Povinelli (2005). Chimpanzees' (*Pan troglodytes*) use of gaze cues in object-choice tasks: different methods yield different results. *Animal Cognition* 8, 84–92.

Barwise, K. J. (1999). Logic. In R. A. Wilson and F. Keil (eds.), *The MIT Encyclopedia of the Cognitive Sciences*, pp. 482–484. Cambridge, MA: MIT Press.

Bates, E., B. O'Connell, and C. Shore (1987). Language and communication in infancy. In J. Osofsky (ed.), *Handbook of Infant Development*, pp. 149–203. New York: Wiley.

Beauquin, C. and F. Gaillard (1998). Responses of class R3 retinal ganglion cells of the frog to moving configurational bars: effect of the stimulus velocity. *Comparative Biochemistry and Physiology: Part A, Molecular and Integrative Physiology* 119(1), 387–393.

Behne, T., M. Carpenter, J. Call, and M. Tomasello (2005). Unwilling versus unable: infants' understanding of intentional action. *Developmental Psychology* 41(2), 328–337.

Bellugi, U., Z. Lai, and P. Wang (1997). Language, communication, and neural systems in Williams Syndrome. *Mental Retardation and Developmental Disabilities Research Reviews* 3, 334–342.

——P. Wang, and T. L. Jernigan (1994). Williams syndrome: an unusual neuropsy-chological profile. In S. Broman and J. Grafman (eds.), *Atypical Cognitive Deficits in Developmental Disorders: Implications for Brain Function*, pp. 23–56. Hillsdale, NJ: Erlbaum.

Beltman, J. B., P. Haccou, and C. ten Cate (2004). Learning and colonization of new niches: a first step toward speciation. *Evolution* 58(1), 35–46.

Benard, J. and M. Giurfa (2004). A test of transitive inferences in free-flying honeybees: unsuccessful performance due to memory constraints. *Learning and Memory* 11(3), 328–336.

Bennett, J. (1988). *Events and their Names*. Oxford: Oxford University Press.

Bergen, J. R. and B. Julesz (1983). Parallel versus serial processing in rapid pattern discrim-ination. *Nature* 303, 696–698.

Bergman, T. J., J. C. Beehner, D. L. Cheney, and R. M. Seyfarth (2003). Hierarchical classification by rank and kinship in baboons. *Science* 302, 1234–1236.

Bergstrom, C. T. and L. A. Real (2000). Towards a theory of mutual mate choice: lessons from two-sided matching. *Evolutionary Ecology Research* 2, 493–508.

Bermejo, M. and A. Omedes (1999). Preliminary vocal repertoire and vocal communication of wild bonobos (*Pan paniscus*) at Lilungu (Democratic Republic of Congo). *Folia Primatologica* 70, 328–357.

Bermúdez, J. L. (2003). *Thinking without Words*. Oxford: Oxford University Press.

Bertram, B. C. R. (1976). Kin selection in lions and in evolution. In P. P. G. Bateson and R. A. Hinde (eds.), *Growing Points in Ethology*, pp. 281–301. Cambridge: Cambridge University Press.

Bickerton, D. (1990). *Language and Species*. Chicago: University of Chicago Press.

——(1995). *Language and Human Behaviour*. London: UCL Press.

——(2005). Language first, then shared intentionality, then a beneficent spiral. *Behavioral and Brain Sciences* 28, 691–692.

——(2007). Language evolution: a brief guide for linguists. *Lingua* 117, 510–526.

Biebach, H., M. Gordijn, and J. R. Krebs (1989). Time-and-place learning by garden warblers, *Sylvia borin*. *Animal Behaviour* 37(3), 353–360.

Bihrle, A. M., U. Bellugi, D. Delis, and S. Marks (1989). Seeing either the forest or the trees: dissociation in visuospatial processing. *Brain and Cognition* 11(1), 37–49.

Blaschke, M. and G. Ettlinger (1987). Pointing as an act of social communication by monkeys. *Animal Behaviour* 35, 1520–1523.

Bodamer, M. D. and R. A. Gardner (2002). How cross-fostered chimpanzees (*Pan troglodytes*) initiate and maintain conversations. *Journal of Comparative Psychol-ogy* 116(1), 12–26.

Boehm, C. H. (1993). Egalitarian behavior and reverse dominance hierarchies. *Current Anthropology* 34, 227–254.

Boesch, C. (2005). Joint cooperative hunting among wild chimpanzees: taking natural observations seriously. *Behavioral and Brain Sciences* 28, 692–693.

Bond, A. B., A. C. Kamil, and R. P. Balda (2003). Social complexity and transitive inference in corvids. *Animal Behaviour* 65, 479–487.

Bonda, E., M. Petrides, D. Ostry, and A. Evans (1996). Specific involvement of human parietal systems and the amygdala in the perception of biological motion. *Journal of Neuroscience* 16(11), 3737–3744.

Bonvillian, J. D. and F. G. P. Patterson (1999). Early sign-language acquisition: compar-isons between children and gorillas. In S. T. Parker, R. W. Mitchell, and H. L. Miles (eds.), *The Mentalities of Gorillas and Orangutans: Comparative Perspectives*, pp. 240–264. Cambridge: Cambridge University Press.

Borer, H. (2005). *The Normal Course of Events.* Oxford: Oxford University Press.

Boroditsky, L. (2000). Metaphoric structuring: understanding time through spatial metaphors. *Cognition* 75(1), 1–28.

Bouchard, T. J. (1994). Genes, environment and personality. *Science* 264, 1700–1701.

Boutsen, L. and G. W. Humphreys (1999). Axis-alignment affects perceptual grouping: evidence from simultanagnosia. *Cognitive Neuropsychology* 16(7), 655–672.

Bowles, S. and D. Posel (2005). Genetic relatedness predicts South African migrant workers' remittances to their families. *Nature* 434, 380–383.

Boyd, R. and P. J. Richerson (1988). The evolution of reciprocity in sizable groups. *Journal of Theoretical Biology* 132, 337–356.

——and P. J. Richerson (1992). Punishment allows the evolution of cooperation (or anything else) in sizable groups. *Ethology and Sociobiology* 13, 171–195.

Boysen, S. T. and G. G. Berntson (1995). Responses to quantity-perceptual versus cognitive mechanisms in chimpanzees (*Pan troglodytes*). *Journal of Experimental Psychology: Animal Behavior Processes* 21(1), 82–86.

——G. G. Berntson, M. B. Hannan, and J. T. Cacioppo (1996). Quantity-based interference and symbolic representations in chimpanzees (*Pan troglodytes*). *Journal of Experimental Psychology: Animal Behavior Processes* 22(1), 76–86.

Brannon, E. M. and H. S. Terrace (2000). Representation of the numerosities 1-9 by rhesus macaques (*Macaca mulatta*). *Journal of Experimental Psychology: Animal Behavior Processes* 26(1), 31–49.

Bräuer, J., J. Call, and M. Tomasello (2005). All great ape species follow gaze to distant locations and around barriers. *Journal of Comparative Psychology* 119(2), 145–154.

Bredart, S., T. Brennen, and T. Valentine (1997). Dissociations between the processing of proper and common names. *Cognitive Neuropsychology* 14(2), 209–217.

Bregman, A. (1990). *Auditory Scene Analysis.* Cambridge, MA: MIT Press.

Brockmann, H. J. (1984). The evolution of social behaviour in insects. In J. R. Krebs and N. B. Davies (eds.), *Behavioural Ecology: An Evolutionary Approach* (2nd edn.), pp. 340–361. Oxford: Blackwell Scientific Publications.

Brosnan, S. F. and F. B. M. de Waal (2002). Regulation of vocal output by chimpanzees finding food in the presence or absence of an audience. *Evolution of Communication* 4(2), 211–224.

——and F. B. M de Waal (2003). Monkeys reject unequal pay. *Nature* 425, 297–299.

——H. C. Schiff, and F. B. M. de Waal (2005). Tolerance for inequity may increase with social closeness in chimpanzees. *Proceedings of the Royal Society*, Series B 272, 253–258.

Brown, C. H. (1982). Auditory localization and primate vocal behavior. In C. T. Snowdon, C. H. Brown, and M. R. Petersen (eds.), *Primate Communication*, pp. 144–164. Cambridge: Cambridge University Press.

Brown, P. and S. Levinson (1987). *Politeness: Some Universals in Language Usage.* Cambridge: Cambridge University Press.

Brownell, C. A., S. Nichols, and M. Svetlova (2005). Early development of shared intentionality with peers. *Behavioral and Brain Sciences* 28, 693–694.

Buckingham, G., L. M. DeBruine, A. C. Little, L. L. Welling, C. A. Conway, B. P. Tiddeman, and B. C. Jones (2006). Visual adaptation to masculine and feminine faces influences generalized preferences and perceptions of trustworthiness. *Evolution and Human Behavior* 27(5), 381–389.

Burge, T. (1973). Reference and proper names. *Journal of Philosophy* 70, 425–439.

Burgess, N. (2002). The hippocampus, space, and viewpoints in episodic memory. *Quarterly Journal of Experimental Psychology* 55A(4), 1057–1080.

Burling, R. (2005). *The Talking Ape: How Language Evolved*. Oxford: Oxford University Press.

Butterworth, G. (2003). Pointing is the Royal Road to language for babies. In S. Kita (ed.), *Pointing: Where Language, Culture, and Cognition Meet*, pp. 9–33. Mahwah, NJ: Lawrence Erlbaum Associates.

—— F. Franco, B. McKenzie, L. Graupner, and B. Todd (2002). Dynamic aspects of visual event perception and the production of pointing by human infants. *British Journal of Developmental Psychology* 20, 1–24.

Butterworth, G. E. and P. Morissette (1996). Onset of pointing and the acquisition of language in infancy. *Journal of Reproductive and Infant Psychology* 14, 219–231.

Buzsaki, G. (1998). Memory consolidation during sleep: a neurophysiological perspective. *Journal of Sleep Research* 7, Supplement 1, 17–23.

Byrne, R. W. (1995). *The Thinking Ape: Evolutionary Origins of Intelligence*. Oxford: Oxford University Press.

—— (1997). What's the use of anecdotes? In R. W. Mitchell, N. S. Thompson, and L. Miles (eds.), *Anthropomorphism, Anecdotes, and Animals: The Emperor's New Clothes?*, pp. 134–150. Lincoln, NE: University of Nebraska Press.

—— (1998). So much easier to attack straw men. *Behavioral and Brain Sciences* 21, 116–117.

—— and N. Corp (2004). Neocortex size predicts deception rate in primates. *Proceedings of the Royal Society of London*, Series B (published online).

—— and A. Whiten (1988). *Machiavellian Intelligence: Social Expertise and the Evolution of Intellect in Monkeys, Apes and Humans*. Oxford: Clarendon Press.

—— and A. Whiten (1992). Cognitive evolution in primates: evidence from tactical deception. *Man* NS 27(3), 609–627.

Call, J. (2006). Descartes' two errors: reason and reflection in the great apes. In S. Hurley and M. Nudds (eds.), *Rational Animals?*, pp. 219–234. Oxford: Oxford University Press.

—— B. Agnetta, and M. Tomasello (2000). Cues that chimpanzees do and do not use to find hidden objects. *Animal Cognition* 3, 23–34.

—— B. Hare, M. Carpenter, and M. Tomasello (2004). 'Unwilling' versus 'unable': chimpanzees' understanding of human intentional action. *Developmental Science* 7, 488–498.

—— Hare, and M. Tomasello (1998). Chimpanzee gaze following in an object-choice task. *Animal Cognition* 1, 89–99.

—— and M. Tomasello (1994). Production and comprehension of referential pointing by orangutans (*Pongo Pygmaeus*). *Journal of Comparative Psychology* 108(4), 307–317.

—— and M. Tomasello (2005). What chimpanzees know about seeing, revisited: an explanation of the third kind. In N. Eilan, C. Hoerl, T. McCormack, and J. Roessler (eds.), *Joint Attention: Communication and Other Minds*, pp. 45–64. Oxford: Oxford University Press.

Calvin, W. and D. Bickerton (2000). *Lingua Ex Machina: Reconciling Darwin and Chomsky with the Human Brain*. Cambridge, MA: MIT Press.

Camaioni, L., M. C. Caselli, E. Longobardi, and V. Volterra (1991). A parent report instrument for early language assessment. *First Language* 11, 345–360.

Camerer, C. and R. Thaler (1995). Ultimatums, dictators, and manners. *Journal of Economic Perspectives* 9, 209–219.

Caramazza, A. (1998). The interpretation of semantic category-specific deficits: what do they reveal about the organization of conceptual knowledge in the brain? *Neurocase* 4, 265–272.

Carnap, R. (1937). *The Logical Syntax of Language*. London: Routledge and Kegan Paul.

—— (1942). *Introduction to Semantics*. Cambridge, MA: MIT Press.

Carnap, R. (1958). *Introduction to Symbolic Logic and its Applications*. New York: Dover Publications.

Carrasco, M. and Y. Yeshurun (1998). The contribution of covert attention to the set-size and eccentricity effects in visual search. *Journal of Experimental Psychology: Human Perception and Performance* 24(2), 673–692.

Carruthers, P. (2003). Monitoring without metacognition. *Behavioral and Brain Sciences* 26(3), 242–243.

Carstairs-McCarthy, A. (1999). *The Origins of Complex Language*. Oxford: Oxford University Press.

Carter, C. S. (1998). Neuroendocrine perspectives on social attachment and love. *Psychoneuroendocrinology* 23(8), 779–818.

Cerella, J. (1980). The pigeon's analysis of pictures. *Pattern Recognition* 12, 1–6.

—— (1986). Pigeons and perceptrons. *Pattern Recognition* 19, 431–438.

Chalmeau, R. (1994). Do chimpanzees cooperate in a learning task? *Primates* 35, 385–392.

—— and A. Gallo (1996). What chimpanzees (*Pan troglodytes*) learn in a cooperative task. *Primates* 37, 39–47.

—— K. Lardeux, P. Brandibas, and A. Gallo (1997). Cooperative problem solving by orangutans, *Pongo pygmaeus*. *International Journal of Primatology* 18, 23–32.

Chalmers, N. (1968). The visual and vocal communication of free living mangabeys in Uganda. *Folia Primatologica* 9, 258–280.

Chan, W. P., F. Prete, and M. Dickinson (1998). Visual input to the the efferent control system of a fly's 'gyroscope'. *Science* 280, 289–292.

Cheney, D. and R. Seyfarth (1990). *How Monkeys See the World: Inside the Mind of Another Species*. Chicago, IL: University of Chicago Press.

Cheney, D. M. and R. M. Seyfarth (1999). Recognition of other individuals' social relationships by female baboons. *Animal Behaviour* 58, 67–75.

Cheng, M. (1992). For whom does the female dove coo? A case for the role of vocal self-stimulation. *Animal Behaviour* 43, 1035–1044.

Cherry, E. C. (1953). Some experiments on the recognition of speech with one and with two ears. *Journal of the Acoustical Society of America* 25, 975–979.

Chomsky, N. (1970). Remarks on nominalization. In A. Jacobs and P. Rosenbaum (eds.), *Readings in Transformational Grammar*, pp. 184–221. Waltham, MA: Ginn and Co.

—— (1975). *Reflections on Language*. Glasgow: Fontana/Collins.

—— (1980). *Rules and Representations*. London: Basil Blackwell.

—— (1995). *The Minimalist Program*. Current Studies in Linguistics, Cambridge, MA: MIT Press.

Churchland, P. S. (1986). *Neurophilosophy: Toward a Unified Science of the Mind/Brain*. Cambridge, MA: MIT Press.

Clark, A. (2000). *A Theory of Sentience*. Oxford: Oxford University Press.

—— (2003). *Natural-Born Cyborgs: Minds, Technologies, and the Future of Human Intelligence*. Oxford: Oxford University Press.

—— (2004). Feature-placing and proto-objects. *Philosophical Psychology* 17(4), 451–477.

Clayton, N. S., T. J. Bussey, N. J. Emery, and A. Dickinson (2003). Prometheus to Proust: the case for behavioural criteria for mental 'time travel'. *Trends in Cognitive Sciences* 7(10), 436–437.

—— and A. Dickinson (1998). Episodic-like memory during cache recovery by scrub jays. *Nature* 395, 272–274.

—— D. Griffiths, N. Emery, and A. Dickinson (2001). Elements of episodic-like memory in animals. *Philosophical Transactions of the Royal Society of London* B 356(1413), 1483–1491.

——J. C. Reboreda, and A. Kacelnik (1997). Seasonal changes in hippocampus volume in parasitic cowbirds. *Behavioural Processes* 41(3), 237–243.

Cleland, A. A. and M. J. Pickering (2003). The use of lexical and syntactic information in language production: evidence from the priming of noun-phrase structure. *Journal of Memory and Language* 49, 214–230.

Clements, K. and D. W. Stephens (1995). Testing models of non-kin cooperation: mutualism and the Prisoner's Dilemma. *Animal Behaviour* 50, 527–535.

Clutton-Brock, T. H. and P. H. Harvey (1976). Evolutionary rules and primate societies. In P. P. G. Bateson and R. A. Hinde (eds.), *Growing Points in Ethology*, pp. 185–237. Cambridge: Cambridge University Press.

Coleman, M. N. and C. F. Ross (2004). Primate auditory diversity and its influence on hearing performance. *The Anatomical Record. Part A. Discoveries in Molecular, Cellular, and Evolutionary Biology* 281(1), 1123–1137.

Collins, S. A. and C. Missing (2003). Vocal and visual attractiveness are related in women. *Animal Behaviour* 65, 997–1004.

Cook, R., M. Brown, and D. Riley (1983). Flexible memory processing by rats: use of prospective and retrospective information. *Journal of Experimental Psychology: Animal Behavior Processes* 11, 453–469.

Cook, R. G., K. K. Cavoto, and B. R. Cavoto (1995). Same–different texture discrimination and concept learning by pigeons. *Journal of Experimental Psychology: Animal Behavior Processes* 21, 253–260.

——and J. Wixted (1997). Same–different texture discrimination in pigeons: testing competing models of discrimination and stimulus integration. *Journal of Experimental Psychology: Animal Behavior Processes* 23, 401–416.

Corballis, M. (2002). *From Hand to Mouth: The Origins of Language*. Princeton: Princeton University Press.

Costa, P. T., Jr. and R. R. McCrae (1992). Four ways the five factors are basic. *Personality and Individual Differences* 13, 653–665.

Coussi-Korbel, S. and D. M. Fragaszy (1995). On the relation between social dynamics and social learning. *Animal Behaviour* 50, 1441–1453.

Cowan, N. (2001). The magical number 4 in short-term memory: a reconsideration of mental storage capacity. *Behavioral and Brain Sciences* 24(1), 87–114.

Cox, C. R. and B. J. LeBoeuf (1977). Female incitation of male competition: a mechanism in sexual selection. *American Naturalist* 111, 317–335.

Craik, K. (1943). *The Nature of Explanation*. Cambridge: Cambridge University Press.

Crockford, C., I. Herbinger, L. Vigilant, and C. Boesch (2004). Wild chimpanzees produce group-specific calls: a case for vocal learning? *Ethology* 110, 221–243.

Cronin, K. A., A. V. Kurian, and C. T. Snowdon (2005). Cooperative problem solving in a cooperatively breeding primate (*Saguinus oedipus*). *Animal Behaviour* 69(1), 133–142.

Cruse, D. A. (1973). Some thoughts on agentivity. *Journal of Linguistics* 9, 11–23.

Cunningham, E. J. A. and T. R. Birkhead (1998). Sex roles and sexual selection. *Animal Behaviour* 56(6), 1311–1321.

Cynx, J. and S. J. Clark (1993). Ethological foxes and cognitive hedgehogs. *Behavioral and Brain Sciences* 16(4), 756–757.

Daly, M. and M. Wilson (1982). Homicide and kinship. *American Anthropologist* 84, 372–378.

Damasio, A. R. (1989). Time-locked multiregional retroactivation: a systems-level proposal for the neural substrates of recall and recognition. *Cognition* 33, 25–62.

Damasio, H., T. Grabowski, D. Tranel, R. D. Hichwa, and A. R. Damasio (1996). A neural basis for lexical retrieval. *Nature* 380, 499–505.

D'Amato, M. R. and M. Colombo (1985). Auditory matching to sample in monkeys (*Cebus apella*). *Animal Learning and Behavior* 13, 375–382.

—— and M. Colombo (1989). On the limits of the matching concept in monkeys (*Cebus apella*). *Journal of the Experimental Analysis of Behavior* 52(3), 225–236.

—— and P. van Sant (1988). The person concept in monkeys (*Cebus apella*). *Journal of Experimental Psychology. Animal Behavior Processes* 14, 43–55.

Darwin, C. (1871). *The Descent of Man, and Selection in Relation to Sex*. London: John Murray. (Repr. Princeton, NJ: by Princeton University Press (1981).)

——(1881). *The Formation of Vegetable Mould, through the Action of Worms*. London: John Murray.

Davidson, D. (1967). The logical form of action sentences. In N. Rescher (ed.), *The Logic of Decision and Action*, pp. 81–95. Pittsburgh, PA: University of Pittsburgh Press. (Repr. in D. Davidson, *Essays on Actions and Events*, pp. 105–123. Oxford: Clarendon Press 1980.)

——(1975). Thought and talk. In S. Gutenplan (ed.), *Mind and Language*, pp. 7–23. Oxford: Oxford University Press.

——(1982). Rational animals. *Dialectica* 36, 318–327.

——(2001a). The emergence of thought. In D. Davidson (ed.), *Subjective, Intersubjective, Objective*, pp. 123–134. Oxford: Oxford University Press.

——(2001b). The myth of the subjective. In D. Davidson (ed.), *Subjective, Intersubjective, Objective*, pp. 39–52. Oxford: Oxford University Press.

——(2004). What thought requires. In D. Davidson (ed.), *Problems of Rationality*. Oxford: Oxford University Press.

Dawkins, R. (1976). *The Selfish Gene*. Oxford: Oxford University Press.

de Blois, S., M. Novak, and M. Bond (1998). Object permanence in orangutans (*Pongo pygmaeus*) and squirrel monkeys (*Saimiri sciureus*). *Journal of Comparative Psychology* 112, 137–152.

de Waal, F. B. M. (1989). Food sharing and reciprocal obligations among chimpanzees. *Journal of Human Evolution* 18, 433–459.

——(1996). *Good Natured: The Origins of Right and Wrong in Humans and Other Animals*. Cambridge, MA: Harvard University Press.

——(1998). *Chimpanzee Politics: Power and Sex among Apes* (rev. edn.). Baltimore, MD: Johns Hopkins University Press.

—— and D. L. Johanowicz (1993). Modification of reconciliation behavior through social experience: an experiment with two macaque species. *Child Development* 64, 897–908.

Deacon, T. (1997). *The Symbolic Species*. London: Penguin.

——(2003). Multilevel selection in a complex adaptive system: the problem of language origins. In B. Weber and D. Depew (eds.), *Evolution and Learning: The Baldwin Effect Reconsidered*, pp. 81–106. Cambridge, MA: MIT Press.

DeBruine, L. M. (2002). Facial resemblance enhances trust. *Proceedings of the Royal Society: B (Biological Sciences)* 269, 1307–1312.

——(2005). Trustworthy but not lust-worthy: context-specific effects of facial resemblance. *Proceedings of the Royal Society: B (Biological Sciences)* 272, 919–922.

Dehaene, S. (1997). *The Number Sense*. New York: Oxford University Press.

—— and L. Cohen (1994). Dissociable mechanisms of subitizing and counting: neuropsychological evidence from simultanagnosis patients. *Journal of Experimental Psychology: Human Perception and Performance* 20(5), 958–975.

—— G. Dehaene-Lambertz, and L. Cohen (1998). Abstract representations of numbers in the animal and human brain. *Trends in Neuroscience* 21(8), 355–361.

Dennett, D. (1991). Granny's campaign for safe science. In B. Loewer and G. Rey (eds.), *Meaning in Mind: Fodor and his Critics*, pp. 87–94. Oxford: Blackwell.

—— (1996). *Kinds of Minds*. London: Weidenfeld and Nicolson.

—— (2003a). Beyond beanbag semantics. *Behavioral and Brain Sciences* 26(6), 673–674.

—— (2003b). *Freedom Evolves*. London: Penguin Books.

—— (1995). *Darwin's Dangerous Idea: Evolution and the Meanings of Life*. London: Penguin Books.

Deputte, B. L. (1982). Duetting in male and female songs of the white-cheeked gibbon (*Hylobates concolor leucogenys*). In C. T. Snowdon, C. H. Brown, and M. R. Petersen (eds.), *Primate Communication*, pp. 67–93. Cambridge: Cambridge University Press.

Deruelle, C. and J. Fagot (1997). Hemispheric lateralisation and global precedence effects in the processing of visual stimuli by humans and baboons (*Papio papio*). *Laterality* 2, 233–246.

—— and J. Fagot (1998). Visual search for global/local stimulus features in humans and baboons. *Psychonomic Bulletin and Review* 5, 476–481.

Dessalles, J.-L. (1998). Altruism, status and the origin of relevance. In J. R. Hurford, M. Studdert-Kennedy, and C. Knight (eds.), *Approaches to the Evolution of Language*, pp. 130–147. Cambridge: Cambridge University Press.

—— (1999). Coalition factor in the evolution of non-kin altruism. *Advances in Complex Systems* 2, 143–172.

—— (2000). Language and hominid politics. In C. Knight, M. S. Kennedy, and J. R. Hurford (eds.), *The Evolutionary Emergence of Language: Social Function and the Origins of Linguistic Form*, pp. 62–80. Cambridge: Cambridge University Press.

Di Paolo, E. (2000). Ecological symmetry breaking can favour the evolution of altruism in an action-response game. *Journal of Theoretical Biology* 203, 135–152.

Dickinson, M. H., F.-O. Lehmann, and S. P. Sane (1999). Wing rotation and the aerodynamic basis of insect flight. *Science* 284, 1954–1960.

Digweed, S. M., L. M. Fedigan, and D. Rendall (2005). Variable specificity in the antipredator vocalizations and behaviour of the white-faced capuchin, *Cebus capucinus*. *Behaviour* 142, 997–1021.

Dobzhansky, T. (1973). Nothing in biology makes sense except in the light of evolution. *The American Biology Teacher* 35, 125–129.

Doherty, J. A. and H. C. Gerhardt (1983). Hybrid tree frogs: vocalizations of males and selective phonotaxis of females. *Science* 220, 1078–1080.

Domb, L. G. and M. Pagel (2002). Sexual swellings advertise female quality in wild baboons. *Nature* 410, 204–206.

Donald, M. (1991). *Origins of the Modern Mind: Three Stages in the Evolution of Culture and Cognition*. Cambridge, MA: Harvard University Press.

—— (2001). *A Mind So Rare*. New York: W. W. Norton & Co.

Dowty, D. (1991). Thematic proto-roles and argument selection. *Language* 67(3), 547–619.

Dretske, F. (1981). *Knowledge and the Flow of Information*. Cambridge, MA: MIT Press.

Driver, J., P. Vuilleumier, and M. Husain (1999). Spatial neglect and extinction. In M. S. Gazzaniga (ed.), *The Cognitive Neurosciences* III, pp. 589–606. Cambridge, MA: MIT Press.

Dudai, Y. (2002). *Memory from A to Z: Keywords, Concepts and Beyond*. Oxford: Oxford University Press.

Dugatkin, L. A. (1988). Do guppies play Tit for Tat during predator inspection visits? *Behavioral Ecology and Sociobiology*, 23 395–399

——(1990). N-person games and the evolution of co-operation: a model based on predator inspection in fish. *Journal of Theoretical Biology* 142(1), 123–135.

——(1997). *Cooperation Among Animals: An Evolutionary Perspective*. Oxford: Oxford University Press.

Dummett, M. E. A. (1993). *The Origins of Analytical Philosophy*. London: Duckworth.

Dunbar, R. I. M. (1996a). Determinants of group size in primates: a general model. In W. G. Runciman, J. M. Smith, and R. I. M. Dunbar (eds.), *Evolution of Social Behaviour Patterns in Primates and Man*, pp. 33–57. Oxford: Oxford University Press.

——(1996b). *Grooming, Gossip and the Evolution of Language*. London: Faber and Faber.

——(1999). Culture, honesty and the freerider problem. In R. Dunbar, C. Knight, and C. Power (eds.), *The Evolution of Culture*, pp. 194–213. Edinburgh: Edinburgh University Press.

Dupré, J. (1996). The mental lives of non-human animals. In M. Bekoff and D. Jamieson (eds.), *Readings in Animal Cognition*, pp. 323–336. Cambridge, MA: MIT Press.

Dusek, J. A. and H. Eichenbaum (1997). The hippocampus and memory for orderly stimulus relations. *Proceedings of the National Academy of Sciences of the USA* 94, 7109–7114.

Edelman, S. (2006). Mostly harmless: review of *Action in Perception* by Alva Noë. *Artificial Life* 12(1), 183–186.

Eggan, F. (1950). *Social Organization of the Western Pueblos*. Chicago: University of Chicago Press.

Egnor, R., C. Miller, and M. Hauser (2006). Non-human primate communication. In K. Brown (ed.), *Encyclopedia of Language and Linguistics* (2nd edn.), pp. 659–668. Amsterdam: Elsevier.

Eichenbaum, H. (2002). *The Cognitive Neuroscience of Memory*. Oxford: Oxford University Press.

Ellington, C. P., C. van den Berg, A. P. Willmott, and A. L. R. Thomas (1996). Leading-edge vortices in insect flight. *Nature* 384, 626–630.

Elugardo, R. (2002). The predicate view of proper names. In G. Preyer and G. Peter (eds.), *Logical Form and Language*, pp. 467–503. Oxford: Oxford University Press.

Emery, N. J. (2000). The eyes have it: the neuroethology, function and evolution of social gaze. *Neuroscience and Biobehavioral Reviews* 24, 581–604.

Enard, W., M. Przeworski, S. E. Fisher, C. S. Lal, V. Wlebe, T. Kitano, A. Monaco, and S. Pääbo (2002). Molecular evolution of *FOXP2*, a gene involved in speech and language. *Nature* 418, 869–872.

Enquist, M. and O. Leimar (1983). Evolution of fighting behaviour: decision rules and assessment of relative strength. *Journal of Theoretical Biology* 102, 387–410.

——and O. Leimar (1993). The evolution of cooperation in mobile organisms. *Animal Behaviour* 45, 747–757.

Erdal, D. and A. Whiten (1994). On human egalitarianism: an evolutionary product of Machiavellian status escalation? *Current Anthropology* 35, 175–183.

Etienne, A. (1973). Developmental stages and cognitive structures as determinants of what is learned. In R. Hinde and J. Stevenson-Hinde (eds.), *Constraints on Learning*, pp. 371–395. New York: Academic Press.

Evans, C. S., L. Evans, and P. Marler (1993). On the meaning of alarm calls: functional reference in an avian vocal system. *Animal Behaviour* 46(1), 23–38.

Evans, H. E. (1977). Extrinsic and intrinsic factors in the evolution of insect sociality. *BioScience* 27, 613–617.

Ewert, J.-P. (1987). Neuroethology of releasing mechanisms: prey-catching in toads. *Behavioral and Brain Sciences* 10, 337–405.

Fagot, J. and C. Deruelle (1997). Processing of global and local visual information and hemispheric specialization in humans (*Homo sapiens*) and baboons (*Papio papio*). *Journal of Experimental Psychology: Human Perception and Performance* 23, 429–442.

——— and M. Tomonaga (1998). Global-local processing in humans (*Homo sapiens*) and chimpanzees (*Pan troglodytes*): use of a visual search task with compound stimuli. *Journal of Comparative Psychology* 113, 3–12.

Fang, F. and S. He (2005). Cortical responses to invisible objects in the human dorsal and ventral pathways. *Nature Neuroscience* 8(10), 1380–1385.

Farah, M. J. (1988). Is visual imagery really visual? Overlooked evidence from neuropsychology. *Psychological Review* 95, 307–317. Cambridge, MA: MIT Press.

——— (1990). *Visual Agnosia: Disorders of Object Recognition and What they Tell us about Normal Vision*. Cambridge, MA: MIT Press.

Fay, N., S. Garrod, T. MacLeod, J. Lee, and J. Oberlander (2005). Design, adaptation and convention: The emergence of higher order graphical representations. (Unpublished paper, University of Edinburgh School of Informatics and ATR Media Informatiion Science Labs, Japan.)

Fehr, E. and S. Gächter (2002). Altruistic punishment in humans. *Nature* 415, 137–140.

Feinberg, D. R., B. C. Jones, L. M. DeBruine, F. R. Moore, M. J. Law Smith, R. E. Cornwell, B. P. Tiddeman, L. G. Boothroyd, and D. I. Perrett (2005). The voice and face of woman: One ornament that signals quality? *Evolution and Human Behavior* 26, 398–408.

——— B. C. Jones, M. J. Law Smith, F. R. Moore, L. M. DeBruine, R. E. Cornwell, S. G. Hillier, and D. I. Perrett (2006). Menstrual cycle, trait estrogen level, and masculinity preferences in the human voice. *Hormones and Behavior* 49, 215–222.

Feldman, M. W. and K. N. Laland (1996). Gene-culture coevolutionary theory. *Trends in Ecology and Evolution* 11, 453–457.

Fischer, J. (2002). Developmental modifications in the vocal behavior of non-human primates. In A. A. Ghazanfar (ed.), *Primate Audition: Ethology and Neurobiology*, pp. 109–125. London: CRC Press.

Fiset, S., C. Beaulieu, and F. Landry (2003). Duration of dogs' (*Canis familiaris*) working memory in search for disappearing objects. *Animal Cognition* 6(1), 1–10.

Fisher, R. A. (1915). The evolution of sexual preferences. *Eugenics Review* 7, 184–192.

——— (1930). *The Genetical Theory of Natural Selection*. Oxford: Clarendon Press.

Fitch, W. T. (2005). The evolution of language: a comparative review. *Biology and Philosophy* 20, 193–230.

Flavell, J. (1979). Metacognition and cognitive monitoring: a new area of cognitive-developmental inquiry. *American Psychologist* 34, 906–911.

Fodor, J. A. (1990). *A Theory of Content and other Essays*. Cambridge, MA: MIT Press.

——— (1998). *Concepts: Where Cognitive Science Went Wrong*. Oxford Cognitive Science Series. Oxford: Clarendon Press.

Fortin, N. J., K. L. Agster, and H. B. Eichenbaum (2002). Critical role of the hippocampus in memory for sequences of events. *Nature Neuroscience* 5(5), 458–462.

Foster, K. R., T. Wenseleers, and F. L. Ratnieks (2006). Kin selection is the key to altruism. *Trends in Ecology and Evolution* 21, 57–60.

Franco, F. and G. E. Butterworth (1996). Pointing and social awareness: declaring and requesting in the second year of life. *Journal of Child Language* 23(2), 307–336.

Freedman, D. G. (1958). Constitutional and environmental interactions in rearing of four breeds of dogs. *Science* 127, 585–586.

Frege, G. (1879). *Begriffsschrift: eine der arithmetischen nachgebildete Formelsprache des reinen Denkens.* Halle: Louis Nebert. (English translation, *Conceptual Notation and Related Articles*, with a biography and introduction, by Terrell Ward Bynum. Oxford: Oxford University Press 1972.)

——(1892). Über Sinn und Bedeutung. *Zeitschrift für Philosophie und philosophische Kritik 100*, 25–50. (Page references here are to *Translations from the Philosophical Writings of Gottlob Frege*, ed. Peter Geach and Max Black. Oxford: Basil Blackwell (1970).)

Fremouw, T., W. T. Herbranson, and C. P. Shimp (1998). Priming of attention to local or global levels of visual analysis. *Journal of Experimental Psychology: Behavior Processes* 24(3), 278–290.

——W. T. Herbranson, and C. P. Shimp (2002). Dynamic shifts of pigeon local/global attention. *Animal Cognition* 5(4), 233–243.

Frost, P. (1994). Preference for darker faces in photographs at different phases of the menstrual cycle: preliminary assessment of evidence for a hormonal relationship. *Perceptual and Motor Skills* 79, 507–514.

Fukatsu, R., T. Fujii, T. Tsukiura, A. Yamadori, and T. Otsuki (1999). Proper name anomia after left temporal lobectomy: a patient study. *Neurology* 52, 1096.

Furness, W. H. (1916). Observations on the mentality of chimpanzees and orang-utangs. *Proceedings of the American Philosophical Society* 55, 281–290.

Gabriel, S. E., K. L. Brigman, B. H. Koller, R. C. Boucher, and M. J. Stutts (1994). Cystic fibrosis heterozygote resistance to cholera toxin in the cystic fibrosis mouse model. *Science* 266, 107–109.

Gagnon, S. and F. Doré (1992). Search behavior in various breeds of adult dogs (*Canis familiaris*): object permanence and olfactory cues. *Journal of Comparative Psychology* 106, 58–68.

Galantucci, B. (2005). An experimental study of the emergence of human communication systems. *Cognitive Science* 29, 737–767.

Gallese, V. (2003a). A neuroscientific grasp of concepts: from control to representation. *Philosophical Transactions of the Royal Society of London*, B 358, 1231–1240.

——(2003b). The roots of empathy: the shared manifold hypothesis and the neural basis of intersubjectivity. *Psychopathology* 36(4), 171–180.

——(2003c). The 'Shared Manifold' Hypothesis: from mirror neurons to empathy. *Journal of Consciousness Studies* 8(5–7), 33–50.

——(2004). 'Being like me': self–other identity, mirror neurons and empathy. In S. Hurley and N. Chater (eds.), *Perspectives on Imitation: From Cognitive Neuroscience to Social Science*. Boston, MA: MIT Press.

——L. Fadiga, L. Fogassi, and G. Rizzolatti (1996). Action recognition in the premotor cortex. *Brain* 119, 593–609.

——and G. Lakoff (2005). The brain's concepts: the role of the sensory-motor system in conceptual knowledge. *Cognitive Neuropsychology* 22(3–4), 455–479.

Gärdenfors, P. (1996). Cued and detached representations in animal cognition. *Behavioural Processes* 35, 263–273.

——(2003). *How Homo Became Sapiens: On the Evolution of Thinking*. Oxford: Oxford University Press.

——(2004). Cooperation and the evolution of symbolic communication. In D. K. Oller and U. Griebel (eds.), *Evolution of Communication Systems*, pp. 237–256. Cambridge, MA: MIT Press.

Gardner, B. T. and R. A. Gardner (1971). Two-way communication with an infant chimpanzee. In A. M. Schrier and F. Stollnitz (eds.), *Behavior of Nonhuman Primates: Modern Research Trends*, Vol. 4, pp. 117–183. New York: Academic Press.

Gasper, K. and G. L. Clore (2002). Attending to the big picture: mood and global versus local processing of visual information. *Psychological Science* 13(1), 34–40.

Geissmann, T. (1999). Duet songs of the siamang, *Hylobates syndactylus*: ii. testing the pair-bonding hypothesis during a partner exchange. *Behaviour* 136(8), 1005–1039.

—— (2000). Gibbon songs and human music from an evolutionary perspective. In N. L. Wallin, B. Merker, and S. Brown (eds.), *The Origins of Music*, pp. 103–123. Cambridge, MA: MIT Press.

Gergely, G. and G. Csibra (2005). A few reasons why we don't share Tomasello et al's intuitions about sharing. *Behavioral and Brain Sciences* 28, 701–702.

—— Z. Nádasdy, G. Csibra, and S. Biró (1995). Taking the intentional stance at 12 months of age. *Cognition* 56, 165–193.

Geurts, B. (1997). Good news about the description theory of names. *Journal of Semantics* 14, 319–348.

Gibeault, S. and S. E. MacDonald (2000). Spatial memory and foraging competition in captive western lowland gorillas (*Gorilla gorilla gorilla*). *Primates* 41, 147–160.

Gibson, J. J. (1979). *The Ecological Approach to Visual Perception*. Boston: Houghton Mifflin.

Giedd, J. N., C. Vaituzis, S. D. Hamburger, N. Lange, J. Rajapakse, D. Kaysen, Y. C. Vauss, and J. L. Rapoport (1996). Quantitative MRI of the temporal lobe, amygdala, and hippocampus in normal human development: ages 4–18 years. *Journal of Comparative Neurology* 366, 223–230.

Gintis, H. (2000). Strong reciprocity and human sociality. *Journal of Theoretical Biology* 206, 169–179.

—— S. Bowles, R. Boyd, and E. Fehr (2003). Explaining altruistic behavior in humans. *Evolution and Human Behavior* 24, 153–172.

Glaeser, E. L., D. I. Laibson, J. A. Sheinkman, and C. L. Soutter (2000). Measuring trust. *Quarterly Journal of Economics* 115, 811–846.

Godwin-Austen, R. B. (1965). A case of visual disorientation. *Journal of Neurology, Neurosurgery and Psychiatry* 28, 453–458.

Goldenberg, G. (1998). Is there a common substrate for visual recognition and visual imagery? *Neurocase* 4, 141–147.

Goldin-Meadow, S. and C. Butcher (2003). Pointing toward two-word speech in young children. In S. Kita (ed.), *Pointing: Where Language, Culture, and Cognition Meet*, pp. 85–107. Mahwah, NJ: Lawrence Erlbaum Associates.

Gómez, J. C. (1990). The emergence of intentional communication as a problem-solving strategy in the gorilla. In S. T. Parker and K. R. Gibson (eds.), *'Language' and Intelligence in Monkeys and Apes: Comparative Developmental Perspectives*, pp. 333–355. Cambridge: Cambridge University Press.

—— (1991). Visual behavior as a window for reading the minds of others in primates. In A. Whiten (ed.), *Natural Theories of Mind: Evolution, Development and Simulation of Everyday Mindreading*, pp. 195–207. Oxford: Basil Blackwell.

—— (1992). *El desarrollo de la comunicación en el gorila*. Ph.D. thesis, Universidad Autónoma de Madrid.

—— (1996). Ostensive behavior in the great apes: the role of eye contact. In A. E. Russon, K. A. Bard, and S. T. Parker (eds.), *Reaching into Thought: The Minds of the Great Apes*, pp. 131–151. Cambridge: Cambridge University Press.

—— (2004). *Apes, Monkeys, Children, and the Growth of Mind*. Cambridge, MA: Harvard University Press.

—— (2005a). Joint attention and the notion of subject: insights from apes, normal children, and children with autism. In N. Eilan, C. Hoerl, T. McCormack, and J. Roessler (eds.),

Joint Attention: Communication and Other Minds, pp. 65–84. Oxford: Oxford University Press.

Gómez, J. C. (2005b). Requesting gestures in captive monkeys and apes: conditioned responses or referential behaviours? *Gesture* 5(1/2), 91–105.

Goodale, M. A., J. P. Meenan, H. H. Bülthoff, D. A. Nicolle, K. J. Murphy, and C. I. Racicot (1994). Separate neural pathways for the visual analysis of object shape in perception and prehension. *Current Biology* 4(7), 604–610.

Goodall, J. (1986). *The Chimpanzees of Gombe: Patterns of Behavior*. Cambridge, MA: Harvard University Press.

Goodglass, H. and E. Kaplan (1983). *The Assessment of Aphasia and Related Disorders*. Philadelphia: Lea & Febiger.

Gopnik, A. (1993). How we know our minds: the illusion of first-person knowledge of intentionality. *Behavioral and Brain Sciences* 16, 1–16.

——and P. Graf (1988). Knowing how you know: young children's ability to identify and remember the sources of their beliefs. *Child Development* 59, 98–110.

Grafen, A. (1990a). Biological signals as handicaps. *Journal of Theoretical Biology* 144, 517–546.

——(1990b). Sexual selection unhandicapped by the fisher process. *Journal of Theoretical Biology* 144, 473–516.

Greene, A. J., B. A. Spellman, J. A. Dusek, H. B. Eichenbaum, and W. B. Levy (2001). Relational learning with and without awareness: transitive inference using nonverbal stimuli in humans. *Memory and Cognition* 29(6), 893–902.

Greenfield, P. M. and E. S. Savage-Rumbaugh (1990). Grammatical combination in *Pan paniscus*: processes of learning and invention in the evolution and development of language. In S. T. Parker and K. R. Gibson (eds.), *'Language' and Intelligence in Monkeys and Apes: Comparative Developmental Perspectives*, pp. 540–578. Cambridge: Cambridge University Press.

Grice, H. P. (1967). *Logic and Conversation*. William James Lectures. (Repr. in H. P. Grice, *Studies in the Ways of Words*, pp. 1–143. Cambridge, MA: Harvard University Press 1989.)

——(1975). Logic and conversation. In P. Cole (ed.), *Syntax and Semantics*, Vol. 3, pp. 41–58. New York: Academic Press.

Griffin, D. (2001). Animals know more than we used to think. *Proceedings of the National Academy of Sciences (USA)* 98, 4833–4834.

Griffiths, D. P., A. Dickinson, and N. S. Clayton (1999). Episodic memory: what can animals remember about their past. *Trends in Cognitive Sciences* 3(2), 74–80.

Grill-Spector, K. and N. Kanwisher (2005). Visual recognition: as soon as you know it is there, you know what it is. *Psychological Science* 16(2), 152–160.

Grim, P., S. Wardach, and V. Beltrani (2006). Location, location, location: the importance of spatialization on modeling cooperation and communication. *Interaction Studies* 7(1), 41–75.

Grossman, M., P. Koenig, C. DeVita, G. Glosser, D. Alsop, J. Detre, and J. Gee (2002). The neural basis for category-specific knowledge: an fMRI study. *NeuroImage* 15, 936–948.

Gurven, M. (2004). To give and to give not: the behavioral ecology of human food transfers. *Behavioral and Brain Sciences* 27, 543–583.

Gust, D., E. St. Andre, C. Minter, T. Gordon, and H. Gouzoules (1990). Female copulatory vocalizations in a captive group of sooty mangabeys (*Cercocebus torquatus atys*). *American Journal of Primatology* 20, 196.

Güth, W. and R. Tietz (1990). Ultimatum bargaining behavior: a survey and comparison of experimental results. *Journal of Economic Psychology* 11, 417–449.

Halliday, M. A. K. (1985). *Introduction to Functional Grammar*. London: Edward Arnold.

Hamao, S. and H. Eda-Fujiwara (2004). Vocal mimicry by the black-browed reed warbler *Acrocephalus bistrigiceps*: objective identification of mimetic sounds. *Ibis* 146, 61–68.

Hamilton, W. D. (1964). The genetical evolution of social behavior. *Journal of Theoretical Biology* 7, 1–16, 17–52. Parts I and II.

——(1970). Selfish and spiteful behaviour in an evolutionary model. *Nature* 228, 1218–1220.

——(1972). Altruism and related phenomena, mainly in social insects. *Annual Review of Ecological Systems* 3, 193–232.

——and S. P. Brown (2001). Autumn tree colors as a handicap signal. *Proceedings of the Royal Society of London* B 268, 1489–1493.

Hamilton, W. J. and P. C. Arrowood (1978). Copulatory vocalisations of chacma baboons (*Papio ursinus*), gibbons (*Hylobates hoolock*) and humans. *Science* 200, 1405–1409.

Hampton, R. R. (2001). Rhesus monkeys know when they remember. *Proceedings of the National Academy of Sciences (USA)* 98, 5359–5362.

Hare, B., E. Addessi, J. Call, M. Tomasello, and E. Visalberghi (2003). Do capuchin monkeys, *Cebus apella*, know what conspecifics do and do not see? *Animal Behaviour* 65, 131–142.

——M. Brown, C. Williamson, and M. Tomasello (2002). The domestication of social cognition in dogs. *Science* 298, 1634–1636.

——J. Call, B. Agnetta, and M. Tomasello (2000). Chimpanzees know what conspecifics do and do not see. *Animal Behaviour* 59, 771–785.

——J. Call, and M. Tomasello (2001). Do chimpanzees know what conspecifics know? *Animal Behaviour* 61(1), 139–151.

——and M. Tomasello (1999). Domestic dogs (*Canis familiaris*) use human and conspecific social cues to locate hidden food. *Journal of Comparative Psychology* 113, 173–177.

——and M. Tomasello (2004). Chimpanzees are more skilful in competitive than in cooperative tasks. *Animal Behaviour* 68, 571–581.

Harms, W. F. (2004). Primitive content, translation, and the emergence of meaning in animal communication. In D. K. Oller and U. Griebel (eds.), *Evolution of Communication Systems: A Comparative Approach*, pp. 31–48. Cambridge, MA: MIT Press.

Harris, M., F. Barlow-Brown, and J. Chasin (1995). Early referential understanding. *First Language* 15(1), 19–34.

Hauser, L. (1995). Doing without mentalese. *Behavior and Philosophy* 23, 42–47.

Hauser, M. D. (1992). Costs of deception: cheaters are punished in rhesus monkeys (*Macaca mulatta*). *Proceedings of the National Academy of Sciences of the USA* 89, 12137–12139.

——(1996). *The Evolution of Communication*. Cambridge, MA: MIT Press.

——(1998a). Functional referents and acoustic similarity: field playback experiments with rhesus monkeys. *Animal Behaviour* 55, 1647–1658.

——(1998b). A nonhuman primate's expectations about object motion and destination: the importance of self-propelled movement and animacy. *Developmental Science* 1(1), 31–37.

——(2003). Knowing about knowing: dissociations between perception and action systems over evolution and during development. *Annals of the New York Academy of Science* 1001(1), 79–103.

——S. Carey, and L. B. Hauser (2000). Spontaneous number representation in semi-free-ranging rhesus monkeys. *Proceedings of the Royal Society of London*, Series B 267, 829–833.

——M. K. Chen, F. Chen, and E. Chuang (2003). Give unto others: genetically unrelated cotton-top tamarin monkeys preferentially give food to those who altruistically give food back. *Proceedings of the Royal Society of London*, Series B 270, 2363–2370.

Hauser, M. D., N. Chomsky, and W. T. Fitch (2002). The faculty of language: what is it, who has it, and how did it evolve? *Science* 298, 1569–1579.

——and P. Marler (1993). Food-associated calls in rhesus macaques (*Macaca mulatta*). I. Socioecological factors influencing call production. *Behavioral Ecology* 4, 194–205.

——and E. Spelke (2004). Evolutionary and developmental foundations of human knowledge: a case study of mathematics. In M. Gazzaniga (ed.), *The Cognitive Neurosciences* III, pp. 853–864. Cambridge, MA: MIT Press.

Healy, S. D. and J. Suhonen (1996). Memory for location of stored food in willow tits and marsh tits. *Behaviour* 133(1–2), 71–80.

Heim, I. (1983). File change semantics and the familiarity theory of definiteness. In R. Bäuerle, C. Schwarze, and A. von Stechow (eds.), *Meaning, Use, and Interpretation of Language*, pp. 164–189. Berlin: Walter de Gruyter.

Henrich, J. (2004). Inequity aversion in capuchins? *Nature* 428, 139.

——and R. Boyd (2001). Why people punish defectors: weak conformist transmission can stabilize costly enforcement of norms in cooperative dilemmas. *Journal of Theoretical Biology* 208, 79–89.

——R. Boyd, S. Bowles, C. Camerer, E. Fehr, H. Gintis, and R. McElreath (2001). Cooperation, reciprocity and punishment in fifteen small-scale societies. *American Economic Review* 91, 73–78.

Herman, L. M., S. L. Abichandani, A. N. Alhajj, E. Y. Herman, J. L. Sanchez, and A. A. Pack (1999). Dolphins (*Tursiops truncatus*) comprehend the referential character of the human pointing gesture. *Journal of Comparative Psychology* 113, 347–364.

Herrnstein, R. (1991). Levels of categorization. In G. Edelman, W. Gall, and W. Cowan (eds.), *Signal and Sense*, pp. 385–413. Somerset, NJ: Wiley-Liss.

Herrnstein, R. J., D. Loveland, and C. Cable (1976). Natural concepts in pigeons. *Journal of Experimental Psychology: Animal Behavior Processes* 2, 285–302.

Hess, J., M. A. Novak, and D. J. Povinelli (1993). 'Natural pointing' in a rhesus monkey, but no evidence of empathy. *Animal Behaviour* 46, 1023–1025.

Hewes, G. (1973). Primate communication and the gestural origin of language. *Current Anthropology* 14, 5–24.

Heyes, C. M. (1998). Theory of mind in non-human primates. *Behavioral and Brain Sciences* 21(1), 101–134.

Higginbotham, J. (1999). Thematic roles. In R. A. Wilson and F. Keil (eds.), *The MIT Encyclopedia of the Cognitive Sciences*, pp. 837–838. Cambridge, MA: MIT Press.

——(2000). On events in linguistic semantics. In J. Higginbotham, F. Panesi, and A. C. Varzi (eds.), *Speaking of Events*, pp. 49–79. Oxford: Oxford University Press.

Hillis, A. E. and A. Caramazza (1991). Category-specific naming and comprehension impairment: a double dissociation. *Brain* 115(5), 2081–2094.

Hirsh, I. J. and C. E. Sherrick (1961). Perceived order in different sense modalities. *Journal of Experimental Psychology* 62, 423–432.

Hobson, P. (2002). *The Cradle of Thought: Exploring the Origins of Thinking*. London: Macmillan.

Hockett, C. F. (1960). The origin of speech. *Scientific American* 203(3), 89–96.

——and S. A. Altmann (1968). A note on design features. In T. A. Sebeok (ed.), *Animal Communication: Techniques of Study and Results of Research*, pp. 61–72. Bloomington, IN: Indiana University Press.

Hodges, J. R. and K. Patterson (1999). Semantic memory disorders. *Trends in Cognitive Sciences* 1(2), 68–72.

Hoffman, M. L. (2004). Communication of where an event occurred by a gorilla (*Gorilla gorilla gorilla*). *Modern Psychological Studies* 10, 61–68.

Hogue, M. E., J. P. Beaugrand, and P. C. Lague (1996). Coherent use of information by hens observing their former dominant defeating or being defeated by a stranger. *Behavioural Processes* 38, 241–252.

Honey, R. and J. Bolhuis (1997). Imprinting, conditioning, and within-event learning. *Quarterly Journal of Experimental Psychology* B 50(2), 97–110.

Hood, B. M., V. Cole-Davis, and M. Diaz (2003). Looking and search measures of object knowledge in preschool children. *Developmental Psychology* 39, 61–70.

Horner, M. D. (1990). Psychobiological evidence for the distinction between episodic and semantic memory. *Neuropsychology Review* 1(4), 281–321.

Horner, V. and A. Whiten (2005). Causal knowledge and imitation/emulation switching in chimpanzees (*Pan troglodytes*) and children (*Homo sapiens*). *Animal Cognition* 8(3), 164–181.

Hoy, R. R., J. Hahn, and R. C. Paul (1977). Hybrid cricket auditory behavior: evidence for genetic coupling in animal communication. *Science* 195, 82–84.

—— and R. C. Paul (1973). Genetic control of song specificity in crickets. *Science* 180, 82–83.

Hubel, D. H. and T. N. Wiesel (1959). Receptive fields of single neurons in the cat's striate cortex. *Journal of Physiology* 148, 574–591.

—— and T. N. Wiesel (1968). Receptive fields, binocular interaction and functional architecture in the cat's striate cortex. *Journal of Physiology* 195, 215–243.

Huber, E. (1931). *Evolution of Facial Musculature and Facial Expression*. Baltimore, MD: Johns Hopkins University Press.

Hughes, S. M., F. Dispenza, and G. G. Gallup (2004). Ratings of voice attractiveness predict sexual behavior and body configuration. *Evolution and Human Behavior* 25(5), 295–304.

Humboldt, W. Von (1836). *Über die Verschiedenheit des Menschlichen Sprachbaues und ihren Einfluß auf die geistige Entwicklung des Menschengeschlechts*. Berlin: Druckerei der Königlichen Akademie der Wissenschaften.

Hume, D. (1739). *A Treatise of Human Nature: Being an Attempt to Introduce the Experimental Method of Reasoning into Moral Subjects*. London: John Noon.

Hummel, J. (1999). Binding problem. In R. A. Wilson and F. Keil (eds.), *The MIT Encyclopedia of the Cognitive Sciences*, pp. 85–86. Cambridge, MA: MIT Press.

Humphreys, G. W. (1998). Neural representation of objects in space: a dual coding account. *Philosophical Transactions of the Royal Society of London*, Series B 353, 1341–1351.

Huntingford, F. A., J. Lazarus, B. D. Barrie, and S. A. Webb (1994). A dynamic analysis of cooperative predator inspection in sticklebacks. *Animal Behaviour* 47, 413–423.

Hurford, J. R. (1989). Biological evolution of the Saussurean sign as a component of the language acquisition device. *Lingua* 77, 187–222.

—— (1991). The evolution of the critical period for language acquisition. *Cognition* 40, 159–201.

—— (1999). Individuals are abstractions. *Behavioral and Brain Sciences* 22(4), 620–621.

—— (2001). Protothought had no logical names. In J. Trabant and S. Ward (eds.), *New Essays on the Origin of Language*, pp. 117–130. Berlin: de Gruyter.

—— (2002). The roles of expression and representation in language evolution. In A. Wray (ed.), *The Transition to Language*, pp. 311–334. Oxford: Oxford University Press.

—— (2003a). The neural basis of predicate-argument structure. *Behavioral and Brain Sciences* 26(3), 261–283.

—— (2003b). Ventral/dorsal, predicate/argument: the transformation from perception to meaning. *Behavioral and Brain Sciences* 26(3), 301–311.

Hurford, J. R. (2007). The origin of noun phrases: reference, truth, and communication. *Lingua* 117(3), 527–542.

——B. Heasley (1983). *Semantics: A Coursebook*. Cambridge: Cambridge University Press.

——and S. Kirby (1999). Co-evolution of language-size and the critical period. In D. Birdsong (ed.), *New Perspectives on the Critical Period Hypothesis and Second Language Acquisition*, pp. 39–63. Mahwah, NJ: Lawrence Erlbaum.

Hurley, K. (2006). Pointing, reference, and the evolution of language: an experimental study on primitive horses' understanding of the human pointing gesture. Master's thesis, University of Edinburgh.

Hurley, S. (2006). Making sense of animals. In S. Hurley and M. Nudds (eds.), *Rational Animals?*, pp. 139–171. Oxford: Oxford University Press.

Inoue-Nakamura, N. and T. Matsuzawa (1997). Development of stone tool use by wild chimpanzees (*Pan troglodytes*). *Journal of Comparative Psychology* 111, 159–173.

Irwin, D. E. and J. R. Brockmole (2004). Suppressing *Where* but not *What*. *Psychological Science* 15(7), 467–473.

Itakura, S., B. Agnetta, B. Hare, and M. Tomasello (1999). Chimpanzee use of human and conspecific social cues to locate hidden food. *Developmental Sciences* 2, 448–456.

Itti, L. and M. A. Arbib (2006). Attention and the minimal subscene. In M. A. Arbib (ed.), *From Action to Language via the Mirror Neuron System*, pp. 289–346. Cambridge: Cambridge University Press.

Jackendoff, R. (1990). *Semantic Structures*. Current Studies in Linguistics, 18. Cambridge, MA: MIT Press.

——(2002). *Foundations of Language: Brain, Meaning, Grammar, Evolution*. Oxford: Oxford University Press.

Janata, P., B. Tillmann, and J. J. Bharucha (2002). Listening to polyphonic music recruits domain-general attention and working memory circuits. *Cognitive, Affective, and Behavioral Neuroscience* 2(2), 121–140.

Jansen, V. A. A. and M. van Baalen (2006). Altruism through beard chromodynamics. *Nature* 440, 663–666.

Jespersen, O. (1922). *Language: its Nature, Development and Origin*. London: G. Allen and Unwin Ltd. (Repr. New York: W. W. Norton & Co. 1964).

Johanson, D. and T. White (1979). A systematic assessment of early African hominids. *Science* 202, 321–330.

Johansson, G. (1973). Visual perception of biological motion and a model for its analysis. *Perception and Psychophysics* 14, 201–211.

John, O. P. (1990). The 'big five' factor taxonomy: dimensions of personality in the natural language and in questionnaires. In L. A. Pervin (ed.), *Handbook of Personality: Theory and Research*. New York: Guilford.

Jokisch, D. and N. F. Troje (2003). Biological motion as a cue for the perception of size. *Journal of Vision* 3, 252–264.

Jolly, A. (1985). *The Evolution of Primate Behavior* (2nd edn.). New York: Macmillan.

Jones, B. C., A. C. Little, L. Boothroyd, D. R. Feinberg, R. E. Cornwell, L. M. DeBruine, S. C. Roberts, I. S. Penton-Voak, M. J. L. Smith, F. R. Moore, H. P. Davis, and D. I. Perrett (2005). Women's physical and psychological condition independently predict their preference for apparent health in faces. *Evolution and Human Behavior* 26, 451–457.

Julesz, B. and R. A. Schumer (1981). Early visual perception. *Annual Review of Psychology* 32, 575–627.

Kahneman, D. and A. Treisman (1984). Changing views of attention and automaticity. In R. Parasuraman and D. A. Davies (eds.), *Varieties of Attention*, pp. 29–61. New York: Academic Press.

—— A. Treisman (1992). The reviewing of object files: object-specific integration of information. *Cognitive Psychology* 24, 175–219.

Kaminski, J., J. Riedel, J. Call, and M. Tomasello (2005). Domestic goats, *Capra hircus*, follow gaze direction and use social cues in an object choice task. *Animal Behaviour* 69, 11–18.

Kamp, H. and U. Reyle (1993). *From Discourse to Logic: Introduction to Modeltheoretic Semantics of Natural Language, Formal Logic and Discourse Representation Theory*. Dordrecht, Holland: Kluwer Academic.

Kant, I. (1781). *Kritik der Reinen Vernunft*. Riga: Johann Friedrich Hartknoch.

—— (1783). *Prolegomena zu einer jeden künftigen Metaphysik die als Wissenschaft wird auftreten können*. Riga: Johann Friedrich Hartknoch. (*Prolegomena to Any Future Metaphysics*, trans. Paul Carus. LaSalle, IL: Open Court 1905.).

Kaplan, G. and L. J. Rogers (2002). Patterns of gazing in orangutans (*Pongo pygmaeus*). *International Journal of Primatology* 23(3), 501–526.

Karakashian, S. J., M. Gyger, and P. Marler (1988). Audience effects on alarm calling in chickens (*Gallus gallus*). *Journal of Comparative Psychology* 102(2), 129–135.

Kastak, C. R. and R. J. Schustermann (2002). Long-term memory for concepts in a California sea lion (*Zalophus californianus*). *Animal Cognition* 5(4), 225–232.

Katz, J. S., A. A. Wright, and J. Bachevalier (2002). Mechanisms of *Same/Different* abstract-concept learning by rhesus monkeys (*Macaca mulatta*). *Journal of Experimental Psychology: Animal Behavior Processes* 28(4), 358–368.

Kaufman, E., M. Lord, T. Reese, and J. Volkmann (1949). The discrimination of visual number. *American Journal of Psychology* 62, 498–525.

Kawecki, T. J. (1991). Sex-linked altruism: a stepping-stone in the evolution of social behavior? *Journal of Evolutionary Biology* 3, 487–500.

Keddy-Hector, A. C., C. Allen, and T. H. Friend (2005). Cognition in domestic pigs (*Sus scrofa*): same-difference relational concepts. Unpub. paper, Texas A & M University.

Keller, L. and K. G. Ross (1998). Selfish genes: a green beard in the red ant. *Nature* 394, 573–575.

Kellogg, W. N. and L. A. Kellogg (1933). *The Ape and the Child: A Study of Early Environmental Influence upon Early Behavior*. New York: McGraw Hill.

Kemmerer, D. (2006). Action verbs, argument structure constructions, and the mirror neuron system. In M. A. Arbib (ed.), *From Action to Language via the Mirror Neuron System*, pp. 347–373. Cambridge: Cambridge University Press.

Kim, J. (1969). Events and their descriptions: some considerations. In N. Rescher (ed.), *Essays in Honor of Carl G. Hempel*, pp. 198–215. Dordrecht, Holland: Reidel.

—— (1976). Events as property exemplifications. In M. Brand and D. Walton (eds.), *Action Theory: Proceedings of the Winnipeg Conference on Human Action*, pp. 159–177. Dordrecht, Holland: Reidel.

King, J. E. and A. J. Figueredo (1997). The five-factor model plus dominance in chimpanzee personality. *Journal of Research in Personality* 31, 257–271.

—— A. Weiss, and K. H. Farmer (2005). A chimpanzee (*Pan troglodytes*) analogue of cross-national generalization of personality structure: zoological parks and an African sanctuary. *Journal of Personality* 73(2), 389–410.

Kinsbourne, M. and E. K. Warrington (1962). A disorder of simultaneous form perception. *Brain* 85, 461–486.

Kirkpatrick, K. (2001). Object recognition. In R. J. Cook (ed.), *Avian Visual Cognition*. Tufts University Psychology Department in cooperation with Comparative Cognition Press. (Cyberbook online at http://www.pigeon.psy.tufts.edu/avc/ .).

Klein, R. G. (1991). *The Human Career: Human Biological and Cultural Origins*. Chicago, IL: University of Chicago Press.

—— (2003). Whither the Neanderthals? *Science* 299, 1525–1527.

Klein, S. B., L. Cosmides, J. Tooby, and S. Chance (2002). Decisions and the evolution of memory: multiple systems, multiple functions. *Psychological Review* 109(2), 306–329.

Knauft, B. M. (1991). Violence and sociality in human evolution. *Current Anthropology* 32, 391–428.

Knight, C. (2002). Language and revolutionary consciousness. In A. Wray (ed.), *The Transition to Language*, pp. 138–160. Oxford: Oxford University Press.

—— (2006). The politics of early kinship. (Class notes, University of East London.)

—— M. Studdert-Kennedy, and J. R. Hurford (2000). Language: a Darwinian adaptation? In C. Knight, M. Studdert-Kennedy, and J. R. Hurford (eds.), *The Evolutionary Emergence of Language: Social Function and the Origins of Linguistic Form*, pp. 1–15. Cambridge: Cambridge University Press.

Kobayashi, H. and S. Kohshima (1997). Morphological uniqueness of human eyes and its adaptive meaning. *Nature* 387, 767–768.

Konishi, M. (1965a). Effects of deafening on song development in American robins and black-headed grosbeaks. *Zeitschrift für Tierpsychologie* 35, 352–380.

—— (1965b). The role of auditory feedback in the control of vocalization in the white-crowned sparrow. *Zeitschrift für Tierpsychologie* 22, 770–783.

—— (1985). Birdsong: from behavior to neuron. *Annual Review of Neuroscience* 8, 125–170.

Kosfeld, M., M. Heinrichs, P. J. Zak, U. Fischbacher, and E. Fehr (2005). Oxytocin increases trust in humans. *Nature* 435, 673–676. (Note corrigendum to a figure appended to the online version of this paper, at http://www.iew.unizh.ch/home/kosfeld/papers/ottrust_nature_.corr.pdf.)

Kosslyn, S. M., (1994). *Image and Brain*. Cambridge, MA: MIT Press.

—— W. L. Thompson, I. J. Kim, and N. M. Alpert (1995). Topographical representations of mental images in primary visual cortex. *Nature* 378, 496–498.

Kotchoubey, B. (2005). Pragmatics, prosody, and evolution: language is more than a symbolic system. *Behavioural and Brain Sciences* 28, 136–137.

Krebs, J. R. and R. Dawkins (1984). Animal signals: mind-reading and manipulation. In J. R. Krebs and N. B. Davies (eds.), *Behavioural Ecology: An Evolutionary Approach*. Oxford: Blackwell Scientific Publications.

Kripke, S. (1980). *Naming and Necessity*. Oxford: Blackwell.

Kuczaj, S. A. and J. L. Hendry (2003). Does language help animals think? In D. Gentner and S. Goldin-Meadow (eds.), *Language in Mind: Advances in the Study of Language and Thought*, pp. 237–275. Cambridge, MA: MIT Press.

Kudo, H. and R. I. M. Dunbar (2001). Neocortex size and social network size in primates. *Animal Behaviour* 62(4), 711–722.

Kuhl, P. K. (1991). Human adults and human infants show a 'perceptual magnet effect' for the prototypes of speech categories, monkeys do not. *Perception and Psychophysics* 50(2), 93–107.

Kyriacou, C. P. and J. C. Hall (1986). Interspecific genetic control of courtship song production and reception in Drosophila. *Science* 232, 494–497.

Lachmann, M., S. Számadó, and C. T. Bergstrom (2002). Cost and conflict in animal signals and human language. *Proceedings of the National Academy of Sciences of the United States of America* 98(23), 13189–13194.

Laeng, B., S. M. Koslyn, V. S. Caviness, and J. Bates (1999). Can deficits in spatial indexing contribute to simultanagnosia? *Cognitive Neuropsychology* 16(2), 81–114.

Laland, K., J. Odling-Smee, and M. W. Feldman (2000). Niche construction, biological evolution, and cultural change. *Behavioral and Brain Sciences* 23(1), 131–175.

Langer, S. K. (1967). *An Introduction to Symbolic Logic* (3rd rev. edn.). New York: Dover Publications.

Leavens, D. A. (2004). Manual deixis in apes and humans. *Interaction Studies* 5(3), 387–408.

——and W. D. Hopkins (1998). Intentional communication by chimpanzees: a cross-sectional study of the use of referential gestures. *Developmental Psychology* 34, 813–822.

——and W. D. Hopkins (1999). The whole-hand point: the structure and function of pointing from a comparative perspective. *Journal of Comparative Psychology* 113(4), 417–425.

——and W. D. Hopkins (2005). Multimodal concomitants of manual gesture by chimpanzees (*Pan troglodytes*): influence of food size and distance. *Gesture* 5(1/2), 75–90.

——and W. D. Hopkins and K. A. Bard (1996). Indexical and referential pointing in chimpanzees (*Pan troglodytes*). *Journal of Comparative Psychology* 110(4), 346–353.

——W. D. Hopkins and K. A. Bard (2005). Understanding the point of chimpanzee pointing: epigenesis and ecological validity. *Current Directions in Psychological Science* 14(4), 185–189.

——W. D. Hopkins and R. K. Thomas (2004). Referential communication by chimpanzees (*Pan troglodytes*). *Journal of Comparative Psychology* 118, 48–57.

——A. B. Hostetter, M. J. Wesley, and W. D. Hopkins (2004). Tactical use of unimodal and bimodal communication by chimpanzees, *Pan troglodytes*. *Animal Behaviour* 67, 467–476.

——J. L. Russell, and W. D. Hopkins (2005). Intentionality as measured in the persistence and elaboration of communication by chimpanzees. *Child Development* 76(1), 291–306.

Leibniz, G. (1714). *Monadologie*. Unpub. in Leibniz's lifetime. See Rescher (1991).

Lempers, J. D., E. R. Flavell, and J. H. Flavell (1977). The development in very young children of tacit knowledge concerning visual perception. *Genetic Psychology Monographs* 95, 3–53.

Lewis, D. (1969). *Convention: A Philosophical Study*. Cambridge, MA: Harvard University Press.

Lewontin, R. C. (1983). Gene, organism, and environment. In D. S. Bendall (ed.), *Evolution from Molecules to Men*. Cambridge: Cambridge University Press.

Liebal, K., S. Pika, J. Call, and M. Tomasello (2004). To move or not to move: how apes adjust to the attentional states of others. *Interaction Studies* 5, 199–219.

Lieberman, P. (1984). *The Biology and Evolution of Language*. Cambridge, MA: Harvard University Press.

Lightfoot, D. (1991). Subjacency and sex. *Language and Communication* 11(1/2), 67–69.

Lim, M. M., Z. Wang, D. E. Olazabal, X. Ren, E. F. Terwilliger, and L. J. Young (2004). Enhanced partner preference in a promiscuous species by manipulating the expression of a single gene. *Nature* 429, 754–757.

Lin, N. and C. D. Michener (1972). Evolution of sociality in insects. *Quarterly Review of Biology* 47, 131–159.

Link, G. (1997). *Algebraic Semantics in Language and Philosophy*. Stanford, CA: Center for Study of Language and Information.

Linnankoski, I., M.-L. Laakso, R. Aulanko, and L. Leinonen (1994). Recognition of emotions in macaque vocalizations by children and adults. *Language and Communication* 14, 183–192.

Lock, A. (1978). The emergence of language. In A. Lock (ed.), *Action, Gesture, and Symbol: the Emergence of Language*, pp. 3–18. New York: Academic Press.

Locke, J. L. and B. Bogin (2006). Language and life history: a new perspective int the development and evolution of human language. *Behavioral and Brain Sciences* 29, 259–280.

Lohmann, H. and M. Tomasello (2003). The role of language in the development of false belief understanding: a training study. *Child Development* 74(4), 1130–1144.

Lombardo, M. (1985). Mutual restraint in tree swallows: a test of the Tit for Tat model of reciprocity. *Science* 227, 1363–1365.

Lorenz, K. (1937). The companion in the bird's world. *Auk* 54, 245–273.

——(1939). Vergleichende verhaltensforschung. *Zoologischer Anzeiger, Supplementband* 12, 69–102. (Journal also referenced as *Verhandlungen der deutschen Zoologischen Gesellschaft* 1939).

Louie, K. and M. A. Wilson (2001). Temporally structured replay of awake hippocampal ensemble activity during rapid eye movement sleep. *Neuron* 29(1), 145–156.

Luria, A. R. (1959). Disorders of 'simultaneous perception' in a case of bilateral occipitoparietal brain injury. *Brain* 83, 437–449.

—— E. N. Pravdina-Vinarskaya, and A. L. Yarbuss (1963). Disorders of ocular movement in a case of simultanagnosia. *Brain* 86, 219–228.

Lyons, J. (1975). Deixis as the source of reference. In E. Keenan (ed.), *Formal Semantics of Natural Language*, pp. 61–83. Cambridge: Cambridge University Press.

——(1977). *Semantics* (2 vols.). Cambridge: Cambridge University Press.

MacDonald, S. E. (1994). Gorilla's (*Gorilla gorilla gorilla*) spatial memory in a foraging task. *Journal of Comparative Psychology* 108, 107–113.

MacNeilage, P. F. and B. L. Davis (2005). The frame/content theory of evolution of speech: a comparison with a gestural-origins alternative. *Interaction Studies* 6(2), 173–199.

Maestripieri, D. (1999). Primate social organization, gestural repertoire size, and communication dynamics: a comparative study of macaques. In B. J. King (ed.), *The Origins of Language. What Nonhuman Primates Can Tell Us*, pp. 55–77. Santa Fe, NM: School of American Research Press.

——(2005). Gestural communication in three species of macaques (*Macaca mulatta, M. nemestrina, M. arctoides*): use of signals in relation to dominance and social context. *Gesture* 5(1/2), 57–73.

Magnan, A. (1934). *Le Vol des insectes*. Paris: Hermann et Compagnie.

Maienborn, C. (2005). On the limits of the Davidsonian approach: the case of copula sentences. *Theoretical Linguistics* 31(3), 275–316.

Mandler, J. M. (1992). How to build a baby II: conceptual primitives. *Psychological Review* 99, 587–604.

——(1994). Precursors of linguistic knowledge. *Philosophical Transactions of the Royal Society*, Series B 346, 1315.

Marcel, A. J. (1998). Blindsight and shape perception: deficit of visual consciousness or of visual function? *Brain* 121, 1565–1588.

Margulis, L. and D. Sagan (1991). *Mystery Dance: On the Evolution of Human Sexuality*. New York: Summit Books.

Marler, P., C. S. Evans, and M. D. Hauser (1992). Animal signals? Reference, motivation or both? In H. Papoucek, U. Jürgens, and M. Papoucek (eds.), *Nonverbal Vocal Communication: Comparative and Developmental Approaches*, pp. 66–86. Cambridge: Cambridge University Press.

Marras, A. (1995). Behaviorism. In R. Audi (ed.), *Cambridge Dictionary of Philosophy*, pp. 67–68. Cambridge: Cambridge University Press.

Martin, A., C. L. Wiggs, L. G. Ungerleider, and J. V. Haxby (1996). Neural correlates of category-specific knowledge. *Nature* 379, 649–652.

Maynard Smith, J. and E. Szathmáry (1995). *The Major Transitions in Evolution*. Oxford: Oxford University Press.

McAndrew, F. T. (2002). New evolutionary perspectives on altruism: multilevel-selection and costly-signaling theories. *Current Directions in Psychological Science* 11(2), 79–82.

—— and M. A. Milenkovic (2002). Of tabloids and family secrets: the evolutionary psychology of gossip. *Journal of Applied Psychology* 32, 1–20.

McComb, K. and S. Semple (2005). Coevolution of vocal communication and sociality in primates. *Biology Letters doi:10.1098/rsbl.2005.0366*. (Published online by the Royal Society.)

McGonigle, B. O. and M. Chalmers (1977). Are monkeys logical? *Nature* 267, 694–696.

McGrew, W. C. (1975). Patterns of plant food sharing by wild chimpanzees. In S. Kondo, M. Kawai, and A. Ehara (eds.), *Contemporary Primatology, Proceedings of the 5th International Congress of Primatology, Nagoya, 1974*, pp. 304–309. Basel: Karger.

McHenry, H. (1996). Sexual dimorphism in fossil hominids and its socioecological implications. In J. Steele and S. Skennan (eds.), *The Archaeology of Human Ancestry: Power, Sex, and Tradition*, pp. 91–109. London: Routledge & Kegan Paul.

McKinley, J. and T. D. Sambrook (2000). Use of human-given cues by domestic dogs (*Canis familiaris*) and horses (*Equus caballus*). *Animal Cognition* 3, 13–22.

McMasters, J. (1989). The flight of the bumblebee and related myths of entomological engineering. *American Scientist* 77, 164–168.

McMullen, P. A., J. D. Fisk, S. J. Phillips, and W. J. Maloney (2000). Apperceptive agnosia and face recognition. *Neurocase* 6, 403–414.

Meacham, J. A. and J. Singer (1977). Incentive effects in prospective remembering. *Journal of Psychology* 97, 191–197.

Mecklinger, A., C. Gruenewald, M. Besson, M.-N. Magnie, and D. Y. V. Cramon (2002). Separable neuronal circuitries for manipulable and non-manipulable objects in working memory. *Cerebral Cortex* 12(11), 1115–1123.

Melis, A. P., B. Hare, and M. Tomasello (2006a). Chimpanzees recruit the best collaborators. *Science* 311, 1297–1300.

—— B. Hare, and M. Tomasello (2006b). Engineering cooperation in chimpanzees: tolerance constraints on cooperation. *Animal Behaviour* 72(2), 275–286.

Meltzoff, A. (1988). Infant imitation after a one-week delay: long-term memory for novel acts and multiple stimuli. *Developmental Psychology* 24, 470–476.

——M. K. Moore (1977). Imitation of facial and manual gestures by human neonates *Science* 198, 75–78.

——M. K. Moore (1983). Newborn infants imitate adult facial gestures. *Child Development* 54, 702–709.

Menzel, C. (2005). Progress in the study of chimpanzee recall and episodic memory. In H. S. Terrace and J. Metcalfe (eds.), *The Missing Link in Cognition: Origins of Self-Reflective Consciousness*, pp. 188–224. Oxford: Oxford University Press.

Menzel, E. (1974). A group of young chimpanzees in a one-acre field. In A. M. Schreier and F. Stollnitz (eds.), *Behavior of Non-human Primates*, pp. 83–153. New York: Academic Press.

Miklosi, A., E. Kubinyi, J. Topal, M. Gacsi, Z. Viranyi, and V. Csanyi (2003). A simple reason for a big difference: wolves do not look back at humans, but dogs do. *Current Biology* 13, 763–766.

——R. Polgardi, J. Topal, and V. Csanyi (1998). Use of experimenter-given cues in dogs. *Animal Cognition* 1, 113–121.

Miles, H. L. (1990). The cognitive foundations for reference in a signing orangutan. In S. T. Parker and K. R. Gibson (eds.), *'Language' and Intelligence in Monkeys and Apes: Comparative Developmental Perspectives*, pp. 511–539. Cambridge: Cambridge University Press.

Milinski, M. (1987). Tit for Tat and the evolution of cooperation in sticklebacks. *Nature* 325, 433–435.

—— K. Külling, and R. Kettler (1990). Tit for Tat: sticklebacks (*Gasterosteus aculeatus*) 'trusting' a cooperating partner. *Behavioral Ecology* 1, 7–11.

Mill, J. S. (1843). *A System of Logic, Ratiocinative and Inductive, being a connected view of the principles of evidence and the methods of scientific investigation*. London: J. W. Parker and Son.

Miller, B. (2002). Existence. In E. N. Zalta (ed.), *The Stanford Encyclopedia of Philosophy, Summer 2002 edition*.

Miller, G. (2000a). Evolution of human music through sexual selection. In N. L. Wallin, B. Merker, and S. Brown (eds.), *The Origins of Music*, pp. 329–360. Cambridge, MA: MIT Press.

—— (2000b). *The Mating Mind: How Sexual Choice Shaped the Evolution of Human Nature*. London: William Heinemann.

Miller, G. A. (1956). The magical number seven, plus or minus two: some limits on our capacity for processing information. *Psychological Review* 63, 81–97.

Millikan, R. G. (1987). *Language, Thought, and Other Biological Categories: New Foundations for Realism*. Cambridge, MA: MIT Press.

—— (1996). Pushmi-pullyu representations. In J. Tomberlin (ed.), *Philosophical Perspectives*, Vol. 9, pp. 185–200. Atascadero, CA: Ridgeview. Repr. in L. May and M. Friendman (eds.), *Mind and Morals*, pp. 145–161. Cambridge, MA: MIT Press.

—— (2004). On reading signs: some differences between us and the others. In D. K. Oller and U. Griebel (eds.), *Evolution of Communication Systems*, pp. 15–29. Cambridge, MA: MIT Press.

Milner, A. D. (1998). Streams and consciousness: visual awareness and the brain. *Trends in Cognitive Sciences* 2(1), 25–30.

—— and M. A. Goodale (1995). *The Visual Brain in Action*. Oxford: Oxford University Press.

Minsky, M. (1991). Logical versus analogical or symbolic versus connectionist or neat versus scruffy. *AI Magazine* 12(2), 34–51.

Mitani, J. C. and P. Marler (1989). A phonological analysis of male gibbon singing behavior. *Behaviour* 109, 20–45.

—— D. A. Merriwether, and C. Zhang (2000). Male affiliation, cooperation and kinship in wild chimpanzees. *Animal Behaviour* 59, 885–893.

Mitchell, R. W. and J. R. Anderson (1997). Pointing, withholding information, and deception in capuchin monkeys (*Cebus apella*). *Journal of Comparative Psychology* III, 351–361.

Mithen, S. (2005). *The Singing Neanderthals: The Origins of Music, Language, Mind, and Body*. London: Weidenfeld and Nicolson.

Montague, R. (1970). English as a formal language. In B. Visentini (ed.), *Linguaggi nella Società e nella Tecnica*, pp. 189–223. Milan: Edizioni di Comunità.

Moore, J. (1984). The evolution of reciprocal sharing. *Ethology and Sociology* 5, 5–14.

—— (2004). The history of human food transfers: Tinbergen's other question. *Behavioral and Brain Sciences* 27, 566–567.

Moriceau, S. and R. M. Sullivan (2005). Neurobiology of infant attachment. *Developmental Psychobiology* 47(3), 230–242.

Moss, S. (2005). Birdwatch. *Guardian*, 19th September 2005, 31.

Mountjoy, D. J. and R. E. Lemon (1996). Female choice for complex song in the European starling: a field experiment. *Behavioral Ecology and Sociobiology* 38(1), 65–71.

Mulcahy, N. J. and J. Call (2006). Apes save tools for future use. *Science* 312, 1038–1040.

Mumford, S. (1996). Virtus dormitiva, ha, ha, ha. *The Philosopher* 84(2), 12–15.

Munakata, Y., L. Santos, E. S. Spelke, M. D. Hauser, and R. C. O'Reilly (2001). Visual representation in the wild: how rhesus monkeys parse objects. *Journal of Cognitive Neuroscience* 13(1), 44–58.

Munn, C. A. (1986a). Birds that 'cry wolf'. *Nature* 319, 143–145.

——(1986b). The deceptive use of alarm calls by sentinel species in mixed species flocks of neotropical birds. In R. W. Mitchell and N. S. Thompson (eds.), *Deception: Perspectives on Human and Nonhuman Deceit*, pp. 169–175. Albany, NY: State University of New York Press.

Myowa-Yamakoshi, M., M. Tomonaga, M. Tanaka, and T. Matsuzawa (2004). Imitation in neonatal chimpanzees (*Pan troglodytes*). *Developmental Science* 7(4), 437–442.

Nakayama, K. and G. H. Silverman (1986). Serial and parallel processing of visual feature conjunctions. *Nature* 320, 264–265.

Navon, D. (1977). Forest before the trees: the precedence of global features in visual perception. *Cognitive Psychology* 9, 353–383.

Neiworth, J., E. Steinmark, B. Basile, R. Wonders, F. Steely, and C. DeHart (2003). A test of object permanence in a new world monkey species, cotton top tamarins (*Saguinus oedipus*). *Animal Cognition* 6, 27–37.

Nettle, D. and R. I. M. Dunbar (1997). Social markers and the evolution of reciprocal exchange. *Current Anthropology* 38, 93–99.

Nishida, T. (1970). Social relationships and relationships among wild chimpanzees of the Mahale mountains. *Journal of Human Evolution* 2, 357–370.

——T. Hasegawa, H. Hayaki, Y. Takahata, and S. Uehara (1992). Meat-sharing as a coalition strategy by an alpha male chimpanzee? In T. Nishida, W. C. McGrew, P. Marler, M. Pickford, and F. B. M. de Waal (eds.), *Topics in Primatology*, pp. 159–174. Tokyo: University of Tokyo Press.

Noë, A. (2004). *Action in Perception*. Cambridge, MA: MIT Press.

Nowak, M. and K. Sigmund (1993). A strategy of win–stay, lose–shift that outperforms tit-for-tat in the Prisoner's Dilemma game. *Nature* 364, 56–58.

Nyberg, L., R. Habib, E. Tulving, R. Cabeza, S. Houle, J. Persson, and A. R. McIntosh (2000). Large scale neurocognitive networks underlying episodic memory. *Journal of Cognitive Neuroscience* 12, 163–173.

O'Connell, S. M. and G. Cowlishaw (1994). Infanticide avoidance, sperm competition and mate choice: the function of copulation calls in female baboons. *Animal Behaviour* 48, 687–694.

Odling-Smee, F. J., K. N. Laland, and M. W. Feldman (1996). Niche construction. *American Naturalist* 147(4), 641–648.

Oliphant, M. (1997). *Formal Approaches to Innate and Learned Communication: Laying the Foundation for Language*. Ph.D. thesis, University of California at San Diego.

——(1999). The learning barrier: moving from innate to learned systems of communication. *Adaptive Behavior* 7(3/4), 371–384.

O'Riordan, C. (2000). A *forgiving* strategy for the Iterated Prisoner's Dilemma. *Journal of Artificial Societies and Social Simulation* 3(4). (Online journal.)

Packer, C. and A. E. Pusey (1983). Adaptations of female lions to infanticide by incoming males. *American Naturalist* 121(5), 716–728.

Palameta, B. and W. M. Brown (1999). Human cooperation is more than by-product mutualism. *Animal Behaviour* 57, F1–F3.

Palmer, C. T. (1991). Kin-selection, reciprocal altruism and information sharing among Maine lobstermen. *Ethology and Sociobiology* 12, 221–235.

Parnell, R. J. and H. M. Buchanan-Smith (2001). An unusual social display by gorillas. *Nature* 412, 293–294.

Parsons, T. (1990). *Events in the Semantics of English: A Study in Subatomic Semantics.* Cambridge, MA: MIT Press.

——(2000). Underlying states and time travel. In J. Higginbotham, F. Panesi, and A. C. Varzi (eds.), *Speaking of Events*, pp. 81–93. Oxford: Oxford University Press.

Peirce, C. S. (1897/1955). Logic as semiotic: the theory of signs. In J. Buchler (ed.), *The Philosophical Writings of Peirce*, pp. 98–119. New York: Dover Books.

Pelamatti, G., M.Pascotto, and C. Semenza (2003). Verbal free recall in high altitude: proper names vs common names. *Cortex* 39(1), 97–103.

Pendlebury, M. (1990). Why proper names are rigid designators. *Philosophy and Phenomenological Research* 50(3), 519–536.

Penton-Voak, I. S. and D. I. Perrett (2000). Female preference for male faces changes cyclically—further evidence. *Evolution and Human Behavior* 21(1), 39–48.

——D. I. Perrett, D. L. Castles, T. Kobayashi, D. M. Burt, L. K. Murray, and R. Minamisawa (1999). Female preference for male faces changes cyclically. *Nature* 399, 741–742.

Pepper, J. W. (2000). Relatedness in trait group models of social evolution. *Journal of Theoretical Biology* 206, 355–368.

Pepperberg, I. M. (2000). *The Alex Studies: Cognitive and Communicative Abilities of Grey Parrots.* Cambridge, MA: Harvard University Press.

——M. Willner, and L. Gravits (1997). Development of Piagetian object permanence in a grey parrot (*Psittacus erithacus*). *Journal of Comparative Psychology* III, 63–75.

Pietroski, P. M. (2002). Function and concatenation. In G. Preyer and G. Peter (eds.), *Logical Form and Language.* Oxford: Oxford University Press.

——(2005). *Events and Semantic Architecture.* Oxford: Oxford University Press.

Pika, S., K. Liebal, J. Call, and M. Tomasello (2005). The gestural communication of apes. *Gesture* 5(1/2), 41–56.

——K. Liebal, and M. Tomasello (2003). Gestural communication in young gorillas: gestural repertoire, learning, and use. *American Journal of Primatology* 60, 95–111.

——and J. Mitani (2006). Referential gestural communication in wild chimpanzees (*Pan troglodytes*). *Current Biology* 16(6), 191–192.

Pinker, S. (1997). *How the Mind Works.* New York: Penguin.

——(2003). Language as an adaptation to the cognitive niche. In M. Christiansen and S. Kirby (eds.), *Language Evolution*, pp. 16–37. Oxford: Oxford University Press.

——and P. Bloom (1990). Natural language and natural selection. *Behavioral and Brain Sciences* 13, 707–784.

Plooij, F. X. (1978). Some basic traits of language in wild chimpanzees? In A. Lock (ed.), *Action, Gesture and Symbol*, pp. 111–131. New York: Academic Press.

Pöppel, E. (1997). A hierarchical model of temporal perception. *Trends in Cognitive Sciences* 1(2), 56–61.

——and M. Wittmann (1999). Time in the mind. In R. A. Wilson and F. Keil (eds.), *The MIT Encyclopedia of the Cognitive Sciences*, pp. 841–843. Cambridge, MA: MIT Press.

Posner, M. I., J. A. Walker, F. J. Friedrich, and R. Rafal (1984). Effects of parietal injury on covert orienting of visual attention. *Journal of Neuroscience* 4, 1863–1874.

Poulshock, J. W. (2006). *Language and Morality: Evolution, Altruism, and Linguistic Moral Mechanisms.* Ph.D. thesis, University of Edinburgh.

Povinelli, D. J. and J. Barth (2005). Reinterpreting behavior: a human specialization? *Behavioral and Brain Sciences* 28, 712–713.

——J. M. Bering, and S. Giambrone (2003). Chimpanzees' 'pointing': another error of the argument by analogy? In S. Kita (ed.), *Pointing: Where Language, Culture, and Cognition Meet*, pp. 35–68. Mahwah, NJ: Lawrence Erlbaum Associates.

——T. J. Eddy (1996). What young chimpanzees know about seeing. *Monographs of the Society for Research in Child Development* 61(2, Serial No. 247).

——and T. J. Eddy (1997). Specificity of gaze-following in young chimpanzees. *British Journal of Developmental Psychology* 15, 213–222.

——and J. Vonk (2003). Chimpanzee minds: suspiciously human? *Trends in Cognitive Sciences* 7, 157–160.

——and J. Vonk (2004). We don't need a microscope to explore the chimpanzee's mind. *Mind and Language*, 19(1), 1–28.

Power, C. (1998). Old wives' tales: the gossip hypothesis and the reliability of cheap signals. In J. R. Hurford, M. Studdert-Kennedy, and C. Knight (eds.), *Approaches to the Evolution of Language*, pp. 111–129. Cambridge: Cambridge University Press.

Premack, D. (1983). Animal cognition. *Annual Review of Psychology* 34, 351–362.

——and A. J. Premack (1983). *The Mind of an Ape*. Hillsdale, NJ: Erlbaum.

——and G. Woodruff (1978). Does the chimpanzee have a theory of mind? *Behavioral and Brain Sciences* 1(4), 515–526.

Price, J. J. and S. M. Lanyon (2004). Patterns of song evolution and sexual selection in the oropendolas and caciques. *Behavioral Ecology* 15(3), 485–497.

Prinz, J. (2006). Putting the brakes on Enactive Perception. *Psyche: an interdisciplinary journal of research on consciousness* 12(1). (Refereed online journal.)

Proverbio, A. M., S. Lilli, C. Semenza, and A. Zani (2001). ERP indexes of functional differences in brain activation during proper and common names retrieval. *Neuropsychologia* 39(8), 815–827.

Provine, R. R. (2005). Illusions of intentionality, shared and unshared. *Behavioral and Brain Sciences* 28, 713–714.

Pusey, A. E. and C. Packer (1997). The ecology of relationships. In J. R. Krebs and N. B. Davies (eds.), *Behavioural Ecology: An Evolutionary Approach*, (4th edn.) pp. 254–283. Oxford: Blackwell Scientific.

Pylyshyn, Z. W. (1989). The role of location indexes in spatial perception: a sketch of the FINST spatial-index model. *Cognition* 32, 65–97.

——(2000). Situating vision in the world. *Trends in Cognitive Sciences* 4(5), 197–207.

——and R. Storm (1988). Tracking multiple independent targets: evidence for a parallel tracking mechanism. *Spatial Vision* 3(3), 179–197.

Quine, W. V. O. (1951). Two dogmas of empiricism. *Philosophical Review* 60, 20–43.

——(1960). *Word and Object*. Cambridge, MA: MIT Press.

Radcliffe-Brown, A. R. (1931). *The Social Organization of Australian Tribes*. Oceania Monographs I. Melbourne: Macmillan.

Ramachandran, V. S. and S. Blakeslee (1998). *Phantoms in the Brain: Human Nature and the Architecture of the Mind*. London: Fourth Estate.

——and E. M. Hubbard (2001). Synaesthesia – a window into perception, thought and language. *Journal of Consciousness Studies* 8(12), 3–34.

Reboreda, J. C., N. S. Clayton, and A. Kacelnik (1996). Species and sex differences in hippocampus size in parasitic and non-parasitic cowbirds. *NeuroReport* 7(2), 505–508.

Reimer, M. (2002). Ordinary proper names. In G. Preyer and G. Peter (eds.), *Logical Form and Language*, pp. 444–466. Oxford: Oxford University Press.

Rescher, N. (1991). *G. W. Leibniz's Monadology*. Pittsburgh, PA: University of Pittsburgh Press.

Ricciardelli, P., G. Baylis, and J. Driver (2000). The positive and negative of human expertise in gaze perception. *Cognition* 77, B1–B14.

Ritchie, G. R. S. and S. Kirby (2007). A possible role for selective masking in the evolution of complex, learned communication systems. In C. Lyon, C. Nehaniv, and A. Cangelosi (eds.), *The Emergence and Evolution of Linguistic Communication*, pp. 387–402. London: Springer.

Rizzo, M. and R. Hurtig (1987). Looking but not seeing: attention, perception, and eye movements in simultanagnosia. *Neurology* 37, 1642–1648.

Rizzolatti, G., L. Fadiga, V. Gallese, and L. Fogassi (1996). Premotor cortex and the recognition of motor actions. *Cognitive Brain Research* 3(2), 131–141.

Roberts, G. (1997). Testing mutualism: a commentary on Clements & Stephens. *Animal Behaviour* 53, 1361–1362.

Robinson, J. G. (1982). Vocal systems regulating within-group spacing. In C. T. Snowdon, C. H. Brown, and M. R. Petersen (eds.), *Primate Communication*, pp. 94–116. Cambridge: Cambridge University Press.

Ross, E. D. (1981). The aprosodias. Functional-anatomic organization of the affective components of language in the right hemisphere. *Archives of Neurology* 38, 561–569.

Rossi, L. N., G. Candini, G. Scarlatti, G. Rossi, E. Prina, and S. Alberti (1987). Autosomal dominant microcephaly without mental retardation. *American Journal of Diseases of Children* 141, 655–659.

Roth, A. E., V. Prasnikar, M. Okuno-Fujiwara, and S. Zamir (1991). Bargaining and market behavior in Jerusalem, Ljubljana, Pittsburgh, and Tokyo: an experimental study. *American Economic Review* 81, 1068–1095.

Rouquier, S., A. Blancher, and D. Giorgi (2000). The olfactory receptor gene repertoire in primates and mouse: evidence for reduction of the functional fraction in primates. *Neurobiology* 97(6), 2870–2874.

Rousseau, J.-J. (1755). *Discours sur l'origine et les fondements de l'inégalité parmi les hommes*. (Repr. Paris: Editions Sociales 1983.)

——(1781). Essai sur l'origine des langues, où il est parlé de la mélodie, et de l'imitation musicale. In P. A. du Peyrou (ed.), *Oeuvres posthumes de J. J. Rousseau, tome III*, pp. 211–327. Geneva.

Rumbaugh, D. M. and J. Pate (1984a). The evolution of cognition in primates: a comparative perspective. In H. Roitblat, T. G. Bever, and H. S. Terrace (eds.), *Animal Cognition*, pp. 569–587. Hillsdale, NJ: Lawrence Erlbaum Associates.

——J. Pate (1984b). Primates' learning by levels. In G. Greenberg and E. Tobach (eds.), *Behavioral Evolution and Integrative Levels*, pp. 221–240. Hillsdale, NJ: Lawrence Erlbaum Associates.

Russell, B. (1905). On denoting. *Mind* 14, 479–493.

Russell, J. L., S. Braccini, N. Buehler, M. J. Kachin, S. J. Schapiro, and W. D. Hopkins (2005). Chimpanzee (*Pan troglodytes*) intentional communication is not contingent upon food. *Animal Cognition* 8(4), 263–272.

Ryle, G. (1949). *The Concept of Mind*. London: Hutchinson.

Sanders, M. D., E. K. Warrington, J. Marshall, and L. Weiskrantz (1974). 'Blindsight': vision in a field defect. *Lancet* 20, 707–708.

Santos, L. R., M. D. Hauser, and E. S. Spelke (2001). Recognition and categorization of biologically significant objects by rhesus monkeys (*Macaca mulatta*): the domain of food. *Cognition* 82, 127–155.

——G. M. Sulkowski, G. M. Spaepen, and M. D. Hauser (2002). Object individuation using property/kind information in rhesus macaques (*Macaca mulatta*). *Cognition* 83, 241–264.

Sarris, V. (1990). Contextual effects in animal psychophysics: a comparative analysis of the chicken's perceptual relativity. *European Bulletin of Cognitive Psychology* 10, 475–489.

——(1994). Contextual effects in animal psychophysics: comparative perception. *Behavioral and Brain Sciences* 17, 763–764.

——(1998). Frame-of-reference effects in psychophysics: new experimental findings with baby chicks. *Psychologia (Greece)* 5(2), 95–102.

——(2000a). The bird's visual psychophysics: a perceptual-cognitive perspective. In *Proceedings of the 16th Annual Meeting of the International Society for Psychophysics*. Online at http://www.psychologie.uni-frankfurt.de/Abteil/sarris/pdf/pdf-sarris/Strasbourg.pdf.

——(2000b). Perception and judgment in psychophysics: an introduction into the frame-of-reference theories. In A. Schick, M. Meis, and C. Reckhardt (eds.), *Contributions to Psychological Acoustics*, pp. 36–62. Oldenburg, Germany: BIS.

——(2006). *Relational Psychophysics in Humans and Animals: A Comparative-Developmental Approach*. London: Psychology Press.

Sassaman, E. A. and A. S. Zartler (1982). Mental retardation and head growth abnormalities. *Journal of Pediatric Psychology* 7, 149–156.

Savage-Rumbaugh, E. S. (1980). Linguistically-mediated tool use and exchange by chimpanzees. In T. Sebeok and J. Sebeok (eds.), *Speaking of Apes*, pp. 353–383. New York: Plenum Press.

——(1986). *Ape Language: From Conditioned Response to Symbol*. New York: Columbia University Press.

——D. M. Rumbaugh, and S. Boysen (1978a). Linguistically-mediated tool use and exchange by chimpanzees (*Pan troglodytes*). *Behavioral and Brain Sciences* 4, 539–554.

——D. M. Rumbaugh, and S. Boysen (1978b). Symbolization, language and chimpanzees: a theoretical reevaluation based on initial language acquisition processes in four young *Pan troglodytes*. *Brain and Language* 6(3), 265–300.

——D. M. Rumbaugh, and K. McDonald (1985). Language learning in two species of apes. *Neuroscience and Biobehavioral Reviews* 9, 653–665.

——D. M. Rumbaugh, S. T. Smith, and J. Lawson (1980). Reference: the linguistic essential. *Science* 210, 922–925.

——S. G. Shankar, and T. J. Taylor (1998). *Apes, Language, and the Human Mind*. Oxford: Oxford University Press.

——B. J. Wilkerson, and R. Bakeman (1977). Spontaneous gestural communication among conspecifics in the pygmy chimpanzee (*Pan paniscus*). In G. H. Bourne (ed.), *Progress in Ape Research*, pp. 97–116. New York: Academic Press.

Sawaguchi, T. (1992). The size of the neocortex in relation to ecology and social structure in monkeys and apes. *Folia Primatologica* 58(3), 130–145.

Scerif, G., J. C. Gómez, and R. W. Byrne (2004). What do Diana monkeys know about the focus of attention of a conspecic? *Animal Behaviour* 68, 1239–1247.

Schacter, D. L. (1987). Implicit memory: history and current status. *Journal of Experimental Psychology: Learning, Memory, and Cognition* 13(3), 501–518.

Schank, R. C. (1982). *Dynamic Memory: A Theory of Reminding and Learning in Computers and People*. Cambridge: Cambridge University Press.

Schein, B. (2002). Events and the semantic content of thematic relations. In G. Preyer and G. Peter (eds.), *Logical Form and Language*, pp. 263–344. Oxford: Oxford University Press.

Scheumann, M. and J. Call (2004). The use of experimenter-given cues by South African fur seals (*Arctocephalus pusillus*). *Animal Cognition* 7(4), 224–230.

Schlottmann, A. and L. Surian (1999). Do 9-month-olds perceive causation-at-a-distance? *Perception* 28, 1105–1113.

Schuster, R. (2005). Why not chimpanzees, lions, and hyenas too? *Behavioral and Brain Sciences* 28, 716–717.

Schwartz, B. L. (2005). Do nonhuman primates have episodic memory? In H. S. Terrace and J. Metcalfe (eds.), *Progress in the Study of Chimpanzee Recall and Episodic Memory*, pp. 225–241. Oxford: Oxford University Press.

—— and S. Evans (2001). Episodic memory in primates. *American Journal of Primatology* 55, 71–85.

—— M. L. Hoffman, and S. Evans (2005). Episodic-like memory in a gorilla: a review and new findings. *Learning and Motivation* 36, 226–244.

—— C. A. Meissner, M. L. Hoffman, S. Evans, and L. D. Frazier (2004). Event memory and misinformation effects in a gorilla (*Gorilla gorilla gorilla*). *Animal Cognition* 7, 93–100.

Searle, J. R. (1969). *Speech Acts: An Essay in the Philosophy of Language*. Cambridge: Cambridge University Press.

—— (1975). A taxonomy of illocutionary acts. In K. Gunderson (ed.), *Language, Mind, and Knowledge*. Minnesota Studies in the Philosophy of Science, Vol. VII, pp. 344–367. Minneapolis: University of Minnesota Press. (Repr. as 'A classification of illocutionary acts' in *Language and Society* 5, 1–23 1976.)

—— (1979). *Expression and Meaning: Studies in the Theory of Speech Acts*. Cambridge: Cambridge University Press.

Sears, C. R. and Z. W. Pylyshyn (2000). Multiple object tracking and attentional processing. *Canadian Journal of Experimental Psychology* 54(1), 1–14.

Seddon, N., J. A. Tobias, and A. Alvarez (2002). Vocal communication in the pale-winged trumpeter (*Psophia leucoptera*): repertoire, context and functional reference. *Behaviour* 139, 1331–1359.

Segal, G. (2001). Two theories of names. *Mind and Language* 16(5), 547–563.

Segerdahl, P., W. Fields, and S. Savage-Rumbaugh (2005). *Kanzi's Primal Language: The Cultural Initiation of Primates into Language*. Basingstoke: Palgrave Macmillan.

Sells, C. J. (1977). Microcephaly in a normal school population. *Pediatrics* 59, 262–265.

Semenza, C. (1997). Proper-name-specific aphasias. In H. Goodglass and A. Wingfield (eds.), *Anomia: Neuroanatomical and Cognitive Correlates*, pp. 115–134. San Diego, CA: Academic Press.

—— and M. Zettin (1989). Evidence from aphasia for the role of proper names as pure referring expressions. *Nature* 342, 678–679.

—— M. Zettin and F. Borgo (1998). Names and identification: an access problem. *Neurocase* 4, 45–53.

Semple, S., K. McComb, S. Alberts, and J. Altmann (2002). Information content of female copulation calls in yellow baboons. *American Journal of Primatology* 56, 43–56.

Senghas, A. (2005). Language emergence: clues from a new Bedouin Sign Language. *Current Biology* 15(12), R463–R465.

Seyfarth, R. M. and D. L. Cheney (1980). The ontogeny of vervet monkeys' alarm calling behavior: a preliminary report. *Zeitschrift für Tierpsychologie* 54, 37–56.

—— and D. L. Cheney (1982). How monkeys see the world: a review of recent research on East African vervet monkeys. In C. T. Snowdon, C. H. Brown, and M. R. Petersen (eds.), *Primate Communication*, pp. 239–252. Cambridge: Cambridge University Press.

—— and D. M. Cheney (2003). The structure of social knowledge in monkeys. In F. B. M. de Waal and P. L. Tyack (eds.), *Animal Social Complexity: Intelligence, Culture, and Individualized Societies*, pp. 207–229. Cambridge, MA: Harvard University Press.

Shannon, C. E. and W. Weaver (1963). *Mathematical Theory of Communication*. Champaign, IL: University of Illinois Press.

Shapiro, A. D., V. M. Janik, and P. J. B. Slater (2003). A gray seal's (*Halichoerus grypus*) responses to experimenter-given pointing and directional cues. *Journal of Comparative Psychology* 117, 355–362.

Shastri, L. (2001). A computational model of episodic memory formation in the hippocampal system. *Neurocomputing* 38–40, 889–897.

——(2002). Episodic memory and cortico-hippocampal interactions. *Trends in Cognitive Sciences* 6, 162–168.

Sherman, P. W. (1977). Nepotism and the evolution of alarm calls. *Science* 197, 1246–1253.

Sherry, D. F. and Schacter, D. L. (1987). The evolution of multiple memory systems. *Psychological Review* 94(4), 469–454.

Sherzer, J. (1973). Verbal and non-verbal deixis: the pointed lip gesture among the San Blas Cuna. *Language in Society* 2(1), 117–131.

——(1983). *Kuna Ways of Speaking: An Ethnographic Perspective*. Austin, TX: University of Texas Press.

——(1993). Pointed lips, thumbs up, and cheek puffs: some emblematic gestures in social interactional and ethnographic context. *SALSA* I, 197–212.

Shettleworth, S. J. (1998). *Cognition, Evolution, and Behavior*. Oxford: Oxford University Press.

——and J. E. Sutton (2006). Do animals know what they know? In S. Hurley and M. Nudds (eds.), *Rational Animals?*, pp. 235–246. Oxford: Oxford University Press.

Shields, J. (1991). Semantic-pragmatic disorder: a right hemisphere syndrome? *British Journal of Disorders of Communication* 26, 383–392.

Sidman, M. S., R. Rauzin, R. Lazar, S. Cunningham, W. Tailby, and P. Carrigan (1982). A search for symmetry in the conditional discriminations of rhesus monkeys, baboons, and children. *Journal of the Experimental Analysis of Behavior* 37, 23–44.

Silk, J. B., S. F. Brosnan, J. Vonk, J. Henrich, D. J. Povinelli, A. S. Richardson, S. P. Lambeth, J. Mascaro, and S. J. Schapiro (2005). Chimpanzees are indifferent to the welfare of unrelated group members. *Nature* 437, 1357–1359.

Simmons, L. W. (2004). Genotypic variation in calling song and female preferences of the field cricket *Teleogryllus oceanicus*. *Animal Behaviour* 68, 313–322.

Simons, D. J. and C. F. Chabris (1999). Gorillas in our midst: sustained international blindness for dynamic events. *Perception* 28, 1059–1074.

——and D. T. Levin (1997). Change blindness. *Trends in Cognitive Sciences* 1, 261–267.

Sinnott, J. M. and T. L. Williamson (1999). Can macaques perceive place of articulation from formant transition information? *Journal of the Acoustical Society of America* 106(2), 929–937.

Skoyles, J. R. and D. Sagan (2002). *Up from Dragons*. New York: McGraw-Hill.

Skyrms, B. (1996). *Evolution of the Social Contract*. Cambridge: Cambridge University Press.

Small, M. F. (1993). *Female Choices: Sexual Behavior of Female Primates*. Ithaca, NY: Cornell University Press.

Smith, C. (1995). Sleep states and memory processes. *Behavioural Brain Research* 69(1-2), 137–145.

Smith, J. D., J. Schull, J. Strote, K. McGee, R. Egnor, and L. Erb (1995). The uncertain response in the bottlenosed dolphin (*Tursiops truncatus*). *Journal of Experimental Psychology* 124, 391–408.

——W. E. Shields, and D. A. Washburn (1997). The uncertain response in humans and animals. *Cognition* 62, 75–97.

——W. E. Shields, and D. A. Washburn (2003a). The comparative psychology of uncertainty monitoring and metacognition. *Behavioral and Brain Sciences* 26, 317–339.

Smith, J. D., W. E. Shields, and D. A. Washburn (2003b). Inaugurating a new area of comparative cognition research in an immediate moment of difficulty or uncertainty. *Behavioral and Brain Sciences* 26, 358–369.

—— and D. A. Washburn (2005). Uncertainty monitoring and metacognition in animals. *Current Directions in Psychological Science* 14(1), 19–24.

Smith, K. (2004). The evolution of vocabulary. *Journal of Theoretical Biology* 228(1), 127–142.

Snowdon, C. T., C. H. Brown, and M. R. Petersen (1982). Social and environmental determinants of primate vocalizations. In C. T. Snowdon, C. H. Brown, and M. R. Petersen (eds.), *Primate Communication*, pp. 63–66. Cambridge: Cambridge University Press.

Soames, S. (2002). *Beyond Rigidity: The Unfinished Semantic Agenda of Naming and Necessity*. Oxford: Oxford University Press.

Sober, E. (1992). The evolution of altruism: correlation, cost, and benefit. *Biology and Philosophy* 7, 177–187.

—— (1993). *Philosophy of Biology*. Boulder, CO: Westview Press.

Sole, L. M., S. J. Shettleworth, and P. J. Bennett (2003). Uncertainty in pigeons. *Psychonomic Bulletin and Review* 10(3), 738–745.

Soproni, K., A. Miklosi, J. Topal, and V. Csanyi (2001). Comprehension of human communicative signs in pet dogs (*Canis familiaris*). *Journal of Comparative Psychology* 115, 122–126.

Sperber, D. and D. Wilson (1986). *Relevance: Communication and Cognition*. Oxford: Blackwell.

Stainton, R. (2004a). In defense of non-sentential assertion. In *Semantics vs. Pragmatics*. Oxford: Oxford University Press.

—— (2004b). The pragmatics of non-sentences. In L. Horn and G. Ward (eds.), *Handbook of Pragmatics*, pp. 266–287. Oxford: Blackwell.

Stamps, J. (1995). Motor learning and the value of familiar space. *The American Naturalist* 146(1), 41–58.

Stander, P. E. (1992). Cooperative hunting in lions: the role of the individual. *Behavioral Ecology and Sociobiology* 29, 445–454.

Stanley, J. and T. Williamson (2001). Knowing how. *Journal of Philosophy* 98, 411–444.

Steels, L. (1999). *The Talking Heads Experiment*, Vol. I: Words and Meanings. Antwerp: Laboratorium. Special pre-edition.

Stein, B. E., M. T. Wallace, and T. R. Stanford (1998). Single neuron electrophysiology. In W. Bechtel and G. Graham (eds.), *A Companion to Cognitive Science*, pp. 433–449. Oxford: Blackwell.

Stevenson, J. G., R. E. Hutchison, J. B. Hutchison, B. C. R. Bertram and W. H. Thorpe (1970). Individual recognition by auditory cues in the common tern (*Sterna hirundo*). *Nature* 226, 562–563.

Stidd, S. C. (2004). Proper names, predicative uses: an essay on logical form. *Language Sciences* 26, 173–215.

Strawson, P. F. (1959). *Individuals: An Essay in Descriptive Metaphysics*. London: Methuen.

Stromswold, K. (2001). The heritability of language: a review and metaanalysis of twin, adoption, and linkage studies. *Language* 77(4), 647–723.

Suddendorf, T. and J. Busby (2003a). Like it or not? The mental time travel debate: reply to Clayton *et al.*. *Trends in Cognitive Sciences* 7(10), 437–438.

—— and J. Busby (2003b). Mental time travel in animals? *Trends in Cognitive Sciences* 7(9), 391–396.

—— M. C. Corballis (1997). Mental time travel and the evolution of the human mind. *Genetic, Social, and General Psychology Monographs* 123, 133–167.

Symons, L. A., K. Lee, C. C. Cedrone, and M. Nishimura (2004). What are you looking at? Acuity for triadic eye gaze. *Journal of General Psychology* 131, 451–469.

Tager-Flusberg, H. and K. Sullivan (2000). A componential view of theory of mind: evidence from Williams syndrome. *Cognition* 76(1), 59–90.

Talmy, L. (2000). *Toward a Cognitive Semantics* (2 vols.). Cambridge, MA: MIT Press.

Tammero, L. F. and M. H. Dickinson (2002). Collision-avoidance and landing responses are mediated by separate pathways in the fruitfly, *Drosophila melanogaster*. *Journal of Experimental Biology* 205, 2785–2798.

Tanner, J. E. and R. W. Byrne (1999). The development of spontaneous gestural communication in a group of zoo-living lowland gorillas. In S. T. Parker, R. W. Mitchell, and H. L. Miles (eds.), *The Mentalities of Gorillas and Orangutans: Comparative Perspectives*, pp. 211–239. Cambridge: Cambridge University Press.

Tanner, N. M. (1981). *On Becoming Human*. Cambridge: Cambridge University Press.

Tavares, M. C. H. and C. Tomaz (2002). Working memory in capuchin monkeys (*Cebus apella*). *Behavioural Brain Research* 131, 131–137.

Thierry, B. (1990). Feedback loop between kinship and dominance: the macaque model. *Journal of Theoretical Biology* 145, 511–521.

Thompson, R., D. Oden, and S. Boysen (1997). Language-naive chimpanzees (*Pan troglodytes*) judge relations between relations in a conceptual matching-to-sample task. *Journal of Experimental Psychology: Animal Behavior Processes* 23(1), 31–43.

Thompson, R. K. R. and D. L. Oden (1998). Why monkeys and pigeons, unlike certain apes, cannot reason analogically. In *Advances in Analogy Research: Integration of Theory and Data from the Cognitive, Computational, and Neural Sciences*. Sofia: New Bulgarian University.

——and D. L. Oden (2000). Categorical perception and conceptual judgments by non-human primates: the paleological monkey and the analogical ape. *Cognitive Science: A Multidisciplinary Journal* 24(3), 363–396.

Thorndike, E. L. (1898). Animal intelligence: an experimental study of the associative processes in animals. *Psychological Review: Series of Monograph Supplements* 2(4), 1–109.

Thorpe, W. H. (1959). Talking birds and the mode of action of the vocal apparatus of birds. *Proceedings of the Zoological Society of London* 132, 441–455.

Tinbergen, N. (1948). Social releasers and the experimental method required for their study. *The Wilson Bulletin* 60(1), 6–51.

——(1952). 'Derived' activities: their causation, biological significance, origin and emancipation during evolution. *Quarterly Review of Biology* 27, 1–32.

——(1964). The evolution of signalling devices. In W. Etkin (ed.), *Social Behavior and Organization among Vertebrates*. Chicago: University of Chicago Press.

Todd, J. J. and R. Marois (2004). Capacity limit of visual short-term memory in human posterior parietal cortex. *Nature* 428, 751–754.

Tolman, E. (1927). A behaviorist's definition of consciousness. *Psychological Review* 34, 433–439.

——(1938). The determiners of behavior at a choice point. *Psychological Review* 45, 1–41.

Tomasello, M. (1990). Cultural transmission in the tool use and communicatory signaling of chimpanzees? In S. T. Parker and K. R. Gibson (eds.), *'Language' and Intelligence in Monkeys and Apes: Comparative Developmental Perspectives*, pp. 274–311. Cambridge: Cambridge University Press.

——(1993). It's imitation, not mimesis. *Behavioral and Brain Sciences* 16(4), 771–772.

——and J. Call (1997). *Primate Cognition*. Oxford: Oxford University Press.

Tomasello, M., J. Call, and A. Gluckman (1997). Comprehension of novel communicative signs by apes and human children. *Child Development* 68, 1067–1080.

—— J. Call, and B. Hare (1998). Five primate species follow the visual gaze of conspecifics. *Animal Behaviour* 55, 1063–1069.

—— J. Call, and B. Hare (2003). Chimpanzees understand psychological states: the question is which ones and to what extent. *Trends in Cognitive Sciences* 7, 153–156.

——M. Carpenter, J. Call, T. Behne, and H. Moll (2005). Understanding and sharing intentions: the origins of cultural cognition. *Behavioral and Brain Sciences* 28, 675–735.

—— D. Gust, and T. Forst (1989). A longitudinal investigation of gestural communication in young chimpanzees. *Primates* 30, 35–50.

Treichler, F. R., M. A. Raghanti, and D. N. van Tilburg (2003). Linking of serially ordered lists by macaque monkeys (macaca mulatta): list position influences. *Journal of Experimental Psychology: Animal Behavior Processes* 29(3), 211–221.

Treisman, A. (1985). Preattentive processing in vision. *Computer Vision Graphics, and Image Processing* 31(2), 156–177.

—— (2004). Psychological issues in selective attention. In M. Gazzaniga (ed.), *The Cognitive Neurosciences* III, pp. 529–544. Cambridge, MA: MIT Press.

—— and G. Gelade (1980). A feature integration theory of attention. *Cognitive Psychology* 12, 97–136.

—— and H. Schmidt (1982). Illusory conjunctions in the perception of objects. *Cognitive Psychology* 14, 107–141.

Trevathan, W. R. (1987). *Human Birth.* New York: Aldine de Gruyter.

Trick, L. M. and Z. W. Pylyshyn (1993). What enumeration studies tell us about spatial attention: evidence for limited capacity pre-attentive processing. *Journal of Experimental Psychology: Human Perception and Performance* 19(2), 331–351.

—— and Z. W. Pylyshyn (1994). Why are small and large numbers enumerated differently? A limited capacity pre-attentive stage in vision. *Psychological Review* 10, 1–23.

Trivers, R. L. (1971). The evolution of reciprocal altruism. *Quarterly Review of Biology* 46(4), 35–57.

Trut, L. N. (1999). Early canid domestication: the farm fox experiment. *American Scientist* 87, 160–169.

Tschudin, A., J. Call, R. Dunbar, G. Harris, and C. van der Elst (2001). Comprehension of signs by dolphins (*Tursiops truncatus*). *Journal of Comparative Psychology* 115, 100–105.

Tulving, E. (1983). *Elements of Episodic Memory.* London: Oxford University Press. 115, 100–105.

—— (1984). Précis of *Elements of Episodic Memory. Behavioral and Brain Sciences* 7, 223–268.

—— (1985). How many memory systems are there? *American Psychologist.* 40, 385–398.

—— (1999). Episodic vs semantic memory. In R. A. Wilson and F. C. Keil (eds.), *The MIT Encyclopedia of the Cognitive Sciences*, pp. 278–280. Cambridge, MA: MIT Press.

—— (2005). Episodic memory and autonoesis: uniquely human? In H. S. Terrace and J. Metcalfe (eds.), *The Missing Link in Cognition: Origins of Self-Reflective Consciousness*, pp. 3–56. Oxford: Oxford University Press.

—— and H. J. Markowitsch (1998). Episodic and declarative memory: role of the hippocampus. *Hippocampus* 8, 198–204.

Tyler, H. R. (1968). Abnormalities of perception with defective eye movements (balint's syndrome). *Cortex* 3, 154–171.

Tyler, L. K., H. E. Moss, M. R. Durrant-Peatfield, and J. P. Levy (2000). Conceptual structure and the structure of concepts: a distributed account of category-specific deficits. *Brain and Language* 75, 195–231.

Uexküll, J. von (1909). *Umwelt und Innenwelt der Tiere.* Berlin: Springer Verlag.

Ujhelyi, M. (1996). Is there any intermediate stage between animal communication and language? *Journal of Theoretical Biology* 180, 71–76.

——(1998). Long-call structure in apes as a possible precursor for language. In J. R. Hurford, M. Studdert-Kennedy, and C. Knight (eds.), *Approaches to the Evolution of Language: Social and Cognitive Bases*, pp. 177–189. Cambridge: Cambridge University Press.

Uvnas-Moberg, K. (1989). Oxytocin may mediate the benefits of positive social interaction and emotions. *Psychoneuroendocrinology* 23(8), 819–835.

Vallar, G. (1998). Spatial hemineglect in humans. *Trends in Cognitive Sciences* 2, 87–97.

Vallortigara, G., L. Regolin, and F. Marconato (2005). Visually inexperienced chicks exhibit spontaneous preference for biological motion patterns. *PLoS Biology* 3(7), e208. (Public Library of Science, online journal.)

VanRullen, R. and C. Koch (2003). Competition and selection during visual processing of natural scenes and objects. *Journal of Vision* 3(1), 75–85.

Vauclair, J. and J. Fagot (1993). Can a Saussurian ape be endowed with episodic memory only? *Behavioral and Brain Sciences* 16(4), 772–773.

Veá, J. J. and J. Sabater-Pi (1998). Spontaneous pointing behaviour in the wild pygmy chimpanzee (*Pan paniscus*). *Folia Primatologica* 69, 289–290.

Vehrencamp, S. L. and J. W. Bradbury (1984). Mating systems and ecology. In J. R. Krebs and N. B. Davies (eds.), *Behavioural Ecology: An Evolutionary Approach*, pp. 251–278. Oxford: Blackwell Scientific Publications.

Victor, M. and P. I. Yakovlev (1955). S. S. Korsakoff's psychic disorder in conjunction with peripheral neuritis; a translation of Korsakoff's original article with comments on the author and his contribution to clinical medicine. *Neurology* 5(6), 394–406.

Vogel, E. K. and M. G. Machizawa (2004). Neural activity predicts individual differences in visual working memory capacity. *Nature* 428, 748–751.

von Fersen, L., C. D. Wynne, J. D. Delius, and J. E. Staddon (1991). Transitive inference formation in pigeons. *Journal of Experimental Psychology: Animal Behavior Processes* 17(3), 334–341.

von Frisch, K. (1974). Decoding the language of the bee. *Science* 185, 663–668.

Vygotsky, L. S. (1988). Development of the higher mental functions. In K. Richardson and S. Sheldon (eds.), *Cognitive Development to Adolescence*, pp. 61–80. New York: Wiley.

Waiter, G. D., J. H. Williams, A. D. Murray, A. Gilchrist, D. I. Perrett, and A. Whiten (2004). A voxel-based investigation of brain structure in male adolescents with autistic spectrum disorder. *Neuroimage* 22(2), 619–625.

——J. H. Williams, A. D. Murray, A. Gilchrist, D. I. Perrett, and A. Whiten (2005). Structural white matter deficits in high-functioning individuals with autistic spectrum disorder: a voxel-based investigation. *Neuroimage* 24(2), 455–461.

Walker, S. (1983). *Animal Thought*. London: Routledge and Kegan Paul.

Wang, P. P., S. Doherty, S. B. Rourke, and U. Bellugi (1995). Unique profile of visuo-perceptual skills in a genetic syndrome. *Brain and Cognition* 29(1), 54–65.

Waser, P. M. (1975). Experimental playbacks show vocal mediation of intergroup avoidance in a forest monkey. *Nature* 255, 56–58.

——(1976). *Cercocebus albigena*: site attachment, avoidance, and intergroup spacing. *American Naturalist* 110, 911–935.

——(1977). Sound localization by monkeys: a field experiment. *Behavioral Ecology and Sociobiology* 2, 427–431.

Washburn, D., R. Thompson, and D. Oden (1997). Monkeys trained with same/different symbols do not match relations. Paper presented at the meeting of the Psychonomic Society, Philadelphia, PA.

Wasserman, E. A., J. A. Hugart, and K. Kirkpatrick-Steger (1995). Pigeons show same–different conceptualization after training with complex visual stimuli. *Journal of Experimental Psychology: Animal Behavior Processes* 21, 248–252.

Watanabe, S., J. Sajamoto, and M. Wakita (1995). Pigeons' discrimination of paintings by Monet and Picasso. *Journal of the Experimental Analysis of Behavior* 63, 165–174.

Watson, J., G. Gergely, V. Csanyi, J. Topal, M. Gacsi, and Z. Sarkozi (2001). Distinguishing logic from association in the solution of an invisible displacement task by children (*Homo sapiens*) and dogs (*Canis familiaris*): using negation of disjunction. *Journal of Comparative Psychology* 115, 219–226.

Weiskrantz, L. (1986). *Blindsight: A Case Study and Implications*. Oxford: Oxford University Press.

——(1997). *Consciousness Lost and Found: a Neuropsychological Exploration*. Oxford: Oxford University Press.

Wells, G. L. and E. A. Olson (2003). Eyewitness testimony. *Annual Review of Psychology* 54, 277–295.

Whitehead, A. N. (1919). *An Enquiry Concerning the Principles of Natural Knowledge*. Cambridge: Cambridge University Press.

Whiten, A. and R. W. Byrne (1988). Tactical deception in primates. *Behavioral and Brain Sciences* 11, 233–244.

——J. Goodall, W. McGrew, T. Nishida, V. Reynolds, Y. Sugiyama, C. E. G. Tutin, R. W. Wrangham, and C. Boesch (1999). Cultures in chimpanzees. *Nature* 399, 682–685.

——V. Horner, and F. B. de Waal (2005). Conformity to cultural norms of tool use in chimpanzees. *Nature* 437, 737–740.

——V. Horner, C. Litchfield, and S. Marshall-Pescini (2004). How do apes ape? *Learning and Behaviour* 32, 36–52.

Whittingham, L. A., A. Kirkconnell, and L. M. Ratcliffe (1992). Differences in song and sexual dimorphism between Cuban and North American Red-winged Blackbirds (*Agelaius phoeniceus*). *Auk* 109, 928–933.

——A. Kirkconnell, and L. M. Ratcliffe (1996). Breeding behavior, social organization and morphology of Red-shouldered (*Agelaius assimilis*) and Tawny-shouldered (*A. humerulis*) blackbirds. *Condor* 98, 832–836.

——A. Kirkconnell, and L. M. Ratcliffe (1997). The context and function of duet and solo songs in the Red-shouldered Blackbird. *Wilson Bulletin* 109, 279–289.

Wilkins, D. (2003). Why pointing with the index finger is not a universal (in sociocultural and semiotic terms). In S. Kita (ed.), *Pointing: Where Language, Culture, and Cognition Meet*, pp. 171–215. Mahwah, NJ: Lawrence Erlbaum Associates.

Wilkins, W. K. and J. Wakefield (1995). Brain evolution and neurolinguistic preconditions. *Behavioral and Brain Sciences* 18, 161–226.

Williams, G. C. (1966). *Adaptation and Natural Selection: A Critique of Some Current Evolutionary Thought*. Princeton, NJ: Princeton University Press.

Williams, J. H., G. D. Waiter, O. Perra, D. I. Perrett, and A. Whiten (2005). An fMRI study of joint attention experience. *Neuroimage* 25(1), 133–140.

——A. Whiten, and T. Singh (2004). A systematic review of action imitation in autistic spectrum disorder. *Journal of Autism and Developmental Disorders* 34(3), 285–299.

Wilson, D. (1999). Relevance and relevance theory. In R. A. Wilson and F. C. Keil (eds.), *The MIT Encyclopedia of the Cognitive Sciences*, pp. 719–720. Cambridge, MA: MIT Press.

Wilson, D. S. (1998). Hunting, sharing, and multilevel selection: the tolerated-theft model revisited. *Current Anthropology* 19(1), 73–97.

——and E. Sober (1994). Re-introducing group selection to the human behavioral sciences. *Behavioral and Brain Sciences* 17(4), 585–654.

Wilson, E. O. (2005). Kin selection as the key to altruism: its rise and fall. *Social Research* 72, 159–168.

—— and B. Hölldobler (2005). Eusociality: origin and consequences. *Proceedings of the National Academy of Sciences of the U.S.A.* 102, 13367–13371.

Wittgenstein, L. (1922). *Tractatus Logico-Philosophicus*. London: Routledge. (Trans. C. K. Ogden from the original German 'Logisch-Philosophische Abhandlung' in *Annalen der Naturphilosophie* 14 (1921), 185–262.).

—— (1953). *Philosophical Investigations*. Oxford: Basil Blackwell. (Trans. G. E. M. Anscombe from the author's *Philosophische Untersuchungen*, unpub. in his lifetime.)

Wolpoff, M. H., B. Mannheim, A. Mann, J. Hawks, R. Caspari, K. R.Rosenberg, D. W. Frayer, G. W. Gill, and G. Clark (2004). Why not the Neandertals? *World Archaeology* 36(4), 527–546.

Wood, D. (1988). *How Children Think and Learn*. Oxford: Basil Blackwell.

Wrangham, R. W. (1975). *The Behavioral Ecology of Chimpanzees in Gombe National Park, Tanzania*. Ph.D. thesis, University of Cambridge.

Wu, X. and W. B. Levy (2001). Simulating symbolic distance effects in the transitive inference problem. *Neurocomputing* 38–40, 1603–1610.

Wynne, C. D. L. (2001). *Animal Cognition: The Mental Lives of Animals*. Basingstoke: Palgrave.

Wynne-Edwards, V. C. (1962). *Animal Dispersion in Relation to Social Behavior*. London: Oliver and Boyd.

Young, M. and E. Wasserman (1997). Entropy detection by pigeons: response to mixed visual displays after same–different discrimination training. *Journal of Experimental Psychology: Animal Behavior Processes* 23, 157–170.

Zahavi, A. (1975). Mate selection—a selection for a handicap. *Journal of Theoretical Biology* 53, 205–214.

—— (1977). The cost of honesty (further remarks on the handicap principle). *Journal of Theoretical Biology* 67, 603–605.

—— and A. Zahavi (1997). *The Handicap Principle: A Missing Piece of Darwin's Puzzle*. Oxford: Oxford University Press.

Zak, P. J., R. Kurzban, and W. T. Matzner (2004). The neurobiology of trust. *Annals of the New York Academy of Sciences* 1032, 224–227.

Zatorre, R. J., A. R. Halpern, D. W. Perry, E. Meyer, and A. C. Evans (1996). Hearing in the mind's ear: a PET investigation of musical imagery and perception. *Journal of Cognitive Neuroscience* 8(1), 29–46.

Zentall, T. R., T. S. Clement, R. S. Bhatt, and J. Allen (2001). Episodic-like memory in pigeons. *Psychonomic Bulletin and Review* 8(4), 685–690.

Zhang, S., F. Bock, A. Si, J. Tautz, and M. V. Srinivasan (2005). Visual working memory in decision making by honey bees. *Proceedings of the National Academy of Sciences of the USA* 102(14), 5250–6255.

Zuberbühler, K., D. L. Cheney, and R. M. Seyfarth (1999). Conceptual semantics in a non-human primate. *Journal of Comparative Psychology* 113(1), 33–42.

Index

Authors of single- and double-authored works are indexed here. For multiple-authored works, only the first author is indexed.

STUDIES IN THE EVOLUTION OF LANGUAGE

General Editors
Kathleen R. Gibson, *University of Texas at Houston*
James R. Hurford, *University of Edinburgh*

PUBLISHED

1
The Origins of Vowel Systems
Bart de Boer

2
The Transition to Language
Edited by Alison Wray

3
Language Evolution
Edited by Morten H. Christiansen and Simon Kirby

4
Language Origins
Evolutionary Perspectives
Edited by Maggie Tallerman

5
The Talking Ape
How Language Evolved
Robbins Burling

6
Self-Organization in the Evolution of Speech
Pierre-Yves Oudeyer
translated by James R. Hurford

7
Why we Talk
The Evolutionary Origins of Human Communication
Jean-Louis Dessalles
translated by James Grieve

8
The Origins of Meaning
Language in the Light of Evolution 1
James R. Hurford

9
The Genesis of Grammar
Bernd Heine and Tania Kuteva

IN PREPARATION

The Evolution of Linguistic Form
Language in the Light of Evolution 2
James R. Hurford

The Invisible Miracle
The Evolutionary Origins of Speech
Peter MacNeilage

PUBLISHED IN ASSOCIATION WITH THE SERIES

Language Diversity
Daniel Nettle

Function, Selection, and Innateness
The Emergence of Language Universals
Simon Kirby

The Origins of Complex Language
An Inquiry into the Evolutionary Beginnings of Sentences, Syllables, and Truth
Andrew Carstairs McCarthy